AMERICA IN THE ROUND

STUDIES IN THEATRE HISTORY AND CULTURE

Heather S. Nathans, series editor

AMERICA

Capital, Race, and Nation at Washington, DC's Arena Stage

DONATELLA GALELLA

IN THE ROUND

UNIVERSITY OF IOWA PRESS, IOWA CITY

University of Iowa Press, Iowa City 52242

Copyright © 2019 by the University of Iowa Press

www.uipress.uiowa.edu

Printed in the United States of America

Design by Richard Hendel

The University of Iowa Press is a member of Green Press Initiative
and is committed to preserving natural resources.

Printed on acid-free paper

Library of Congress Cataloging-in-Publication Data

Names: Galella, Donatella, 1987– author.

Title: America in the round : capital, race, and nation at Washington, DC's
Arena Stage / Donatella Galella.

Description: Iowa City : University of Iowa Press, 2019. | Series: Studies in theatre
history and culture | Includes bibliographical references and index. |
Identifiers: LCCN 2018025275 (print) | LCCN 2018028721 (ebook) |
ISBN 978-1-60938-626-9 | ISBN 978-1-60938-625-2 (pbk. : alk. paper)
Subjects: LCSH: Arena Stage (Organization : Washington, DC)—History—
20th century. | Arena Stage (Organization : Washington, DC)—History—
21st century. | Theater and society (Organization : Washington, DC)
Classification: LCC PN2277.W22 (ebook) | LCC PN2277.W22 A7335 2018 (print) |
DDC 792.09753—dc23
LC record available at https://lccn.loc.gov/2018025275

Parts of chapter 1 were originally published as
"Making Art and Making Money: Arena Stage in the 1960s" in *The Sixties, Center Stage*
(University of Michigan Press). Parts of chapter 4 were originally published as "Playing
in the Dark / Musicalizing *A Raisin in the Sun*" in *Continuum.* Parts of chapter 6 were
originally published as "Redefining America, Arena Stage, and Territory Folks
in a Multiracial *Oklahoma!*" in *Theatre Journal.*

For Zelda

CONTENTS

ACKNOWLEDGMENTS

his book would not exist if I had not interned in dramaturgy at Arena Stage in the summer of 2009. As absurd as it sounds, at Arena I learned that professional theatre and in some ways life itself exist beyond New York City. This transformative experience opened my eyes to the importance of having women/queer folks/people of color in leadership positions, to the economies of regional theatre, and to the centrality of blackness to Americanness. So first and foremost, I would like to thank Arena Stage, the subject of and the inspiration for this study, and Janine Sobeck Knighton for hiring me. I am sincerely grateful for the many people connected to the company who shared their experiences and insights with me, particularly the three artistic directors of Arena Stage—Zelda Fichandler, Doug Wager, and Molly Smith—who were generous with their time and knowledge. In addition, archivists from UC Irvine to the Schomburg Center assisted me with primary sources, and I want to single out for special thanks those who manage the Arena Stage records at George Mason University.

My home institutions gave me the necessary resources to conduct my research. The Graduate Center at the City University of New York granted me fellowships that enabled me to visit archives and complete my dissertation. At UC Riverside, I have been lucky to find stability and community, formations that challenge, sharpen, and make space for my thinking.

I would be lost without my colleagues and mentors, and I offer them my thanks. At the Graduate Center, David Savran changed the way that I perceive society, and Kandice Chuh taught me to seek the material conditions that make an institution possible and to imagine conditions otherwise. Close friends rooted for me and my project. I appreciate our friendships and our conversations. In particular, Janet Werther and Chris A. Eng even read the entire manuscript and pushed me toward clearer articulations of my historical-theoretical approach. Judy Milhous, Tammy Ho, Stephen Sohn, Brian E. Herrera, Faedra Chatard Carpenter, and all of my teachers and coconspirators at the Graduate Center and UC Riverside provided support and mentorship on the publishing process.

The team at the University of Iowa Press believed in this book and made it as strong as it could be. My deep thanks especially to Studies in Theatre History and Culture editor Heather Nathans and the manuscript readers who really know black theatre and/in Washington, DC.

Finally, I must thank my family and my partner, Ross Wolfarth. Ross has read my work (including this page) and talked with me about Arena Stage for a decade, as I moved toward social justice and honed my radical thinking. And you can be my sidekick.

AMERICA IN THE ROUND

INTRODUCTION

n 2000, Arena Stage and the Library of Congress coproduced a historic concert reading of *Polk County*, a play by Zora Neale Hurston long thought to be lost. After a retired copyright expert had unearthed Hurston's unpublished plays, Arena Stage's literary manager Cathy Madison read them all and was particularly struck by *Polk County*. Set in a sawmill camp and juke joint in Depression-era Florida, the play weaves early blues, folk, and church culture into a story of romance, colorism, and competition between working-class African Americans. It is a world where a character named Dicey Long can fight with Leafy Lee over the same man and threaten, "Don't git bigitty wid nobody and let your head start more than your rump can stand."[1] A black artist and ethnographer, Hurston researched the first incorporated black township in the United States and folk songs about subjects from Jesus to John Henry. Written in 1944, the play never received a production.[2] But Arena Stage and the Library of Congress kept the archive alive. Molly Smith, the artistic director of Arena, remarked in the concert playbill, "*Polk County* is a perfect example of an undiscovered classic. How thrilling to be part of this resurrection of a great author's previously unproduced play," as the Washington, DC-based theatre celebrated its fiftieth anniversary and the library celebrated its bicentennial.[3] Nonprofit resources and black representation united in this momentous staging of U.S. Americanness, just as the people of *Polk County* used performance to form their community. After the concert played to standing ovations, Smith programmed a full production of *Polk County* the following season.

The staging joined a resurgence of literary and theatrical interest in Hurston's work and a larger discourse of what constitutes real blackness.[4] In her lifetime, Hurston was caught between black intellectuals who critiqued her portrayals of unsophisticated black folks and white liberals who eagerly consumed these images. Staking a claim to black authenticity with the then-common term "Negro," Hurston's *Polk County* bears the subtitle "A Comedy of Negro Life on a Sawmill Camp with Authentic Negro Music in Three Acts."[5] Queer black performance artist and scholar E. Patrick Johnson contends that people define blackness differently to demarcate their own credibility versus that of others, instead of blackness being a stable, agreed-upon term: "Authenticity, then, is yet another trope manipulated for cultural capital."[6] According to African Americanist John Lowe, Hurston "had nothing but scorn for the white-dominated 'Negro' musicals being produced on Broadway."[7] The copy of *Polk County* held in the Library of Congress names as an additional author Dorothy Waring, the white wife of a theatre producer, but "Hurston's role in the collaboration seems to have been dominant,"[8] while Waring's contributions remain speculative.[9] When she pressed Hurston "to keep a 'sort of Gershwinesque feeling' about their *Polk County* musical, Zora's reply was, 'You don't know what the hell you're talking about.'"[10] Hurston scholar Pamela Bordelon suggests that Hurston "spoke around" her specific experiences of oppression as an educated black woman so as not to alienate white patrons.[11]

The balance of producing acceptable blackness for commercial and critical viability speaks to Arena Stage's development process and durability. As dramaturg, Madison adapted the script for Arena with director Kyle Donnelly. She recounted some uneasiness going into the production:

> There was a lot of tension going into the project, with the black staff at Arena really wanting to be supportive, but really being afraid because not only was it a white director with a black show, but it was a folksy show. . . . These were black people from the early half of the twentieth century and poor as poor can be, just dirt poor, undereducated. So there was a real fear about representing those people correctly.[12]

Madison articulated the difficulty of black representation, and those few opportunities were overdetermined by stereotypes and bourgeois respectability politics. The black actors seemed to embrace the folk culture of the play at first but then appeared uncomfortable working under a predominantly white administration, while she was one of the few black members of the creative team. Madison's collaborator Donnelly recalled, "Being the only white person in the room for the most part [and] directing a group of African American actors and musicians was challenging yet exhilarating."[13] She had directed many Arena productions, primarily Western classics. White music director and composer Stephen Wade had a long history with the company, including his solo show *Banjo Dancin'* (1981), which played at Arena for a decade. Based on Hurston's suggestions in the script, he selected the songs and composed some of his own. Wade worked with a band of local black blues musicians, but just prior to the opening of *Polk County*, he allegedly alienated some black members of the production by suggesting that he knew more about black music than they did.[14] The production mediated racial politics amid artists who struggled over authorship and authenticity.

Arena Stage's production of *Polk County* represents what happens when funding, prestige, and black storytelling create a constellation of the American public, both the bright possibility of racial equity within the nation as well as the flickering tenuousness of that possibility. A critical hit, *Polk County* earned six Helen Hayes nominations and won the Charles MacArthur Award for Outstanding New Musical, the premier awards for professional performance in Washington, DC. The play received productions at the McCarter Theatre in New Jersey and Berkeley Repertory Theatre in California. Madison and Donnelly continued to strengthen the work with a new music director, Chic Street Man, a black artist who had previously collaborated on Hurston's *Spunk* with George C. Wolfe at the Public Theater in New York. *Polk County*'s transfer to other major regional theatre companies and its ticket sales and awards showcase the economies of theatrical production, and it reveals the appeal of certain black musicals to black and white audiences at traditionally white institutions.

Its performance in the nation's capital works toward the inclusion of blackness in the definition of the United States, though that inclusion comes at a price. Arena Stage has produced both *Polk County* by Hurston and *The Originalist* by John Strand (2015), whose work humanizes conservative Supreme Court Justice Antonin Scalia and defends his anti-gay-marriage stance.[15] Citing listening to multiple sides as a value, the play "extends its hand across the aisle and finds the humanity in our civil discourse," even though the right wing dehumanizes women, people of color, and LGBTQ people.[16] The theatre adopts a progressive-centrist position, not a decidedly leftist one committed to social justice. This is not necessarily a compromise but what the institution promotes to have broad appeal.

How has Arena Stage sustained itself since its opening in 1950? What does its flourishing reveal about U.S. theatre and racial and national formations, given the exigencies of capitalism? Arena has carefully navigated economic, racial, and national dynamics. It was the first professional resident theatre in Washington, DC, the first one in this city to admit a racially integrated audience, the first to send a new play production to Broadway to immense commercial and critical acclaim, the first to win the Tony Award for best regional theatre, and the first to perform behind the Iron Curtain. Defined by its location in Washington, DC, this theatre has the potential for tangible impact on U.S. governmental policies and symbolic impact on national discourses. In response to economic and political demands, Arena Stage's mission has changed from producing the European and U.S. American canon with an emphasis on Russian culture during the Cold War to building a multicultural canon with an emphasis on African American culture since the late 1980s. Today Arena is one of few large regional theatres that strategizes to include African Americans onstage, backstage, and in the audience beyond Black History Month. The institution performs Americanness as a black-white dialectic and celebrates individual inclusion through popular genres such as the musical. Far from radically upturning racial hierarchy and the profit motive, the theatre has been financially and artistically viable due to its careful calculation of risk and project of racial liberalism. Arena Stage capitalizes on stories of racial integration, the black middle class, the symbolism of the nation's capital, and a disavowal of financial interests.

Spotlighting Arena Stage illuminates examinations of a financially successful, racially integrated theatre and the terms and limits for that success and integration. Instead of advocating for an uncritical recuperative project, *America in the Round: Capital, Race, and Nation at Washington, DC's Arena Stage* engages with operations of power. The company merits investigation for how it negotiates different forms of capital as well as racial and U.S. American identities, not only challenging norms but also socially reproducing them. Arena wields nonprofit status yet mobilizes for-profit thinking. It has done more than many of its peer institutions to incorporate blackness for half a century yet still centers on whiteness. It imagines a more perfect union through racial diversity, though often without reckoning with racial hierarchies. Arena stages, opposes, and shifts what it means to be nonprofit, black, and U.S. American; its history from administrative decisions to artistic programming to audience building shows the economics of theatre, racial liberalism, and U.S. nationalism at work. Yet the institution has received little scholarly attention.

Modeling a materialist history of regional theatre, this study uses sociology of culture, theatre and performance studies, and critical race theory to read theatrical productions, archival texts, and interviews. It examines the Arena Stage records held by George Mason University, including meeting minutes, correspondence, audience responses, in-house studies, financial documents, newspaper clippings, production files, advertisements, photographs, and videos. These materials suggest how productions developed, how the institution branded itself, and how audiences responded to performances. Reviews provide insight into how critics received Arena's productions and policed blackness and Americanness. Interviews with more than two dozen associates of Arena Stage, including all three of the theatre's artistic directors, Zelda Fichandler, Douglas Wager, and Molly Smith, accentuate the voices of artists and decision-makers. Finally, my own experiences having seen many of Arena's productions and having worked in the artistic development department in 2009, when the company renovated its building and its branding under the banner "Arena Re-Staged," offer an insider's perspective at a crucial moment in Arena's history.

REGIONAL THEATRE AND RACIAL LIBERALISM

Contemporary U.S. theatre history often focuses on literary, experimental, and social justice–oriented theatre. Many scholars have written on artists from Eugene O'Neill to Off-Off-Broadway companies, privileging New York City and avant-garde productions over regional theatre. Others have sometimes examined culturally specific theatres without attending to their complicity with power. U.S. performance studies scholar David Román calls this "indigenous theatre . . . presumed to have remained uncontaminated by commercialism, commodity culture, or mainstream tastes."[17] Scholars typically find large regional theatres, productions, and patrons too bourgeois, safe, and white. They rationalize that highly "artistic" theatres are most deserving of investigation, thus seeking to legitimize U.S. theatre and its study. Itself a dominantly white bourgeois establishment, the theatre academy uses its privileged yet seemingly neutral lens to spread its tastes and values, based on experiences with and access to theatre.[18] This scholarship frequently adopts a celebratory tone as if the worth of sanctioned artists is already obvious, rather than interrogating the terms of worthiness.

Regional theatre routinely appears in opposition to avant-garde theatre and theatre for social change. Theatre historian Hillary Miller observes, "In theater studies, dominant paradigms used to historicize theaters of OOB [Off-Off-Broadway] measure their radicality—in terms of politics or the commercial theater or prior stage conventions—through a model of autonomy and resistance to institutions."[19] In *The Sixties, Center Stage*, James M. Harding and Cindy Rosenthal document the scholarly bias toward avant-garde theatre, which has overshadowed more popular theatre.[20] As a result, academics have devoted less attention to what the authors call "mainstream experimental" theatre, institutions and productions that challenge the simplistic divide between boundary-pushing art and commercially successful entertainment. Moreover, Harding and Rosenthal suggest that the prioritization of white, allegedly more masculine, raw performance has sidelined productions that have had racially diverse audiences and companies spearheaded by women artistic leaders.

As a result of these biases, there is a dearth of recent scholarship on U.S. regional theatre, and what exists is rarely critical. The central text of the field, Joseph Zeigler's *Regional Theatre: The Revolutionary Stage*, is an invaluable survey, but it lacks sociological theorization and is now more than forty years old.[21] More recent histories serve as chronicles of artists and productions with thematic analyses.[22] Regional theatres such as the Goodman Theatre in Chicago have published their own illustrated histories, and so has Arena Stage, whose former literary manager Laurence Maslon organized *The Arena Adventure: The First 40 Years*.[23] This text demonstrates how Arena's leaders wished to portray and remember themselves. Despite the popularity and longevity of regional theatres, there are no published scholarly manuscripts providing critical histories of leading companies like the Guthrie Theater in Minneapolis, the Mark Taper Forum in Los Angeles, or the Alley Theatre in Houston.

U.S. regional theatre necessitates greater investigation because of what theatre theorist David Savran dubs middlebrow anxiety:

> Middlebrow cultural producers, consumers, and critics alike are always looking over their shoulders; always fearful of encroachments from above or below; always uneasy about their own class positionality and their own tastes; always trying to negotiate between creativity and the exigencies of the marketplace, between politics and aesthetics, between an art that requires studied investment and the desire for untrammeled pleasures.[24]

Professional, noncommercial theatres across the United States occupy a fraught position between forms like opera and pop concerts.[25] As Savran notes, regional theatres in the 1960s and 1970s moved toward the upper-middlebrow end of the spectrum due to their nonprofit status and productions of "serious drama."[26] Yet this position remains shaky. Top regional theatres accept funding from Broadway producers and send world premieres to the Great White Way, and their cachet relies on these relationships with commercial producers and New York City. This middlebrow anxiety relates to the institution's very institutionalization, a dependence on not only the box office, donations, and grants, but also status quo, apparently apolitical politics. In his critique of the theatre as a public sphere, Christopher B. Balme observes, "The term institution is inimical to our preferred understanding of theatre as a bubbling cauldron of resistance, subversion and perpetual innovation."[27] Large companies require widespread consumer and critical approval. Cynics imagine them as too benign to be progressive and therefore insignificant. Savran avers that regional theatre is not activist theatre because consuming nonprofit theatrical productions is not equivalent to igniting revolution or even voting.[28] Regional theatres are too popular to be sources of high art and yet not popular enough to be researched as mass pop culture. This very in-betweenness demands attention as exemplary of the dynamics of U.S. theatre, culture, and politics.

Some regional theatre founders, like Robert Brustein of the Yale Repertory Theatre, believe that contemporary nonprofit theatres have lost their way. In 2016, when celebrating Yale Rep's fiftieth anniversary, he lamented that regional theatres "are becoming more commercial and now look more toward Broadway—which is the exact opposite of what their original intention was."[29] He rhapsodized on the mid-twentieth century, when regional institutions from Margo Jones's Theatre '47 in Dallas to Trinity Repertory Company in Providence sought to professionalize theatre beyond Broadway. He framed this as a period of producing pure art that took risks without consideration of ticket sales.

The case of Arena Stage disrupts this Golden Age narrative. While it is true that nonprofit theatres work increasingly with for-profit producers, the distinction between for- and not-for-profit was never stark, and the collaboration is far from new. The romantic history presumes that regional theatres sat outside of capitalism, as if these institutions were not interested in ticket sales and prestigious grants. In fact, they have always resided within what sociologist Pierre Bourdieu dubs "the field of cultural production," existing in relation to one another and within a larger field of power.[30] Bourdieu theorizes that economic capital, or money, has an inverse relationship to symbolic capital, or prestige, so that cultural productions can earn only one or the other, not both. If a play is a commercial smash, then it is unlikely to be a critical hit as well. Arena Stage has strategically mobilized Bourdieu's art versus commerce logic to distinguish nonprofit regional theatres as specially deserving of grants, donations, and tax breaks due to the artistic risks that they take. The theatre also challenged this binary by producing plays that gained both high ticket receipts and favorable critical attention. As cofounder of Arena, Zelda Fichandler wrote of these contradictions, "While theatre is a business, its business is art, not business."[31] The company established a model for nonprofit theatres, leading the U.S. regional theatre movement. It sent world premiere plays to New York City while at the same time acting as if season selection did not factor in the possibility of for-profit transfers. The first play that Arena transferred to Broadway, *The Great White Hope* by Howard Sackler, epitomizes how the theatre's worth has relied on a performed disinterest in making money and a political project of racial liberalism.

According to philosopher Charles W. Mills, who originated the notion of the "racial contract," racial liberalism proposes moral equality for all people, but its "terms originally restricted full personhood to whites (or, more accurately, white men) and relegated nonwhites to an inferior category, so that its schedule of rights and prescriptions for justice were all color-coded."[32] In the twentieth-century United States, racial liberalism entails the enfranchisement of people of color to gain civil rights, integration, and equal opportunity. It endorses reform rather than revolution or even reparations to create a society without prejudice. Trusting the educated elite and their technocratic solutions, adherents to this ideology look optimistically to the U.S. government to enforce compliance with nondiscrimination laws as a principal way to redress racial inequality. They also believe that rational discourse, such as staging progressive plays and hosting postshow talkbacks, will teach people to not discriminate against others.

But racial liberalism has restrictions. Rather than overturning tables, it offers more seats at the table for certain people deemed worthy. The terms of inclusion preserve a white center, which others join, and whites determine the timetable for justice. In this philosophy, discrimination against people of color is seen as not fundamental to the United States but as an aberration. Everyone is equal in theory yet not treated so in practice. Perhaps best epitomized by sociologist Gunnar Myrdal whose *An American Dilemma* has shaped U.S. policies of racial liberalism since the mid-twentieth century, "Myrdal believed that blacks desired complete assimilation into the mainstream white culture and that distinctive patterns of Afro-American culture were a pathological vestige of slavery and segregation that would soon fade away."[33] Instead of antiblack policies like denying Social Security benefits and affordable mortgages being the problem, black people themselves seemed to be the problem. Racial liberalism considers the U.S. nation-state good, and good at extending equality to those willing to adhere to its dictates.

For Arena Stage to preserve itself as a viable theatre institution, it has capitalized on racial liberalism in its location, season programming, and patronage. From the start, the theatre admitted a racially integrated audience, although people of color did not attend in significant numbers until the 1960s. At that point, the company began producing black plays legible to white audiences and casting multiracially in canonical white plays. These theatrical productions can celebrate yet flatten difference, as they deracinate specificity and suggest that everyone has equal struggles. English scholar Cathy Irwin and performance studies theorist Sean Metzger contend that, at U.S. regional theatres, "ethnic difference sells when it is equated with the general feeling of difference everyone occasionally experiences. But leveling all difference and forgetting the uneven power dynamics accorded by categories of race and ethnicity, gender and class, can leave some very unsettling impressions."[34] Racial liberalism overstates the playing field as level. Even though it means well in welcoming and representing people of color, it fails to understand racism as structural, historic, and deliberate, or to see people and institutions as complicit with systemic oppression.

Racism mobilizes race as a technology for creating and maintaining privileges. For black theatre scholar Harvey Young, "an awareness of race becomes racism when a person insists that one particular group of people, one 'race,' is better than another."[35] In their foundational study on racial formation, sociologists Michael Omi and Howard Winant conceive race as both social construct and material lived experience rather than biological essence. Omi and Winant historicize what they call "racial projects," which can conform to and/or challenge racial hierarchies because they are "simultaneously an interpretation, representation, or explanation of racial dynamics, and an effort to reorganize and redistribute resources along particular racial lines."[36] Plays and policies, representations and redistribution of resources, constitute racial projects.

Racism is not mere prejudice, personal feelings of hatred or fear, but what geographer Ruth Wilson Gilmore calls "the state-sanctioned or extralegal production and exploitation of group-differentiated vulnerability to premature death."[37] It is a power structure that teaches and rationalizes whose lives matter. Although scholars such as Cedric J. Robinson have pointed to racial-ethnic differentiation and valuation dating back to ancient times, the iteration of racism in the United States as manifested in the history of Arena Stage from 1950 onward is founded on dispossessing, enslaving, killing, and exploiting people of color to create a hierarchy that enacts racial difference and justifies the unequal distribution of power according to those differences.[38] In this case, "systemic racism" and "institutional racism" specifically refer to white supremacy because of this temporal-spatial context of white dominance. Sociologist Eduardo Bonilla-Silva defines this racial structure as *"the totality of the social relations and practices that reinforce white privilege."*[39] On a structural level, white people have the privilege to obtain better jobs, homes, education, treatment, and health outcomes than people of color. They can amass more resources and pass them down to the next generation. White privilege entails not only material benefits but emotional ones, what W. E. B. Du Bois and David Roediger have called the "wages of whiteness."[40] Naming white privilege is not a personal insult but a diagnosis of the pattern by which biases and policies favor people with white skin. People become part of this racial hierarchy by internalizing its logic that lighter skin is superior to darker skin and then spreading this logic. White supremacy manifests in institutions to which people are hailed. Individuals cannot opt out, yet they can attempt to change from within or make new spaces.

When companies like Arena Stage engage in the racial project of racial liberalism, they both advance antiracist politics by expanding the stage to black people and curtail these advances by permitting entry on the terms of sustaining white supremacy and the U.S. state. This theatre exemplifies not only the achievements of white liberal leaders and the presence of people of color among plays, practitioners, and patrons, but also the workings of institutional racism. That has been the recipe for Arena's stability as an institution. For example, Arena would probably never produce Amiri Baraka's *Slave Ship*, because that in-your-face radical black 1960s play dramatizing the institutionalization of slavery and calling for violence would make white people uncomfortable, curtailing ticket sales and grants.

Many scholars of black American performance have observed that black cultural productions earn critical approval and box office success when they reify various hierarchies. In *Forgeries of Memory and Meaning: Blacks and the Regimes of Race in American Theater and Film before World War II*, Robinson traces historic racial regimes through white representations of blackness on stage and screen that gained traction from commercial structures seeking to support themselves and justify white supremacy.[41] Even black artists and producers have participated in upholding power structures. African American Studies scholar Stephanie Batiste has analyzed early twentieth-century black American productions that celebrated U.S. imperialism and positioned black Americans above other minoritized groups like Asians and Native Americans.[42] Historicizing the same period, scholar Adrienne

Macki Braconi argues that Harlem's black middle class mobilized their capital and respectability politics to stage their values and viewpoints, and that they failed to reach the black masses.[43] Black American performance can both contest and socially reproduce structural racism. As demonstrated by Arena Stage, middlebrow black productions that stride the liberal-center can receive loud praise and high ticket sales on the basis of that middle ground.

STAGING THE NATION IN THE CAPITAL

Arena Stage's position in Washington, DC, has significantly shaped its racial politics. Since Arena opened its doors in 1950, it has been a liberal integrationist theatre. In that period, Washington was 65 percent white and 35 percent black. Within ten years, the white population had dipped to 45 percent and the black population increased to 54 percent as whites fled from the city proper.[44] Arena has thrived in large part thanks to finally reaching out to a black bourgeois audience. Unique among large, traditionally white resident theatres, Arena deserves credit for institutionalizing black inclusion, though that came at a cost. To secure nonprofit status in 1959, Arena used its white privilege to garner patrons, grants, and the very land in Southwest, DC that the theatre now occupies, which had belonged to low-income black residents. The theatre, its leadership, and its supporters did not have deliberately racist intentions, and they did not personally exclude black people, but instead they contributed to racially unequal outcomes. In another example, since the downsizing of Crossroads Theatre Company in New Jersey in the late 1990s, there have been no black-specific LORT (League of Resident Theatres) member regional companies. As August Wilson so passionately argued in his 1996 "The Ground on Which I Stand" manifesto, funding that might otherwise go toward black theatres went toward diversifying traditionally white institutions, like Arena Stage. That diversification has been gradual yet crucial to the company's identity and viability. The company both embraced blackness and extracted resources from black people.

As demographics changed and as the theatre experienced its first deficit in the 1960s, Arena started to stage classics and new plays with, by, and about people of African descent. Blackness gave this theatre the edginess that nonprofit companies needed to appear risk-taking and thus obtain significant grants, even as black productions were critically and commercially successful. When Doug Wager took up the leadership in 1991, he committed to a U.S. multiculturalist repertory, ensemble, and audience. The black middle class provided the backbone to the theatre, effectively subsidizing the institution. In 1998, Molly Smith, the third artistic director, increased this commitment to U.S. American work, especially with black musicals that earned more than almost any other kind of production. By this point, Washington had become increasingly gentrified—white, wealthy, and educated— and able to support approximately ninety professional theatres.[45] In the early 1980s, the number of playing weeks for professional touring productions in the nation's capital was higher than that of any other city.[46] In 2012, the *Washington Post* reported that more than two million local theatre tickets are sold each year and, since 2000, hundreds of millions of dollars have been invested in new theatre complexes.[47] This proliferation of theatres led Arena to articulate its own niche, focusing on new and classic U.S. drama, particularly with stories of people of color, and this mission gains deeper resonance in the nation's capital.

Arena Stage positions itself as a platform for U.S. political discourse. The theatre bestows the American Voice Award to politicians who advocate for the arts and arts education, and recipients span the political spectrum from Senator Tim Kaine (D-Virginia), 2016 vice presidential nominee, to Senator Lisa Murkowski (R-Alaska). The community engagement department has hosted annual fundraising galas in which politicians performed in original, campy plays like *Conniver*, a parody of the reality competition series *Survivor*. Arena has publicized the attendance of Supreme Court justices. (Ruth Bader Ginsburg even officiated Molly Smith's marriage to Suzanne Blue Star Boy.) Arguably the closest institution the U.S. has to a national theatre, Arena fits Marvin Carlson's definition of "a monumental edifice located in a national capital, authorized, privileged and supported by the government, and devoted wholly or largely to productions of the work of national dramatists."[48] Now housed within the multimillion-dollar Mead Center for American Theater, Arena embodies this national stage.

Branding itself as the largest U.S. theatre dedicated to "American voices," Arena represents a site of struggle over what constitutes Americanness.[49] In 2018, its website proclaimed, "Arena Stage's vision is to galvanize the transformative power of theater to understand who we are as Americans."[50] This forceful diction privileges theatre as "transformative" in its affect and production of knowledge. The presumptive "we" situates Arena's artists, administrators, and audiences as U.S. Americans. Through this vision, Arena Stage imagines a community; the performative utterance of "American" and performances of, by, and for Americans make Americans and make their respective nation.[51] This articulation unites people around a national identity and idea, an act that potentially erases other identifications, material differences, and inequalities.[52] Arena's usage of "American" denotes "of the United States of America," obscuring the rest of North America and all of Central and South America, regions rarely represented at this theatre.[53] Its mission statement asserts:

> Arena Stage is alive as a center for American Theater in our nation's capital with productions, diverse and innovative works from around the country and the nurturing of new plays. Our focus is on American artists. We produce and present all that is passionate, exuberant, profound, deep and dangerous in the American spirit. We explore issues from the past, present and future that reflect America's diversity and challenges. These are voiced through the productions we create, the work we develop, the presentations that move beyond our stages and community and education programs that engage artists, students and audiences.[54]

From the start, the statement positions Arena as a "center" of American national identity because of its American repertory and location in the nation's capital. The theatre emphasizes "diversity" in both the "works" and "issues" onstage. By not naming minoritized people, "diversity" becomes a nebulous catch-all value that includes everyone, even those with privileges, and offends no one.[55] Although Arena's artistic leaders have understood race, particularly blackness, as an indelible part of Americanness, the institutional branding celebrates abstract nationalism. The diction glosses the American spirit in both celebratory terms—"exuberant"—and condemnatory ones—"dangerous"—resonating with allegedly U.S. American characteristics and histories of pioneering, exploring, and dominating. Invoking the "past, present and future," the mission statement grounds the foundation of American identity in classic and contemporary U.S. dramas and in an imagined future. Finally, the theatre names its development, production, presentation, and education practices that form the pillars to support the institution and its performances of Americanness. A container of U.S. history, Arena is precisely the theatre where the material conditions make possible a coproduction of *Polk County* with the Library of Congress to revive and change U.S. theatre.

AMERICA IN THE ROUND

America in the Round takes its titular cue from the primary Arena Stage space, a theatre in the round now named for the company's cofounder, Zelda Fichandler. By staging national identity "in the round," Arena opens up multifaceted perspectives of who comprises the nation and under what circumstances. Fichandler observed: "Since it has no back, front or sides, the arena becomes a highly democratic form for the audience, it is true that the individual witnesses the stage life from one particular point of view. . . . But he [*sic*][56] has, kinesthetically and emotionally, fundamentally the same experience wherever he is sitting."[57] Evoking U.S. sentiments of democracy and equality, the arena gives every spectator a similarly good view of the stage. Audience members form the backdrop, holding space and holding each other accountable as they encircle the playing space. Together, they perform U.S. national identity *and* perform their own Americanness. Spectators cannot help but see one another across the stage. In the late 1960s, when black patrons began to come to Arena to watch stories about black people, Fichandler suddenly noticed the white homogeneity of her institution, and she worked to change that. Analyzing Arena and the United States of America "in the round" opens critical examinations of this theatre company, nation, and citizen-spectators.

To work through a critical history of Arena Stage, *America in the Round* adopts an innovative "in the round" approach to structure the storytelling. When a spectator sits on different sides of the stage, they can see in the central playing space the faces of some actors and the backs of others. Then, when they choose a seat in another section, their perspective changes, even as the bodies onstage stay still. This book likewise looks at the company from multiple points of view—capital, race, and nation—as if these were three interrelated actors. They form thematic sections on how Arena produced nonprofit status, black drama, and U.S. identity, focusing on the periods of roughly 1950–70, 1970–90, and 1990–2010, respectively. In the first part, the reader sees the "face" of the economic actor but the "backs" of the racial and national actors. These dynamics are all in play, yet one receives primary attention. In the next section, the racial actor appears more clearly to the reader while still existing in relation to the imperatives of the economy and nation. And so on. Each section theorizes capital, race, and nation, though these organizing axes intersect. The totality of the histories, productions, and thematic through-lines offers a 360-degree picture of institutional dynamics.

Because the object of study, Arena Stage, remains the same while the viewpoint changes, the book necessarily occasionally revisits earlier moments in the company's history. Later chapters return to certain texts and flashpoints in order to ground the context of the present exploration and offer new ways of understanding the past, ultimately moving the narrative forward. Retreading steps is essential to comprehending Arena's trajectory. Meanwhile, the earlier chapters covering 1950 to 1990 commence with more contemporary anecdotes before going back in time; the flash-forward anecdotes serve as launch sites to ponder how Arena reached those points.

Each capital, race, and nation section includes one history chapter and one case study. The histories provide the landscape, whereas the case studies zoom in on key details. The former is not a season-by-season gloss of productions. Instead, the historical chapters document twenty-year patterns in the company's image, repertory, and audiences to contextualize the case studies. Then the case study chapters highlight the major productions that mark turning points in and are representative of Arena's practices within those periods: *The Great White Hope* (1967) by Howard Sackler inspired a national trend toward transfers from regional theatres to Broadway; *Raisin* (1973), the musical adaptation of Lorraine Hansberry's *A Raisin in the Sun* with book by Robert Nemiroff and Charlotte Zaltzberg, music by Judd Woldin, lyrics by Robert Brittan, and direction and choreography by Donald McKayle, continued this trend and sparked a new one in staging a popular, liberal black musical; and Richard Rodgers and Oscar Hammerstein II's *Oklahoma!* (2010) as directed by Molly Smith solidified the theatre's commitment to imagining the United States as multiracial via color-conscious cast musicals. To consider production and consumption, the case study chapters each include production histories, close textual readings, and critical responses.

The case studies of *The Great White Hope*, *Raisin*, and *Oklahoma!* suggest what has made Arena Stage profitable, black, and American. These works represent parts of a typical season of plays under Smith's leadership: a new U.S. play that deals with racial politics, an uplifting black musical, and a multiracial production of a classic American musical. In their time, they were among the most successful shows in the theatre's history. Each theatrical text looks back at U.S. history to understand its contemporary moment: *The Great White Hope* turns to the early twentieth century when Jack Johnson became the first black heavyweight champion, *Raisin* turns to the 1950s when a black family challenged housing segregation, and *Oklahoma!* turns to the 1900s when the Oklahoma and Indian Territories transformed into a state. All three productions staged the trials and beauty of interracial union standing in for not only the United States but also Arena Stage. Racial integration was performative, made tangible on the theatrical stage, in the audience surrounding the stage, and on the national stage. Yet the conditions for this interracial harmony have tended to be elisions of the depths of structural inequality. These productions enacted the aesthetics and affects of racial liberalism, moving critics, patrons, and donors to support Arena Stage for decades.

Focusing on the 1950–70 period, the first chapter traces Arena Stage's turn from for-profit to nonprofit and argues that there was little difference in programming—except for racial difference. Producing director Zelda Fichandler deftly accumulated income and accolades to balance the budget and define nonprofit institutional practices. *The Great White Hope*, the attendant case study to unpack nonprofit status and racial liberalism, is the basis of chapter 2. Signaling the potential for works honed in regional theatres to transfer to Broadway, the play offered an antiracist critique of white supremacy policing the black protagonist and his white lover as well as a rehearsal of white supremacy in centering whiteness and denying the importance of race. Chapter 3 historicizes 1970 to 1990, when the theatre increasingly presented itself as a global company and, by the end of the Cold War, replaced its slots for Russian and Eastern European plays with African American plays. The fourth chapter investigates *Raisin*, which marked the company's first foray into black musicals, a genre that would become a significant part of its repertoire, attract a racially diverse audience, and bankroll the theatre. Chapter 5 historicizes 1990 to 2010, when Arena Stage passed to Doug Wager and Molly Smith and began to center on U.S. American theatre. While Wager developed new multicultural initiatives to manage diversity, Smith successfully capitalized on racial diversity, specifically blackness, as a selling point and as integral to U.S. identity. The final chapter provides a close reading of Arena Stage's multiracial production of *Oklahoma!* in 2010. Its story of U.S. nation formation populated by multiracial settlers staged a utopian performative of inclusion, yet it also covered up historic oppression of indigenous people and continuing settler colonialism and racial strife.

By producing racially liberal dramas, capitalizing on black audiences, using the assets of Washington, DC, adapting and distinguishing its mission as U.S. American, and accumulating economic and symbolic capital, this flagship company, Arena Stage, has steered a viable course for nearly seventy years. Arena produces capital, race, and nation in the round and demands critical attention to intersections of power. Through a balancing act of art, politics, and finances, of recognizing and regulating racial difference, Arena stages an inclusive definition of the United States. At the expense of radical change, the company has gained longevity. The theatre enacts multiracial understandings of American representation uniquely situated in the nation's capital, where Americans attend performances, participate in discourse, and shape policy.

PART ONE

Capital

CHAPTER ONE

NEGOTIATING NONPROFIT THEATRE

n 1967, critic Martin Gottfried argued in *A Theater Divided: The Postwar American Stage* that U.S. theatre fell into two camps. The right camp produced new comedies and musicals from Broadway to summer stock, staged legitimate theatre such as Chekhov's *The Cherry Orchard* in a professional manner, and subscribed to *Variety*—in short, for-profit theatre. Meanwhile, the left camp produced classical and experimental work in a more amateurish fashion, renounced wide appeal, and subscribed to *TDR*—in short, nonprofit theatre. According to Gottfried,

> The *left* wing includes most of the newer resident theaters that have developed in the United States. These theaters are concerned with producing theater art—the classical literature in particular. They are not nearly so adventurous as they think and their work is concentrated in war-horse classics (Chekhov, Shaw, O'Neill and Shakespeare), but their object is serious, and their directors are usually bright and talented young men [*sic*] who became disenchanted with Broadway (to a degree because they couldn't get any work there) and left for art's sake.[1]

Although Gottfried presents the right and left as opposing forces, he also demonstrates how they overlap. He chastises the self-importance of regional theatre artistic directors, many of whom were actually women, whose tastes and resumes were at once rooted in Broadway and disdainful of Broadway. Both right and left wings produce "classical literature" as well as new avant-garde plays. Both are "accepted by the public, the government, the powers that be" if in different ways through ticket sales, donations, grants, and newspaper and academic reviews.[2] Both seek profit. Their artistic and economic practices are not as separate as Gottfried initially portrays them. Indeed, he names regional theatre, specifically Arena Stage, as the intersection between right and left, money and art, profit and nonprofit, because in his view Arena had become "institutional" by the 1960s.[3] How did this trailblazing company straddle these apparent oppositions and become firmly established?

Many regional theatres from Arena to the Alley Theatre developed professional theatre outside of New York City. Martin Gottfried and Richard Schechner initially welcomed these companies as alternatives to Broadway in the early 1960s. Yet a few years later, they accused artistic directors of selling out by selecting repertories based on what might thrive on Broadway or receive foundation and government grants.[4] These critics viewed economic capital (ticket sales) and symbolic capital (positive reviews, awards, grants from prestigious organizations) as antithetical.[5] In contrast to this narrative of a tragic fall from art to commerce, Vincent Landro critiques the critics for romanticizing the origins of regional theatre and reifying the idea that a theatre can have *either* artistic or commercial success, "a simplistic bipolar model of theatre history typical of the polarized thinking in the 1960s."[6] Institutionalizing, professionalizing, and maintaining a balanced budget did not necessarily mean reducing artistic standards and experiments.

But it was this presumed opposition between art and money that helped to give Arena Stage its longevity. As one of the forerunners of regional theatre, Arena was key to the invention of viable U.S. nonprofit theatre through its acts of distinction, negotiation, and contradiction. Founded as a for-profit corporation in 1950, the company became the first professional resident theatre in the nation's capital. Producing director and cofounder Zelda Fichandler had big ambitions. She envisioned a large, in-the-round, accessible theatre that staged entertaining comedies; challenging, contemporary works; and classics that spoke to present issues, almost all written by acclaimed white men. She wanted to imitate European theatres that boasted resident acting companies and, to do so, she needed a permanent home. To raise funds for these projects, Arena Stage reorganized as a nonprofit theatre, a relatively new idea in 1959 that has now become the dominant model. The theatre's success flowed from Fichandler's accumulation and negotiation of various kinds of capital with the help of her economist husband and company executive director, Thomas Fichandler, as well as the head of the Humanities and the Arts division of the Ford Foundation, W. McNeil "Mac" Lowry.

I chart the history of Arena Stage from 1950 to 1970, focusing on the intersections of commerce, aesthetics, and race that materialized Zelda Fichandler's ideas. Pierre Bourdieu's concepts of different capitals, the Economic World Reversed, and relations of agents in the field of cultural production provide a foundation for understanding the economics of this theatre. Next, an overview of precursors to regional theatres in the United States helps to situate Arena Stage's history and negotiation of nonprofit status. The material conditions that made the construction of this company possible include the specific political landscape of Washington; the racial, economic, and educational privileges of the founders and patrons; and the widely accepted but untrue art versus commerce binary. The only major programming changes after receiving nonprofit tax status were the production of more left-leaning theatre and then, after the deficit, the extension of more opportunities to black people. Although Fichandler sought to distinguish her nonprofit theatre from for-profit Broadway, that distinction is a blurry yet powerful one to generate different kinds of capital. In this way, the term "nonprofit theatre" becomes capacious, challenging the implicit idea that symbolic capital and contributions are not kinds of profit.[7] Arena invented the viable nonprofit model by investing in what were considered more risky, artistic, left-leaning endeavors yet remained well within the bounds of popular acceptance and profit.

ORIGINS OF U.S. REGIONAL THEATRE IN THE FIELD OF CULTURAL PRODUCTION

Pierre Bourdieu's sociological approach to the economies of culture helps to explain how Arena Stage harvested income and accolades in the field of cultural production. Bourdieu conceives this field as comprising of the relations between different agents (individuals and institutions), their positions, how those positions historically came to be possible, and how this field sits in the larger field of power. Habitus emerges from agents' social class among other dispositions, producing behaviors and tastes that seem second nature. Capital requires flow because it is risked to try to generate more capital. Capital is unevenly

distributed due to a history of privatization and class oppression inter-
sected with hierarchies of gender, race, sexuality, and ability status.
Agents compete over resources categorized as different kinds of capital, and they can sometimes exchange one kind of capital for another
kind of capital.

Arena competes with other theatres and other kinds of cultural institutions as well as leisure activities for economic capital and symbolic capital. Economic capital includes the formalized money earned
in wages or ticket sales. Money becomes capital when reinvested rather
than hoarded. Symbolic capital represents the prestige, celebrity, and
honors from consecrating institutions such as awards committees and
the academy. Because grants from prestigious foundations offer literal
money *and* cachet, they constitute both economic and symbolic capital. Symbolic capital rests on a production of belief in which agents engage in "struggles for the monopoly of power to consecrate, in which
the value of works of art and belief in that value are continuously generated."[8] Moreover, this value derives from a practiced disinterestedness, a disavowal of the desire to accumulate economic capital. If an
agent has obvious commercial aims, then it is harder for them to attract critical acclaim. This apparent opposition between economic and
symbolic capital is the "winner loses" logic of what Bourdieu calls the
"Economic World Reversed." Agents can accumulate economic capital at the expense of symbolic capital, or they can accumulate symbolic
capital at the expense of economic capital.

Yet, at the center of these intersections, Arena Stage demonstrates
that theatre, in its middlebrow position, complicates the art-commerce
binary. The company claims nonprofit status along with gifts like grants
and donations by acting disinterested in money yet still selects plays
that attract wide audiences. According to Bourdieu, "The theatre, which
directly experiences the immediate sanction of the bourgeois public,
with its values and conformisms, can earn the institutionalized con-
secration of academies and official honours, as well as money."[9] The
model of the "Economic World Reversed" is less predictable than Bourdieu claims. His theory describes the art industry of the late nineteenth
century, while it does not wholly account for the 1960s when movements like camp and regional theatres complicated delineations between high and low art. But because the presumption of economic and

symbolic capital as opposites still pervaded 1960s culture, Arena Stage was able to capitalize on this idea and generate both kinds of income.

Setting the stage for Arena and the regional theatre movement decades earlier, little theatres practiced the economic versus symbolic capital logic and laid the foundations for decentering professional theatre, cultivating white middle-class audiences, and implementing nonprofit structures. Little theatres emerged in the 1910s and lasted through the 1920s, the most famous being the Boston Toy Theatre, Chicago Little Theatre, and Provincetown Players. According to theatre historian Dorothy Chansky, George Pierce Baker's playwriting workshops, publications such as *Theatre Arts*, and new high school and university drama courses helped to form a national bourgeois theatergoing audience at a time when radio and film began to compete with theatre.[10] Such initiatives distinguished between—and often derided—lowbrow mass entertainment and highbrow inaccessible art, teaching audiences to replicate bourgeois taste and social class. Sociologist of culture Paul DiMaggio illustrates how little theatres turned nonprofit to imitate museums and symphonies.[11] However, few survived into the second half of the twentieth century, namely the Cleveland Play House and the Pasadena Playhouse. Regional theatre leaders such as Zelda Fichandler cited European national theatres such as the Comédie-Française, Berliner Ensemble, and Moscow Art Theatre as influences more frequently than they did little theatres. Still, these early twentieth-century U.S. companies modeled an art theatre and developed audiences outside the theatrical center of New York City.

Another forebear of regional theatres, the Federal Theatre Project, brought professional theatre to working-class audiences beyond New York City, often for the first time.[12] This Depression-era federal program also included the Negro Unit, giving dedicated resources to black American artists. These initiatives did not produce long-lasting institutions, but like the little theatres, they demonstrated that nonprofit-run professional theatre could find regional support and that black performance beyond minstrelsy could find patrons. In addition, they provided training for artists such as Margo Jones, who along with Fichandler, would become known as a matriarch of regional theatre.[13]

In Dallas in 1947, Jones founded the in-the-round Theatre '47, and Fichandler soon followed her example in Washington, DC. In her influential tract *Theatre-in-the-Round*, Jones asserted that a theatre created as a for-profit company could work as long as the investors did not compromise artistic standards for big dividends. Such a belief suggests that art and money constitute opposite goals, and investors and administrations should lean toward the side of art. Jones had previously worked in commercial theatre. She codirected the original Broadway production of Tennessee Williams's *The Glass Menagerie*, and it was partially through her Broadway connection that she gained legitimacy for her work in Dallas. Meanwhile, she opened her theatre as a nonprofit institution when theatre in general had not yet joined the solidly nonprofit ranks of the symphony and opera house. Nevertheless, Jones insisted, "Unlike many nonprofit organizations, a theatre should and can make enough money to pay for itself, provided an initial sum is raised to start it."[14] She distinguished between theatre and other arts: theatres, she believed, should raise money principally through capital campaigns, not on an ongoing basis, and then continue to support themselves through the box office. Despite advocating for nonprofit status and art above money, she perpetuated the underlying conviction that theatre should be able to support itself financially. As conceived by Jones, for-profit theatre and nonprofit theatre were not so different from each other, and Arena Stage illustrates this point from its earliest years.

WASHINGTON, DC, AND THE OPENING OF ARENA STAGE

Arena Stage arose during the Jim Crow era, when theatre in Washington was racially segregated. In 1939, Constitution Hall, administered by the Daughters of the American Revolution, infamously rejected having an integrated audience for black opera singer Marian Anderson. She performed outside the Lincoln Memorial instead. In 1947, when the National Theatre, the chief touring house in Washington, refused to sell tickets to black patrons, the Committee for Racial Democracy and the National Association for the Advancement of Colored People (NAACP) picketed the theatre.[15] Committed to social justice, Zelda Fichandler and other artists joined the picket line. Actors' Equity Association began calling for its members to boycott the National Theatre. Rather than admit an integrated audience or weather the boycott and lose theatre ticket sales, the National Theatre became a movie house from 1948 to 1952.

In 1950, Arena emerged as Washington's leading racially integrated professional resident theatre. By opening its doors to everyone, the theatre made a liberal political statement, even if it catered to white interests and did not have many black patrons. Director and George Washington University theatre professor Edward Mangum and his graduate student Zelda Fichandler cofounded Arena Enterprises Inc. He proposed that they follow the model of Margo Jones. Unlike Jones, though, Mangum insisted on starting as a for-profit venture. He remarked, "I knew of no one who wanted to contribute his [sic] hard-earned cash to a nonprofit enterprise as shaky as a legitimate theatre can be. I did know some friends who were willing to gamble on my making a success of a new kind of theatre."[16] Despite the history of little theatres, U.S. theatre was still cast in commercial terms, and according to Mangum, a nonprofit theatre was riskier than a for-profit one. At the time, Washington had no professional resident theatre. The Gayety Theater, originally a burlesque house, had transformed into a touring house under the Shubert conglomerate.[17] For amateur performance, locals could visit colleges such as Catholic University and historically black Howard University. The Mount Vernon Players, a community theatre, had provided experience for Arena's founding members including Mangum and Vera Roberts.

To launch their for-profit enterprise, Mangum and Fichandler raised $15,000 from forty stockholders whose occupations ranged from ambassador to carpenter, a point that Arena's own narratives use to underscore the company's populist beginnings.[18] The founding members initially bought a boat, the SS *Potomac*, on which they hoped to perform plays, but they were unable to find a suitable place to dock their show boat. The members located a movie theatre, the Hippodrome, in the Northwest quadrant and transformed it into a 247-seat theatre-in-the-round. Because theatres were required to have a fire curtain, and Arena could not have one due to its in-the-round playing space, the institution legally could not use the word "theatre" in its name, hence Arena Stage. The company produced a repertory representing the educated, white, middle-class habitus of the company's founders and patrons. The first season boasted seventeen productions, including Oliver Goldsmith's *She Stoops to Conquer*, Oscar Wilde's *The Importance of Being Earnest*, and William Shakespeare's *Twelfth Night*, which were so popular that they were brought back the next season. By staging canonical works by white Western male playwrights, this budding theatre could appeal to the local elite and gain sound financial footing. Arena achieved Equity status after its first year, meaning that all the actors were professionals. In 1952, when Mangum left for other ventures in Hawaii, Zelda Fichandler co-led the company with Alan Schneider, who eventually directed more than thirty productions at Arena Stage.[19] After four more years with Fichandler at the helm, the company's corporate worth nearly doubled.[20]

Fichandler's social class, education, and cultural upbringing shaped her taste in programming and her ability to take on leadership of a professional theatre company in the first place. Born Zelda Diamond in 1924, she hailed from a middle-class immigrant family in Boston, Massachusetts. Both her parents had emigrated from Russia, and both were Orthodox Jews. They met when they were studying at the Massachusetts Institute of Technology. When her father, Harry Diamond, took a job at the National Bureau of Standards, the family moved to Washington, DC. He went on to become an important engineer. When Zelda was around seventeen, she defied her parents, who had wanted her to remain in Washington and marry like "a regular girl."[21] She attended Cornell University, where she originally followed a pre-med path, but an upper-level program on contemporary Soviet culture changed her direction. She penned Russian translations, wrote her thesis on Shakespeare and the Soviet Union, and read Chekhov in Russian. During the early Cold War, she translated Russian missives for the U.S. government. This background gestures toward her repertory, which prominently featured Shakespeare and Chekhov, playwrights whose works would become staples at regional theatres. After college, in 1946, she married Thomas Fichandler. An economist, he supported her artistic leadership of Arena Stage and managed the company's finances, an increasingly complex job as the theatre grew. Although Zelda had racial, class, and educational privileges, she had to contend with systemic misogyny and antisemitism. When people outside Washington took notice of her, they expressed skepticism that a woman steered this flagship institution. Fichandler recounted, "They would say, 'Well, who runs this place?' And I would say, 'Well, my name is on the pro-

Arena Stage cofounder Zelda Fichandler in front of the company's first theatre venue, the Hippodrome, in 1950. Photo courtesy of Arena Stage.

gram. I don't know, I think I do.' And they'd say, 'No, but I mean really, make the hard decisions, like what plays you're gonna do, how much money you're gonna spend?' And I said, 'Well, I think I *do*.'"[22]

In 1955, Zelda Fichandler persuaded the stockholders to move Arena Stage to a larger space, arguing that more seats would generate more income. This income would go back into the theatre because it "has entailed too many hardships, including that of low salaries, the pressures of constant bargain hunting in all departments, and the necessity to make too many artistic judgments on the basis of the dollar sign alone."[23] This was not a typical corporation calculating every decision to increase the economic value of its holdings and distribute those dividends to investors regularly. This was also not a romantic valorization of the starving artist. Instead, Fichandler asserted that theatre thrives on well-paid employees, reduced anxiety over finances, and decisions not beholden to the box office and production costs, such as selecting plays with small casts and few costume changes. She conceived of economic capital being in service to her artistic choices. However, even sold-out runs like the Washington premiere of *The Crucible* in 1954 lost money. Arena was willing to keep ticket prices low, produce work at an immediate financial loss, and stage this anti-McCarthy play that had fared poorly on Broadway. In a time of containment of threats within and beyond the United States, the Federal Bureau of Investigation scrutinized Fichandler and her husband for producing this particular play by Arthur Miller.[24] But she did not shrink. In her five-year report to the stockholders, she imagined Arena Stage at age ten with a permanent acting ensemble, a playwright in residence, and educational initiatives, programs that later became the purview of nonprofit theatres.

In 1956, Arena moved to Foggy Bottom, also in Northwest. They occupied a former brewery and fitted it with five hundred seats, twice the size of the previous theatre. The company dubbed the building the Old Vat in reference to the Old Vic in London and the leftover vats of beer. The theatre continued to produce white middlebrow plays by the likes of Sean O'Casey, George Bernard Shaw, and Agatha Christie. But because that building was soon slated for demolition to make way for a new bridge across the Potomac River, the company had to move again. This time, the company sought a stable home and nonprofit status. Both could bestow greater security: a space owned by the company, tax exemptions, and foundation grants. During a meeting with the board of directors in 1958, Zelda Fichandler "pointed out that we were at present in an anomalous position, being set up as a private-profit making venture, and yet by our aims and policy not seriously expecting to make any sizeable private profits, but rather attempting primarily to furnish the Washington area with high caliber theatre fare."[25]

Although Fichandler appeared uninterested in making "any sizeable private profits," Arena had a preexisting relationship with commercial theatre. The company gained a reputation for reviving Broadway flops such as the acclaimed Australian drama *The Summer of the 17th Doll* by Ray Lawler. Its production, directed by Alan Schneider in 1958, was so successful that commercial producer Sidney Bernstein proposed that he transfer and coproduce the show with Arena Stage Off-Broadway. After considering the potential high prestige and low financial risk, the board of directors voted to cover half of the capitalization.[26] The fact that the play had not done well at the Broadway box office and was moving to the less explicitly commercial clime of Off-Broadway likely helped to justify this decision. A few years later in "A Permanent Classical Repertory Theatre in the Nation's Capital," part of the application for Arena to obtain nonprofit status, Fichandler indicted Broadway and articulated the art versus commerce binary: "Broadway's objective is not culture at all. Its objective is commodity."[27] In her speeches to board members, she repeatedly linked New York, specifically Broadway, to a money-making machine—and a broken one at that, pointing out the high rate of flops in the late 1950s. She contrasted this image with regional theatre as the new site for art. Regional theatre and Off-Broadway, even though they produced the same plays that had premiered on Broadway, were considered distinct from Broadway.

While Fichandler tried to stake a claim to professionally produced serious drama outside of New York, many critics deemed Washington a cultural backwater. In 1959, Howard Taubman of the *New York Times* asked, "In Culture, Is Washington a Hick Town?" and implicitly answered yes.[28] Critiquing Taubman's article, Fichandler remarked, "He shows a lack of specific knowledge about the dynamics of the situation when he calls Washington's record in theatre 'poor' and at the same time fails to note that between 1950 to 1960 Arena Stage went from $67,000 to almost a quarter-of-a-million dollars at the box office and . . . went from 30,000 to over 100,000 in attendance."[29] She pointed out that Washington had (and has) more theatre playing weeks than comparable cities such as Dallas and a professional audience eager for professional theatre. She understood the power of critics from New York as well as local ones such as Richard Coe of the *Washington Post* in consecrating her institution and city.[30] In the 1950s, reviews by *New York Times* critic Brooks Atkinson and articles in *Theatre Arts* helped to legitimize Arena and position it as an exceptional regional theatre.

Fichandler also critiqued her bourgeois audience and their reliance on critical approval. The critics' power was not natural or immutable but granted

by a by-and-large immature, commodity-oriented public who, for both psychological and economic reasons, are loathe to make independent choices as to how to spend their time and money. "Daddy" must tell them whether or not this production of *Hamlet* is worth the price of two tickets as against a new gadget for the

barbecue pit and worth three or four hours time as against weed-
ing out the crabgrass.[31]

Fichandler reveals a Bourdieusian understanding of the field of cultural production and habitus. Using her sarcastic wit and betraying
her own ambivalence about the audience, she mocks the bourgeoisie's
deliberate calculation of capital accumulation. This ambivalence—
wanting a public theatre but also rebuking the public—recurred
throughout Fichandler's tenure and negotiation of non- and for-profit.
She resented commodifying art but understood that doing so was a
material condition for her productions to score critical approval and
ticket sales. During these transitional years, Fichandler acknowledged
the continued importance of "unpretentious entertainment."[32] Speaking like a producer, she stated, "Success is the first law of the theatre,
profit or nonprofit."[33]

To help shield the theatre from negative reviews and to keep it financially afloat, Fichandler built a subscription base. Instead of buy-
ing single tickets for specific, attractive productions, patrons could
purchase tickets for the entire season. Beginning in 1957, the theatre
could count on subscribers to pay for and fill seats, whether or not the
individual production was well-liked, paralleling the audience model
of other performing arts nonprofits. When speaking of subscriptions,
Fichandler was fond of quoting French theatre artist Jean Louis Bar-
rault: "A theatre's duty was 'to strive unbendingly to attract the devoted adherent as opposed to the transient public interested only in
the hits.'"[34] She attributed the theatre's success in the 1959–60 season to subscribers and community-oriented programs, including "pre-
view performances for government workers" and "the teen ticket plan
for high school students and teachers."[35] By cultivating this educated
audience, Arena appeared less commercial than other endeavors yet
had reliable income.

Zelda Fichandler's husband, Thomas Fichandler, undoubtedly
played a huge part in researching the financial planning, though it is
sometimes difficult to determine which Fichandler was responsible for
which fiscal policy. He served as Arena's executive director and had
previously worked for the Twentieth Century Fund, a progressive think
tank that focused on policy issues from poverty to global security. With
their economic savviness, the Fichandlers forged a sustainable stage,

but Zelda wanted to take more risks and to reach more people, which could be done more easily under the banner of nonprofit. Nonprofit status would allow the company to receive grants; donations; and new tax breaks on income, property, mailers, and tickets. According to Zelda Fichandler, "The reason we moved from 247 to 800 [seats] was because we weren't taking enough in to do what we wanted to do, and we were selling out. It was success that turned us into nonprofit."[36] In 1959, the Fichandler duo persuaded the stockholders to dissolve the corporation and transfer assets to the new nonprofit Washington Drama Society. This change was a bold experiment.

Zelda Fichandler subsequently applied for Arena Stage to become a not-for-profit 501(c)3 organization. Part of gaining nonprofit status entailed Arena's assertion that it was already not in the business of making substantial economic profits but of benefiting the community with professional theatre. Fichandler emphasized Arena's pedagogical objectives. She recounted that she "wrote a long document to the Department of the Treasury, supporting theatre as an instrument of education. . . . The document happened to land on the desk of an Arena subscriber! And was read into the Congressional Record. We've been nonprofit ever since."[37] Her argument and her repertory appealed to a governmental worker with a similar habitus as an educated professional. A circle of privileged people in key positions made way for nonprofit regional theatre. Reincorporation as a nonprofit gave Arena security through the potential of not only tax exemptions and grants but also a permanent home.

It was important for Arena to establish itself as a durable institution, and for Washington to showcase its sole resident professional theatre. With the National Theatre and Ford's Theatre closed in 1950, U.S. politicians needed a cultural center where they could take diplomats, so they had a vested interest in supporting a local, professional theatre. Arena's 1981 application for landmark status boasts of foreign visitors and newspaper coverage from Italy to Hong Kong in the early 1950s.[38] During the Cold War, the U.S. government wanted to counter the Soviet Union with artistic achievements in its own capital. While Russian culture was associated with elite art, U.S. cultural products were associated with mass culture. To gain more symbolic capital, U.S. political leaders wanted to shift their branding toward higher-class fare. Moreover, the visible impoverishment of the city embarrassed them.

According to historian Howard Gillette Jr., two factors motivated infrastructure policy in the nation's capital: social justice for the advancement of racial equality and aesthetic beauty for the advancement of state power.[39] Arguments for the latter often outweighed the former.

The derelict state of the U.S. capital had much to do with the demographics of the Washington metro area. From 1940 to 1950, the surrounding suburbs of Montgomery, Prince George's, Arlington, and Fairfax Counties doubled in size.[40] In 1950, whites made up 65 percent and blacks made up 35 percent of the city proper.[41] One decade later, the percentage of whites dropped to 45 percent, and black people became the majority. When segregation was no longer legally upheld, white residents moved to the suburbs, aided by real estate agents and federal policies such as redlining to preserve white homogeneity and wealth. Completed in 1964, the "Beltway," a new major highway encircling the city, facilitated suburban sprawl. The population of Washington steadily decreased from this point on to 2000, when gentrification caused the numbers to climb again. With a less affluent tax base and no major industry outside of government, the city had fewer resources and its residents had little say over how to use those resources. According to longtime journalists Harry Jaffe and Tom Sherwood, "No one can understand Washington without appreciating the debilitating impact of federal control that has been at various times patronizing, neglectful, and racist."[42] Since the end of Reconstruction in the 1870s, Washington was ruled by a presidentially appointed board of commissioners. The city did not gain home rule, an elected mayor and council, until one century later. The capital's residents still lack voting representation in Congress.

In 1950, this top-down effort to beautify Washington came in the form of the Redevelopment Land Agency to package and resell the land in Southwest to developers and eventually to Arena Stage.[43] Since the Great Migration of the early twentieth century, Southwest attracted a significant concentration of poor African Americans. Many residents lived in substandard housing, which did not provide a pretty picture when politicians looked from the Capital toward Southwest. Rather than improve existing structures, developers called for the total destruction of the area in order to build anew. Mid-twentieth-century urban renewal efforts used eminent domain to evict people and raze their homes, leading to even more overcrowding in surrounding neigh-borhoods.[44] According to political theorist Margaret E. Farrar, policy-makers cast "the problem of urban poverty in the rationalized lan-guage of 'blight' and 'slums' [which] allowed the subjects of discourse to disappear . . . [and] erase the distinction between public and pri-vate space, so that all urban spaces were available for their appropria-tion."[45] The Redevelopment Land Agency authorized the demolition of 99 percent of the buildings in Southwest DC and then the construc-tion of 5,900 housing units. This resulted in the displacement of 23,500 residents, three-quarters of whom were black. The new units were in-tended to entice back the high-income white residents who had fled to the suburbs of Virginia and Maryland.[46] This development project, the largest in U.S. history at that point, became known as "Negro re-moval."[47] After clearing the area of low-income black residents, the Agency promised to sell the land at a reduced cost to Arena if it were a nonprofit organization.

The price for nonprofit status and a permanent home was the dis-placement of poor black residents. In *How Racism Takes Place*, Ameri-can Studies scholar George Lipsitz analyzes the racialization of space and the spatialization of race.[48] He demonstrates how what he calls the "white racial imaginary" rests on financially, juridically, and politically constructing and policing areas to the benefit of white Americans. The U.S. government literally pushed out black people and sold the land to white artist-administrators at a discount. Officials hoped that the theatre would gentrify the area, whitening the space and enriching the already rich. Even though Arena technically welcomed racially inte-grated audiences and did not personally evict black residents, in prac-tice the theatre carved out a largely separate whitened space within the black urban environment. The institution's racial integration would not materialize for many more years. In the autumn of 1961, the Arena Stage Theatre became the first theatre built in Washington since 1895, the first arena-style theatre built for a U.S. company, and the largest theatre for a resident U.S. professional company.[49] Designed by Harry Weese, who also designed the Washington Metro, the in-the-round space mirrored Arena's past stages and Fichandler's vision.

With nonprofit status, Arena Stage obtained funding that had not been available to the institution as a for-profit enterprise. One foundation after another (the Rockefeller Foundation, the Old Dominion Foundation, and the Meyer Foundation) contributed to the capital campaign. Arena also raised funds by soliciting donations from loyal patrons, former stockholders, and members of the new board of trustees. In addition, administrators sold bonds to the public, making the theatre more of a community-driven initiative and financial investment. Although the company was left with many hundreds of thousands of dollars of debt, the press celebrated the financial security that the permanent home promised. Reporters hardly discussed potential artistic changes that the new building and nonprofit status would make possible, reinforcing the notion that Arena had been behaving like a not-for-profit company that would continue business as usual.

Arena received substantial economic security in 1962 when the Ford Foundation granted $863,000. It covered the mortgage, bonds, and site acquisition for the theatre and left more than $150,000 in reserve. W. McNeil "Mac" Lowry, the head of the Humanities and the Arts division of the Ford Foundation from 1957 to 1965 and later a vice president of the organization, had previously given grants to Zelda Fichandler to enhance her skills as a director. In 1962, Zelda and Thomas Fichandler told the board of trustees that Lowry had consulted them on the state of regional theatre and was funding their own institution as part of a new initiative.[50] Between 1962 and 1971, the Ford Foundation gave $2,659,450 to Arena, out of a total $16 million distributed among seventeen regional theatres.[51] The only regional theatre that received more money was the Alley Theatre. In "Theatre Reawakening: A Report on Ford Foundation Assistance to American Drama," the foundation repeatedly cited Arena as an exemplar.[52] The impact of the Ford Foundation's financial support cannot be overstated in giving Arena ownership over the means of production and what Zelda Fichandler called the "freedom to fail," a prerogative of the nonprofit.

For the Ford, the economic plight of Arena Stage and the budding regional theatre movement provided opportunities to make a significant impact on the performing arts field. In contrast with symphonies and opera houses, theatres were generally poorly funded. Spending this economic capital could earn the Ford corporation symbolic capital as forward-thinking and humanist. A tax shelter for the profits from the car conglomerate, Ford boasted the largest foundation in the world in the mid-twentieth century.[53] Vast income from stock dividends and stock sales combined with the end of the McCarthy era to embolden the foundation to make gigantic donations. Scholar-activist Ruth Wilson Gilmore argues that "foundations are repositories of twice-stolen wealth—(a) profit sheltered from (b) taxes—that can be retrieved by those who stole it at the opera or the museum."[54] Capitalists skim the surplus value off of their laborers' productivity instead of paying their full share in wages. Their foundations protect their profits from taxation. Instead of the general populace deciding where that communal tax money should go, the wealthy are able to funnel their foundation funds into their own causes, ultimately subsidizing themselves: "The majority of grants go to universities, hospitals, research, and the arts, while barely 1.7 percent goes to fund civil rights and social action."[55] Foundations are required to spend a percentage of their annual income, and later tax codes placed greater restrictions on giving grants to individuals, thereby favoring institutions like Arena Stage.

Scholar of arts philanthropy Sheila McNerney Anderson argues that "Lowry shaped arts policy and institutional development in the performing arts community in the United States more than any other single individual."[56] Lowry was particularly interested in the development of European-inspired acting companies, "noncommercial theatre," "classics," and the "creation of a new body of American classics."[57] Part of a liberal political project, these endeavors promised to bolster the production and reputation of arts in the United States at a time when politicians felt that they were losing on the cultural front of the Cold War. As a result, Arena received more money to train and retain talented actors for its permanent ensemble. Zelda Fichandler recounted, "It never entered my head to start a theatre without an acting company. . . . The acting company is the center of the theatre because it is the acting company that contacts the audience and the audience who responds back and the actors who respond back to the response back and forth and back."[58] With a resident company, Arena could cultivate ongoing relationships between artists and audiences, making the company and Washington a home. By paying Equity cardholders season-long contracts as opposed to offering single-show contracts, the regional theatre could dissuade actors from going back to New York City. Company veterans like Richard Bauer, who played more than one hundred roles at Arena Stage from the 1960s to the 1990s, remarked, "Arena develops the whole artist rather than an actor who can play a single role in a given play."[59] The resident ensemble would become important to Arena's reputation. The theatre also began to support playwrights in residence. Nonprofit status thus generated even more economic capital and symbolic capital in the form of grants from prestigious foundations to underwrite ambitious artistic programs.

With support from patrons, critics, government agencies, and foundations, Fichandler chose more artistically and politically challenging plays. In 1961, she opened the new space with what was billed as the U.S. premiere of Bertolt Brecht's *The Caucasian Chalk Circle* (but was actually the premiere of John Holmstrom's translation). Directed by Alan Schneider, this parable about law versus righteous justice signified the type of work that Fichandler wanted to promote. Fichandler used the play as a framing device for her introduction to the theatre's self-produced commemorative book *The Arena Adventure: The First 40 Years*. Reflecting on the 1961 production, she noted that "there was some consternation about picking this particular then-avant-garde play by this particular East German writer for so spotlighted an event," especially considering that the Berlin Wall had been erected a couple of months earlier.[60] In the week leading up to the launch of the theatre and *The Caucasian Chalk Circle*, the *Washington Post* printed several articles about Arena Stage, its new building, and Brecht, as well as a positive review by Richard Coe. In the *New York Times*, Howard Taubman compared Washington favorably to New York for producing Brecht and having such a stellar resident acting ensemble. The production was a hit, but writing to Lowry, Fichandler claimed that audiences were coming to see the new theatre building, not the play.[61] This was probably true to an extent, yet it was also likely a tactic to continue asking the Ford Foundation for targeted artistic grants.

In its first seasons at the permanent home, Arena earned more box office income than ever before. The company continued to produce eight-show seasons but for more weeks and seats. Brecht's *Caucasian Chalk Circle* and Marc Blitzstein's adaptation of Brecht and Kurt Weill's antibourgeois musical *The Threepenny Opera* had the highest ticket sales in the 1961–62 and 1962–63 seasons, respectively.[62] Such

CAPITAL

financial success prompted a reevaluation of how to price tickets and which patrons to prioritize. Thomas Fichandler had recommended raising ticket prices for *Threepenny* because of the high cost of hiring an orchestra. However, the board of trustees insisted on the theatre's duty as a nonprofit to make tickets affordable to more people. They ultimately defeated his motion.[63] According to Zelda Fichandler, maintaining low ticket prices was one of her greatest achievements because "everybody can come," opening up the possibility for dialogue and transformation.[64] But "everybody" is an overstatement. In 1962, single Arena Stage tickets cost $2–$3.95, several times the cost of movie tickets.[65] According to a study conducted in 1964, more than half the company's patrons had some graduate school education and their average family income was $15,000, approximately twice the Washington average.[66]

Fichandler surely produced Brecht and Brecht-inspired plays because their politics, prestige, and music appealed to middlebrow audiences in the 1960s. In his study of U.S. reception, Siegfried Mews adds, "The general acceptance of Brecht by white, mostly affluent, middle-class audiences who support the regional theaters was most likely aided by noncontroversial productions."[67] In 1967, a decade after Brecht's death, theatre theorist Martin Esslin commented on Brecht's growing popularity in U.S. academic publications. In an essay in *TDR*, he posed the question "Has the significance of Brecht engendered the Brecht industry, or has the Brecht industry made Brecht seem so significant?"[68] *Threepenny* was one of the most frequently produced works at regional theatres in the late 1960s.[69]

Thinking of Brecht as an "industry" and possibly "American" seems strange, yet his works' circulation between Washington, New York, and other U.S. cities suggests his strong presence in U.S. theatre, and Arena Stage took part in his institutionalization. Fichandler likely knew of the popular production of *The Threepenny Opera* in New York, where it ran for nearly three thousand performances Off-Broadway at the Theater de Lys from 1954 to 1961. After Arena opened with *The Caucasian Chalk Circle*, that play was produced soon afterward at the Actor's Workshop in San Francisco, the Guthrie Theater in Minneapolis, and Lincoln Center in New York, among other regional theatres. Fichandler also prided herself on producing *Galileo* (Charles Laughton's version) "before it did the resident theatre circuit."[70] Such negotiations draw attention to competing claims to owning Brecht as well as a system of programming beyond Broadway. Moreover, play selection was not a simple matter of choosing between high art and high box office receipts. Politically progressive and popular, these plays linked Arena's artistic mission and commercial needs.

In the mid-1960s, Fichandler moved the repertory further in this direction. She produced contemporary European plays including *The Hostage* by Brendan Behan, *Oh! What a Lovely War* by Joan Littlewood and the Theatre Workshop, and *Serjeant Musgrave's Dance* by John Arden. The former plays were two of the most produced works across the United States in the mid-1960s.[71] In *The Hostage*, Behan dramatizes Irish Republican Army members who take a young British soldier hostage after an Irish youth has been arrested. Littlewood spearheaded the English adaptation by the Theatre Workshop, with which she also developed *Oh! What a Lovely War*. This play explores and sends up the causes of World War I through upbeat period songs punctuated by offstage sounds of explosions, while news items are projected onto a back screen. In *Serjeant Musgrave's Dance*, Arden critiques militarism when a group of soldiers, devastated by colonialism and imperialism, call for further violence. Whereas the early marketing downplayed the antiwar messages of these works, Arena's productions themselves seem to have been provocative, or they are at least reframed that way in retrospect. Covering the 1965–66 season, *The Arena Adventure* spotlighted only *Oh! What a Lovely War* and *Serjeant Musgrave's Dance* and declared that "Arena kept pace with the country's growing skepticism about armed conflict in Indochina by offering two distinctly different anti-war plays."[72] The productions were particularly topical in the context of the nation's capital and U.S. military actions. According to staff meeting minutes, during the run of *Serjeant Musgrave's Dance*, Arena planned to put photographs of the Vietnam War and other wars in the lobby.[73] *Washington Post* critic Geoffrey A. Wolff observed that Arden's play "obviously speaks to our moral dilemmas in Vietnam."[74] Programming these plays capitalized on the audience's mostly liberal politics, which were not limited to Off- and Off-Off-Broadway but very present in 1960s regional theatre.

Sixteen years after its opening, Arena Stage experienced its first deficit, and the blame went to the 1965–66 season's experimental and progressive repertory. The theatre was in the red for approximately $50,000, and its subscription base dipped for the first time. In 1963, Thomas Fichandler explained that the company regularly lost half of its subscribers each season: one quarter because of the transient nature of political Washington, and the other quarter for no known reason.[75] But this time, Zelda Fichandler claimed that Arena lost half its subscribers because conservative audiences disliked the previous season, which included short works by Eugène Ionesco (*The Lesson*) and Harold Pinter (*The Collection*) in addition to *Oh! What a Lovely War* and *Serjeant Musgrave's Dance*.[76] According to *The Arena Adventure*, including these antiwar plays in "this banquet gave some subscribers indigestion and they left the table. More traditional fare was added."[77] As noted earlier, this same commemorative book describes these antiwar plays as reflections of popular U.S. sentiment. Here, however, the book positions these plays as unpopular in a strictly commercial sense. In *The Making of Theatrical Reputations*, Yael Zarhy-Levo uses Joan Littlewood's Theatre Workshop and John Arden as her two case studies for illustrating how artists' aesthetics and politics resulted in mixed reviews and denials of governmental grants.[78]

But in Arena's case, the claims about losing money and losing subscribers seem exaggerated if not plain false, even though they feel true due to Bourdieu's Economic World Reversed idea. In total, Arena Stage had only four hundred fewer subscribers than the year before, coming to the still sizable total of sixteen thousand in the 1966–67 season. Throughout the mid-1960s, the audience typically filled 90 percent of the house, suggesting the challenging repertory proved popular among many subscribers and individual ticket buyers.[79] Pinter's plays *The Birthday Party* and *The Homecoming* were among the most frequently staged at regional theatres in the mid 1960s.[80] *Oh! What a Lovely War* was the biggest box office draw of Arena's 1965–66 season, bringing in more than $90,000, second only to *The Threepenny Opera* years earlier.[81] Admittedly because of the hired band and projections, *Oh! What a Lovely War* had additional expenses. It also had fewer available seats due to one section of seating being removed, the first and only time when the theatre has done this, to create a thrust stage and area for projections. Still, *Oh! What a Lovely War* was the single production whose image graced the brochure for subscribers to renew for the following season, perhaps the reason why some subscribers "left the table."

Despite the fiscal success and entertainment value of *Oh! What a Lovely War*, the widely held belief that provocative, higher art cannot also be commercially viable permitted Fichandler to blame the deficit on the supposed rejection of the artistically and politically challenging repertory. In 1967, she delivered a speech to the American Educational Theatre Association, an audience likely receptive to praises of avant-garde and antiwar plays. Critics have quoted this speech unquestioningly for decades. She disclosed that Richard Schechner, creator of the avant-garde Performance Group, admired most of her company's productions such as *Oh! What a Lovely War* but derided what he called the "Marshmallow Theatre" movement and absence of working-class audiences. Fichandler countered by underlining the absence of wealthy donors to support a populist theatre and claiming that she had received complaints from her audience about the repertory becoming too "specialized" and not enough "fun."[82] She asserted that to survive, "what we *had to do* was to acknowledge that the audience was our Master (oh oh oh six o'clock and the master's not home yet, pray God nothing's happened to him crossing the Potomac River. If anything happened to him we'd all be inconsolable and have to move to a less desireable [*sic*] residence district!)"[83] Using racialized diction, Fichandler positioned Arena as a black servant and its patron as a white master, which was somewhat ironic given the lack of blackness on her stage. She acknowledged loyal subscribers as the backbone of her theatre, but she also resented their influence and critiqued their frankly white, middlebrow tastes. She later reflected in "Whither (or Wither) Art?," "What I learned was that while I was entitled to enjoy the freedom to fail, it was anticipated that I would not indulge in it too frequently. Further, that it would be much more comfortable for me if the failure could be attributed to some outside power—the Republicans, the snow, a parade, a flood in the Potomac River—and not to my own bad judgment or creative misstep."[84] Even as a nonprofit, Arena had to demonstrate that it made fiscally sound decisions and hold accountable an imagined unappreciative audience that wanted safe entertainment.

This did not mean that Fichandler produced more canonical fare against her own wishes. There was no conservative board of trustees imposing its will, an accusation used against nonprofit theatres since the 1960s.[85] According to regional theatre scholar Joseph Zeigler, who interned at Arena Stage in 1962, the "board may technically employ Zelda and fix her salary, [but] she controls the board. Arena Stage is a ladylike autocracy."[86] The theatre kept staging Renaissance comedies such as *Volpone* and *The Taming of the Shrew* into the '60s because Fichandler wanted to stage such work. Before and after the move to the new building, some of Arena's most commercially successful shows were comedies. In her essay "Theatres or Institutions?" among other speeches and publications, Fichandler actively advocated for classics that spoke to contemporary audiences, and she defended 1930s farces for their aesthetics as well as their box office appeal.[87] From the opening of the new building in 1961 to 1970, Arena produced four plays by Shakespeare and three each by Shaw and Chekhov. This period also included multiple productions of plays by Brecht, Georges Feydeau, Luigi Pirandello, Eugene O'Neill, Howard Sackler, Jean Anouilh, and George Kaufman and Moss Hart. Following the deficit year, the 1966–67 season reined back slightly yet continued to produce works about abuses of power such as *Macbeth*, *The Crucible*, and *The Inspector General* and fewer plays in total. This programming attracted more subscribers while remaining within the bounds of Fichandler's artistic preferences.

Although Arena had to appear disinterested in economic profit, the theatre still had to focus on selling tickets because the fundraising safety net was relatively small. Arena Stage's contributed income from grants and donations accounted for 11 percent of total income in the 1961–62 season and increased to 32 percent by the end of the decade.[88] The box office supplied the vast majority of income. In *The Subsidized Muse*, Dick Netzer notes of the 1973–74 season that the company's continued heavy reliance on ticket sales was rather unusual in contrast to theatres such as Trinity Repertory Company in Providence, Rhode Island, which had an even split between box office and contributed income.[89] Artistic and foundation leaders, such as Lowry, frequently pointed to Arena's early financial stability as evidence of a theatre not needing to raise money after an initial capital campaign.

Many theatres used individual, foundation, and government contributions to construct permanent homes, and as with Arena's new model, they established themselves as nonprofits in the 1960s. According to the 1965 Rockefeller Fund study *The Performing Arts: Problems and Prospects*, "More than half the professional theatre projects outside New York—and almost all the major ones—have been created as nonprofit undertakings."[90] The Guthrie Theater in Minneapolis is a frequently cited example.[91] Founded by Sir Tyrone Guthrie, Oliver Rea, and Peter Zeisler, the company sought out foundation and civic funding from the very beginning. On a panel about "The Community and Festival Theaters" in 1963, Fichandler distinguished the opening of the Guthrie, "that is, full-blown from the head of Zeus" from the emergence of her own theatre, "slowly, painfully, organically," arguing that her experience of navigating profit accumulation and institutionalization was the more common.[92] But both theatres were uncommon in their extraordinary financial and artistic success. According to the Rockefeller report, only three regional theatres ran surpluses in 1963: Arena Stage, the Guthrie Theater, and UCLA Theatre Group.[93] Reversing earlier ideas about theatre sustainability, the report concluded in bold italics: "This panel believes that as a general principle the non-profit performing arts organizations should not be expected to pay their way at the box office. Indeed, they cannot do so and still fulfill their true cultural mission."[94] Moving from "should not" to "cannot," the panel argued that the "true cultural mission" of nonprofit theatres was at odds with selling out at the box office.

The Rockefeller Panel's beliefs and recommendations were supported by William Baumol and William Bowen in their 1966 landmark study *Performing Arts: The Economic Dilemma*. The Princeton economists dispelled the 1960s cultural boom myth: U.S. Americans were not spending more on cultural activities with respect to percentage of income, and the percentage of people attending performing arts events had not increased in preceding years. The difference between an institution's expenditures and box office income became known as the "income gap," and Baumol and Bowen argued that the nonprofit theatre's income gap would worsen over time. They reasoned that technology would not meaningfully improve productivity in theatre, a relatively

CAPITAL

small, hand-crafted medium, so production costs would continue to increase. Ticket prices could not keep up with inflation, production costs, and salaries while remaining low enough to attract economically diverse audiences.[95] An analysis of the income gap in the 1966–67 season illustrates that the Guthrie ended with a $224,700 gap between expenses and ticket sales and a $22,500 season deficit, thanks to significant foundation grants.[96] Meanwhile, Arena had an income gap of $43,300 with almost no donations or grants leading to a $41,800 deficit.[97] According to Zeigler, on average, the income gap for eighteen regional theatres from 1966 to 1970 was $165,000, and the average "Fund Raising" was $138,000, leaving a net deficit of $27,000.[98]

The reports by the Rockefeller Foundation and Baumol and Bowen came at precisely the moment when Arena Stage suffered its first deficit and needed a rationale for that deficit. Nonprofit regional companies subsequently cited these studies and changed the language of their grant requests to accept deficits as the natural condition of nonprofit theatres, not a fault of mismanagement.[99] Rather than asking for donations for only capital campaigns, nonprofits created fundraising initiatives to maintain the regular operations of their theatres. By disavowing high ticket sales, yet still depending on them, they maneuvered to attract more grants and donations. This tactic gave theatres more money to reinvest in apparently riskier initiatives like experimental and leftist plays, which reaffirmed an apparent disinterest in economic profit and continued this cycle of capital production. To establish Arena as nonprofit and thus raise donations and win grants, Fichandler mobilized the assumption that she lost money and subscribers due to her production of antiwar plays with antirealist aesthetics. But plays like *Oh! What a Lovely War* were in fact commercial hits. Playing both sides, Fichandler cleverly accumulated income from donors and foundations as well as from the box office.

EMBRACING THE DEFICIT AND RACIAL DIVERSITY

Zelda Fichandler mobilized the deficit to secure more funding from foundations and install ambitious programs.[100] She explained, "Every time the box office caught up with our intentions, our intentions grew."[101] Because having a deficit became acceptable by the mid-1960s, she could implement the plans that she had envisioned years earlier as well as new ones responding to contemporary politics. She could position education, art, and social justice as having higher callings than commerce. What truly distinguished Arena as a nonprofit from the mid-1960s forward was not only the staging of more left-leaning and aesthetically challenging plays, but also the active incorporation of black stories, artists, and locals for the first time. The rumblings of black liberation stirred Fichandler. No longer needing to end the season in the black, Fichandler could add blackness to her season. What could appear riskier than a white institution staging integration?

In the wake of civil rights legislation and white flight, Arena began concerted efforts to reach out to black communities. In 1966, white actor-director Robert Alexander founded the Living Stage Theatre Company under Arena's umbrella. Located in a renovated jazz club, Living Stage worked with local community members such as public school students coming from predominantly of-color and low-income backgrounds. They improvised plays dealing with their racial, economic, and gendered struggles.[102] Alexander believed that everyone had important stories to tell and that creative self-expression could lead to empowerment. By launching this theatre for social change as an educational program, Arena helped the disenfranchised in Washington in a way that was liberal and legible, creating a platform for their voices rather than just giving resources. In addition, Living Stage granted Arena greater legitimacy as a public-serving institution. According to Zeigler, "The concept of public service is partly an insurance policy for the regional theatre institution. By serving, it hopes to provide for itself and its public an alternative to the 'hit-or-miss' psychology of the commercial theatre."[103]

Grants to subsidize the world premieres of plays also served as "an insurance policy" because untested works were fiscally risky endeavors. As a for-profit in the 1950s, Arena had produced a handful of premieres, including Robert Anderson's domestic drama *All Summer Long*, which subsequently moved to Broadway. As a nonprofit in the 1960s with targeted grants for new work, the company produced one or two world premiere plays each season with varying degrees of success. Fichandler secured funding from the newly founded National Endowment for the Arts (NEA) for Howard Sackler to write *The Great White Hope*, a new play based on the life of black American boxing champion Jack Johnson.[104] She admired *The Great White Hope* for its commentary on contemporary racial dynamics based in the struggles of a black man and his romance with a white woman. When the play opened in 1967, Arena had staged only one other play out of 150 productions that dealt with black-white politics—*Othello*—and that was merely five years prior. By being nonprofit and securing grants for new play development, Arena had a financial cushion. The theatre could worry less about covering the costs of an interracial story that might alienate the white critical establishment and subscriber base. But the play became a critical hit, and it appealed to both white subscribers and new black audiences. Fichandler found the theatre to be "most alive" in its eighteen-year history when it attracted this unprecedented racially diverse audience.[105] *The Great White Hope* became one of the centerpieces of Arena's self-narrative for helping to launch James Earl Jones as a star, transferring to Broadway, and winning the Pulitzer Prize. But it ended up as only the third-highest grossing play for Arena in the 1967–68 season. The next chapter further explores the economics, reception, and racial liberalism of *The Great White Hope*.

Several of Arena's productions had moved to New York years before, but the success of *The Great White Hope* crystallized the idea that a regional theatre could gain national attention and substantial profits from a Broadway transfer. Arena soon afterward produced the U.S. premiere of Arthur Kopit's *Indians*, which tackled Buffalo Bill's complicity with indigenous oppression. The production moved to Broadway in 1969. From 1969 to 1970, "15 percent of all plays on the main stages of theatres were new plays—triple the percentage in the two seasons before *The Great White Hope*," and more regional theatre productions transferred to Broadway or Off-Broadway.[106] These changes provoked some critics such as Martin Gottfried to accuse regional theatre artistic directors of producing plays for their commercial rather than artistic potential, again as if these are opposing qualities.[107] The overwhelming majority of these transfers did not turn an economic profit. Instead, they offered regional theatres prestige by association. New York, specifically Broadway, remains at the top of the theatrical hierarchy, in spite of attempts by regional theatres to legitimize themselves through their nonprofit status, riskier plays, and community service.

In the late 1960s, Arena Stage produced edgy, contemporary plays alongside classics and comedies but now with racial difference. Critic Julius Novick wrote in 1968, "More and more, the Arena is expanding beyond its old preoccupation with familiar plays for its contented middle-class audience."[108] According to Thomas Fichandler, "We have lost some subscribers as expected. There was some resentment to the integration of the cast and some negative reactions to *Marat/ Sade*."[109] In addition, *No Place to Be Somebody* (1969) provoked hostile mail from audience members because of what some patrons viewed as its racist portrayal of whites. Written by Charles Gordone, *No Place to Be Somebody* followed the struggles of a masculinist black barkeep in Greenwich Village. It was the first play by a black writer to win the Pulitzer Prize, and Gordone was the first black playwright produced at Arena Stage. The only earlier time when the theatre produced a work by a playwright of color was in 1952 with the spoken drama version of the Chinese opera *Lady Precious Stream* by S. I. Hsiung. Even then, the white cast performed the play in yellowface, a common practice in the age of *The King & I*.[110] *No Place to Be Somebody* and *The Great White Hope* signaled Arena's growing interest in cultivating stories centered on African Americans.

Fichandler's most ambitious program to mobilize her nonprofit status and reach out to black communities was her exceptional call for a racially integrated acting ensemble. Few other major regional theatres had similar initiatives. Founded in Mississippi in 1963, the Free Southern Theater began with an integrated ensemble performing plays like *Waiting for Godot* but then became exclusively black. In Washington, Fichandler observed a "profound aesthetic dislocation" between the whites onstage and in the audience of Arena versus the majority-black population outside.[111] Aside from *The Great White Hope*, stories of racial anxieties were not being told at Arena Stage, yet they were staged in marches on the National Mall in 1963 and in race riots following the assassination of Martin Luther King Jr. in 1968. For her art to remain relevant, Fichandler awoke to the pressing need for her theatre to address race relations: "Our national life is finding its identity within the inter-relationships of black and white people. And a living theatrical art can hardly do other than follow the example of the life it seeks to illuminate."[112] Her solution to Arena being stagnant and "divorced from reality" was the training and hiring of fourteen black actors to join the existing company of sixteen white actors, which would still keep whites in the majority.[113] Fichandler's integrated ensemble would perform antirealistic works from the Greeks to Shakespeare. Her vision was far from colorblind: she considered the racialized readings of, for instance, casting the underdog scoundrel Macheath as black versus the controlling Peachum family as white in *The Threepenny Opera*.

Fichandler emphasized that artistic reasons superseded social justice ones. She understood that black actors likely had less dramatic instruction than more privileged artists, so she budgeted for voice, movement, improvisation, and Shakespeare teachers. In "Toward a Deepening Aesthetic," a lengthy essay in her funding application to Ford in 1968, she insisted that she had "no sociological motive behind" the racially mixed acting ensemble; "the motivation is not to employ Negro actors for their own good or out of impulses of white guilt or social generosity or responsibility. . . . Nor do we have in mind enticing the middle-class Negro dollar into the box office till."[114] Perhaps to appeal to white funders, Fichandler disavowed the possibilities of hiring black actors as an act of reparations or of capitalizing on black bourgeois patrons. In fact, this proposal did reallocate resources to black artists and bring in new revenue from the black middle class. She emphasized that she wanted Arena to avoid "aesthetic death," linking blackness with liveliness.[115] Yet she still centered whiteness. When Fichandler cited Afro-Caribbean psychiatrist and intellectual Frantz Fanon in her application, she did so to suggest that a presumed white spectator has much to learn about black psychology. She firmly positioned the theatre on the side of art and humanism, not commerce and social justice, as a strategic way to raise money and integrate blackness into this traditionally white institution. Fichandler's strategy was hugely successful: she obtained a $250,000 grant from the Ford Foundation to bring African Americans into the resident ensemble.

Arena's program and the Ford Foundation's support were parts of a pattern of racial liberalism, the development and implementation of technocratic solutions by well-educated, well-meaning, mostly white leaders that would ensure greater peace, prosperity, and opportunity without radically changing existing racial hierarchies. Radical American Studies scholar Dylan Rodríguez critiques the nonprofit industrial complex (NPIC) that relies on foundations, whose "overall bureaucratic formality and hierarchical (frequently elitist) structuring . . . has institutionalized more than just a series of hoops through which aspiring social change activists must jump—these institutional characteristics, in fact, *dictate the political vistas of NPIC organizations themselves*."[116]

As 501(c)3s, nonprofits must accept terms such as how they are permitted to lobby the government. Liberal philanthropy and the state shape the horizons of nonprofit organizations and limit the extent to which they can otherwise imagine themselves or solutions to systemic oppression. When foundations like Ford give money to nonprofits like Arena, the nonprofits' financial stresses ease, but such grants do not eradicate material inequality on the terms of maintaining institutions of power. In addition to Arena's integrated ensemble, Ford simultaneously funded the Negro Ensemble Company and the New Lafayette Theatre in New York but not the radical Black Arts Movement. In *Top Down: The Ford Foundation, Black Power, and the Reinvention of Racial Liberalism*, Karen Ferguson historicizes how the foundation repeatedly invested in policies that championed charismatic, exceptional black men and treated black Americans as worthy yet immature people who needed separate, special refinement until they could join the white mainstream with significant white support.[117] The Arena proposal was unique among Ford-sponsored artistic endeavors because integration was at its core. But this integration took the form of assimilating black actors into performances of the white repertory. In part because Fichandler believed canonical Western plays to be universal, she wrote, "The matter of plays that 'speak to Negro concerns' comes very much second" to the acting company.[118]

Reactions to the multiracial ensembles in *Six Characters in Search of an Author, King Lear,* and a new production of *Threepenny Opera* were mixed. Richard Coe acknowledged the integrated ensemble near the end of his reviews of *Six Characters* and *Threepenny*, which ran in rotating repertory, but claimed that the integration had zero effect on the productions.[119] In his review of *King Lear* later that season, he did not mention race, perhaps as a way to perform how he liberally saw past race, or because it had become well known that Arena boasted a black and white ensemble.[120] On the other hand, some audience letters in the Arena Stage archives reveal discomfort and anger about the casting, particularly when family members in the plays were of differing races. One patron complained, "We find your policy of enforced integration to be artificial and distracting. Certainly a policy of nondiscrimination is highly desirable, but your discriminatory policy (in reverse) interferes substantially with one's concentration upon the theatrical aspects of the production."[121] Other letters accused the black actors of being less talented, or at least less trained, criticizing their diction. Even though the success of works like *Oh! What a Lovely War* proved that artistic experimentation and commercial popularity are not necessarily at odds, there were still limits: in this case, many patrons were unwilling to pay to see black actors in classic Western plays.

And the Ford Foundation was unwilling to pay beyond the first year of this program, so the integrated ensemble folded. In a letter to the foundation, Fichandler called the program a temporary failure and reported that she did not think that black artists and audiences were interested "in our kind of repertory" but in the Black Arts Movement.[122] She did not implicate white audiences but cited the failure to attract a sizable black audience—implicitly blaming black people. Meanwhile, at a board of trustees meeting in 1968, Thomas Fichandler explained the deficits and decreases in subscriptions by highlighting "the April disturbances and the consequent reluctance of many people to come into the inner city in the evenings."[123] His word choice glosses the riots as "disturbances" and "people" as suburban, wealthy whites. At the annual membership meeting in 1969, Zelda Fichandler added that finding and keeping qualified black actors was difficult, and that the integrated company was "several years ahead of its time," yet she and the Ford Foundation "felt it was a worthwhile attempt and did not regret trying it."[124] Reflecting on the integrated ensemble in 2012, she remarked, "It was always called an experiment. It's the only thing that rescued me when it fell apart."[125] Despite the discontinuation of the program, Arena's experiment with an integrated acting ensemble was historically significant, especially considering DC's racial climate. Fichandler would launch another concerted attempt to integrate the resident ensemble in the 1980s when she oversaw NYU's graduate acting program and won a significant grant for cultural diversity.

By the late 1960s, there was more competition over local theatre audiences and national theatre grants. The number of regional theatres had dramatically increased from a handful in 1950 to a few dozen by 1970. In addition, there were more professional theatres in Washington. The National Theatre reopened as a touring house in 1952, and Ford's Theatre reopened in 1968. A new local professional theatre called the Washington Theatre Club was founded in 1957 and filled a niche for smaller plays as Arena transitioned to its larger, permanent home. The company won the Margo Jones Award for its commitment to new U.S. plays years before Zelda Fichandler did. Finally, after years of promising to build a cultural center in the nation's capital but refusing to fund it, Congress moved forward with the Kennedy Center after the assassination of President John F. Kennedy. The center opened in 1971 to showcase music, dance, and theatre by local and touring companies, and to memorialize Kennedy, who had long been tied to cultural aspirations.

In 1970, Arena expanded by opening the Kreeger Theater, a second stage with a flexible proscenium/thrust space meant for more experimental work and named for a major donor, David Lloyd Kreeger. Meeting minutes reveal that Zelda Fichandler had been planning this new theatre since the mid-1960s, precisely when her theatre first moved toward a deficit model. She insisted, "We need to test the resources of the community vis-à-vis the major foundations' attitudes towards grants."[126] Such statements demonstrate her use of the accepted deficit to execute her larger vision by this point. In 1969, Thomas Fichandler wrote to Mac Lowry for more funding and ultimately received a combined $900,000 from the Ford Foundation and NEA to help cover the $1.5 million cost of the new building.

This time, these organizations stipulated that Arena could not ask for more money for several years because they viewed theatres as having grown overly dependent on grant money and engaging in irresponsible, unsustainable financial practices. The timing of the Ford Foundation pulling back its contributions was far from coincidental. The Tax Reform Act of 1969 taxed foundations' net income, limited their business dealings, and required more transparency in spending. Cutting down on donations was a problem when Baumol and Bowen had shown that performing arts nonprofits would need more financial support beyond the box office. Moreover, the thrift and long-term planning that capitalists valorize are at odds with both producing risky art and maintaining unpredictable theatre businesses. These funding organizations demanded that nonprofit theatre adhere to businesses' best practices of professionalism and stability. Dorothy Chansky notes that many professional theatre organizations such as the League of Resident Theatres and Theatre Communications Group originated in the 1960s, as companies were taught to prioritize the bottom line over artistry, humanism, and social justice.[127] Theatre scholar Margaret M.

Cofounders Tom and Zelda Fichandler during the construction of
the Kreeger Theater in 1971. Photo courtesy of Arena Stage.

Knapp points out that "the 'theatre industry' became more than a
metaphor when theatre companies took their places alongside other
American businesses, conforming to the rules of the capitalist marketplace in order to receive corporate and governmental funding."[128] Although training and hiring black actors for Arena's resident ensemble
was a boon for racial justice, it was not sufficiently profitable in a system that values economic capital. Foundations and the state wanted
nonprofits to act more like for-profits to demonstrate their fiscal responsibility. Theatre economist Jack Poggi warned in 1968, "There is a
danger in mammoth subsidy: it tends to turn theaters into Institutions.
. . . The larger and more complex the operation, the more likely a theater is to shift its major emphasis from putting on plays to insuring its
growth and survival as an institution."[129]

In "Theatres or Institutions?," published in 1970, Zelda Fichandler
questioned pitting theatres and institutions against each other. She
articulated the fundamental need for funding: "There are other signs
that money will not right, but which cannot be righted without money
since money is the exchange commodity of our life."[130] Concerned
about "the hand that rocks the cradle," she felt uncomfortable about
the audience donating to the theatre and dictating the repertory.[131] In

Negotiating Nonprofit Theatre   (53

The Arena Stage campus after the 1971 opening of the
Kreeger Theater. Photo courtesy of Arena Stage.

time, however, individual, local donors would mostly fill the financial gap created by foundation retreat. Fichandler was willing to make
what she considered more commercially driven decisions, as long as
they did not jeopardize her artistic integrity. She endorsed classics and
comedies as vital to the repertory, the human spirit, the public, and the
subsidizing of new work and other programs. She confessed, "I cling to
European institutional models—the subsidized, well-staffed, anything-
that-money-can-buy theatre," but she also recognized that "we have
had to teach ourselves to be independent of European models . . . [to]
be conceived more fluidly," adhering to the demands of capitalism.[132]

CONCLUSION

Arena Stage gradually figured out the limits to its costly, adventurous
artistic programs and new spaces. In 1970, income met expenditures
for the first time in years, not counting the new building-related costs.
That year, the theatre also lost subscribers, increased ticket prices,
and still lacked a formal fundraising department. All the while, Zelda
Fichandler leveraged the deficit to conduct artistic experiments, implement racial integration, and ultimately fortify her theatre institution within the demands of show business. Although she deferred the

dream of a multiracial ensemble due to restricted resources, she slowly began to stage more works centering on black experiences to make Arena reflect its environment and attract new sources of capital. Negotiating the meaning and model of the viable nonprofit regional theatre, she, along with her husband Thomas Fichandler and patron Mac Lowry, sustained Arena Stage with careful appeals to artistry, calculations of profit, and new yet limited black inclusion.

Arena's sustainability was also made possible by a set of contradictory economic and racial conditions. First, white privilege, educational capital, and the removal of poor black residents enabled Arena's leaders to secure the stability of nonprofit status and a permanent home that later started to welcome black artists. Second, belief in the Economic World Reversed philosophy allowed them to capitalize on the theatre's first deficit and expand the organization, even though the productions were actually box office hits. The line between for- and not-for-profit is a blurry one. Arena did not start out as a totally avant-garde, anti-Broadway, nonprofit art house, and such classifications obscure the relations of capital in cultural production. Instead, the company began as a for-profit corporation that behaved much like what would become the norm of a nonprofit theatre with its eclectic repertory of classics, comedies, and new work; resident acting ensemble; and other innovative programs alongside ties to commercial theatre in New York. Its productions of antiwar plays were very profitable, and to believe that they were otherwise perpetuates oversimplified assumptions about the cultural values of art. Too often, art and commerce are pitted against one another. Using nonprofit status, Zelda Fichandler mobilized this binary logic to build a theatrical home and accumulate ticket sales, grants, and prestige. And yet Arena's programming remained remarkably consistent from the 1950s to the 1960s. Perhaps the biggest difference between Arena before and after it gained nonprofit status was that the theatre began to stage narratives centered on black protagonists, like *The Great White Hope*.

CHAPTER TWO

CAPITALIZING ON RACIAL LIBERALISM
IN *THE GREAT WHITE HOPE*

Often hailed as the first new play to transfer from a regional theatre to Broadway, *The Great White Hope* is a heavyweight in the history of U.S. theatre and the mythos of Arena Stage. Seventeen years after Arena opened, the institution staged its first-of-now-many new plays centering on a black character. Arena marked its fiftieth anniversary and its identity with a new production of this play in 2000. In the program, artistic associate Steve Samuels penned a paean to the company's many firsts; he asked, "How much shock and exultation were caused by the cross-color kiss shared by James Earl Jones and Jane Alexander when Howard Sackler's *The Great White Hope* premiered December 7, 1967, and when the production moved to Broadway, establishing Arena and the suddenly burgeoning resident theater network as the primary source of new American plays?"¹ Accompanied by interviews with playwright Sackler and revival director and artistic director Molly Smith, the program celebrated Arena as a leader in the realms of racial progress and cultural production. Smith employed larger-than-life diction to underscore the play's importance: *The Great White Hope* was a "wonderful, passionate epic play," a "legend" thanks to the "audacious achievements of Zelda and Tom Fichandler."²

The original production of *The Great White Hope* effectively shifted the site of new play development and signaled the potential for works honed in nonprofit sectors beyond the Great White Way to garner not only high ticket sales and movie deals but also Tony Awards and the Pulitzer Prize. *The Great White Hope* generated this economic and symbolic capital through its politics of racial liberalism. Exploring the potentials and pitfalls of integration, the play's "cross-color kiss" facilitated the move to Broadway. Playwright Howard Sackler dramatized the struggles of Jack Jefferson in the boxing ring and in his intimate relationship with Ellie, a white woman. Sackler based Jack Jefferson on Jack Johnson, the first black man to win the world heavyweight title in boxing and in so doing challenged scientific rationalizations of racial hierarchy as natural in the early twentieth century.[3] Because of Johnson's sexual relationships with white women and his boxing victories, the U.S. government persecuted him to police his body and remove his title. His life was ripe for drama.[4]

But the "legend" of Sackler's play obscures its actual origins. As the previous chapter demonstrates, *The Great White Hope* was far from the first play to premiere at Arena Stage and subsequently move to New York. Moreover, Arena was not the only nonprofit regional theatre involved with Broadway. Six months before the play opened on the Great White Way in 1968, the musical *Man of La Mancha* transferred to Broadway from the Goodspeed Opera House in Connecticut. A "legitimate" play rather than a musical, *The Great White Hope* represented a new mode of play production and economic and critical "success." The scare quotes highlight the arbitrariness of legitimacy and success: in the end Arena Stage lost $50,000 on its premiere of the play, while Sackler received an advance of $550,000 to adapt the play for Hollywood. The regional theatre nevertheless gained symbolic capital. The lights of Broadway, the Pulitzer committee, and the Tony Awards shone on *The Great White Hope* and thus Arena.

What were the material conditions through which these apparent firsts and honors were made possible? Amid calls for civil rights, Arena's nonprofit status cushioned the company in taking the moderate risk of staging a world premiere play of black-white racial intimacy and strife. This play subsequently enabled Arena to gain more resources yet also rationalize its identity as noncommercial. By staging this racially liberal drama of integration, the company hit on a recipe for success: the nonprofit theatre disavowed interest in financial gain, and the playwright disavowed interest in racial justice, so *The Great White Hope* could accrue both artistic prestige and broad popularity. Those conditions paradoxically equipped the production to earn a lot of money and to discuss racial politics.

There is little scholarship on this important play, and what exists is largely bifurcated. Scholars of Theatre Studies focus on the economics of the nonprofit/for-profit production, while scholars of Performance Studies focus on Jack Johnson's real-life racial performances. For example, in *Regional Theatre: The Revolutionary Stage*, Joseph Zeigler deems *The Great White Hope* the "fourth major turning point of the regional theatre because it proved the national power of new plays" without attending to its racial politics.[5] On the other hand, Performance and American Studies scholars Harvey Young,[6] David Krasner,[7] and Theresa Runstedtler[8] unpack Johnson's bouts in the ring as black performance interventions into U.S. American and global white supremacy in the early twentieth century. In the fifty years that scholars have been writing about the play, much has changed in the way they understand its significance in the American repertoire.

This chapter addresses this gap in scholarship by exploring the interrelations of profit and racial hierarchy in *The Great White Hope* as produced by Arena Stage. Pierre Bourdieu's concepts of different capital and habitus provide the groundwork for understanding Arena's investment and the critical and commercial success of this play.[9] Scholars such as Harvey Young signify on[10] Bourdieu in Young's formulation of black habitus, which "allows us to read the black body as socially constructed and continually constructing its own self."[11] A close reading of the play and the discourses around it reveal that its allure was based on its narrative possibilities for interracial union and black triumph but ultimate foreclosure of those possibilities. Howard Sackler highlights the social construction of white supremacy and critiques its impact on black and white bodies, resonating with then current events from Muhammad Ali's defiance of the draft to the Supreme Court case for interracial marriage, *Loving v. Virginia*. At the same time, the play emphasizes whiteness and black downfall, leaving little room for radical change led by black actors in solidarity with whites. Practicing ambivalence, the play airs racialized gender and middlebrow anxieties concerning the play's central interracial relationship and cultural categorization. In addition, Sackler and Jones publicly and repeatedly rejected the salience of race and racism in order to frame the play as a generalizable man-versus-society epic, which enticed rather than alienated white bourgeois audiences and sanctioning institutions. Just as Sackler and his play practiced ambivalence, the critics struggled with reconciling the play as both for-profit and nonprofit, and both racial and colorblind. The few who pushed back against the play and its politics tended to be radical black feminists.

To achieve critical acclaim and box office appeal, *The Great White Hope* advanced a project of popular racial liberalism. It offered sympathetic characters and challenges to systemic racism without proposing structural change. Like a boxing match, the form of this chapter exchanges jabs back and forth to exhibit the play as a site of struggle with differing position-takings that availed audiences of multiple ways to interpret and appreciate this play as legitimate theatre and popular culture. Originally staged in the round at Arena, the play literally welcomes 360-degree vantage points. *The Great White Hope* illuminated the structure of white supremacy, critiqued it, socially reproduced it, and disavowed it in order to produce profit for Arena Stage and Howard Sackler.

NAVIGATING BLACKNESS, BROW LEVEL, AND THE MARKETPLACE

Sackler's dramatization of a black boxer navigating global white supremacy in *The Great White Hope* manifests what Young calls black habitus. Young articulates blackness through a racialized performative repetition or feel of the game. He theorizes, "If we identify blackness as an idea projected across a body, the projection not only gets incorporated within the body but also influences the ways that it views other bodies."[12] Although blackness is a social construct, its habitual performance generates material, patterned effects. Structural antiblackness circumscribes movements and representations, yet provides space for challenges and dynamic change. The structure shapes the individual, and the individual shapes the structure. Black habitus connects Jack Johnson's, Jack Jefferson's, and Muhammad Ali's similar experiences in and out of the boxing ring.[13] Another black boxing champion, Ali went to see *The Great White Hope* on Broadway several times. After one performance, he staged "a scene from the play with himself in the role of Jack Jefferson. . . . Ali remarked that he knew the story of Johnson because it was his story. All a person had to do was to replace white women with Ali's contemporary issues around the draft to see the similarity."[14] Ali chose stillness, refusing to step forward and become inducted into the U.S. military to fight in the Vietnam War. Johnson chose matches with white boxers and sex with white women. Both were imprisoned. Young's framework links critical memory, blackness, and individuality.

Part of that constellation, the play, as well as reactions to it, illustrates the workings of the nonprofit world as a prime example of middlebrow theatre and its attendant anxieties over race, sexuality, and capital. The term "middlebrow" comes from phrenology, marking the space in between the alleged "highbrow" of white bodies and supposed "lowbrow" of black bodies to rationalize racial hierarchy on a biological basis.[15] As a middlebrow text, *The Great White Hope* has these racial connotations but not necessarily the derogatory value judgments that often stick to this term. Instead, this designation by producers and critics opens up analysis of the struggles over legitimacy. According to Bourdieu, "The field of cultural production is the site of struggles in which what is at stake is the power to impose the dominant definition of the writer and therefore to delimit the population of those entitled to take part in the struggle to define the writer."[16] When authors and authorizing institutions bestow *The Great White Hope* with capital, they enrich themselves as tastemakers and implicitly reveal that no art is innately praiseworthy. David Savran writes:

> The theorization of middlebrow as a site of struggle allows one to recognize that the multifarious makers of theater are by no means free and independent agents. . . . What we call "drama" can be theorized only by reference to the positionalities of the agents who make it in response to these impossible demands, to theater's relationship with other cultural forms, to an audience whose tastes and expectations can never be completely known in advance, and to the variable amounts of capital—economic, cultural, social, and symbolic—at risk in any performance.[17]

The middlebrow indexes an anxious in-between state of race, gender, sexuality, class, and cultural hierarchies. Middlebrow cultural productions are both too low and too high, emblematized by Sackler's inclusion of both blackface minstrelsy as well as a whole scene spoken in Hungarian. Because of *The Great White Hope*'s critical and commercial success, it is difficult to categorize the play as it upends the "Economic World Reversed," the belief that an artwork can be either a boundary-pushing experiment or a comfortable moneymaker. Produced at a nonprofit regional theatre and on for-profit Broadway, this text provides a valuable site for teasing out contradictions.

The play is especially important in marking a turning point for the Pulitzer Prize in Drama. In *A Queer Sort of Materialism*, Savran analyzes the musicals *South Pacific* and *Rent*, whose formal and racial miscegenation, coupled with anxieties over authenticity and commodification of art, emblematize the tensions of the middlebrow and the qualities of Pulitzer Prize–winning plays.[18] *The Great White Hope* follows the thematic pattern. Since 1969, almost every play that has won the Pulitzer had its world premiere at a nonprofit theatre. In the 1970s, such plays included *No Place to Be Somebody*, *That Championship Season*, and *A Chorus Line* (originally produced by the Public Theater, New York) as well as *The Effect of Gamma Rays on Man-in-the-Moon Marigolds* (the Alley Theatre, Houston) and *Buried Child* (the Magic Theater, San Francisco). Sackler's collection of awards, including the Tony and the Outer Critics Circle Award, is largely due to his successful navigation of middlebrow themes, values, forms, and politics as policed by critics and committees. And Sackler gained this capital thanks to Arena.

Sackler's play came to Zelda Fichandler at a key point, when her theatre suffered its first deficit and when she realized the incongruity of her white stage situated in a black city. A white American whose background was in radio, Howard Sackler began working on *The Great White Hope* in the early 1960s. When Arena Stage produced his play *Mr. Welk and Jersey Jim* in 1966, he showed Fichandler his draft of *Hope*. Attracted to its racial themes, she agreed to produce the play the following year. She sought to distinguish what made nonprofit theatres specially deserving of grants, and a crucial part of that distinction was the integration of blackness into a historically white institution. As Arena's first world premiere centering on a black protagonist, *The Great White Hope* could be both nonprofit and for-profit for its trailblazing yet cautious aesthetics and politics. The narrative focus on the obstacles that a black man faces gave the play an edge, the appearance and actuality of riskiness suggesting that the producing theatre could not survive on box office receipts alone. Yet the play was far from the radical cry of the Black Arts Movement. Its authorship by a white male playwright, epic and realist dramaturgical structure, and ultimate reining in of its black protagonist tempered the play's antiracist potential. Still within racially liberal norms, the play could appeal to Arena's typical white bourgeois audience. The white privilege of Sackler, Fichandler, and Arena Stage endowed *The Great White Hope* with the ability to make a limited, antiracist critique and to earn various kinds of capital.

Fichandler took an active role in the development of *The Great White Hope*. With 240 roles and more than sixty actors, the play initially had a running time of three hours and forty-five minutes. By the end of the Arena run, the production team had shaved off twenty minutes, and when the play reached Broadway, it ran under three hours. In a fourteen-page letter commenting on the first draft of the play in 1966, Zelda Fichandler and director Ed Sherwin said little of the thematic elements but advised Sackler on the several scenes that he should tighten or cut because they did not advance the narrative.[19] The playwright rarely took their advice. Having directed some two hundred dramas for audio recording, including many of Shakespeare's plays, Sackler was used to sprawling dramatic structures that changed settings almost every scene.

Supportive of new work engaging with racial politics, Fichandler sought substantial funding for Sackler and his playwriting. After her initial proposal to the newly created NEA was denied, she rallied again and secured a $25,000 grant to support the production. Post-Federal Theatre Project, *The Great White Hope* became the "first play born through the federal government's latent interest in the arts," or more precisely the government's interest in racial liberalism at home through the arts.[20] Seven thousand dollars went directly to Sackler as his commission, and he earned an additional $1,000 per week for the six-week run from December 1967 to January 1968. This amount is considerable, given that the average national income at that time was roughly $6,000, and that the average commission for plays as late as 2010 was $3,000 to $5,000.[21] Without informing Arena's leadership team, Sackler sold the film rights of *The Great White Hope* to 20th Century Fox. He received an advance of $550,000 with the potential of doubling that amount depending on box office receipts. Sackler then moved forward with a Broadway transfer using much of the same cast, creative team, costumes, and set pieces from Arena Stage. He invested $225,000 in the Broadway staging and partnered with experienced producer Herman Levin, who contributed $25,000; they agreed to split the profits 75/25. During the Broadway run from October 3, 1968, to

January 31, 1970, Sackler earned approximately $7,000 per week, at a capacity weekly gross of $73,000. Arena Stage, by contrast, lost $50,000 on its production.

These numbers may be surprising, since *The Great White Hope* is often remembered as the germination of profitable nonprofit/for-profit collaborations. But Arena Stage did not secure subsidiary rights or potential financial profits from future productions because there had been no need with earlier plays that it had sent to New York. The theatre also lost many of its resident ensemble members to the Broadway production, a huge blow to Zelda Fichandler for the time, money, and effort that she had put into cultivating a local acting company. She had to rebuild. Although the regional theatre was not listed in the Broadway billing, it still gained prestige from New York critics and awards. The script did in fact make a lot of money. It just did not go to the originating theatre. Arena occupied an ambivalent and precarious position as a nonprofit organization that actively sought economic as well as symbolic capital to institutionalize the theatre.

Sackler's economic success led to a public tussle explicitly about compensation for Arena Stage and implicitly about the nonprofit theatre's legitimacy. Arena attempted to obtain 10 percent of the profits from the Broadway production. Sackler and Levin offered only 5 percent of the royalties, up to a maximum of $50,000. Arena would have broken even. But as the manager of the theatre's finances, Thomas Fichandler refused the offer as insufficient. He repeatedly called attention to the substantial economic needs of the regional theatre, which he defined as not designed to generate large incomes: "We think it's unfortunate that a deficit-operated theater like the Arena Stage, which, like all noncommercial theaters is in need of sustenance, is not participating in the success of 'The Great White Hope.'"[22] In 1968, the newly created League of Resident Theatres met, and as the inaugural president of the organization, Thomas Fichandler along with other regional theatre leaders "decided at that time that premieres should be accompanied by some sort of contractual protection."[23] He specified that "a New York lawyer is currently drawing up a model contract that will call for 5–10% of future earnings, with an option for Arena to produce the play on Broadway."[24] He followed through in 1969 in the contract for *Indians* by Arthur Kopit, Arena's next new play that transferred to Broadway.

The regional theatre blurred the nonprofit/for-profit line. While Thomas Fichandler stressed Arena's integral role as a nonprofit theatre launching, developing, and funding *The Great White Hope*, the *New York Times* used language that positioned the theatre as for-profit. Reporter Sam Zolotow called Arena a "tryout" space distinctly beyond Broadway.[25] Critic Howard Taubman noted that *The Great White Hope* "was received so well that the Arena Stage did something unusual for an out-of-town resident company. It took a substantial ad in the *New York Times* on a Sunday to proclaim its success."[26] In a personal letter to Levin, Zelda Fichandler again argued for financial compensation by pointing out how the commercial production rested on the nonprofit production:

> You capitalize on Arena Stage's production in the ads. You also lean on "America's burgeoning theatre movement" which, in this context, is put forth as a noteworthy item—good for its prestige value, good for ballyhoo and drum-beating, good for selling tickets and making money. But, ironically and unjustly, not good enough to have been tangibly recognized for what it did to make the Broadway production happen![27]

Even though Fichandler knew that her institution must rely on a practiced disinterestedness, she too was interested in financial gain. In addition, she did not want Arena's name in promotional materials because she did not have a hand in further changes to the script on Broadway. Arena had invested its economic and symbolic capital, and it desired a return on that investment once the play's representation of racial dynamics proved to be popular among the white bourgeoisie.

RACIAL REPRESENTATION AND DISAVOWAL

By dramatizing the contours of white supremacy on the body of Jack Jefferson but also disavowing race and systemic racism, *The Great White Hope* advances both progressive politics of racial struggle and reproduces racist logics. The play's dramaturgical structure, use of stereotypes, and interracial relationship form a recipe for popular racial liberalism. The audience witnesses an individual navigating systemic oppression and comes to sympathize with him, as his doomed interracial relationship and lost title result in a tragic fall that restores the status quo. White consumers can feel good about feeling bad for Jack without threats to their privilege. The very terms of inclusion, be it Jack's reentry into the United States, into Arena, and into Broadway, rest on an aesthetic and political ambivalence in order to win liberal hearts, minds, awards, and ticket sales.

Sackler exhibits a black body for a mostly white audience and from a largely white perspective, though he also draws attention to the very construction of this frame. From the first scene to the last, the audience's experiences are mostly mediated by white character-spectators. The play begins with Tom Brady, a stand-in for real-life white boxer Jim Jeffries. White men and a persuasive letter from Washington, coax him out of retirement to retrieve the heavyweight title from Jack Jefferson and restore white supremacy. Tom relents and revels in his whiteness: "And it's gonna be a pleasure! Tell your n*gger[28] I said so!"[29] The scenes of federal and judicial officials developing ways to arrest Jack and take back the heavyweight title further reveal the workings of the white supremacist state. In the district attorney's office, civic leaders voice their concern that Jack and Ellie's relationship is "repulsive to every decent Caucasian in America," and the attorney and detective plot ways to find evidence of "coercion" or "abduction" to make sense of Ellie's attraction to Jack and to stop this interracial intimacy.[30] Citing the Mann Act, which was intended to regulate the trafficking of white women for sex work, the state arrests Jack supposedly for driving his lover across state lines but in reality for being a black man while winning the heavyweight title and a white woman. After Jack flees the country, officials persuade boxing promoters to refuse Jack work. As a result, they starve him out and force him to accept the U.S. government's terms: if Jack loses a match and the heavyweight title, then he can gain reentry into the country. The audience hears descriptions of the boxing match via white spectators when he loses in the end. This storytelling reveals the mechanisms that sustain systemic racism yet does so in such a way that prioritizes the impact of Jack's victories on white men.

The Arena staging supports this interpretation. In scene 2, Jack shows off to the press as white men, his white lover Ellie, his black common-law wife Clara, and his black trainer encircle him. He draws the gaze of the other characters, just as he does of the theatre patrons

James Earl Jones (center), Jane Alexander (right of center),
and ensemble in *The Great White Hope* at Arena Stage in
1967. Photo by Fletcher Drake courtesy of Arena Stage.

forming another circle around him. They become intimately involved
and implicated in the action, as Sackler presumes a white gaze. But because they are in the round, they can see their peers, becoming aware
that they are watching a performance. They can become aware of the
construction of race, storytelling, and power structures.

But Sackler does not show Jack's concrete blows to systemic oppression. As theatre historian David Krasner observes of the early twentieth century, "Boxing would provide visible 'proof' of race-based theo-
ries through performative style," but Jack Johnson challenged white
hegemonic understandings of the body through his supremacy over
white bodies and through his use of improvisation in the ring, as opposed to the supposed fixity of whiteness.[31] State laws suppressed the
distribution of films over state lines that documented Johnson's winning of the heavyweight title because of a fear that these films would
inspire black spectators to rise up and overthrow racial hierarchy. The
fact that there is no actual boxing onstage in *The Great White Hope* is
hugely significant.[32] James Burns and Abel Bartley point out that even
the film version shows only the final fight, which Jack loses or throws.[33]
In addition, the juridical implementation of the Mann Act does not in-

volve a dramatization of Johnson's legal arguments. In the play, Jack never boxes any white men literally in the ring or figuratively in the courts. He never wins. Sackler chooses to focus on the tragic repercussions of the black boxer's achievement, indicting racial hierarchy but also obscuring small victories.[34]

For much of the play, Jack tries to escape from the institutions of white supremacy to no avail, a pattern of black habitus. African American literature scholar Carol Bunch Davis has argued that Jack productively rejects the burdens of the "race man" and respectability politics with his postblack individualism.[35] But as African American Studies scholar Erica Edwards has critiqued, this political strategy extols extraordinary, charismatic black men who appear to have transcended systems, as if one could easily remove the shackles of historic anti-blackness.[36] Within the liberal frame of *The Great White Hope*, Jack feels that he can create his own social rules in his nightclub and in his bedroom. But in both spaces, whites intrude and restrict his mobility. When he celebrates the opening of his club in Chicago by wearing his finest and doing the cakewalk, a dance that historically mocks whites, he performs the freedom of his middle-class status and blackness. Here is the intimacy and looseness afforded by what Shane Vogel calls "everynight life."[37] Cathy J. Cohen further articulates queer politics as able "to create a space in opposition to dominant norms, a space where transformational political work can begin."[38] With his extraordinary body and sexual deviance, Jack transgresses racial-sexual norms and performs other ways of being and moving. However, temperance protesters interrupt the proceedings, and Mrs. Bachmann demands her daughter Ellie. In the second half of the play, Jack leaves the country for Europe and then Latin America only to discover the global reach of racism and the long arm of the U.S. state. A series of unfortunate events happen *to* him, leading up to his defeat in the ring. His mother and his white mistress die, incidents which intensify the drama yet do not match the order of events in Jack Johnson's actual life. By delimiting Jack's ability to drive the story, Sackler dramatizes the tensions of black movement and stillness that black performance studies scholars such as Jayna Brown,[39] Daphne Brooks,[40] Soyica Diggs Colbert,[41] and Harvey Young have analyzed. He shows the audience survival strategies, a move that illuminates power structures but evacuates the ability to change such structures.

Sackler offers no escape. Rather than being solely a sociopolitical drama, the play becomes an inevitable tragedy of an individual, terms that many critics used in their understanding of the play. When Jack loses the heavyweight title, Sackler generates ambivalence rather than affirmation that, at the very least, Jack *chose* to lose the fight in exchange for a more lenient prison sentence back in the United States. In the final tableau, Jack does not wink at the audience when he appears to be knocked out, but a young black Cuban boy spits on a smiling Jack as a group of white men prop up the bloodied white boxer deemed the Great White Hope. This overdetermined image welcomes varying interpretations from a scathing critique of racial hierarchy—look at the violence done to black bodies—to a preservation of focus on white actors—look at the triumph of white bodies—and precisely this multi-pronged view opened the play to economic viability.

Throughout the play, Sackler similarly practices ambivalence by both condemning and reproducing black stereotypes. He shows how journalists framed Jack as a minstrel character: "He's still got that big banjo smile on him."[42] In addition, he includes a character in black-face that performs minstrel humor and mocks Jack for the enjoyment of white spectators just prior to a boxing match. This awareness of how minstrelsy haunts black performance turns into a critique of symbolic violence and the marketplace when boxing promoters refuse to hire Jack. His only way to earn money is by performing in *Uncle Tom's Cabin*. Jack plays Uncle Tom, and over the course of the vaudeville performance, he quietly expresses his displeasure, while his white mistress plays Eva and his trainer plays Topsy. As the orchestra performs "Old Black Joe," "Jack tries to escape," and the audience groans throughout the show.[43] He is bad at acting this part he does not want to play. By staging this play within the play, Sackler comments on the degrading labor and roles that black people take on to survive, revealing the scripts and inequalities of racial hierarchy and class exploitation. He redirects the sentimentality of this famous abolitionist text to have the audience sympathize for Jack, yet just like *Uncle Tom's Cabin*, *The Great White Hope* proffers racist images.

Audiences are open to interpreting blackface in different ways, and Sackler was himself influenced by the minstrel tradition. Indicating the potential for producing uncritical pleasure, critic Richard Coe observed the double standards of the largely white liberal audience at Arena Stage enjoying this minstrelsy: "How unthinking it seemed, after all the head-noddings of approbation, to hear roars of laughter over 'darky' humor and struts."[44] In addition, Jack speaks with a dialect raced as black and classed as working class, occasionally verging into minstrelsy with malapropisms. When English officials attempt to deport Jack "for moral deficiency flaunted at the public," he responds, "Ah ain't flung no fish at no public!"[45] While it is true that the real-life Jack Johnson played the minstrel at times, he did so in particular situations such as in the boxing ring to antagonize his opponent. He was a highly literate man who was familiar with French, and at times he affected an English accent to disassociate himself from the United States. Sackler's decision to emphasize Jack's charisma, which is shaped by racialized narratives, and yet not include these deliberate performances of race, class, and nationality in the written text suggest that the playwright, like Jack, cannot escape from minstrelsy.

Still, the script offers opportunities for black performers. The original production launched the career of James Earl Jones, and when Arena Stage revived the play in 2000, Mahershala Ali made his professional stage debut. Jones had space to show that he was putting on a show, and some critics interpreted this metaperformance as sending up stereotypes. When interviewed by journalists on whether he is "the Black Hope," Jack wittily replies, "Well, I'm black and I'm hopin'."[46] The character spotlights and subverts the burden of representation. Because the play contains monologues and moments when characters break the fourth wall, highlighting the construction of racial representation is fitting. On the other end of the dramatic spectrum, Sackler invites the audience into domestic realism and tragedy when focusing on the interracial relationship between Jack and Ellie.

In *Imperfect Unions*, Diana Rebekkah Paulin contends that after the Civil War,

> the performative trope of miscegenation continued to ignite the regenerative flames of the black-white binary and the culturally powerful image of racial intermingling as a threat not only to U.S. nationhood but also to the progress of Western civilization.... At the same time, however, the exaggerated spectacle of miscegena-

Jane Alexander and James Earl Jones sharing a moment of intimacy in
The Great White Hope. George Tames / *The New York Times* / Redux.

tion also allowed for other types of cultural work that crossed
racialized boundaries to remain less visible and therefore also
under the protection of the "cover story."[47]

Paulin suggests that representations of interracial intimacy can both
uphold and disturb white supremacy. In the second scene of the play,
the audience meets Jack, who is shadowboxing half-naked while his
lover Ellie watches him and stands in for the white gaze. During the
1969 Tony Awards broadcast, James Earl Jones and Jane Alexander
performed this scene and shared a passionate, sweaty kiss, the first of
its kind on national television.[48] This powerful act transgressed racial
boundaries and bourgeois propriety. During the rest of this scene
in *The Great White Hope*, Jack's white manager attempts to hide the
boxer's interracial relationship from the press, and then Clara, Jack's
black common-law wife, barges in to attack Jack and Ellie. Sackler
stages white and black anxiety over Jack's relationship with Ellie. Promoting segregation, Clara replicates the troubling racialized and gendered type of the irrational, angry black woman, and she receives little
attention in the play. Meanwhile, Sackler constantly shows audiences
the feelings and actions of whites. He devotes several scenes to the dis-

comfort of Ellie's mother, meetings between federal employees and concerned citizens, an interrogation of Ellie, and most melodramatically the scene of arresting Jack under the Mann Act for "immoral" usage of a white woman transported across state lines.

This moment resonated with the sociopolitics of the late 1960s, specifically the case *Loving v. Virginia*. In bed together in the middle of the night, Jack and Ellie flirt and discuss how their skins sunburn differently. Audiences gasped, and Zelda Fichandler said she wished she could have recorded that reaction, the "sound of the city."[49] Suddenly, law enforcement officials infiltrate their bedroom. This scene gives the audience the titillating and transgressive pleasure of interracial intimacy as well as its policing. Outside the theatre, a white man and a black woman had married in Washington and were arrested in Virginia, where antimiscegenation laws remained, having been put in place at the time of Jack Johnson's preeminence and in part because of his interracial intimacies. The couple painted the real-life scene this way:

> The three law officers entered the Lovings' bedroom and awakened them that July night (July 11, 1958). "We were living with my parents," where "we had a guest bedroom downstairs," Mildred Loving later recalled. "I woke up and these guys were standing around the bed. I sat up. It was dark. They had flashlights. They told us to get up, get dressed. I couldn't believe they were taking us to jail."[50]

The scene in the play is extremely similar, and its staging in Washington, where the Lovings were able to live together instead of in Virginia, provided local resonance. In 1967, the same year as the premiere of *The Great White Hope*, the verdict in favor of the Lovings allowed for interracial marriages across the nation. Literature scholar Aliyyah I. Abdur-Rahman argues that mid-twentieth-century African American texts often engaged the trope of black-white relationships because "representations of cross-racial *sexual* desire provide a space for black writers to investigate—and to interrogate—broader possibilities for meaningful civil cooperation and political equality between the races."[51] Read in this way, *The Great White Hope*, though written by a white playwright, offers a loving black-white romance signifying integration and the violent state apparatus preventing such unions.

But the play also replicates the trope that cultural theorist Celia R. Daileader calls Othellophilia, based on Shakespeare's *Othello*. Othellophilia is the popular narrative of a black man sexually engaged with a white woman in which the former is portrayed as beastly, while the latter is tainted and doomed to die by the relationship.[52] This racist-misogynist narrative works to justify violent punishment of both parties, fortify white hetero-cis-patriarchy, and obscure a history of white masters assaulting enslaved black women. Jack's sexual relationships with white women threatened the white patriarchy, which believed that all women belong to white men and often used the fiction of black men raping white women to rationalize lynching in the Jim Crow era. The hegemonic white imagination could not fathom the boxer being in a loving marriage with a white woman. In the play, Jack and Ellie never marry. In the penultimate scene, almost out of nowhere, Jack repeatedly orders Ellie to leave him and "Stay wid you own," whips her with a towel, and verbally abuses her.[53] She finally responds with hatred and threats:

ELLIE: Oh, I despise you—
JACK: Right, like all resta ya—
ELLIE: Oh, I'd like to smash you—
JACK: Me an evvy udder dumb n*gger who'd letya! Now go on home an hustle one up who doan know it yet, plenty for ya, score em up—*watch out, brudders!* Oughta hang a bell on so dey hear you comin.[54]

Throughout the play, Sackler depicts Ellie as a kind of saint who is sullied and sexualized by her interracial relationship. This contrast amplifies Jack's villainy. This ultimately drives Ellie to commit suicide, as if moralizing on how mixed-race romances are hopeless. Sackler is again ambivalent, because this death can be read as either by Jack's hands or by the hands of racial hierarchy and hetero-cis-patriarchy. In fact, the first white wife of Jack Johnson did kill herself because of the backlash against her. By having Ellie commit suicide, Sackler forecloses radical interracial love, although he also gives audiences glimpses of this possibility. It was not by coincidence that critics compared the play to *Othello*. Prior to *The Great White Hope*, *Othello* was the only play that Arena had staged about a black protagonist.

Jane Alexander's testimony to her experience with *The Great White*

Hope further elucidates the complex workings of white supremacist patriarchy. Playing Ellie, she did not receive hate mail when at Arena Stage, but on Broadway she "got tons of mail from white bigots, and two death threats."[55] She was accused of being a traitor to her race, and she was sometimes followed after leaving the theatre.[56] She categorized the New York audiences as "predominantly white" at first, but "by the end of the year they were predominantly black":

> The white audience was very, "Yes, yes, we're very racially understanding," patting themselves on the back and cheering about the play and all that. And then the black audiences looked at my character as the trouble—the total troublemaker who had caused all the problems for this guy, which in some ways is true. And they used to boo me, and they used to cheer when I died. And this was very hard for Jimmy [Jones] to take, because he saw the play as a love story as much as anything else, and was very angry that the black audience could not get past my color.[57]

The mail and threats that Alexander received indicate that the staging of this interracial relationship deeply disturbed overt racist-sexists. In this passage, Alexander critiques self-congratulatory liberal white audiences. She shows some understanding of black audiences' objections as if Ellie caused Jack's downfall, rather than structural oppression, but decries their cheering and booing as inappropriate because she values colorblindness, implying that they are the real racists. Finally, she notes that Jones viewed *The Great White Hope* as a "love story," troublingly erasing race. The differences in reactions to and interpretations of Jack and Ellie's relationship underscore struggles over legitimate uses of racialized, gendered bodies with consequences beyond the theatre. Yet reviews almost never mentioned *Loving v. Virginia* and the interracial relationship as such. Aside from outright bigoted outliers and spectators' gasps during the bedroom scene, the intimacy between Jack and Ellie was not overwhelmingly threatening to liberal, middle-class theatre audiences but desirable and profitable. Because he loses her and loses the heavyweight title, their precarious, taboo relationship can be more pleasurable. *The Great White Hope* perhaps marked a turning point in the dramatization and consumption of popular interracial romance.

The racially liberal marketing of *The Great White Hope* focused less

ARENA STAGE 67/68

ZELDA FICHANDLER, PRODUCING DIRECTOR

WORLD PREMIERE

THE GREAT WHITE HOPE

By HOWARD SACKLER

DECEMBER 7, 1967-JANUARY 14, 1968

Arena Stage playbill for *The Great White Hope*, 1967. Courtesy of Arena Stage
and Special Collections Research Center, George Mason University Libraries.

on interracial love and more on interracial struggle, which opened up interpretations of the play as about a larger, universal battle that could resonate with everyone, no matter one's skin color. The playbill for the Arena Stage production displays a black-and-white drawing of a black man and a white man boxing each another. The former wears white shorts, while the latter wears black shorts. Color coded as opposites, they represent blackness and whiteness as mutually exclusive and yet also mutually constitutive. They are at once pummeling each other, embracing each other, holding each other up, resting on each other, and using the strength of the other's body in order to do damage to that body. They are locked in a Hegelian struggle, suggesting equal push and pull. This dynamic represents a racial struggle but also an individual struggle between two men of apparently equal power. Like *The Great White Hope*, the image provokes raced and erased meanings, appealing to multiple audiences—a specific critique of systemic white supremacy or a generalization of the universal battle against personal obstacles, as if material equality has already been achieved.

Sackler disavowed racial themes as being central to *The Great White Hope* and instead positioned the "universal" theme of man versus society as the main point. In a profile piece for the *New York Times*, Sackler asserted that he researched the play between 1961 and 1965, as if to confirm that he had not been thinking of Muhammad Ali, who refused to be inducted into the U.S. military in 1967.[58] Moreover, Sackler repeatedly insisted, "I consider this not to be about blacks and whites. It's a metaphor of struggle between man and the outside world."[59] This is, however, ambivalent because the "man" in this case is black, and "the outside world" is framed as white. In the script he typically referred to unnamed white characters as "WOMAN ONE," while black characters were designated as "NEGRO," leaving whiteness unmarked, while blackness—and not gender—defined the black personage. Sackler rejected any association of his play with a liberal project: "Some people spoke of the play as if it were a cliché of white liberalism. But I kept to the line right through, of showing that it wasn't a case of blacks being good and whites being bad, I was appalled at first at the reaction."[60] While it is true that Sackler showed characters from different racial groups as multitudinous in their views, such as a black bourgeois character who condemns Jack's sexual behavior, his equation of "white liberalism" with "good blacks" and "bad whites" is reductive. In another interview in 1975, Sackler reiterated his position: "My goal in dealing with any subject for a play is to take it and raise it to the level of metaphor, to take it from the level of history or anecdote to the level of universal experience."[61] He positions himself, his play, and his politics to move into the higher realms of art and universalism, apparently untethered by power. By writing a highly specific play that engages with historical and contemporaneous race relations and at the same time disavowing its explicit content, he creates a seductive narrative. He can accumulate symbolic capital and economic capital. He successfully appeals to a range of people, from those who actively advocate for racial equality to those who prize supposedly "neutral," great art over politics, as if these qualities are separate and objective.

James Earl Jones, who became a star playing Jack Jefferson, also helped the project of favoring universalism over explicit racial politics, yet he embodied the contradictions therein. In 1968, Jones married a white woman, the actress who played Desdemona to his Othello in 1964, Julienne Marie. In an interview with the *New York Times*, his wife said, "When we got married, we never discussed race as a social issue."[62] Like his character in *The Great White Hope*, Jones rejected demands that he be a "race man" responsible for racial uplift. He resented when the Citizen's Committee for Hubert Humphrey asked for his help: "They make it sound like if I don't use my influence to get black votes, Wallace will get in. Well I'm not so sure that's such a bad idea for this country at this time. I don't know."[63] By suggesting that George Wallace, the infamous segregationist governor of Alabama, might not be "such a bad idea for this country" as president, Jones revealed either extreme right-wing politics or political apathy. In 2000, when Arena revived *The Great White Hope*, Jones echoed Sackler's rhetoric about "the story of a man who was up against the system."[64] He went further to dismiss race as a theme: "That was bullshit then, and it is now."[65]

But Jones has also indicated his consciousness of racial politics and his place within them. He exemplifies the anxieties of the hypervisible black body.[66] In the same interview with the *New York Times* in 1968, he said, "The public hates Muhammad Ali's guts because he doesn't conform. They like me because my social mask is a gentleman. I don't like to offend people. But I don't blame Muhammad Ali for being himself. Here I am married to Julienne, but I don't know if we should take an auto ride together through Mississippi."[67] He knew that his success was contingent on his respectable behavior. In another interview, he asserted that playing Jack Jefferson onstage was more productive than marching for the civil rights movement in order to justify his perceived lack of participation in the struggle for racial equality.[68] Like the real boxer Jack Johnson, he navigated his own black habitus and desired colorblind treatment for his exceptionalism. He declared both "I would like to be a great actor and recognized as that, and not just as a great black or just a black actor"[69] and "My Negro-ness does not rule my life."[70] He both recognized how white supremacy impeded him and rejected how blackness shaped his identity.

CRITICAL DEBATE

This discourse from the artists behind *The Great White Hope* likely primed the critical reception of the play, particularly assessing whether it qualified as nonprofit or commercial and as racially specific or colorblind universality. Dozens of newspaper reviews spanning from New Haven to St. Louis indicated the growing importance of Arena as a site for new work and the special attention given to this story of black struggle. The reviews almost uniformly celebrated *The Great White Hope*. Martin Gottfried commended the play, "probably the most important new American play ever to come out of any resident theatre."[71] Critics have a direct impact on the Pulitzer Prize for Drama, whose symbolic capital became extremely desirable to nonprofit companies attempting to replicate the success of *The Great White Hope*. The play's racial liberalism appealed to the white establishment, while radical black feminists were far more critical. When the play won the Pulitzer Prize, it provoked dialogue about changes in the new play ecosystem.

When *The Great White Hope* premiered at Arena Stage, critics debated the relative economic and artistic positions of regional theatre and Broadway. Thomas Shales of the *DC Examiner* lauded the play for its "tremendous popular appeal"; he added, "'Great White Hope' could, quite single-handedly in fact, deal a welcome and devastating blow to the intellectual snobbery which has so saturated many of the past productions at Arena Stage."[72] He distinguished *The Great White Hope* from what he considered "the intellectual snobbery" that Zelda Fichandler typically produced, perhaps alluding to *Serjeant Musgrave's*

Dance and *Oh! What a Lovely War.* Gottfried exclaimed, "Now, with the presentation of a new and excellent play—a play that would probably have a commercial success in New York—resident theatre becomes an alternative to the commercially produced new play and a force that Broadway has to contend with. That contention will be healthy."[73] By stressing nonprofit regional theatre and for-profit New York theatre as alternate sites of new play production, Gottfried positioned these institutions in the field of cultural production as quite similar and as healthy capitalist competition. Peter Altman of the *Minneapolis Star* similarly extolled the play, saying, "It is the first new play I have ever seen in such a playhouse that has the scope, topicality, and excellence of production that could earn a successful Broadway run."[74] These critics framed the Arena premiere as a pre-Broadway tryout, much as the *New York Times* did.

Different critics averred that *The Great White Hope* was a nonprofit cultural production with values opposed to the market. Don Rubin of the *New Haven Register* insisted that it "is precisely the kind of play which could only be staged by a noncommercial producing group," and it "is clearly not a commercial venture and would probably never find a production in a commercial theater because of its immense size and scope. That Arena Stage is bold enough and skilled enough to mount this play is to its great credit."[75] With such deliberate diction as "precisely" and "clearly," he named the artistic scope and financial riskiness of the play as the characteristics of nonprofit productions. Rubin added, "Arena officials—before the show even opened—expected to lose somewhere about $35,000 on 'The Great White Hope.'"[76] Russell Shaw of the *St. Louis Review* argued, "It bears little resemblance to the conventional Broadway hit, nor does it seem a likely candidate for Hollywood. (Sidney Poitier is, for one thing, too light to play a heavyweight.)"[77] William J. Eaton remarked in the *Chicago Daily News*, "Such a play would not be commercial enough for Broadway, yet the theater would be poorer without it, in Arena's view."[78] Eaton's comment replicated a value system that pits economic capital against symbolic capital. Yet his use of "poorer" and his appendage of "in Arena's view" acknowledged how value depends on perspective and the nature of profit.

Most critics also mentioned the NEA grant that supported the production. In *Women's Wear Daily*, Gottfried opined, "That the National

　　　　　CAPITAL

Endowment has forked over 25,000 taxpayer dollars to mount a play that would probably infuriate most of those taxpayers' conservative hearts is reason enough for hope that Government subsidy can be reasonable and artistically promotional."[79] Naming the grant from the new agency served to celebrate this kind of left-leaning play honed in a nonprofit environment. In Gottfried's tacit assessment, the play's racially liberal politics would alienate white supremacist conservatives, and that this was the kind of integrationist-but-not-quite work that the federal government should endorse in nonprofit theatres.

Critics often performed their tolerance of black Americans, but only when they were portrayed in certain ways. In "Is All Black Theater Beautiful? No," Gottfried argued that by 1970, "standards of writing, production, performance and judgment are being lowered for blacks and it is prejudice all over again, inverse this time."[80] Ever the fan of false dichotomies, Gottfried juxtaposed pure (white) art against (black) politics and insinuated that white writers were losing out to mediocre black artists: "Hundreds of years of oppression, in and out of the theater, cannot be used as an excuse to overlook lapses in craft."[81] He also objected to black critics reviewing black plays because this implied he was not qualified to assess black craft. He saw himself as objective. Sympathetic whites might use different tools such as political efficacy or Afrocentrism to evaluate plays, but Gottfried rejected considerations of power dynamics in the evaluation of artwork. While he echoed the praise for Sackler and *The Great White Hope*, he dismissed praise for Charles Gordone's *No Place to Be Somebody* as overwrought white guilt. These plays won back-to-back Pulitzer Prizes. Arena staged *No Place to Be Somebody* in 1970, a few years after *The Great White Hope*, suggesting a new trend in these sanctioned black works coming from nonprofit, predominantly white climes.

Most critics celebrated *The Great White Hope* for its racial liberalism. Russell Shaw began his review claiming: "The most effective commentary on the country's racial crisis currently available here is being delivered nightly in a small but elegant theater a few blocks from the Capitol."[82] By highlighting the theatre's location in Washington, Shaw linked the play with national governance as well as recent events such as the March on Washington and the passage of civil rights legislation. In his review, William J. Eaton named the apparent contradiction between U.S. democracy and inequality by dubbing *The Great White*

Hope "an exciting new drama about the old American dilemma—racial degradation despite egalitarian ideals" and its theme "the moral destruction of a man, because of his race, by a white supremacist world."[83] James Earl Jones also received tremendous praise for his powerful performance as Jack. *Boston Herald* critic Samuel Hirsch wrote, "He has bubbling humor and common sense, raising loud laughter with his deft self-mockery of Negro stereotypes."[84] To Hirsch, Jones's performance critiqued rather than reiterated stereotypes.

But the critics also betrayed the limits of racial liberalism. Shaw concluded his review by writing, "It is an extraordinary powerful study of America's sickness on the subject of race," framing structures of racial hierarchy as "sickness" rather than as historically invented and actively maintained.[85] Systemic racism is not a cold that a country catches. Others counseled Sackler to cut the scene between Jack and a young African student in Germany[86] or the monologues of Jack's mother and of Scipio, which reminded them of Marcus Garvey and more contemporary black power leaders.[87] These recommendations hint at some white critics' minimal interest in or inability to perceive the importance of black intraracial dynamics. Moreover, these critics cited Scipio's critiques of African American assimilation as senseless. Harry MacArthur of the *Washington Star* mentioned "a strange character named Scipio, who keeps turning up to make ranting Black Power speeches which confuse virtually everybody."[88] His comment begs the question, who counts as "everybody"?

A few critics also argued that Sackler exaggerated the perniciousness of white supremacy. Although *Washington Daily News* critic Tom Donnelly admitted that his argument was based on "very scanty research," he claimed, "Mr. Sackler has romanticized his black hero and has, just possibly, made Jack's white oppressors more oppressive than they actually were,"[89] and it is worth noting that even some reviews of the revival production in 2000 judged the portrayal of racism in the script unrealistic (judgments that say more about the critics' reluctance to acknowledge the extent of white supremacy than the historical record).[90] Writing in 1968 for the left-leaning *Nation*, Jules Novick practiced self-reflection on racial liberalism, and he had difficulty grappling with inequality as deliberate rather than a miscalculation. It is worth quoting him at length as a representative of this prevalent ideology:

CAPITAL

I had it in my mind to accuse Sackler of catering to the absurd, ugly and dangerous kind of Negro paranoia that considers family planning a genocidal plot against the colored races. But then I thought of Adam Clayton Powell and, even more, of Cassius Clay, who has recently been sentenced to a $10,000 fine and five years in prison for refusing induction into the army. The play is by no means a calm and balanced assessment of the situation, but it seems clear to me that what Sackler implies is at least basically true; ours is still a racist society.[91]

Novick tried to position himself as reasonable and balanced by showing his thinking process. In so doing, he recognized white complicity in the persistence of racism after the Civil Rights Act yet prized an allegedly nonpartisan view that championed civil discourse over social justice. He simultaneously advocated for performing *The Great White Hope* for Congress to educate them on race relations and, elsewhere, derided Trinity Repertory Company's initiatives for "academically retarded Negro slum children" in Providence.[92] This belief in education and tolerance for whites only as strategies for racial equality exemplifies the paradox of racial liberalism.

Critics drew parallels between the early twentieth century and the late 1960s, yet they often used broad strokes to universalize the play. *New York Times* critic Clive Barnes called the subject matter "fascinating and relevant. In these liberal times we can accept a black heavyweight champion, but can we accept a *Black Muslim* heavyweight champion?"[93] He connected *The Great White Hope* to late 1960s racial politics, even as he centered whiteness by framing the readers as "we" (presumably whites) accepting them (presumably black Muslims). Almost every review cited the similarities between Jack Jefferson and Muhammad Ali as black boxers oppressed by systemic racism. Some named Stokely Carmichael, again suggesting the shared experiences of black male habitus. Instead of unpacking the subtleties of racial dynamics, some critics devoted equal if not more column space to "universal themes." Martin Gottfried observed, "The threat and doom of Stokely Carmichael and H. Rap Brown are there too, and the fate of Muhammad Ali. And beyond all that, the grim capture of any man caught in too-powerful circumstances, aching only to live his own life with some privacy and just a little joy."[94] Gottfried dismissed the relevance of race and ignored the fact that Jack actively sought the spot-light. By framing the narrative as a man "caught in too-powerful cir-cumstances," Gottfried focused on the tragic individual without the possibility of social change. Peter Altman also worked to personalize *The Great White Hope* to include all men: "And the story is not just political allegory; it is the portrayal of one man's search for fulfillment in love and work, not as a member of a race but as an individual. It is a personal tragedy."[95] These strategies at once acknowledged and disavowed the importance of race and systemic racism to focus on the universal and the individual, replicating narratives by Sackler and Jones. Summarizing the reviews by whites, Carol Bunch Davis wrote, "In demonstrating regret for historical wrongs against Johnson and linking them to Ali in the then-current moment, *The Great White Hope*'s reviews served as a racial repentance that ultimately elide the complexities of African American subjectivity as they are staged in the play."[96]

Radical black feminists have assessed why *The Great White Hope* appealed to white bourgeois audiences. In *Ain't I a Woman*, bell hooks argues, "The public's acceptance of these movies [*Guess Who's Coming to Dinner* and *The Great White Hope*] indicates that it no longer feared black males and white females uniting."[97] Although hooks overstates "the public's acceptance" of these films, given that *Guess Who's Coming to Dinner* was not screened in some places in the South, her argument that black men and white women together were accepted by norma-tive U.S. society in part because they each have some privilege (male and white, respectively) is compelling.[98] In 1970, Toni Cade Bambara praised *The Great White Hope* as "the least harrowing example I know of of whites hustling Black material. And for the first time in my ex-perience of white-on-black theater, it was the drama of the playwright that captured my attention, rather than the comic-tragedy of the Black players trying to cope with bullshit without losing their credibility as either actors or Black people."[99] Her appraisal suggests that she found the play surprisingly sensitive in its portrayals of black characters and gave good opportunities to black actors. The *Washington Informer*, a black newspaper founded in 1964, marveled that the Broadway audi-ence accepted this "forthright play" "with the most outspoken dia-logue I've yet to hear in a theatre" regarding racial dynamics, indicat-ing that Sackler advanced palatable antiracist discourse, and that this amazed some black writers.[100] However, Bambara also critiqued what she viewed as the hypocrisies of racial liberalism: "Some critics have called the play the great hope for the white liberal, offered as they are a chance to flagellate themselves. . . . Of course it doesn't cost anything to cheer the innocent beast/transhuman archangel in the dark of the theater."[101] She questioned the political efficacy of *The Great White Hope* in inspiring white spectators to engage in direct actions to dismantle the structures of white supremacy when they leave the theatre; instead, she believed that the play offered white patrons an affective experience of guilt, sympathy, and expiation.

Bambara and others also offered critical interpretations of the text. Bambara pointed out that the black women in the play serve as tools in Sackler's dramaturgy: Jack's estranged wife Clara is the "Evil Black Bitch," and his mother is the stereotypical religious "Black Mother."[102] When the play toured to the Ahmanson Theatre in Los Angeles in 1969, Dan Sullivan reported that the Afro-American Cultural Association distributed leaflets attacking Sackler. Devoted to African American uplift, appreciation, and knowledge, the black activist group objected to the portrayal of Jack as "stupid, boorish, a collector of 'neurotic and psychotic white women' and, in general, a traitor to his race and his country" in contrast with the historic figure of Johnson who was "intelligent, sensitive, heroic, and loved by 'all kinds, classes, and colors of women.'"[103] By contrast, Clive Barnes found the protagonist to be "whitewashed" as "almost too good, too noble, to be true," illuminating how people with different positions can have discrete views of Jack.[104] In the aptly titled review "Black Woman Examines Two Plays by White Men," Mildred Pitts Walter viewed Jack as an "arrogant buffoon" whose "incredible dialect revealed his state of dehumanization" and internalized racism.[105] She worried that these characterizations would prompt white audiences to "indulge their own racist attitudes" separated by the "comfortable lenses of the early 1900s."[106] Walter advocated for more complex dramatizations of black characters, and she diagnosed that the self-hating characters and historical distancing seen through a white male gaze were precisely what made the play score box office receipts and win accolades: "This is a white man's work: I now understand why this play got the Pulitzer Prize."[107]

The Great White Hope's middlebrow appeal in being both nonprofit and commercial, black and unmarked white, made it viable for awards.

With its huge scope of history and setting, the play is, in dramaturgical terms, epic. In a lengthy piece for the *New York Times*, Walter Kerr pontificated on the play's intensity, "Mr. Sackler's ambition is staggering: He is out for total immersion—in the period, in the problem, in the experience. Nothing that can be known of all the factors that went into a horrifying case history, nothing that the theater can do or say in its intimate, artificial, privileged way, is to be left out."[108] The play was sprawling not only in location but also in languages, among them French, German, Spanish, and Hungarian, without English translations across several scenes. Some critics compared the drama to Greek and Shakespearean tragedies.[109] Others linked Sackler to the "father" of legitimate, literary U.S. theatre, Eugene O'Neill, and specifically to *The Emperor Jones* and *The Hairy Ape*, plays that were likely chosen for their racial resonances.[110] Through these associations, *The Great White Hope* gained proximate legitimacy. Many touted the importance of this new play, given recent seasons of unsatisfying theatre from U.S. playwrights. Between 1963 and 1968, the Pulitzer Prize for Drama was awarded only twice: to Frank Gilroy for *The Subject Was Roses* (1965) and to Edward Albee for *A Delicate Balance* (1967). By 1968, critics developed more interest in transfers from England such as Tom Stoppard's *Rosencrantz and Guildenstern Are Dead* and Harold Pinter's *The Homecoming*.[111]

Hope appeared well positioned to win the Pulitzer Prize in Drama, yet its eligibility revealed tensions between nonprofit regional theatres and New York City commercial theatres. The play's chief competitor was the musical *1776*, book by Peter Stone, music and lyrics by Sherman Edwards, which also engaged with U.S. identity and progressive politics, implicitly critiquing the Vietnam War and directly addressing the nation's founding on slavery. In the end, the play won over the musical. Savran argues that the Pulitzer "functions primarily to reaffirm the critics' authority by turning their reviews into self-fulfilling prophesies and to reward those plays that have most fortuitously balanced 'educational value' against commercial viability."[112] *The Great White Hope* achieved high "educational value" and "commercial viability" by historicizing Jack Johnson and engaging with contemporary racial politics. The Broadway production was one of the first two plays that the Theatre Development Fund supported by purchasing $10,000 worth of tickets and distributing them to students.[113] In "It's

Time the Pulitzer People Woke Up," Richard Coe called for the committee to look beyond Broadway productions.[114] The three jurors were all white male New York critics: Walter Kerr of the *New York Times*, Richard Watts Jr. of the *New York Post*, and Brendan Gill of the *New Yorker*. Sackler's win called into question the preeminence of Broadway as the incubator of worthy new U.S. plays and New York critics as the sole judges. The *Washington Post* took great pleasure in the honors heaped on *The Great White Hope* and criticized New York newspapers for downplaying the production's origins. After Sackler won the Best Play Tony Award, the "Around Town" section asserted, "Our pride in this collective, home-grown achievement is, we must confess, singed ever so slightly by New York's characteristic attitude that it, it first and it alone had the perception and enterprise to see a major artistic work be born," and then pointed out that *1776* had also debuted in Washington.[115]

The 1969 Tony Awards broadcast highlighted certain racially liberal politics of integration. When James Earl Jones, Jane Alexander, and Howard Sackler won awards, the latter two thanked Arena in their speeches. The platform of Broadway and this national broadcast put the spotlight on the regional theatre in the nation's capital. Jones became the first black performer to win the Tony for Best Actor in a Play. That night, a special Tony went to the Negro Ensemble Company. Artist-activist Harry Belafonte introduced the multiracial cast of *Hair* by making oblique references to the "confusing, polarizing times" and how audiences must listen to the younger generation.[116] Black-white pairs of musical stars such as Pearl Bailey and Robert Preston flirted with each other while copresenting awards. Finally, the award show was hosted by Alan King and Diahann Carroll, and the young boy who played the black actress's son on the television show *Julia* brought the couple together at the start and end as if to suggest a peaceful interracial family. Yet the terms "race," "racism," "black," and "white" were never uttered during the broadcast. This mix of racialized bodies and silent discourse in both the ceremony and in *The Great White Hope* lays out the contours for racially liberal projects: it calls attention to racial injustice, suggests interracial harmony, and accrues ticket sales and awards but avoids talking about racism in a way that would make white audiences feel too uncomfortable.

Although Arena Stage helped to decenter the production of new U.S. plays with its premiere of *The Great White Hope*, the company's and the play's legitimacy still rested on a relation to New York City. At the same time, the Broadway production might not have been possible without Arena and its aura of nonprofit status. Arena's practiced disinterest in making money invited critics' praise, which could then lead to making more money. Sackler's and Jones's professed disinterest in race permitted dramatizing race relations, attracting both spectators who might not otherwise want to see an overtly antiracist play and those who wanted to see racial politics onstage. To many critics, the play both mediated late 1960s racial politics and transcended its historical subject. These combinations enabled the play to be a commercial and critical hit. It was not a coincidence that Arena's first original play about a black protagonist was its first to reach the Great White Way but a crucial condition of its success. Ultimately, *The Great White Hope* generated symbolic capital for Arena through its accolades, transfer to Broadway, and navigation of racial dynamics, distinguishing this nonprofit regional theatre; these acts further blurred the arbitrary line between for-profit and not-for-profit. *The Great White Hope* established a precedent for Arena's future productions that capitalized on nonprofit status, commercial potential, and black-white racially liberal politics.

PART TWO

Race

GLOBALIZING THE STAGE FROM RUSSIA AND EASTERN EUROPE TO AFRICA AND THE BLACK DIASPORA

n 1991, Zelda Fichandler sat down to an interview with critic and scholar Edwin Wilson to discuss the economic and racial politics of Arena Stage. She spoke of Washington's "mostly black government, mostly black city" and the public school system in which 90 percent of the students were black.[1] She concluded, "As time goes by, it becomes more and more incongruent and ridiculous for this theatre to be a little white, western theatre perched in the center of a city in turmoil."[2] Her repertory had originally embraced not only Western European and American classics but also Russian and Eastern European plays, which were her special expertise. During the Cold War, audiences in Washington took great interest in these productions. But by the time the Berlin Wall came down in 1989, the U.S. state had become less interested in funding them. Fichandler followed the money and filled the season slots once occupied by artists such as Polish playwright Sławomir Mrożek with artists such as African American playwright August Wilson.

But Arena's commitment to African and African diasporic theatre was not initially a clearly articulated, purposeful mission. From the late 1960s through the early 1990s, the theatre produced multiple plays by Athol Fugard, Derek Walcott, and Mustapha Matura, yet meeting minutes, letters, and promotional materials do not reveal a consciously coordinated connection between these playwrights. Instead, these documents dramatize the theatre's anxiety at not being a more racially integrated environment and uncertainty in how to proceed. Racial liberalism provided an answer that accommodated local and global politics without radically upending the theatre. American Studies scholar Jodi Melamed asserts, "At racial liberalism's core was a geopolitical race narrative: African American integration within U.S. society and advancement toward equality defined through a liberal framework of legal rights and inclusive nationalism would establish the moral legitimacy of U.S. global leadership."[3] Arena produced works from South Africa and the Caribbean for a range of reasons including advocating for racial equality, commenting on U.S. race relations (from the safer distance of apartheid and European colonialism), and attracting black audiences with ostensibly black theatre. The strategy also branded the theatre and U.S. nation as global, and accumulated economic and symbolic capital. By both including and sidelining this repertory, the theatre does not seem to have conceived of African/Caribbean/American theatre as part of its bent toward international work. Arena exemplified a push-pull relationship with incorporating black theatre stories, artists, and audiences into its community onstage, on staff, and in the seats of the theatre. Cognitive, materialist theatre scholar Bruce McConachie describes this phenomenon as "containment liberalism."[4]

Scholarship that emphasizes particularity and solidarity to theorize the black diaspora helps to illuminate links between the black plays that Arena Stage presented or produced. In his study of black Francophone literature, *The Practice of Diaspora*, Brent Hayes Edwards uses the framework of diaspora because "it makes possible an analysis of the institutional formations of black internationalism that attends to their constitutive differences" and exchanges.[5] People with African heritage who experienced either forced or voluntary migration can bond over racialized identities and cultures, but they are not inevitably the same. There is no single, easily apprehensible genre of black diasporic theatre. African American theatre scholar Sandra Richards provides a multivalent definition of diaspora that spans communal affect, time, and space:

> (a) a "backward" glance and affective affiliation with the site of collective origin; (b) alienation from, varying degrees of accommodation to, and critical appropriation or creolization of, norms of the host nation, which is ambivalent about the presence of diasporans within its borders; (c) subjective experience of identity as both rooted or fixed in a distinctive history, and routed or continually (re)articulated in relation to intersections of local, regional, national, and global particularities; (d) recognition of affinity with other ethnonational communities displaced from the original homeland, accomplished by privileging similarity and

unity over difference; and (e) identification and nurturance of a home in the world.[6]

Richards conceives black diaspora as dynamic, as between past and present, between an avowed origin and new home. The people and plays that make up the diaspora community exist in relation to other people from other places, yet they often work together. Through both commonality and specificity, people of the black diaspora articulate their identity. In Washington, black communities from the literary salons of the early twentieth century to African refugees of the Eritrean-Ethiopian War found continuity. Arena capitalized on the black bourgeoisie linked by their interest in African and black diasporic drama. There are similarities across the plays because they resonated with the company's artistic leadership and audiences and were viewed through a lens of U.S. racial politics. A global theatre on the performance and political fronts of the Cold War, Arena Stage produced a diasporic black aesthetics and politics mostly welcomed by middle-class white audiences and growing black audiences.

The theatre's programming, branding, and patronage from 1970 to 1990 shifted from classic and contemporary European theatre to African and African diasporic dramas, artists, and audiences. During this period, Arena increasingly positioned itself as an international company in the sense that it staged plays from around the world but most prominently from the USSR and Eastern Europe. At the same time, it represented the United States to those abroad. The historic tour of *Our Town* by Thornton Wilder and *Inherit the Wind* by Jerome Lawrence and Robert E. Lee in Moscow and Leningrad in 1973 put Arena Stage on the map. Arena also fashioned itself as a global center by producing and presenting some works by African and black diasporic artists, but they were held at arm's length; they were not explicitly part of the international branding. Stories of black-white struggle authored by whites hailed regional theatres and the critical establishment. Additionally, the space of the nation's capital and the stage performed the black diaspora as spatial-temporal imaginings of black collectivity and racial difference for black audiences. Behind the scenes, the theatre staff debated how the company could attract *more* black artists, employees, trustees, and spectators. By the end of the Cold War and the beginning of the age of multiculturalism, Arena Stage increasingly institutionalized black inclusivity. It definitively committed to cultural diversity, which had become a U.S. value worth funding. Blackness subsidized this traditionally white regional theatre.

ON THE INTERNATIONAL STAGE

Cold War cultural politics shaped the United States' artistic exports and strengthened Arena Stage's reputation. After World War II, the U.S. state funded artwork to showcase excellence in U.S. culture and distinguish its aesthetics from Soviet realism. A production of *Hamlet*, produced by the Barter Theatre, an early regional theatre in Virginia, was "the first production to tour abroad with official support from the US government" when it played at the Elsinore Festival in Denmark in 1949, and it "demonstrated that there was profit for everyone in such collaborations" between the federal government and nonprofit theatre.[7] Moreover, the State Department sought control over the international narrative of the civil rights movement to exert greater influence in nonaligned nations.[8] It mobilized stories of racial equality to combat Soviet propaganda, which highlighted the violence of institutional antiblack racism from Little Rock to Selma. The United States sponsored tours of black musicians such as Dizzy Gillespie and the opera *Porgy and Bess* "to redefine an image of American nationhood [as] more inclusive and integrated than the reality."[9] Theatre historian Charlotte Canning contends that the U.S. government became a "cultural ministry" during the Cold War.[10] In 1969, the State Department abruptly canceled a tour to South Asia and Eastern Europe of the Los Angeles–based Mark Taper Forum's "New Theatre for Now," a series of short plays by prominent playwrights including Lanford Wilson, Adrienne Kennedy, and Martin Duberman because officials and artists like Robert E. Lee found the plays too full of sex, expletives, and antiestablishment rhetoric.[11]

As a model for regional theatre, Arena Stage fit the State Department's agenda for promoting cultural prestige, Americanness, and racial harmony. Officials surveyed major regional theatres and selected Arena for its productions of *Our Town* and *Inherit the Wind*. Wilder's realist-expressionist classic explores life in the small town of Grover's Corners, New Hampshire. In *Inherit the Wind*, Lawrence and Lee dramatize the arguments for and against teaching about evolution via the

92)   RACE

famous Scopes Monkey Trial. The Department of State had considered the Guthrie Theater in Minneapolis and the American Conservatory Theater (ACT) in San Francisco as its U.S. regional theatre representative; however, Soviet cultural attachés responded poorly to the former's production of *Of Mice and Men* and determined that ACT's productions were insufficiently "American." Meanwhile, the wife of one of the attachés found Arena's *Our Town* moving and reminiscent of Chekhov.[12] The selection of Arena Stage also likely involved a consideration of Zelda Fichandler's and Alan Schneider's backgrounds. Fichandler had studied Soviet culture; worked for U.S. military intelligence; taught Stanislavski-inspired acting techniques; and produced plays by Anton Chekhov, Nikolai Gogol, and Ivan Turgenev. She was of Russian descent, while Schneider was born in Ukraine. They both assisted with the Russian translations of *Our Town* and *Inherit the Wind*. In addition, Arena was renowned for its resident acting ensemble, and these productions featured Robert Prosky and Dianne Wiest. The integrated company boasted a couple of African American actors, likely appealing to the State Department's desire to impart a diverse, friendly vision of the United States. As with *The Great White Hope*, the theatre's inclusion of blackness within a white frame enabled their productions to circulate further. Staging the U.S. as multiracial, *Our Town* idealized integration, emblematized community-building, and dramatized domesticity with metatheatrical critique.

The financial investment in and promotion of the Arena Stage tour suggest its importance. The Department of State agreed to cover the estimated cost of the tour, nearly $150,000.[13] This included travel and accommodations for sixty-eight actors and crew members, sets by Ming Cho Lee, and even a monkey for *Inherit the Wind*. Under the 1972–73 Exchanges Agreement, Arena would be joined by the Thad Jones-Mel Lewis Orchestra, the New York City Ballet, the José Limón Dance Company, the San Francisco Symphony Orchestra, and Holiday on Ice.[14] Fichandler remarked with some bite that the Russians "had never known that there was anything besides musicals from the United States."[15] By picking Arena Stage and its productions of *Our Town* and *Inherit the Wind*, the Department of State sought to showcase more "legitimate" U.S. theatre. As Gad Guterman observes, *Inherit the Wind* had more economic capital than cachet among theatre circles, yet the play also entailed political capital.[16] The press release for the tour underscored "efforts to increase understanding by strengthening through educational and cultural exchanges ties that bind the American people with the peoples of other nations" that would help lead to "an improved climate for international cooperation."[17]

In the fall of 1973, Arena became the first regional theatre to perform behind the Iron Curtain. The company played for one week at the Moscow Art Theatre and one week at the Pushkin Theatre to wide acclaim and sold-out houses.[18] While the actors performed the plays in English, the audience members listened to a Russian translation via headsets. Arena Stage received significant political approbation for the tour. Shortly before the company departed for the Soviet Union, Mayor Walter Washington declared September 27, 1973, to be Arena Stage Day. Walter Mondale, Hubert Humphrey, Jacob Javitz, and others sent the theatre letters of congratulations on the successful tour. On Capitol Hill, Senator Charles Percy of Illinois called for two news articles on Arena's tour to be entered into the Congressional Record. Representative George Hansen of Idaho made explicit political points about how *Inherit the Wind* "cannot fail to have made an imprint on the capital of a country which is wracked with internal tension caused by the challenge of dissident intellectuals. Its theme is freedom of speech, a freedom denied citizens of the U.S.S.R."[19] He congratulated the company for "representing the American people by carrying in their persons and in the words of American plays, a message of good will from the citizens of the United States."[20] For many, the company and its plays symbolized an ideal U.S. culture emblematized by supposed freedom in contrast with the Soviet Union.

After the trip to the Soviet Union, Zelda Fichandler sought more opportunities for touring around the world. According to meeting minutes, in 1976, "Gene Feist of Roundabout Theater called to say he would like to be Arena's New York outlet," and the transcriber noted, "This is not a focus point now. Zelda would rather go to Holland, Poland, Romania & Israel—more important to this company."[21] The Holland Festival invited Arena to present *Death of a Salesman* as the sole representative of U.S. theatre for the American bicentennial.[22] But limited funding barred the trip, because Holland would cover only $14,000 in local expenses. Arena did present Miller's *After the Fall,* as well as George S. Kaufman and Moss Hart's *You Can't Take It with You,* at the

Hong Kong Arts Festival in 1980. Seven years later, the company took *The Crucible* to the Israel Festival in Jerusalem.

The Soviet tour produced more season programming and directing opportunities geared toward Russian and Eastern European artists. *The Arena Adventure* argues that Arena's commitment to contemporary political plays from Eastern Europe distinguished the company from other regional theatres.[23] Even before the 1973 tour, Fichandler had produced classic plays such as *The Cherry Orchard* and *A Month in the Country*. In the early 1970s, she staged lesser-known works, namely *Wipe-Out Games* by Eugene Ionesco and *Enemies* by Maxim Gorky. After the tour, having seen *The Ascent of Mount Fuji* by Chingiz Aitmatov and Kaltai Mukhamedzhanov in the USSR, Fichandler directed it in 1975, making it the first new Soviet play produced in the U.S. since 1967.[24] From the 1970s through the '80s, Arena produced three plays by Polish playwright Sławomir Mrożek, *Enchanted Night*, *The Police*, and *Emigrés*, and three by Hungarian playwright István Örkény, *The Tot Family*, *Catsplay*, and *Screenplay*. In 1978, Fichandler directed the world premiere of *Duck Hunting* by Alexander Vampilov, a meditation on the post-Stalinist generation, and in 1981, Arena staged Richard Nelson's adaptation of *The Suicide* by Nikolai Erdman, a play that had been suppressed by Stalin. Many of these productions were U.S. premieres, and their themes of political struggle likely resonated with DC audiences after the Vietnam War and Watergate scandal and in the context of the Cold War. Fichandler reflected that plays from Eastern Europe appealed to her because they dramatized the "explosion of human psyche under repression."[25]

In addition, Arena Stage developed relationships with Eastern European directors. Romanian director Liviu Ciulei made his U.S. directing debut at Arena in 1974 with *Leonce and Lena* by Georg Büchner and subsequently directed several other productions that decade including *The Lower Depths*, *Hamlet*, and *Don Juan*. When Ciulei became the artistic director of the Guthrie in the 1980s, Fichandler visited Minneapolis and saw the company's production of *Tartuffe* directed by Lucian Pintilie, Ciulei's student from the Bulandra Theatre in Romania. Fichandler brought Pintilie to Arena to direct *Tartuffe* and *The Wild Duck*. Having met Yuri Lyubimov during the USSR tour, she also brought him and his adaptation of *Crime and Punishment* to Arena

Stage in 1987, which was during the period when he had lost his citizenship and directorship of the Taganka Theatre in Moscow.

Arena's tour had a lasting impact on the theatre's reputation. In 1974, the Theatre Panel of the NEA recommended that Arena Stage be awarded $200,000, $50,000 more than the Endowment's ceiling grant.[26] This grant suggested recognition of the company's achievements and of its difficulty fundraising in Washington, given the city's lack of a local arts council. In 1976, following the tour and Broadway transfers of *The Great White Hope, Indians, Moonchildren, Raisin,* and *Zalmen, or The Madness of God,* Arena Stage received the first Tony Award given to a regional theatre. This symbolic capital granted the institution greater legitimacy and national attention. In notes from a staff meeting, Fichandler pondered, "How to react to award—important to be recognized by establishment forces, esp. for funding. Change in reaction to regional theaters—now benign recognition by forces that were hostile, before that indifferent."[27] She recognized the legitimation of her company and regional theatres in general, and how this symbolic capital had potential to turn into economic capital. Director of Public Relations Alton Miller cautioned against over publicizing the award because of the irony of gaining such legitimacy from Broadway, an institution against which Fichandler had positioned herself.[28]

Yet the Tony and the tour became indelible parts of Arena's self-promotion. "The Arena Stage Story," a self-narrative covering 1950 through 1976, emphasizes the company's national and international repute: "Today, in its 27th year, Arena Stage is variously described as 'a national institution,' as having 'a worldwide reputation,'" and its "landmarks" include the first Tony Award for a regional theatre; its productions that went on to Broadway, film, and television; and the fact that it was "selected as the first 'ambassador' theater company to tour the Soviet Union in 1973."[29] An advertisement for *Our Town* and *Inherit the Wind* as part of the theatre's regular season declared, "You Don't Have to Go around the WORLD to See the First American Drama in the USSR."[30] The subscription mailer for the 1981–82 season pronounced, "One of the world's best theater companies is just around the corner," at once signaling world-class theatre, global programming, and local accessibility.[31] *The Arena Adventure* highlights the repertory's international reach: "New plays from England, Canada, France, Germany—East and West, Switzerland, Austria, Poland, Hungary, Romania, the Soviet Union, and Australia broadened Arena's scope and were greeted enthusiastically by the cosmopolitan audience from the nation's capital."[32] But there is a glaring omission from this list of countries. African and black diasporic work did not gain legibility as such until the late 1980s, when the theatre and U.S. culture at large began to name cultural diversity, which in the case of Arena Stage and context of Washington was code for blackness.

PRESENTING AFRICAN AND
BLACK DIASPORIC PERFORMANCE

From the late 1960s to the late 1980s, Arena Stage sporadically included black-centered narratives by African, Afro-Caribbean, and African American artists. Rather than homegrown productions by Arena, they were often presentations from other theatre companies that were included in the regular subscription series and toured to various U.S. cities. This model of welcoming certain individuals while holding groups at a distance dramatized the dynamics of racial liberalism. Most of the African works were penned by white South African playwright Athol Fugard, and the Afro-Caribbean works were typically adaptations of canonical Western plays and forms. They staged racial integration on white terms. Well-liked by audiences and critics, these plays effectively financed the rest of Arena's white repertory. Although the plays were not explicitly marketed as part of the theatre's global branding, they nevertheless helped to position the company as a center for international performance in the 1970s and 1980s.

For example, after the Arena run of *The Great White Hope* in 1967, James Earl Jones remained with the company for *The Blood Knot* by Athol Fugard. In this play about two coloured[33] brothers, one white-passing and one black-passing, in apartheid South Africa, Jones performed the role of Zachariah, which he had previously done Off-Broadway. In a letter to subscribers, Thomas Fichandler framed this one week of performances in January 1968 as a special "Subscriber Bonus" to see "Athol Fugard's universal drama."[34] The production was received fairly positively and set the stage for future critical vocabulary that moves back and forth between the constructed poles of art and politics, at once acknowledging South African apartheid and disavowing it for allegedly universal, humanist, and personal themes—

the tenets of racial liberalism. Between 1968 and 1992, Arena presented four more works by Athol Fugard, two of which were collaborations with black South African artists John Kani and Winston Ntshona.

In the early 1970s, Zelda Fichandler began to provide a stage for stories by African Americans. The first was the Pulitzer winner *No Place to Be Somebody* in 1970. Written by Charles Gordone, the play was a meditation on black masculinity in a competitive, corrupt system with more than a dozen characters brought together in a Greenwich Village bar. In 1971, Arena produced *The Sign in Sidney Brustein's Window* by Lorraine Hansberry, a cerebral exploration of bohemian life and socialism. Arena worked with Hansberry's ex-husband and estate manager, Robert Nemiroff, again in 1973 on *Raisin*, the musical adaptation of *A Raisin in the Sun*, the subject of chapter 4. The next season, Fichandler hired Glenda Dickerson to direct the newly initiated Black Writers Project. The Project included a brief run of Dickerson's adaptation of *Their Eyes Were Watching God* by Zora Neale Hurston and a staged reading of *East of Jordan* by Evan Walker, whose work had been previously produced by the D.C. Black Repertory Company.

In 1969, Robert Hooks left the Negro Ensemble Company in New York to launch the D.C. Black Repertory. His mission was to develop and produce black artists, administrators, and audiences in the nation's capital, where he was born. In 1970, he reached out to Arena Stage for usage of the Kreeger Theater and administrative offices during the summer when the theatre was dark.[35] But, according to Zelda Fichandler, "it turned out he wanted us to finance [the company]."[36] The D.C. Black Rep ran as a production company for only six years, closing in 1978. As case studies, these companies suggest that while a separate black-specific theatre was unsustainable in Washington, a predominantly white institution that included certain black representation and patronage could prove a stable nonprofit model.

It may be that because Hooks opened his company to stage new plays and musicals by African Americans that Arena Stage produced less black theatre during the mid-1970s. In 1976, for example, Arena celebrated the U.S. bicentennial with its mature resident acting company performing an "All American Rep," *Death of a Salesman*, *Our Town*, and *The Front Page*. Here, "American" means white and male. Although the season featured other canonical U.S. plays such as Eugene O'Neill's *Long Day's Journey into Night*, the season also boasted European works, including Henrik Ibsen's *An Enemy of the People*, Samuel Beckett's *Waiting for Godot*, and George Bernard Shaw's *Heartbreak House*, emphasizing Arena's continuing international connections. Fichandler's letter to subscribers advertising this season pronounced, "The accent is American; the playwright may be American or Russian or Hungarian or South African or English."[37] In other words, some of the plays were written by non-American artists, but they dealt with American themes. Just not necessarily people of color.

During the late 1970s through the late 1980s after the D.C. Black Rep had closed, Arena Stage presented rather than produced African American–centered productions. In 1979, the company brought in the Negro Ensemble Company's production of *Nevis Mountain Dew* by Steve Carter. Part of Carter's Caribbean trilogy, the play examines a Caribbean American family dealing with a paralyzed patriarch. The Negro Ensemble Company returned in 1982 with *Home* by Samm-Art Williams, who had been in the cast of *Nevis Mountain Dew*. Book-in musicals in the 1980s included *One Mo' Time*, *The Gospel at Colonus*, *Beehive*, *The Late Great Ladies of Blues and Jazz*, and *Abyssinia*. Most of these musicals were revues, an accessible form that celebrated popular black jazz standards (*One Mo' Time*, *The Late Great Ladies of Blues and Jazz*) and '60s girl group songs (*Beehive*). By offering these works and companies such as the Negro Ensemble Company on its stages, Arena Stage could claim a history of including African Americans, though the act of presenting, and irregularly at that, suggested that African Americans were infrequent guests invited to the theatre rather than an integral part of the Arena family.

Part of the increase in book-in shows came about because of the opening of the Kreeger Theater in 1971, which meant that Arena Stage had to juggle two large spaces, the 800-seat in-the-round theatre and the 500-seat thrust-proscenium theatre. In 1975, the company opened another venue, a 150-seat space called the Old Vat Room for presentations of small shows and bare bones productions of new work. Book-in productions kept down Arena's costs and offered the potential of high box office income with a built-in subscriber base. The new spaces also provided flexibility for different running lengths in case productions turned out to be financially successful. For instance, the one-man show *Banjo Dancing* by folk musician Stephen Wade ran in the Old Vat Room for a decade. With multiple spaces, the resident acting ensemble could perform in back-to-back productions and rehearse simultaneously. Presenting work by other companies provided the resident actors with some time to recharge. By using the Kreeger as a proscenium space to showcase international touring productions, Arena competed with the Kennedy Center and the National Theatre as a world-class venue. The regional theatre distinguished itself, however, with black productions that exhibited virtuosic spectacle and overt politics. Scholar of African theatre Catherine M. Cole explains that "theater in the form of touring performances travels beyond Africa only rarely," in contrast with play scripts and recordings, making the African tours at Arena Stage particularly remarkable.[38]

In February 1975, Arena Stage presented the U.S. premiere of the Yoruba opera *Oba Koso*. Writer, director, and performer Duro Lapido had popularized this form and this particular opera about the leader-deity Shango, having toured the production in Africa, Asia, and Europe. Arena's press release emphasized *Oba Koso*'s authenticity, spectacle, and exoticism; the company included the Elewe War Dancers of King Oba Adetona Ayeni as well as Lapido's wives.[39] The presentation became a commercial and critical hit. According to Arena meeting minutes, "*Oba Koso* was a great success—we made a good deal of money from those performances which will help to reduce our deficit."[40] This black production helped to cover the shortfall from white plays produced that season. Several critics framed *Oba Koso* as a special cultural, educational, and entertaining event not to be missed, especially considering Washington's makeup. Critic Richard Lebherz wrote:

> One leaves the theatre as if one had just paid a long visit to an African museum. For the white man, he may admire the colors, the energy, the drumming skill, and he is quite patient with their almost childish desire to please. To the black, I imagine two things. He experiences a certain uncomfortableness on the other hand, [sic] (setting [sic] there in an elegant tuxedo) and a certain yearning, on the other hand, for a world that was as simple as the one depicted in "Oba Koso."[41]

Lebherz believed *Oba Koso* to be for everyone, or at least rich white and black men. He posited different racialized perspectives from the white person's cultivated, even patronizing appreciation of aesthetics to the black person's alleged innate cultural primitivism. His allusion to museums and the government proved prophetic. Arena held a benefit performance for the Museum of African Art attended by ambassadors and politicians. *Oba Koso* brought Yoruba culture to critics, diplomats, and DC audiences and generated box office income for Arena Stage, foreshadowing future success with these sorts of productions. When planning *Oba Koso* and Glenda Dickerson's *Jump at the Sun* at a meeting in 1974, Zelda Fichandler noted, "There are now 2 works of interest to the black community," presuming a correlation between black artists and audiences across the diaspora.[42] This season also included *The Last Meeting of the Knights of the White Magnolia*, part of Preston Jones's Texas trilogy. While Washington critics applauded Jones's play, Fichandler's comment about featuring only two plays of interest to the black community implied that black audiences would not be interested in a comedy about a group of white men in a KKK-like organization.[43]

ATHOL FUGARD, DEREK WALCOTT, AND THE APPEAL OF RACIAL LIBERALISM

Also in 1975, the company presented John Kani, Winston Ntshona, and Athol Fugard's *Sizwe Banzi Is Dead* and *The Island* in repertory. *Sizwe Banzi* dramatizes a black South African man's decision to take up the identity of a dead man whose passbook will grant him work and greater mobility. Based on real events, *The Island* focuses on two inmates passing time by rehearsing *Antigone* at Robber Island, where antiapartheid political prisoners were detained. Both plays emerged from collaborations between actors Kani and Ntshona improvising with Fugard's guidance. In the context of a non–South African audience, the plays took on a didactic quality of educating attendees about the daily life of black men under apartheid. The advertising meanwhile celebrated the Tony-winning actors and their indomitable "human dignity" and "human spirit."[44] Critics raved about Kani and Ntshona's affective and effective performances. David Richards of the *Washington Star* concluded, "What the two plays reveal about South Africa is appalling. But what they reveal about men in appalling circumstances is exalting."[45] When one dissenting spectator wrote to Arena's artistic leadership that *Sizwe Banzi Is Dead* was "in poor taste" and "most shallow," Thomas Fichandler wrote back noting the wide praise from the general audience: "Performance after performance, the audience has stood and cheered and more people have thanked us for bringing them this play than almost anything else we have done."[46]

While Washington critics connected the plays to South African politics and humanist values, others attempted to make connections with African American politics. According to Douglas Wager, who worked as the stage manager for these productions and would later become artistic director of Arena Stage, Kani and Ntshona "played to a largely African American audience."[47] He recounted, "I remember sitting in the green room with John Kani and having him excoriate the people. He—he had no time for the African American people who came back stage and tried to identify their experience with his. And he said to me, he said, 'We were never slaves.'"[48] His account suggests a need from African American audiences in Washington to identify with black theatre about racial struggle, despite the differences between the United States and South Africa. The text of *Sizwe Banzi* in particular invited comparisons, such as when the characters discuss black Americans engaging in acts of defiance versus black South Africans performing subservience for whites; the photography studio owner Styles relates an anecdote: "Gentlemen, he says we must remember, when Mr. Ford walks in, that we are South African monkeys, not American monkeys. South African monkeys are much better trained."[49]

The double production toured to other regional theatres, including the Guthrie, ACT, Seattle Repertory Theatre, and the Mark Taper Forum, indicating its popularity and accessibility. When John Kani and Winston Ntshona were imprisoned in South Africa in 1976, Thomas Fichandler in his capacity as the president of the League of Resident Theatres wrote to the South African embassy and the government of Transkei. At a meeting with the Arena board of trustees, he reported "with some satisfaction that partly due to the action of the League of Resident Theatres," Kani and Ntshona were released from prison.[50] His letter underscores the important relationship between U.S. regional theatres and these artists. Yale Repertory Theatre, for example, became a home for Fugard in premiering his plays and publishing scholarly articles about them. In the mid-1990s, William Morris Agency and Samuel French received many requests from regional theatres to stage Fugard's plays, requests second only to Edward Albee's works.[51] Arena was not alone in its presentation of plays from South Africa; however, the differences of location and audience shaped context and reception. When Arena produced Fugard's plays and Washington critics praised them, they drew attention to apartheid for a theatergoing audience in the nation's capital, for diplomats and elites who held sway, and for residents who experienced racial segregation.

In 1984, Arena presented *Woza Albert!* by Percy Mtwa, Mbongeni Ngema, and Barney Simon. Like *Sizwe Banzi Is Dead* and *The Island*, *Woza Albert!* dramatizes apartheid and toured to New York, Los Angeles, San Francisco, Seattle, and Washington. Once again, two black actors worked with one white director from South Africa's famous Market Theatre. Arena again framed the production as a special event in its mailers.[52] Some critics put these plays in conversation with each other, though David Richards argued, "The difference, however, is that Fugard is a playwright (maybe the world's best right now), and that he molded and fixed what was most pertinent in his actors' improvisations. No one connected with 'Woza Albert!' seems to have his rigorous eye."[53] Richards preferred the more linear, coherent narrative, which he attributed exclusively to Fugard rather than his black collaborators, an attribution that is not without racial valence.[54]

Much of Fugard's celebration by the U.S. critical establishment had to do with his white identity, racially liberal politics, and writing in a Western tradition. Literary scholar Jeanne Colleran argues that Fugard's works were extraordinarily popular among U.S. regional theatres in the 1980s and 1990s because the plays and productions dehistoricized South Africa and advocated for gentle reform.[55] Fugard's aesthetic and politics allowed for an easy mapping of U.S. racial politics onto apartheid and called for individual freedom rather than radical, collective redistribution of power. As demonstrated by *The Great White Hope*, racially liberal dramas by white male playwrights could accrue significant economic and symbolic capital from white U.S. audiences. Fugard scholar Russell Vandenbrouke reasons that of Fugard's works *Sizwe Banzi Is Dead* appealed to rather than alienated whites outside of South Africa because they did not feel "personally threatened or castigated. Despite moments of caustic condemnation and unbridled anger, *Sizwe Banzi* is more loving and ingratiating than strident; it embraces man instead of rejecting him."[56] Thanks to the civil rights movement, many white American audiences may not have felt directly implicated in apartheid, despite ongoing racial material inequality and segregation in Washington. *Sizwe Banzi* fit in with Arena's repertory, which largely eschewed radical dramas from the Black Arts Movement. Fugard's collaborations with Kani and Ntshona employed comedy, sympathetic characters, virtuosic performances, realism, and symbols to dramatize stories of resistance instead of revolution. Influenced by Samuel Beckett, Bertolt Brecht, Albert Camus, and Jerzy Grotowski, Fugard hailed from a tradition of Western drama. His work was first produced by the Royal Court Theatre in London in 1973.

Lauded by white patriarchy, Fugard and his plays had the privilege of being interpreted as universal. Many critics used language that acknowledged the politics of his plays but also praised their aesthetic transcendence and personal grounding. In *Truths the Hand Can Touch*, Vandenbrouke contends that "race is only one component of the human condition; the suffering and degradation rife throughout Fugard's work is, finally, a poetic image of the plight of all men."[57] In this "all lives matter" interpretation, race, white supremacy, and apartheid are reduced to symbols for all plights and all men. Indeed, the title of Vandenbrouke's monograph on Fugard, which comes from a self-reflective quotation by Fugard, suggests that the playwright can locate "truths" and make them tangible to everyone. Albert Wertheim similarly asserts in his own book on the playwright, "The reality is that Fugard is a world-class playwright, who often uses the South Africa he knows so intimately as a setting for more universal examinations of human life, human interactions, and the powers of art."[58] Fugard himself encourages both personalized and explicitly political readings of his work. When he called for an artistic boycott of South Africa, a position that he later retracted, he became an icon of social consciousness. At the same time, as Mel Gussow wrote in an extensive *New Yorker* profile, "he is seldom an activist."[59] Fugard's identity, actions, and art positioned him as a liberal playwright ripe for traditionally white institutions.

After its success with Fugard's work in the 1970s, Arena Stage subsequently produced *A Lesson from Aloes* (1981) and *My Children! My Africa!* (1991). Doug Wager directed the former, starring Zakes Mokae, and he described his admiration for the playwright: "Fugard was . . . sort of singularly committed to theatre for cultural change. . . . He was able to capture—to do what theatre could do, which was to create a safe place for talking about dangerous things."[60] *A Lesson from Aloes* centers on Piet, a white bus driver, who is inspired by Steve, a black man, to join the antiapartheid movement. Literature scholar Rita Barnard has critiqued Fugard's celebration of art as a tool for individual liberation and reduction of "complicated political realities to homespun analogies" like the fable of the aloe plant.[61] Fugard took his inspiration from real-life incidents that he recorded in his diary, and Arena Stage reprinted excerpts from his diary in the program, encouraging spectators to understand the play through his personal lens. Edward Merritt of WAMU Public Radio praised Arena's production for its "overwhelming argument of individual values and the human spirit" in contrast with "the gross, filthy and self-serving plays of such as Leroi Jones," who preferred to be known as Amiri Baraka.[62] In several reviews of Arena's productions that stage blackness from the 1960s to the 1980s, critics used Baraka as a negative foil to plays by Fugard and Sackler or musicals like *Raisin* that they preferred.

My Children! My Africa! provides yet another example of Fugard taking a literary, didactic approach to ending apartheid. He dramatizes the relationships and debates between a black teacher called Mr. M, his black student Thami, and a white student Isabel in response to a new policy conferring second-tier, whitewashed schooling on black South Africans. Mr. M advocates reform through racial integration and education. Although Thami initially agrees, he comes to see the limits of his colonized education, and he calls for violent revolution. Wertheim observes that liberal spectators may too easily applaud Mr. M and therefore themselves while they condemn Thami, but he argues that the play offers a more complex lesson: "Actions and words—can educate and spur reform even as Fugard's own playwriting can educate and suggest reform through its combination of dialogue and physical action."[63] Meanwhile, Colleran critiques the play's liberal "middle position" of "nonalignment" that "reduces active social and ideological conflicts to isolated instances" and questions of what constitutes proper behavior, rather than taking a stand for the redistribution of resources to black South Africans.[64] In both *A Lesson from Aloes* and *My Children! My Africa!*, Fugard features highly literate characters who recite English poetry and encourage dignified perseverance under systems of oppression, incorporating blackness into white institutions under the tenets of individual, rights-based, calls-for-common-humanity that define racial liberalism.

Arena's mission to produce contemporary, international, left-leaning, nonprofit theatre still centered on the canon. The most produced playwrights of Arena Stage's subscription seasons from 1970 to 1991 were William Shakespeare, Bertolt Brecht, George Bernard Shaw, Samuel Beckett, Athol Fugard, Molière, Anton Chekhov, Arthur Miller, Christopher Durang, Sam Shepard, István Örkény, and Lorraine Hansberry, in that order, representing a classic and contemporary repertory of mostly white, male writers.[65] Many of the African and black diasporic plays that Arena staged were adaptations of canonical Western works: *The Island* and *Gospel at Colonus* were partly adapted from Ancient Greek tragedies, Derek Walcott drew from British and Greek traditions for *Pantomime* and *The Odyssey*, respectively, and Mustapha Matura transposed *Playboy of the Western World* by John Millington Synge and *Three Sisters* by Anton Chekhov to Trinidad.

Derek Walcott has been widely celebrated for his founding and leadership of the Trinidad Theatre Workshop, but he also actively sought opportunities and legitimacy beyond the West Indies. Born in St. Lucia, Walcott emerged as a major literary voice with the help of the Rockefeller Foundation, which provided him with substantial funding for his art, travels, and studies. He networked with major regional theatre directors including Tyrone Guthrie and Andre Gregory. Influenced by West Indian culture and the European traditions of Brecht, Artaud, Shakespeare, and the Abbey Theatre, Walcott penned intercultural dramas that appealed to local West Indian and global audiences. *Dream on Monkey Mountain*, *Ti-Jean*, and *The Charlatan* were developed and produced by the O'Neill Playwriting Center, Public Theater, and Mark Taper Forum, respectively, in the late 1960s and early 1970s. This popularity, however, had a drawback because Walcott found U.S. actors and audiences lacked an understanding of West Indian culture. He described the Los Angeles production of *Dream on Monkey Mountain* thus: "Rather than being a West Indian play it has become an American production of a play by a West Indian performed in a mixture of American-Method Naturalism, Kabuki, and Martha Graham with an imitation of dialect rhythms and ethnic music."[66] According to Bruce King's monograph on Walcott, the playwright also resented the expectations that he felt were placed on him "to be 'black' and write protest plays and comedies on racial themes."[67] The perspective of the black diaspora, overdetermined here by African American aesthetics and politics, shaped how producers and patrons read Walcott's works. Stressing both specific cultural setting and general humanism, his plays were reminiscent of Fugard, Kani, and Ntshona's works and therefore appealed to the same institutions that had staged plays like *Sizwe Banzi Is Dead*.

In 1981, Arena Stage produced Walcott's *Pantomime*, a two-hander about a white hotel proprietor and a black servant and their collaboration on a racially themed pantomime based on Robinson Crusoe. In the program for the original production, Walcott said, "It may also be a political play, with its subject independence; but that process first has to be human before it can become political."[68] Playing on the racialized master-slave dialectic, *Pantomime* suggests liberal notions of equality and humanity appealing to Arena Stage's audiences. The program for the company's production provided a history of the pantomime form, framing the play as one about theatre rather than postcolonial politics. James Lardner of the *Washington Post* cheered Arena Stage for continuing its productions of contemporary global drama: "It's not every day of the theatrical week that you get to see a play from Trinidad. . . . Arena should be saluted for this latest evidence of an internationalist spirit that has already given us a Russian play ('The Suicide') and a French play ('Kean') this season."[69] Arena did not produce another drama by Walcott, *The Odyssey*, until the early 1990s, by which point the theatre had begun a concerted effort to include black artists and audiences.

THE RACIAL GAP: INSIDE VERSUS OUTSIDE ARENA STAGE

While Arena produced a handful of plays dealing with black-white politics, internal meeting minutes, letters, and reports reveal that Arena's artistic leadership was concerned about the dearth of African Americans among the theatre's staff, trustees, patrons, and play selections. In 1972, the top staff members met, and one declared, "Arena Stage is too white an organization. We should have more blacks in the technical area and in the company. We will have one black in the shop and, hopefully, 3 in the company this coming season but we should have more."[70] Even as the staffer diagnosed racial inequity, they imagined black employees as only members of production teams, not as administrators. Another staff member stressed the importance of retaining the people of color currently on staff and named three people, implying that the other 150 or so nonacting employees of Arena Stage were white.[71] To begin to redress racial inequality in hiring, staff members planned to contact historically black colleges and universities with theatre departments and young people of color already in the company's intern program.

In the 1970s, Arena Stage also confronted the whiteness of its board of trustees but in ways that disavowed responsibility and stressed finances rather than social justice. On April 14, 1977, the board began its meeting by announcing possible collaborations with the Negro Ensemble Company and then ended by discussing Arena's racial politics. One member articulated the challenge as Arena's "image" rather than the theatre's white repertory or ticket prices.[72] Thomas Fichandler repeatedly defended Arena by noting its attempts to produce black plays and integrate the acting ensemble. He judged that there were few "good black plays."[73] Zelda Fichandler's archived papers contain *Black Theater: A Resource Directory*, published by the Black Theatre Alliance in 1973, and its pages list black theatre companies, directors, playwrights, plays, administrators, and technicians.[74] This suggests *she* must have been aware of the larger field of black theatre. Another trustee added that the board must avoid tokenism and instead recruit several black members, recommending that recruitment and retention work best with cohorts. However, this individual also identified the "problem" as one of attracting black audiences, not the axes of oppression that form barriers to access. This rhetorical maneuver of putting the responsibility on black patrons to show interest instead of on the white institution to redistribute resources toward people of color occurs repeatedly in meeting minutes well into the late 1980s.[75]

Arena exhibited deep concern about the homogeneity of its audience. In 1978 and 1980, the director of public relations conducted surveys to determine the theatre's demographics. One-third worked in government, one-third worked in a nongovernment professional capacity, and three-quarters had at least some graduate education.[76] The typical Arena patron was (and is) much more privileged than the typical U.S. American. The quality that most appealed to spectators was Arena's variety, indicating that eclecticism was a value if not a marker of distinction for this theatre company. A report in 1985 affirmed prior studies: "Most people who have been to the Arena in the last year are white (93%), earn over $50,000 a year (51%) and have a graduate or professional degree (61%)."[77] This survey appeared to be the first time when Arena's patrons were asked to identify their race, meaning that, by the mid-1980s, it was worthwhile for the institution to have these numbers ready when planning seasons and applying for grants. Other U.S. theatre institutions similarly had subscriber bases that were "white, middle-class, educated people over 45."[78] With an almost entirely white audience, it is unsurprising that theatres catered to them with plays centered on white experiences.

On the one hand, Arena Stage attempted to portray its patrons as diverse. "The Arena Stage Story," written in 1976, describes "A Profile of Arena's Audience" as "largely upper middle-class, white, in the 18–60-year-old range."[79] Immediately afterward the profile asserts, "Black support and attendance is increasing significantly. In 1975 and 1976, the Council of the District of Columbia and the Office of the Mayor issued proclamations and resolutions 'calling upon all of our citizens to join in expressing appreciation to this excellent theatrical company for its role in giving vitality to the artistic life of our Nation's Capital.'"[80] By pointing to local black officials like Mayor Walter Washington, the narrative highlights approval from black institutions.

On the other hand, Zelda Fichandler was fairly open about the lack of audience diversity. At a meeting with the artistic directors of ACT, the Guthrie, and the Mark Taper Forum in 1974, Fichandler discussed her audience versus the demographics of Washington. She remarked bluntly, "Except for the times when we do black plays, we play to a suburban audience," meaning whites.[81] She added, "We found that when we did 'The Great White Hope,' 'Raisin,' 'No Place to Be Somebody,' in varying degrees we had a large black audience depending upon what part of their lives we were hitting them. For 'No Place' we had about a 90% black audience. 'Raisin' had a 75% black Audience [sic]. 'The Great White Hope' had a 50% black audience."[82] Her numbers do not quite add up with other sources, but they underscore the notion that black actors onstage attracted black patrons because the latter desired representations of themselves.[83] Among the directors at the 1974 meeting, Fichandler seemed uniquely concerned about audience racial composition, while the other regional theatre leaders spoke mostly of the difficulties balancing their budgets. They all relied on their subscriber base, which was likely almost entirely white and deliberately kept that way. In the 1970s, many of them drew on Danny Newman's book *Subscribe Now!* Newman encouraged nonprofit arts companies to mail subscription advertisements using lists "based on people's annual income, how much the house they live in costs, whether they live 'on the right side of the tracks,' and so on."[84] In this racially coded language, Newman encouraged cultivating patrons from certain high-earning, implicitly white zip codes. But Arena considered different tactics.

After the D.C. Black Repertory closed, Arena's staff meeting minutes reveal more discussions about the need to produce black plays to draw black spectators. On May 4, 1979, Edith Cohen, who was in charge of group ticket sales, repeatedly brought up "that there should be a steady program of presenting black plays in order for Arena to develop a solid black audience."[85] Others said that the institution had been attempting to recruit black audiences for years, a "frustrating goal," and pointed to the Negro Ensemble Company's *Nevis Mountain Dew*, which had "drawn disappointingly from the black community."[86] Two weeks later, Cohen argued that "we must make a firm commitment to develop local black audiences," by inviting the Negro Ensemble Company back to Arena.[87] Another staff member "insisted that we need to develop black audiences to come and see 'plays,' not exclusively 'black plays,'" while Thomas Fichandler "countered that the Arena, historically, has never drawn a black audience *without* a black play."[88] Resident directing assistant Benny Sato Ambush said, "The Arena is, to Washington black residents, a white institution," and he recommended "that blacks must be 'baited' to attend shows here, then that their interest be prolonged and encouraged by the Arena's interest in having them become a part of the organization."[89] Of African American and Japanese descent, Ambush was one of very few people of color at the theatre. He said that interim producing director David Chambers "opened the door to me, to Arena Stage," after he had tried entering other regional theatres where there were few opportunities for entry-level directing apprenticeships.[90] By bringing in Ambush even for one year, Arena's leaders demonstrated a genuine interest in hearing a different voice. He researched pre–World War I plays by black artists for production consideration. In his pitch, Ambush highlighted that approximately 71 percent of Washington residents were black;

specifically, "the Southwest D.C. area is largely inhabited by blacks who almost never so much as cross the street to participate in theatre at Arena Stage."[91] These internal documents illustrate a discursive struggle over black audiences—what would attract them, what would keep them at Arena, how the institution had attempted to reach such audiences historically, and to what extent Arena truly is and/or appeared to be white and to whom. The staff members repeatedly argued that plays with black characters and actors would attract black spectators who would hopefully become subscribers to the rest of the white season. But little was done to address these concerns on a systemic level, and when Zelda Fichandler took a sabbatical from 1978 to 1980, director David Chambers led the company and added more spectacle, launching works including *Tintypes* and *The 1940's Radio Hour*, both of which transferred to Broadway.[92]

THE BLACK BOURGEOISIE IN WASHINGTON

Arena staff sensed a potential audience among the black bourgeoisie in Washington, which has long been a center in the black American public sphere. In 1867, Congress approved the founding of Howard University to educate, principally, freed black people. In *Chocolate City: A History of Race and Democracy in the Nation's Capital*, Chris Myers Asch and George Derek Musgrove contend that, during early Reconstruction, Washington served as a laboratory for radically antiracist measures including black male suffrage and integrated public and private spaces.[93] African Americans obtained high-status positions such as ambassadorships to Haiti and supervisory roles in the federal government. Federal institutions such as the postal service integrated as well. But in the racist backlash that ended Reconstruction, black residents lost civil rights, and in the 1910s, Woodrow Wilson fully resegregated government offices and replaced black workers with whites. Still, the city's location, educational opportunities, and federal jobs attracted working-class and middle-class African Americans during the Great Migration of the early- to mid-twentieth century, and a black professional class concentrated in Washington.[94] Although Harlem claimed the title of epicenter of African American culture in the 1920s, the nation's capital "was the locale for drama" thanks to playwright Georgia

Douglas Johnson, who held salons with black playwrights and intellectuals such as W. E. B. Du Bois and Alain Locke.[95] Meanwhile, Duke Ellington played on U Street, known as Black Broadway.

After segregation was legally struck down in the 1950s, whites fled to the suburbs, and Washington became the first large city with a majority-black population. With ratification of the Twenty-Third Amendment in 1961, DC residents won the right to vote in presidential races for the first time since 1800. In 1967, after a century without substantial local governance—a strategy that denied black sovereignty—President Lyndon B. Johnson appointed Walter Washington as mayor-commissioner. In 1973, the city gained home rule with an elected mayor and city council. Washington, the first black mayor of a major city, made the nation's capital what singer George Clinton called a "Chocolate City." However, this representation was more symbol than substance. Locally elected officials had little power to govern the district, the new House delegate for DC lacked voting privileges, and white middle-class flight left a reduced tax base for funding public services such as education. But in the remains, the new black music, dance, and fashion culture of go-go emerged.[96]

At the same time, black suburbs grew in numbers and importance. Bart Landry calls this post-1960s social formation the "new black middle class" that rose due to the economic boom and elimination of legalized antiblack discrimination.[97] As African American Studies scholar Mark Anthony Neal notes, "Like the mass migrants of the early twentieth century, black middle-class people in the late 1960s and 1970s were driven by aspirations to improve their quality of life, often at the risk of hurting communal and familial relations."[98] Many professional, highly educated African Americans moved out of inner city Washington and into Prince George's County in Maryland, staying within the metropolitan area. There they developed their own dominantly black, wealthy enclave: "Prince George's County is the only county in the country in which the median income of residents continued to rise as the suburb transitioned from majority white to majority black."[99] Sociologist Karyn R. Lacy has found that late twentieth-century Washington-area middle-class black people valued black spaces as important for their racial identity, even as they engaged in what she calls "strategic assimilation" to navigate the white world beyond the black suburbs. They "are firm in their belief that it is possible to minimize the probability of encountering racial discrimination if they can successfully convey their middle-class status to white strangers."[100] Bryant Keith Alexander dubs this "boojie performativity," "those perceived repetitive actions performed by black people, plotted within grids of power relationships and social norms that are presumably relegated exclusively to white people" and thus often seem racially inauthentic, a response that presumes black equals folk.[101] After the end of juridical segregation, the new black middle class expanded their social life to more public spaces, and though only 5-6 percent of them went to the theatre, that equaled approximately the same percentage as for whites.[102]

In addition, Washington received new immigrants from Africa and the Caribbean. Immigration reform in 1965 abolished previous quotas and exclusions of African and Asian people. As a result of independence movements in the late 1950s through the 1960s, embassies for new African nations appeared in the U.S. capital, "setting the stage for the arrival of more African-born immigrants who, in the 1970s and 1980s, built on established networks of compatriots to create new communities."[103] For decades, the DC metro area has had one of the highest concentrations of African immigrants in U.S. cities, including many refugees from the Eritrean-Ethiopian War (1961-91).[104] The economic downturn in Caribbean nations in the 1970s through the 1980s prompted more working-class people to immigrate to the United States. Students from Jamaica, Trinidad, and Tobago also arrived in Washington to study at Howard University.[105] By the late 1980s, Arena Stage became more attentive to black internationalism and actively sought to change the culture of the institution. As Doug Wager noted, "Because of the embassy world and the ambassador world, there was *a lot* of interest in international work. And Zelda knew that from the get-go, and part of the reason [Arena Stage] succeeded earlier on, and [was] sort of looking at that kind of work in a way that no other theatre in the country was looking at, was because we were in DC."[106]

SEEDING INSTITUTIONAL CHANGE

In the mid- to late 1980s, Arena Stage took deliberate steps to cultivate a more racially diverse workforce and audience. The fact that change took so long indicates institutional inertia, if not active resistance to social change. In 1986, the administration sent a memo to all staff members requiring that job postings include an equal opportunity clause and be distributed to local black organizations like Howard University.[107] The staff underwent training to become more sensitive to and knowledgeable about cultural differences. Some resented the training, while others appreciated the inclusive gesture. Recognizing that memos and exercises were not enough to create a more diverse and welcoming institution, some staff members initiated a Cultural Diversity Committee. Committee members researched racial minority recruitment procedures and pinpointed a need for "a well-worded mandate to our staff in order to change the attitude that there are no qualified and interested minority candidates out there."[108] They produced an in-house publication titled *The Arena Arrow* that sought to educate staff members about histories of people of color in the United States and anecdotes of perseverance and microaggressions that staff of color had personally experienced. The theatre celebrated Black History Month in February 1987 with staged readings of plays by African American authors, symposia on African diasporic dramas and influences, and lobby displays of black art. Furthermore, the theatre formed an Outreach Advisory Committee consisting of several people of color from local institutions.

These outreach initiatives complemented more racially diverse programming onstage. An in-house document entitled "Arena Stage: 1987–88, toward Cultural Diversity" attempted to soften the transition and define "cultural diversity" broadly: "In the past we have looked into and through the eyes of European and Russian culture. Today we turn to the cultures present within our own country and community. Not to limit our field of vision but to enlarge it. We do not give up the vision of Chekhov when we welcome the vision of August Wilson."[109] Despite the assurance that changing the repertory is not a zero-sum game, works by African Americans did indeed replace the slots previously reserved for Russians and Eastern Europeans. Arena was engaging in a real shift of resources from whites to blacks. For the 1987–88 season, the theatre produced an unprecedented three plays written and directed by African Americans: *Joe Turner's Come and Gone*, written by August Wilson and directed by Lloyd Richards; *Les Blancs*, written by Lorraine Hansberry and directed by Harold Scott; and *Checkmates*, written by Ron Milner and directed by Woodie King Jr. August Wilson's play follows the spiritual journey of Herald Loomis, who has traveled up north as a part of the Great Migration in the 1910s. It had premiered at Yale Rep before moving to Arena, other regional theatres, and then Broadway, a path that became typical for Wilson's Pittsburgh cycle. Hansberry's *Les Blancs*, a critique of Jean Genet's *The Blacks*, built on Arena's previous engagement with Hansberry and plays that engaged with colonialism and imperialism. Set in a two-family home in Detroit, *Checkmates* was a rare play "about black urban professionals and what they're going through," in King's estimation.[110] As part of the Stage Four series for developing and producing new work, *Checkmates* attracted significant ticket sales, donations, and attention from the black media, particularly with the help of its star, Ruby Dee. Meeting minutes suggest that this trio of productions helped to build consistent African American audiences. Arena's archival file on cultural diversity includes *A Basic Guide to Audience Diversity*, developed by the Virginia Commission for the Arts in 1988.[111] The document offers strategies on marketing to black audiences in Virginia, and the copy in the Arena archives shows ideas for developing an advisory committee and marketing to black churches underlined, tactics that Arena put into action. The following season, the theatre brought in *Abyssinia*, a musical about a Job-like woman with a gift for singing in an all-black town in Oklahoma in the early twentieth century. Director Tazewell Thompson became actively involved with Arena Stage, though he was also reluctant to be subsumed by the institution. At a celebration for Zelda Fichandler in 2016, he recalled a colossal argument that he had with her in which he declared, "I want to be free from the Arena Stage plantation," but he stayed and called this the "best decision."[112]

In 1988, Thompson directed *Playboy of the West Indies* by Mustapha Matura, a production that prompted much discussion about Arena's commitment to black work. The theatre coordinated with local Caribbean American institutions to give the production more dramaturgical authenticity and attract new audiences. Arena hired Von Martin, the host of the local radio show *Caribbeana*, who helped the actors with Trinidadian dialects and shared his collection of Caribbean newspapers. The Embassy of Trinidad and Tobago hosted a reception with Matura and Arena Stage's artistic leaders. Black newspapers including the *Washington Afro-American*, *Washington Informer*, and *Caribbean Sun* covered this special event. Using a different marketing technique, the company obtained the embassy's mailing list of local Trinidadians and sent flyers to Caribbean restaurants, stores, and lawyers. But the coverage of *Playboy of the West Indies* was not entirely positive. In "Arena's Other Worlds on Stage" in the *Washington Post*, Arena's Outreach Committee member Stella Gomes, the assistant director for education of homeless children in the nation's capital, indicted the theatre for doing "too little, too late" and for presenting a play set in a rum shop because of the potential to reify Caribbean stereotypes of drunkenness.[113] But another committee member, James Early, the Smithsonian deputy assistant secretary for public service, maintained that Arena's leaders "are beyond the stage of rhetoric. They are actually implementing many of the ideas."[114] Thompson recounted that after a performance a Trinidadian woman said to him, "I can't believe someone is doing a play set in the West Indies. I've been here a long time and never seen anything like this. It's very important that my children know what it was like to grow up there."[115] *Playboy* enabled black diasporic audiences to see themselves.

Local critics praised the play not only for its representation of black life but also for its comedy and impressive transposition of *Playboy of the Western World*. Like other reviewers preoccupied with issues of adaptation and exoticizing the Caribbean, David Richards of the *Washington Post* used food images, commenting on the "cinnamon-flavored English patois."[116] Critic Bob Mondello meditated on the production's relation to Arena's cultural diversity objective: "The play is a near perfect reflection of Arena's strategy for reaching D.C.'s huge, largely untapped black audience. Its appeal is obvious: This *Playboy* has an all-black cast, is based on a modern classic, and (having premiered just a few years ago in London) is practically brand new, which means Arena can use it to fulfill three different mandates at once."[117]

Mustapha Matura's work was an obvious match for Arena Stage's mission. The theatre had produced a monologue he penned, *Nice*, in 1980, and then reached out to his agent years later. Matura was born in Trinidad and, like Derek Walcott, had gained prominence and legitimacy when his work was produced in London. His adaptation of Synge's play came about when he won a playwriting grant from the UK Arts Council.[118] Matura soon began a similar treatment of *Three Sisters* called *Trinidad Sisters*, which had its U.S. premiere at Arena Stage in 1992. The theatre then commissioned him to write an original play, *A Small World*, about a long-lost pair of Caribbean Americans, which debuted in 1994. Preferring to call *Playboy* a "translation" rather than an "adaptation" because he believed that he did not stray far from the original text, Matura still noted his allusion to escaped slaves and "a black Americanness" in the Arena Stage production.[119] The lens of the black diaspora highlighted similarities across experiences but within the framework of African American history. In 2014, Matura sounded much less positive when he recounted, "My experience working at Arena was non engaging, there was no meeting of [m]inds, was like a big factory assembly line," and he suspected that "black plays were done to meet some political agenda."[120] He believes that his plays were used for utilitarian ends, not for artistic, personal collaborations.

In the late 1980s, on the acting front, more performers of color joined the resident ensemble. Black actor Teagle F. Bougere, who had studied under Fichandler at NYU, recalled the value of company membership in providing both a "classroom . . . with those great actors" and a regular paycheck.[121] Although Bougere said that he did not experience racial tensions, the increase in productions of classics with actors of color and of new plays by writers of color triggered some ill will within the company. For example, when a white actress in the company was finally the appropriate age to play Amanda in *The Glass Menagerie*, the role went to Ruby Dee in an all-black version of the play.[122] To some of the white actors, actors of color seemed to receive more opportunities. When the Cultural Diversity Committee hired Mitchell Hammer, a sociologist of race studies, he encouraged the staff to discuss openly their "feelings about the apparent lack of interest shown by those (particularly those at the upper levels of the organization) who did not attend," their diversity meeting, indicating continued resistance within the administration.[123]

Some subscribers also disliked the theatre's new direction, while others appreciated it. Letters from Arena's patrons illustrate the stage as a site of struggle over politics, representation, and the ideal spectator, as they shaped to what extent the theatre would be antiblack or antiracist. Most of the letters in the archive express objections rather than approval. Zelda Fichandler had begun receiving complaints about "the antiwar, antiestablishment theme" of her increasingly leftist repertory from the 1960s onward.[124] During the 1970s and '80s, when Arena presented and produced more black works, the theatre had to negotiate racial hierarchy through longtime patrons who wanted fewer and new patrons who wanted more. One person sent back the 1988–89 season subscription mailer after having crossed out August Wilson's *The Piano Lesson* and written in the margin, "Dear Madam Fichandler, please no more than *one* play by *black authors*!!"[125] Another remarked that Lorraine Hansberry's work should be "left on the cutting room floor."[126] On the other hand, one patron had subscribed to the theatre with "the understanding that there would be at least three play [*sic*] with Afro-American themes," but when *The Piano Lesson* was ultimately not included in the 1988–89 season, the patron canceled their subscription.[127] One single-ticket buyer congratulated the company on presenting *Joe Turner's Come and Gone* and added, "As a black person, if you can integrate a play or two like this in your season, I would again become a regular subscriber."[128] This patron wrote on stationery from the law school of the Catholic University of America, suggesting that Arena was successfully tapping into the black bourgeoisie market.

Arena's commitment to the local black community was driven in part by social conscience but also by economics. After the company's tour to the USSR and production of the musical *Raisin* in 1973, the institution had more than sixteen thousand subscribers and filled approximately 90 percent of the seating capacity.[129] By 1980, however, the theatre had begun to lose subscribers and fill only 77 percent of its houses. Meeting minutes with staff during the 1980s include panicked notes about potential cuts to the NEA by the Reagan administration, cuts that would actually manifest in the Republican Revolution of 1994. Minutes from the board of trustees reveal deep anxieties about cost-saving measures, fundraising activities, and artistic decisions guided by limited budgets. The theatre experienced six-figure deficits. Furthermore, when new professional theatres such as the Studio Theatre and Woolly Mammoth Theatre Company emerged in Washington in 1978 and 1980, respectively, Arena faced increased competition.

Zelda Fichandler also received less support for her interests in Soviet culture as the Cold War cooled down. In the late 1980s, Arena attempted another USSR tour, in which Arena would perform *The Crucible* and, in turn, the Taganka Theatre would come to Washington to perform two Russian works. Elspeth Udvarhelyi, Arena's director of development, wrote to David O. Maxwell of Fannie Mae, "The USIA [United States Information Agency] has designated the Arena-

Taganka exchange as 'part of the official program of cultural exchange between the US and the USSR.' This doesn't mean whole lot as there is no money attached to it. But, it might impress someone."[130] This tour never materialized because, despite extensive outreach, neither the Department of State, major corporations such as American Express, nor philanthropists such as George Soros were willing to fund Arena. Since the mid-1970s, the Department of State had found cultural exchanges to be less urgent.

Making a commitment to black diaspora drama instead of Russian and Eastern European drama provided a financial, ethical, and cultural solution to addressing the theatre's increased expenses. In remarks to Arena's Finance Committee in 1987, Fichandler asserted,

> There is a strong sense, and it is justifiable, that we are inadequately addressing the interests of the black community. . . . At bottom, it's a question not of public relations or of box office, but of exchanging energies between an art institution and its community in the interest of both becoming more fully alive. Black playwrights can deepen Arena's aesthetic and sense of reality even as they broaden its audience base.[131]

As in her essay "Toward a Deepening Aesthetic" to integrate her ensemble twenty years before, Fichandler framed Arena's reenergized dedication to black Americans in humanist terms: "community," "aesthetic," and "fully alive," instead of the practicality of "public relations" and "box office." Not surprisingly, since she was addressing the Finance Committee, she also linked black artists and residents to "audience base." But the nonprofit values of engaging with "the black community," specifically the black middle class, could help to sell more seats as well as "deepen" the cultural productions. According to Fichandler, African diasporic works at Arena from 1987 to 1989 "brought in third world and primarily black audiences; several of these productions played to 95 percent capacity."[132] Even if this claim is an exaggeration, the perception of black plays as popular enabled Arena to continue staging the rest of its traditional Western repertory. In the theatre's season programming, Matura sat beside Luigi Pirandello, Jean Anouilh, and Alan Ayckbourn. In sum, the production of certain racially liberal plays about black experiences subsidized the maintenance of Arena as still a dominantly white institution. By incorporating black producers and consumers, Arena Stage could then apply for diversity-driven grants and raise more income.

During the 1988–89 season, the theatre's leadership and development office rallied for sustained funding to produce, attract, and employ people of color. They approached organizations that had previously sponsored Arena's diversity endeavors, including the Ford Foundation, the NEA, the Hitachi Foundation, and the Lila Wallace-Reader's Digest Fund. Hitachi, a Japanese conglomerate, had supported Tadashi Suzuki's *Tale of Lear* at Arena, while Lila Wallace had supported new play development. Addressing the Ford Foundation, Fichandler began her speech by citing studies of racial inequality. Her personal files include hundreds of newspaper articles about racial disparities across fields such as media representation, employment, and education. She underscored Washington census data of 70 percent of residents being black, citing a "cultural apartheid," the gap between white institutions and the world beyond these institutions, and the urgent need to bridge this gap, "if not out of conscience, compassion, and good citizenship, then for reasons of economic survival and the very perpetuation of these institutions."[133] The theatre needed black artists and the black bourgeoisie not just to enliven the repertory but to keep the institution alive.

The grant applications shared a particular narrative to distinguish Arena Stage. They emphasized the theatre's history of reaching out to African Americans, beginning with the racially integrated acting ensemble in the late 1960s. The history then jumps to the mid-1980s, not acknowledging the African, Caribbean, and African American works between these periods. This erasure suggests that the artistic leaders did not claim these productions as part of a thread of cultural diversity and Arena's identity, in part because many of them were touring presentations rather than homegrown productions and because they did not necessarily connect the dots of African diaspora performance. The narrative then locates the shift to a distinctly U.S. cultural diversity in 1984 when Fichandler took on the chair of the graduate acting program at NYU. She noticed that few students of color applied to, were accepted to, and thrived in the program, and she investigated the underlying problems rooted in racial hierarchy. Arena Stage subsequently produced and presented five works by and/or about black people within two seasons. In addition, the institution began to recruit people of color. The proposals demonstrated a complex understanding of institutional racism. In a letter to the director of the challenge grant program at the NEA, Udvarhelyi adopted some of Fichandler's language: "It is still difficult, very difficult, to locate and support young, talented minority artists and administrators. It's the cycle, the circle, we know about. They don't emerge because they see no place for themselves. There is no place for them because they haven't emerged."[134] Instead of blaming people of color, Udvarhelyi located barriers in power structures. She added, "Arena is well positioned to break this cycle. We hope that our experience and achievement will help other theaters towards similar goals."[135] The theatre staff mobilized Arena's history of engagement with black people, underlining the context of Washington as the nation's capital and as a majority-black city, to situate the theatre as uniquely qualified for leading the charge in cultural diversity.

Soon afterward, the NEA granted Arena Stage $1 million in a three-to-one matching challenge to generate a total of $4 million for the theatre's ambitious cultural diversity agenda. The new fellowship program was named for Allen Lee Hughes, an African American lighting designer who first came to Arena as an intern in 1969 and continues to design for the company to this day. The first initiative of its kind to give dedicated opportunities to young people of color in professional theatre, the Allen Lee Hughes Fellowship provided mentorship, $10,000 season-long salaries, and on-the-ground education from stage management to literary management. The program actively recruited young people of color. Coordinator Willa Taylor explained, "I think it's a problem not just of trepidation, but theater work is hard, the hours long and the pay low, and minority people who go to college have big financial loans to meet."[136] Over twenty-five years, Arena trained approximately seven hundred fellows, the vast majority of whom went on to careers in the theatre, and some even rose up the ranks at Arena Stage itself.[137] A uniquely antiracist initiative, the Allen Lee Hughes Fellowship directly addressed the whiteness of institutional theatre and dedicated resources to people of color in order to build systemic change. With this immense support from the NEA, Arena also commissioned more playwrights of color, starting with African American writer Cheryl West. Finally, Arena promoted Tazewell Thompson to artistic associate, coinciding with more productions of black drama, multiracial versions of canonical plays, and all-black takes on U.S.

classics. These productions built on others from the 1980s to develop a staying, significant black audience. Articulating Arena Stage's mission for the theatre's fortieth anniversary, Fichandler emphasized commitment to artists and audiences of color, "The institution seeks now to transform itself in order to be responsive to the significant minority populations who constitute its community. . . . Minority exclusion and disengagement can only be changed by means of deep and real revision in the institutions through which we lead our lives."[138] When she had tried to integrate the resident ensemble twenty years earlier, she did not receive sustained support. But the political climate had changed.

By the late 1980s, other regional theatres started to take more seriously the racial inequality within their ranks, as they argued that cultural diversity was "necessary for the survival of the theatre as a vital, relevant art form."[139] When Theatre Communications Group convened meetings with artistic directors in 1987, theatre institution expert Todd London found that "they adamantly concur that they and their institutions have generally done far too little to promote and provide access for minority, ethnic and (until recently, some argue) women artists."[140] To diversify the audience, they looked to theatres like the Mark Taper Forum, Milwaukee Repertory Theatre, and Goodman Theatre that altered their marketing strategies, casting policies, and programming, initiatives that Arena had helped to inaugurate.[141] Partial inclusion of people of color allowed Arena Stage and others to remain financially afloat and politically relevant.

CONCLUSION

At the end of the 1990–91 season, Fichandler stepped down as producing director. The culture wars, emblematized by the Robert Mapplethorpe controversy and right-wing attacks on the so-called NEA Four, had taken a toll on Fichandler and jeopardized arts funding sources. Fichandler reflected, "I didn't know exactly why I left at [that] point. I just thought, I'm not pushing this. I'm not starting at the bottom again and pushing this rock up the hill."[142] Doug Wager, who had been a part of Arena Stage since he was an intern in the early 1970s, became the artistic director. According to Wager, "When Zelda left, it wasn't so much a changing of the guard as a passing of the torch. Or, as she said, maybe I'm not passing the torch. I'm just passing the fire."[143]

The 1970s through the 1980s marked a major transition for Arena Stage. The racially liberal politics of Arena's productions and artistic leadership, as well as funding concerns, drove the theatre further in the direction of engagement with black artists, audiences, staff, and stories. This programming on- and offstage in the late 1980s provided space for more work by artists of color, especially African Americans, over the next twenty years. Although Zelda Fichandler left Arena Stage in 1991 and passed away in 2016, the institution continues her spirit of inquiry and liberalism but has moved increasingly toward an image as an "American" theatre centering on blackness.

CHAPTER FOUR

CULTIVATING *RAISIN* AND
THE POPULAR BLACK MUSICAL

O n January 4, 2010, Arena Stage hosted a salon to discuss race onstage with artistic staff and actors from its multiracial production of Harvey Schmidt and Tom Jones's *The Fantasticks*, a classic musical that follows a young couple coming of age. During the open forum, an Arena sales associate described his interactions marketing group tickets to black churches: when a church member asked why her congregation should be interested in *The Fantasticks*, the associate pointed to the casting of an African American actor in one of the lead roles. In so doing, he suggested that black audiences desire seeing people who resemble themselves onstage, and that black actors can turn a "Golden Age" implicitly white musical into a black musical.[1] To the surprise of the salon attendees, this sales associate revealed that black musicals comprise most of the top ten highest-grossing productions in Arena's history.

Popular black musicals have a storied history at Arena Stage, dating back to the 1973 production of *Raisin*, the musical adaptation of Lorraine Hansberry's *A Raisin in the Sun*. To contemporary audiences, the existence of this musical often comes as a surprise, but in its time, the musical overshadowed the play.[2] *Raisin*'s immense success foreshadowed that of similar productions. The musical ran for a then-unprecedented 110 performances, becoming "the most successful show" in the company's history.[3] *Raisin* received glowing reviews from DC-area critics. The production transferred to the Walnut Street Theatre, a prominent touring house–turned–regional theatre in Philadelphia whose proscenium theatre provided a transitional space for new staging. After that, the musical headed to Broadway, won multiple Tony Awards, and went on an extensive national tour.

Raisin is crucial to understanding Arena Stage's investment in black musicals. This case study builds on the previous chapter by zeroing in on a key production that staged blackness, garnered critical acclaim and commercial success, and mobilized black patrons. Just as *The Great White Hope* gave Arena entrée to Broadway, *Raisin* gave entrée to black musical theatre. Through this production, the institution articulated a genre of black musicals that would become a significant part of its repertoire and attract a more racially diverse audience. Because black musicals have been so popular at Arena, it is important to unpack what the genre entails. It is also vital to explore what blackness means, who decides, and why. Hansberry's original play, contemporaneous black musicals, and Washington in the early 1970s help to contextualize Arena's production. The development of the musical and a close reading of this adaptation reveal that the very act of musicalization, haunted by minstrelsy, as well as other creative decisions, deradicalized the core text, which offered feminist, antiracist, and anticapitalist critiques. *Raisin* became a feel-good, liberal musical that many audiences welcomed in an era of economic recession, racial upheaval, Watergate, and the Vietnam War. Through standing ovations and joyous diction, spectators embodied and expressed the positive effect of this production, whereas other critics questioned the authentic blackness of the musical. Audiences' responses and critical discourse, from stage manager reports to reviews, illustrate how various players contested the definitions of black musicals as they positioned *Raisin* and thereby positioned themselves and Arena Stage.

WHAT MAKES A MUSICAL BLACK?

Zelda Fichandler did not like musicals—at least musicals not of the big Broadway variety. In the first twenty-three years of Arena Stage, the only musical that she had produced was *The Threepenny Opera* in 1963. Instead of producing another musical, Fichandler staged *Threepenny* a second time five years later. Not a traditional musical comedy with chorus girls and a show business plot, Brecht and Weill's piece both alienated and entertained with its discordant score and harsh criticisms of the hypocrisy of the bourgeoisie. Fichandler's taste in musicals was limited to critical, experimental ones. Reflecting on how nonprofit companies have become increasingly imbricated in commercial theatre, she said, "It's total irony, or maybe the word is travesty, that the nonprofit theatre was established in reaction to and away, away from the Broadway theatre, now needs it for money in order to do what? In order to do less and less of what it was intending to do and more and more of what they need to get the money, which is mostly musicals."[4] If she were to stage a musical, then it must have a social conscience, and it must have an unusual dramaturgical structure. Ironically, Fichandler contributed to the theatrical economy she criticized when her nonprofit production of *Raisin* ended up on Broadway. For Fichandler, a critical approach to capitalism and blackness could endow musicals with the edginess and seriousness that she thought they needed.

What constitutes real blackness in theatre remains up for debate and is often mobilized by producers to their own ends. Over the years, artists and scholars have staked out various definitions of blackness, locating it in certain racialized bodies and cultural expressions as well as deconstructing it as an arbitrary yet powerful, material signifier. Many practitioners and academics cite W. E. B. Du Bois's formulation that black theatre should be about us, by us, for us, and near us, "us" being black people,[5] though Koritha Mitchell points out that this definition is not universal but historically located in lynching dramas in early twentieth-century literature.[6] Allen Woll employs a similar understanding as Du Bois does in his survey *Black Musical Theatre: From "Coontown" to "Dreamgirls,"* yet opens up the possibility of collaboration with nonblack artists, producers, and spectators as still counting as black theatre.[7] In an analysis of Melvin van Peebles's early 1970s meditation on black struggle *Ain't Supposed to Die a Natural Death*, theatre historian Sam O'Connell insists on the blackness of soul music because of its political and musical style in contrast with what he considered pseudo-black musicals like the black take on *The Wizard of Oz* called *The Wiz*.[8] In "Africanisms in African-American Music," Portia K. Maultsby delineates distinct African and African American qualities of soul, jazz, and gospel such as improvisation, syncopation, and call and response, and she argues for black collectivity through music.[9] These articulations codify blackness in complex yet still limited ways. Many of them presume an essential, steady, and legible racialization of bodies that directly translates to the art those bodies produce and consume, and the implication is that black people authorize black art.

But race is invented, dynamic, and contingent. In their foundational text *Racial Formation in the United States*, sociologists Michael

Omi and Howard Winant argue that race is overdetermined by social construction, historical context, macro state structures and policies, and micro daily lived experiences.[10] In "New Black Math," playwright Suzan-Lori Parks famously complicates one-to-one correlations of black bodies with black theatre:

> A black play doesnt have anything to do with black people.
> Im saying *The Glass*
> *Menagerie* is a black play.
> SAY WHAT?
> EXCUSE ME?!?!?![11]

She throws into confusion stable, singular definitions of "black" by avowing that white-authored plays can be considered black.[12] Against "white racial amnesia," musical theatre scholar Eric M. Glover insists, "US musicals are always black," pointing to the form's foundation in black artists as well as black music and repetition and revision.[13] In her analysis of *Jelly's Last Jam*, a musical about jazz musician Jelly Roll Morton, Kathryn Edney argues that the black artistic creators "stake a particularly African American claim for the history of the American musical."[14] During the mid-1980s, New Black Aesthetic and Post-Soul Aesthetic discourses emerged among black artists who rejected essentialized definitions of blackness and the burden of racial uplift.[15] At the turn of the twenty-first century, "postblack," not to be equated with "postrace," has gained currency beginning with curator Thelma Golden and the "Freestyle" exhibition at the Studio Museum in Harlem. According to Golden, postblack "was characterized by artists who were adamant about not being labeled as 'black' artists, though their work was steeped, in fact deeply interested, in redefining complex notions of blackness."[16] Performance scholars such as Harry J. Elam Jr. and Douglas A. Jones Jr. have taken up the term to denote a postmodernist aesthetic of black artists in a post–civil rights era.[17] Finally, because a history of slavery grounds concepts of citizenship, freedom, and personhood in the United States, the meaning of U.S. blackness often stands in relation to the meaning of whiteness. As thinkers and artists like Toni Morrison have explored, black and white appear both mutually exclusive and mutually constitutive.[18]

Blackness is relational. In *Scenes of Subjection*, Saidiya V. Hartman identifies performances of blackness as enactments marking "a social relationship of dominance and abjection and potentially one of re-dress and emancipation; [blackness] is a contested figure at the very center of social struggle."[19] In *Appropriating Blackness*, queer black performance studies artist-scholar E. Patrick Johnson theorizes black-ness as unstable, dependent on sociopolitical factors, and historically contested by agents with different investments. Johnson argues that "the mutual constructing/deconstructing, avowing/disavowing, and expanding/delimiting dynamic that occurs in the production of black-ness is the very thing that constitutes 'black culture.'"[20] By defining blackness through claims to authenticity, agents position themselves and others: "Individuals or groups *appropriate* this complex and nu-anced racial signifier in order to circumscribe its boundaries or to ex-clude other individuals or groups."[21] These boundaries are malleable yet material, as artists, producers, spectators, and critics designate what "black is" and what "black ain't."[22] These definitions of black-ness index the periods from which they emerge. No single definition of "black" is the correct one; rather, various positionings produce a spectrum of blackness.

Fichandler navigated the parameters of what she considered real blackness in *Raisin*. She also made a distinction between what she considered "black" versus "Black." In a letter on the 1973–74 season, she asserted, "I think it bad if we don't do a black play somewhere in there next season. I wanted to do one this season (I mean outside of *Raisin* which, as black goes, is not really Black), but was unable to find one that suited or satisfied."[23] She implied that the musical, as a typi-cally spectacle-driven and commercial form, gave *Raisin* less authen-ticity. In addition, the musical's authorship made *Raisin* black but "not really Black." The musical was written by a mostly white production team: Robert Nemiroff and Charlotte Zaltzberg penned the book, Judd Woldin the music, and Robert Brittan the lyrics, while African Ameri-can artist Donald McKayle directed and choreographed. But because Fichandler presumed blackness as the presence of black people on-stage, sounds inspired by black musical traditions, and stories drama-tizing the struggles of working-class black people, she still considered the musical "black." In contrast, capital-B "Black" referred to the radi-cal politics of Black Power and avant-garde aesthetics of the Black Arts Movement. She articulated a careful calculation of b/Blackness and a compulsion to stage a "black play," not a "Black play." The admission that she could not find a black play that "suited or satisfied" says less about black theatre and more about her arbitrary yardstick for measuring theatre and blackness for Arena's repertory and patronage. The artists, producers, and critics of *Raisin* the musical repeatedly invoked the terms "black" and "universal" to make claims about the authenticity and wide appeal of the adaptation. The press packet for the national tour anticipated the first question to come up in interviews, "Is it a Black show?" to which the artists were coached to respond, "Yes. It is. Very Black. And it is *also* universal."[24] Although the packet used "Black," not "black," it tempered possible discomfort of white audiences by insisting on the musical's universality beyond race.

PRODUCTION HISTORY

The same dual definitions of "black" and/yet "universal" had been applied to Lorraine Hansberry's drama almost fifteen years before. When *A Raisin in the Sun* had opened on Broadway in 1959, critics recognized the watershed moment of producing the first Broadway play written by a black woman, and the first Broadway production directed by a black man, Lloyd Richards. The play offers a serious, realist, domestic drama about a working-class African American family, the Youngers, who live on the South Side of Chicago. When Big Walter dies, the matriarch, Lena, decides they should use the insurance money for her daughter Beneatha to attend medical school and for a down payment on a house in a white neighborhood, whereas her son Walter wants to use the money to open a liquor store. American Studies scholar Robin Bernstein contends, "The play's ability to appear to encapsulate 'Negro experience' in the readily knowable, digestible, and nonthreatening form of theatrical realism . . . constituted the primary reason for the play's success among white audiences."[25] Black Studies specialist Tricia Rose adds, "The terms of [Hansberry's] celebration and embrace rested on the interpretation that *Raisin* was a universal story, that it revealed that Blacks were 'just like whites' and suggested that full integration could take place without substantial disturbance to or sacrifice of the status quo of white privilege," when in actuality Hansberry offered "(inter)personal justice" as necessary for consciousness raising, black love, and freedom.[26] Drawing black audiences as well, "the production demonstrated the desire to see black life."[27] While some black radicals such as Harold Cruse and Amiri Baraka condemned the play as "bourgeois" at the time, Harilaos Stecopoulos argues that the play "is less a symptom than a diagnosis of the black ambivalence about normative (white) notions of embourgeoisement."[28] Stecopoulos points to Hansberry's use of 1930s leftist, white ethnic melodrama such as Clifford Odets's work to center domestic women and critique capitalism and systemic racism. Theatre theorist Aaron Thomas notes that most theatre scholarship erases Hansberry's communist ethos.[29] A queer black woman, Hansberry advocated for social justice for women-identified, black, queer, and working-class people and intersections therein.[30] Her radical politics led the FBI to investigate her, but they did not perceive anticapitalist content in *Raisin*. Probably because the play lent itself to different interpretations, Hansberry won the New York Drama Critics Award, becoming the first black playwright to do so.

After Hansberry died of cancer in 1965, her ex-husband Robert Nemiroff devoted himself to producing her legacy.[31] A white Jewish American man, Nemiroff had a history of profiting off of black cultural productions. With Burt D'Lugoff in 1956, he cowrote the top-40 hit "Cindy, Oh Cindy," a romantic song whose melody they took from black diasporic stevedores in their song "Pay Me My Money Down." The payment that Nemiroff received for "Cindy, Oh Cindy" gave Hansberry the time to write *A Raisin in the Sun*. Following her death, he adapted Hansberry's writings into *To Be Young, Gifted, and Black* (1969) and edited *Les Blancs* (1970) in collaboration with his creative consultant Charlotte Zaltzberg. As part of promoting the wider dissemination of her work, Nemiroff pitched a musical adaptation of *A Raisin in the Sun* to commercial producers for years before Arena Stage agreed to develop and stage it.[32]

Producers initially hesitated to support a musicalization of Hansberry's play, but black musicals gained greater prominence after 1970. According to Allen Woll, black musicals written by whites in the 1960s, such as *Kwamina*, *No Strings*, and *Hallelujah, Baby!*, flopped because they avoided dealing with the complexities of contemporary racial dynamics. However, the latter two musicals earned Tony Awards in acting for Diahann Carrol, Leslie Uggams, and Lillian Hayman. Woll cites the musical *Purlie* in 1970 as a turning point marking the revitalization of successful black musicals. When Ossie Davis replaced Sidney Poitier in *A Raisin in the Sun* on Broadway, he persuaded the producer

to stage his play *Purlie Victorious*. The musical version of *Purlie* arguably facilitated the production of the musical *Raisin*. Woll also cites
the growing number of black dramas of the 1960s, foundation of the
Negro Ensemble Company, and support from the Ford Foundation as
reasons for the renewed popularity of black musicals by the 1970s.[33]
Ain't Supposed to Die a Natural Death, *The Wiz*, and the Fats Waller
revue *Ain't Misbehavin'* became part of this trend. In addition, musical scholar Elizabeth Wollman notes the increase in black theatergoing
at this time.[34]

Broadway was not the only site for original musical productions
with black artists. In Washington, theatre companies produced world
premieres of black musicals. In 1971, the newly reopened Ford's Theatre premiered Vinnette Carrol's *Don't Bother Me, I Can't Cope*, a revue
that engaged with poverty, black power, women's liberation, and other
experiences of modern African Americans. The musical transferred to
the Great White Way, making Carrol the first African American woman
to direct on Broadway. Three years later, Ford's Theatre revived the
production. In 1975, the company staged Carrol's musical telling of the
book of Matthew, *Your Arms Too Short to Box with God*, moved it to
Broadway, and presented an encore production in 1976. Meanwhile,
Robert Hooks founded the D.C. Black Repertory Company in 1972 and
produced musicals including an adaptation of Gwendolyn Brooks's
poetry entitled *Among All This You Stand Like a Fine Brownstone*; a
revue of original songs about the daily life of people in Washington
called *A Day, a Life, a People*, by civil rights activist–scholar–musician
Bernice Reagon; and *Changes*, by playwright–arts administrator Vantile Whitfield, which "was considered the most successful of the D.C.
Black Rep's musical productions."[35] Although the theatre held a fund-
raiser with singer Isaac Hayes, the fundraising was insufficient, and the
company closed in 1978. In deciding to produce *Raisin*, Arena Stage
followed a course set by other Washington institutions.

GROWING *RAISIN*

The musicalization of *Raisin* developed over nearly a decade before
landing at Arena and then Broadway. The project began when emerging composer Judd Woldin and lyricist Robert Brittan met in Lehman
Engle's BMI Musical Theatre Workshop and wrote a musical treatment

of *A Raisin in the Sun*. They sent their songs to Robert Nemiroff, who asked to see more. When the producer heard "A Whole Lotta Sunlight," Lena's anthem for cultivating her plant and her family, he became devoted to the project. As heir to Hansberry's estate and a seasoned producer of her work, he supervised the musical and cowrote the book with Charlotte Zaltzberg. He reached out to choreographer Donald McKayle, with whom he had worked on *Kicks & Co.*, a musical that opened in Chicago in 1961 but never reached Broadway.[36] When Nemiroff secured a producing agreement with Arena Stage, he treated the theatre company as more of a presenting house than a coproducing organization.

Arena, however, sought greater control. The company paid for a license to stage *Raisin* and would later receive subsidiary rights, while Nemiroff promised $60,000 to offset additional costs.[37] *Raisin* marks an early example of a Broadway musical tryout via a nonprofit theatre company, an arrangement that has become commonplace at Arena Stage and other regional and Off-Broadway theatres.[38] Letters between Thomas Fichandler and lawyers negotiating the contract indicate that more than economic capital was at stake. He wrote, "Nemiroff's credit should not be as associate producer: Zelda will never agree to this. Nor should we endanger our tax-exempt status. Arena Stage is the producer. The words should be 'by arrangement with Robert Nemiroff,' and the size should be the same as afforded to Zelda Fichandler as Producing Director."[39] To avoid appearing as a commercial touring house, Arena had to be credited as the producer. The theatre may have been sensitive because by 1973 Arena Stage had a regular presence on Broadway. In a playbill for *Raisin*, Zelda Fichandler boasted,

> *Raisin*, now in its second extension and one of a list of productions created for Washington audiences by Arena Stage is one of the most successful new productions in the theater's history. The Arena production of *Raisin* is now scheduled to open on Broadway in October. In this route it follows such previous Arena premieres as the *Great White Hope, Indians*, and *Moonchildren*.[40]

She touted Arena's productions as both Washington-specific and national in their scope. And yet, when Nemiroff picked up the Tony Award for Best Musical, he thanked Zelda and Thomas Fichandler, but he did not name Arena Stage.

Arena was far from merely a venue for *Raisin* because the space and artistic leaders shaped the musical production. Neither Zelda Fichandler nor Robert Nemiroff desired a "traditional musical," by which they meant a splashy production, a point that they made to distinguish themselves from musicals like the Carol Channing vehicle *Lorelei*, which was running in Washington the same season. Nemiroff described his early libretto as "rather old-fashioned with elaborate production numbers involving heavy sets, wagons, flies, and a large cast," whereas the new book was closer to "STORY THEATER" due to its fluidity and nearly bare stage.[41] The latter was more attuned to the setup of the arena, economized budget, and Fichandler's aesthetic. During the rehearsal process, McKayle removed more and more physical objects, freeing up the space and creating abstract movement.

In November 1972, Nemiroff sent Fichandler an outline of the musical book, and she sent back an eighteen-page memo voicing concerns about the art and politics of *Raisin*. She repeatedly asked questions within a liberal, sociological understanding of an individual's choices amid material conditions, or character's motivation given the circumstances: "What choices does Walter have in being a man-father? Who keeps him from these choices? How are Walter's own choices limited by the kind of mother and father he had and the kind of choices available to them? How did the white people, how do the white people, affect these choices? How can they be reclaimed by black people?" and "how does Walter's fantasy get theatrically embodied in such a way that it is sophisticated, personal, related to his son, anti-white-capital and yet doesn't end up by making him seem like all he wants to do is take over white values??????"[42] Here she framed choices as both dramatic and systemic. Throughout the memo, she posed black values as the opposite of white values, which align with capitalism. In so doing, she constructed white/black, capitalism/anticapitalism binaries. In another example of her attentiveness to politics, Fichandler pointed out that cutting the character of Beneatha's wealthy romantic interest George Murchison and Ruth's abortion left act 2 with too little dramatic action and too little resonance with the contemporary issue of women's liberation.[43] According to Steven Carter, who dealt extensively with Nemiroff when writing *Hansberry's Drama*, "To gain time for the music, large chunks of the play, such as Ruth's deliberations about abortion, Asagai's male chauvinist speeches, everything relating to George Murchison, and the bulk of Lindner's first visit, had to be eliminated."[44] Although Carter has a point about time constraints, dropping those overtly political parts was a deliberate decision that resulted in a safer cultural production.

Originally entitled *A Long Time Comin'*, evoking both the civil rights movement and Sam Cooke's song "A Change Is Gonna Come," early drafts of *Raisin* magnified Hansberry's text and feminist politics. The musical began with Mama singing "A Whole Lotta Sunlight," centering her as the heart of the show. Beneatha sang a sarcastic duet with her brother Walter, "Please Forgive Me," to introduce their gendered conflict; she refers to him as the "massa" and the "hero of the story," as he keeps insisting that she should either get a job like a nurse or get married.[45] She had another duet with George, her rich, assimilationist suitor. Like Walter, he insisted to Beneatha, "Turn on the girl for me. / Let Mother Nature appear," while she cites Harriet Tubman and Simone de Beauvoir.[46] In addition, Mama, Ruth, and Beneatha shared a trio called "In My Time" in which they expressed the social mores for dating across their separate generations. Beneatha launched her feminist critique of women's imprisonment in patriarchal domesticity:

> Here we go again—the answer must be men—
> The marriage routine!
> Why should women think when there's a kitchen sink
> To say what they mean.
> If you don't know what to do,
> Have another kid or two.
> You won't go out of use when you can reproduce
> Just like a machine.[47]

Her caustic words underscored the household and reproductive labor that women often do instead of pursuing higher education. Beneatha's cynical, biting tone throughout these numbers rubbed up against the feel-good, male-centered narrative that the musical would become.

By the spring of 1973, the musical was retitled *Raisin*, and the creative team expanded the theatrical world and reduced Hansberry's dialogue and Beneatha's role. The new title kept the sense of raisin' or racial uplift of *A Long Time Comin'* but connected the musical more identifiably with the play. The producers wanted to capitalize on but also distinguish themselves from *A Raisin in the Sun*. For the musical translation, Nemiroff, Fichandler, and McKayle sought song-and-dance opportunities for the ensemble beyond the confines of the Youngers' apartment. For example, Nemiroff's personal script from April and May 1973 included this early scene: "Chicago—as observed thru the windshield of WALTER's limousine—and in his mind. A production number in the course of which the blacks of the Southside are transformed via movement and masks, into the shoppers and businessmen of the affluent, successful 'white' Chicago at work and play."[48] This number became "Running to Meet the Man," in which the black ensemble did not portray and satirize the white bourgeoisie but instead played black blue-collar workers. These scenes perform the intersection of race with class, linking white people to the bourgeoisie and black people to the working class. Of the previous songs mentioned, only "A Whole Lotta Sunlight" remained in the Arena production, and it was no longer the opening number. Instead, the musical as premiered focused on Walter. Some of Beneatha's songs may have been removed because the creative team found it difficult to work with the original actress, Shezwae Powell, who was replaced by her understudy Debbie Allen.[49] But their decisions on which parts to cut, add, and develop demonstrate an attempt to produce a popular, liberal black musical and a struggle to articulate blackness.

POPULARIZING *RAISIN*

Raisin performed blackness in ways that affirmed hegemonic expectations of black working-class struggle, masculinity, religiosity, savagery, and inherent musicality, yet also contested assumptions of authenticity by drawing attention to the constructions of performance and race. The production signaled from the start that it would expand on *A Raisin in the Sun* to musicalized and danced representations of not only the Younger family but also the black community. During the overture, which interweaves jazz and blues themes from the score, the ensemble dances a minidrama, a supposedly typical night on the South Side of Chicago in the 1950s, and perhaps more closely Washington and New York City in the 1970s. This includes "groovy cats" wearing "doo-rags," attractive "chicks," a drunk, a drug pusher, and his "victim."[50] The dance-drama evoked *West Side Story* and showcased McKayle's expertise as a choreographer. By confirming typical representations of poor, black neighborhoods, the setting establishes conditions that an exceptional and aspirational black family like the Youngers would want to leave.

When the spotlight shifts to the Younger family, Walter emerges as the protagonist. During the scene when the family readies for the day ahead, he sings the first song, "Man Say," which uses much of Hansberry's dialogue set to a Calypso tune. The song dramatizes normative gender roles, as if Ruth is the nagging wife holding back her husband: "Man say, 'I got me a dream!' / Woman say,—(*Mimicking.*) 'Pass the cream!'"[51] While Ruth speaks her lines urging Walter to come down to earth, Walter and his triumphant, horn-backed music in this I am / I want song easily overcome her, letting the audience know that they should be on his side. He sings eight songs, whereas the play emphasizes the power of the female characters, Lena, Ruth, and Beneatha. Many critics viewed *A Raisin in the Sun* as a struggle between Walter and Lena due in part to battles between the stars, Sidney Poitier and Claudia McNeil, and in part to the interpretation that Mama stood in the way of her son's manhood.[52] But African American literature scholar Julie M. Burrell argues that the characters wield competing visions: "Mama's, a masculinity that stems from a life-affirming Black tradition; Walter's, a capitalist masculinity that depends upon being the family's sole provider and a wealthy power player."[53] By diminishing the roles of women, including Lena, the musical leans more heavily on Walter's side and insistence on the man as head of household.

Hegemonic claims to authentic blackness often prioritize working-class heteronormativity and masculinity. E. Patrick Johnson offers as examples Harlem Renaissance artists like Langston Hughes, who located true blackness in the "folk," and Black Arts Movement artists like Amiri Baraka, who prioritized male leadership and denigrated women and queer-identified people in order to advance the race.[54] Minoritized groups such as working-class, straight, black men can mobilize what privilege they do have to promote themselves at the expense of maintaining certain hierarchies. As black feminist scholars such as Kimberlé Crenshaw have pointed out, identity formations and structures of oppression are intersectional.[55] Race, class, gender, sexuality, and ability status are neither separate nor separable. In *Aberrations in Black*, sociologist Roderick Ferguson demonstrates that, in the 1960s and 1970s, the hetero-patriarchal through-line of black nationalism worked in tandem with the Moynihan Report, a sociological study of black families that ended up pathologizing black female-headed households so as to regulate racialized gender roles and queer sexuality.[56] In the musical, Lena is not an even match for Walter. She sings as a principal in only two songs. Her soundscape tends to be bluesy and full of nature imagery, grounding her as opposed to the rollicking sound of Walter's music. In addition to her longing for "A Whole Lotta Sunlight" for her plant and her family, she sings "Measure the Valleys," urging Beneatha not to judge her brother for his faults alone but also for his highpoints: "Measure the valleys, measure the hills."[57] Her songs concern other family members, not herself. By prioritizing Walter and his point of view, *Raisin* accorded with contemporary expectations of normative hetero-patriarchal blackness.

The musical also boasts a gospel number, "He Come Down This Morning," which plays on popular African American music and religiosity. The number is full of call-and-response, repetition, a certain idiolect ("He Come Down" instead of "He Came Down"), movement, and virtuosic vocal performances. This second-act opener welcomes the audience back into a comfortable theatrical world where the black community minus Walter and Beneatha sing and dance the gospel. African American gospel plays have proved financially successful among African American audiences.[58] Scholar of "Chitlin Circuit," or urban theatre, Rashida Z. Shaw contends that these plays offer "another way of going to church, of getting religious instruction. They're validating and validated entertainment."[59] While Shaw's argument is compelling, the fact that the *Raisin* audience was majority white raises questions about who or what was being "validated" through the production. As scholar and designer Kathy A. Perkins notes on the popularity of the gospel musical *Crowns*, "It's not just black people, you know, white people want to come hear black church music or whatever."[60]

Two pseudo-African numbers in the musical further complicate authenticity and audience. When Asagai explains to Beneatha the meaning of the name that he has given her, Alaiyo, he drapes traditional cloth on her as drums begin to play in the background. His lyrics name these drums: "Heartbeats tell me . . . / Beating like drums of my home / Calling my name / We have made our two diff'rent worlds the same, Alaiyo."[61] This is a didactic song meant for Beneatha and for the

Photo of original cast of *Raisin*, "African Dance" with Debbie Allen (center), Joe Morton (center), and ensemble at Arena Theatre, Washington, DC, 1973. Donald McKayle, director/choreographer. Photographer unknown. Courtesy the Donald McKayle Legacy Trust archives.

audience, who can assemble the clothing, musical, and linguistic signifiers of essentialized Africa. As the song progresses, the orchestrations become fuller, resembling descent-into-the-jungle motifs, as a flute sounds an exotic bird. Shortly thereafter, an extended sequence directly from Hansberry's text shows Beneatha criticizing Ruth for listening to "*assimilationist* junk," popular blues, instead of "real music," which was Michael Olatunji's "Drums of Passion" in the original musical production.[62] When Beneatha performs what she believes are African dances, Ruth in turn criticizes her and the problem of appropriating culture.

This salient critique, however, becomes muddled in the musical. On Walter's drunken entrance, the stage becomes full of African warriors. A production still shows that the ensemble wore little more than thongs, reinforcing the idea of Africans as tribal and barbaric. By manifesting Walter's drunken vision of Africa, the musical implicitly undermines Hansberry's critique of stereotypical portrayals of Africa. In an earlier scene in both the play and the musical, Beneatha lectures her mother on how most people think only of Tarzan when they think of Africa rather than the rich history and culture of specific tribes, and modern Africans such as Asagai who are resisting colonial governments. Mc-Kayle insisted that the performance reveals Walter's skewed imagination, not reality.[63] Still, it could provide audiences the pleasure of consuming bare black bodies. For example, critic Allen Lewis wrote for the *New Haven Register*, "The equally obligatory African dance seemingly divorced from the main story line, came alive in its own right."[64] He found the number expected in a clichéd way and convincing. An image of this number figured prominently in many print advertisements. When *Raisin* moved to Broadway, producers aired television commercials consisting primarily of this dance number.[65] The advertising choice represents one of the earliest television commercials for a Broadway musical and indicates the imagined appeal of these black images and sounds to U.S. audiences. This commercial may also have discouraged African Americans who viewed the musicalization as denigrating to Hansberry's critical play.[66]

As a musical, *Raisin* purported to deliver real black music. For Walter and Ruth's romantic duet, "Sweet Time," the stage directions advised: "Musically, the quality should be Black—the Blackest interpretation possible—a cry from the heart with all the subtleties, the broken lines and jagged edges and, where appropriate, the freely improvised quarter-notes of Soul. But none of this for embellishment—only where and to the extent it enhances true feeling."[67] The underscoring of soul music and soulful feeling relate to O'Connell's definition of an authentically black musical. Improvisation and unadorned emotion translate the black body to black sound. The rawness in musical style works against musical theatre's associations with whiteness and a polished, allegedly inauthentic quality.[68] In a critique of putting black diaspora culture into essentialized national-identity boxes, Paul Gilroy observes, "Black music is so often the principal symbol of racial authenticity."[69] The creative team likely emphasized authenticity because they themselves were almost entirely white.

But the director-choreographer, music director, members of the orchestra, and the cast were black. By 1973, McKayle was a renowned choreographer known for compositions such as *Ring 'Round My Shoulder* (1959) that incorporated African-inspired movement and African

American-specific social formations. He choreographed the Broadway musical *Golden Boy*, which in 1964 starred Sammy Davis Jr. His Tony nominations for his direction and choreography for *Raisin* made him the first black artist to receive these honors. He recalled in an interview in 2002, "The show I'm most attached to is *Raisin*. Part of it was I was able to completely formulate how it would be viewed and set the style of that show."[70] Joyce Brown had also worked on *Golden Boy* and later *Purlie*, becoming the first African American woman to conduct the opening of a Broadway show.[71] For *Raisin*, Brown served as the music director, vocal arranger, conductor, and pianist. When hiring local musicians for each stop of the national tour, the production team emphasized employing black musicians because of morale, scrutiny from the black press, and *Raisin*'s identity as a "black show": "It is *important that there be as many excellent Black, female and minority-group players in the pit as possible* . . . BUT DO NOT HIRE SOMEONE BECAUSE OF IT IF THEY ARE *NOT* AMONG THE BEST PLAYERS AND READERS."[72] The principal actors, Virginia Capers (Lena), Joe Morton (Walter), Ernestine Jackson (Ruth), Debbie Allen (Beneatha), and Ralph Carter (Travis), all had Broadway credits, and some went on to have starring roles on television: Allen in *Fame*, Carter on *Good Times*, and Morton on *Scandal*. The black artists on- and offstage authenticated the music composed and written by white artists.

The musical further constructs blackness by juxtaposing a silent and largely absent white world with singing black characters. The only white character in the musical is Karl Lindner, who does not sing. When he enters the Youngers' home, the reprise of Walter and Ruth's romantic duet "Sweet Time" ends abruptly, emphasizing Lindner's dramaturgical function as a nonmusical force. In contrast with Hansberry's long, intricate scene in which Lindner articulates concern for the Youngers and for himself, Lindner barely speaks in the musical. His dialogue is full of ellipses, dashes, "ah"s, and stage business such as clearing his throat, until he says that he is from the Clybourne Park Improvement Association, at which point *"with controlled anger, Walter takes a step towards him, brandishing the card almost under his nose, and Lindner draws back,"* and the scene ends suddenly.[73] Perhaps the deletion was due to a presumption that the audience was already familiar with Lindner's intentions to buy out the Youngers so that they will not move to his all-white neighborhood, as Walter seems to be here. Nemiroff appears to have had little concern for this character. In a memo to Zelda Fichandler, he said that the cast should have twenty or fewer actors, and "Lindner would presumably be an assistant stage manager."[74] As a consequence, Lindner's seemingly benign but deeply antiblack outlook is not taken as seriously in the musical.

Walter, Ruth, and Beneatha mock Lindner to Lena in what may be the most radical song in the score, "Not Anymore." The characters pretend that they are the Clybourne Park welcoming committee by whiting up. Performed by Morton, Walter adopts a nasally voice with a clipped cadence on the cast recording, affecting what Faedra Chatard Carpenter calls "linguistic whiteface," "a form of disidentification, aurally articulating the popularized view that whites and blacks necessarily speak differently. Yet the presentation of linguistic whiteface simultaneously reveals the black body's inherent ability to create 'white sounds,' therefore further demonstrating that any white-bodied proprietary claim on aural whiteness is a faulty one."[75] In "Not Anymore," the characters sing of racist acts they do not do anymore ("We didn't bring no rope!"), though the mock-hymn, vaudeville-style music, and exaggerated movements act as punchlines (*"The three hang themselves—one arm up taut, the other at the neck, head dangling limp"*).[76] But perhaps the most critical part of the song is the point at which the characters exalt the NAACP, Lena Horne, and Harry Belafonte, popular representations of blackness. Beneatha remarks, "I wouldn't mind *him* livin' next door to me!" while the song ends with the characters insisting that they will pay to keep their neighborhood white.[77] Walter, Ruth, and Beneatha demonstrate whites' hypocrisy by pointing out how whites disavow race and structural racism except for a few comfortable examples of blackness. Meanwhile, their gestures counter their lyrics; they did bring rope. Many of the lyrics are spoke-sung and taken from Lindner's speech in the original play. "Not Anymore," a kind of reverse minstrel song, reveals the complex layers and instability of performing race: black actors playing black characters impersonating white characters and performing a song written by white artists using lines from a black playwright.

On the other hand, "Not Anymore" is rather moderate within its political and historical context. Unlike *A Raisin in the Sun*, the musical emerged after the civil rights movement. Liberal spectators could take on the privileged position of believing themselves to be not racist, not like those evil white people being mocked in the song. Attending *Raisin* the musical involves a self-selecting audience that would likely be at least sympathetic to African Americans. But again, the song does not challenge the spectator to become not only *not* racist but *anti*-racist; it does not directly implicate the audience in the structures of white supremacy. Because the musical is set in the 1950s, the audience might believe that by 1973 the lyrics are no longer true. Segregation had been juridically struck down. Whites could congratulate themselves on their liberal tolerance of black people, even as they fled Washington for the suburbs and returned only to work and attend productions at Arena Stage. *Raisin*'s message of integration and musical presentation provided comfort and entertainment.

Raisin completes Walter's journey by mobilizing silence to indicate where he has gone wrong and then redeem him with music. After Walter loses the money for his business and Beneatha's education, he tells his family that he will call Karl Lindner and accept his offer. Instead of singing, he speaks over the musical underscoring, but that turns to silence when Walter begins to perform minstrel tropes. The silence clarifies for the audience that they should condemn this unsympathetic portrayal of a black man. In the end, Walter changes his mind and asserts his pride, masculinity, and decision to move to Clybourne Park. During this transition, Lena hums and the orchestra plays "He Come Down This Morning," which locates the influence of God in this outcome "to show His children the way."[78] Instead of the final tableau of Hansberry's script depicting Mama retrieving her potted plant alone, Walter picks it up and gives it to her, spotlighting Walter's dramatic arc. The musical concludes on a note of optimism for the future of the Younger family integrating a white neighborhood.

POSITIONING *RAISIN* AND BLACK MUSICALS VIA REVIEWS

Critics positioned *Raisin* in various ways as they contested what makes a black musical and who authorizes which definition. Dozens of reviews from across the country illustrate the national attention given to Arena Stage and *Raisin* even before the transfer to Broadway. Wollman assesses that successful black musicals like *Raisin* "appealed to whites and blacks alike, with upbeat plots, lots of jokes, and catchy music carefully diluting any polemics."[79] While most white review-ers lauded the musical for its humanity, joy, and black score, others deemed *Raisin* whitened and inauthentic. But white and black critics did not have the same responses within and between groups.

Much of the discourse surrounding *Raisin* focused on its "humanity" as if to assure white spectators of the musical's universality and to as-sure black spectators of its liberalism. Donald McKayle's note in the program primed audiences' interpretations of the Arena production: "Because [*Raisin*] is so basically human, it contains man's tears and pain as well as his laughter. Because it is black, it is filled with the rich heritage of black music—blues, gospel, jazz, and the polyrhythms of Africa."[80] He gendered people as male, equated feeling with humanity, and defined blackness musically. According to CBS radio critic Mike Heid, "The playwright avoids caricatures, drawing for us *vibrant beings*—not just black beings, but beings. As *Fiddler on the Roof* en-veloped us with its sense of Jewishness, so *Raisin* envelops us with its blackness, but transcends all racial bounds to bring us a poignant series of encounters."[81] By suggesting that blackness, not systemic racism, forms a limiting barrier to humanity, he reproduced a racial-ized logic that distinguishes "black beings" from implicitly white, un-encumbered "beings," and celebrates assimilation. He also gestured toward a history of portrayals of African Americans as "caricatures" and supported *Raisin*'s liberal project of realizing black subjectivity. Clive Barnes of the *New York Times* argued that the libretto was stronger than Hansberry's original play, and in a universalist-colorblind turn claimed, "Today it is not the color of the piece that overwhelms one but its tremendous story."[82] *Washington Star* critic David Richards, who would come to be the dominant local critic when he moved to the *Washington Post*, wrote somewhat reductively that *Raisin* "views its characters as simple human beings,"[83] and concluded, "Perhaps the most rewarding discovery is that *Raisin*'s humanity is still an essential one, rooted in a firm belief in human dignity."[84] By invoking and eras-ing race, the critical discourse for *Raisin* the musical resembled that of the play, which many critics viewed as specific to the "Negro ex-perience" or "universal"; the former essentialized blackness, while the latter erased blackness.[85]

Despite these appeals to universalism, "dignity" has a particular black bourgeois connotation, and the word appeared several times in reviews. Clifford A. Ridley of the *National Observer* argued that *Raisin* boasts "a deeply felt salute to human dignity."[86] Another critic admired the "sense of dignity with which the characters fill their roles."[87] Charles B. Jones, editor of the African American newspaper the *Amsterdam News*, used his editorial to praise the black family values of *Raisin* in contrast to other popular black cultural productions: "In this age of exploitative Black movies, it is rejuvenating and inspiring to return to images of human dignity."[88] With its respectability politics, the musical ennobled a working-class black American family in a performance context haunted by blackface minstrelsy, and white and black journalists found this representation remarkable and desirable. But the desire for humanizing and dignifying black people via racial and class uplift onstage betrays a belief that they are not already human; furthermore, the production presumes having a middle-class audience mired in white supremacy from which black people must gain approval.

Critics distinguished *Raisin* from more radical theatrical works representing black people. For example, Ernest Schier separated Hansberry and *Raisin* from "newer, militant playwrights like Ed Bullins."[89] *Catholic Review* critic Gerard Perseghin wrote, "In comparison to the real-life visual drabness of other black shows of recent years, 'Raisin' makes them all seem lumpenprol. It is beautiful in sight and sound."[90] David Richards asserted, "There may be a few grumblings among those who expect black theater to be abrasive and accusatory, and who will hence be impatient with the love and humanity that fill the theater to the bursting point," contrasting the heartwarming musical with what he perceived as the typical Black Arts play that harangues and implicates white audiences.[91] Critic Philip F. Crosland preferred *Raisin* to the D.C. Black Repertory Company's production of Jean Genet's *The Blacks* in part because it was difficult "to become emotionally involved" in the latter.[92] At the same time, critics such as Elliot Norton of the *Boston Herald* also distinguished *Raisin* from bubbly black musicals: "We have had many black musicals, full of bouncing tunes, paced at a swift tempo by kinetic drum beats. This 'Raisin' has the bounce and the beat but it has also things like 'Measure the Valleys' which none of the others had."[93] Both comforting and challenging, *Raisin* represented a satisfying black musical in between radical Black Arts Movement theatre and light entertainment. In the context of the Vietnam War and

Black Power, it is not surprising that critics would favor upbeat, emotionally rich integration narratives and more palatable representations of African Americans, especially through a musical. Roy Meachum of *Metromedia News* wrote, "Only the most radical black or deeply racist white can possibly resist its strength, visceral beauty, the musicality and movement in the Arena production."[94]

The musical produced, for many, a sense of uplift and profound, emotional movement. David Richards illustrated his longing for such affect when he detailed his experience of the act 2 opener, "He Come Down This Morning":

> Normally, I consider my privacy in a playhouse inviolate, and take fierce umbrage at any performer who insists on sitting in my lap, kissing me, accusing me of war crimes, or any of the thousand and one participatory acts the theater seems bent on cooking up these days. But at Arena, I wanted to shake the hands of all the performers who passed my way. And I wasn't the least bit self-conscious about returning the smile.[95]

The audience regularly gave the Arena production standing ovations, which were rare at the time. Leonard Probst of NBC Radio pronounced, "*Raisin* succeeds in raisin' your spirits."[96] Moreover, for some critics, the musicalization provided additional emotional colors that felt more authentic than the original play: *New Haven Register* critic Allen Lewis remarked, "The Musical version masks the weaknesses, highlights the strengths and transforms a grim realistic drama into a multi-dimensional deeply moving theatrical experience."[97] Underscoring *Raisin*'s difference from radical theatre of the Black Arts Movement, Perseghin claimed, "Where other shows have made a point of getting across the black experience by depressing, 'Raisin' exhilarates by serving up the spirit of the American negro. And in the spirit, there seems to be more truth."[98]

Critics' attention to the musical's optimism suggests that D.C. audiences needed cultural productions to provoke happy feelings. In the Broadway souvenir program, Nemiroff shared "A Personal Note from the Producer": "We sense somehow that what the audience is applauding is not a show, not us, not even Lorraine, but in a sense themselves; the best part of themselves as they would like to be, as they would wish *America* to be. And that—in this particular hour, this age of Watergate when so many find it so difficult to believe in anything any longer—is no small thing."[99] *Raisin* should make spectators not only feel good but feel good about themselves.

Part of the pleasure came from viewing what many critics considered nonstereotypical blackness. Critic Emory Lewis remarked, "Here are no Porgys or Besses rolling their eyes in green pastures, but honestly etched black people."[100] With her closed eyes, rocking back and forth in her chair, Virginia Capers created a serious portrayal of the matriarch Lena, offering a contrast to the mammy stereotype often seen in popular depictions of black motherhood.[101] Her performance earned the best actress in a musical Tony Award. According to critic Richard Lebherz, "There was something brutal and unpleasant about Claudia McNeil's Mama in the original production, but Virginia Caper's Mama has all the warmth, confusion and beauty that she was meant to have."[102] By adding "that she was meant to have," he became an arbiter of what constitutes acceptable black womanhood, and he collapsed the play character and the musical character, although the latter wielded significantly less power. Charles Farrow of the *Washington Afro-American* acknowledged type as opposed to stereotype when he complimented Capers: "When they talk about the classic, strong black woman, they are probably talking about the 'Mama' Lena Younger as played by the brilliant actress Virginia Capers. By her forceful stage wisdom and voice, she has moments of incandescent beauty, and insight."[103]

Critical discussions about racializing the score also reveal deep fissures in interpretations of black authenticity. Perhaps because he wrote for a black newspaper, Farrow was one of few critics to note the race of white composer Woldin and lyricist Brittan before stating that they "have created [a] fairly representative 'soul' quality."[104] Gerard A. Perseghin applauded the "Afro-influence music," particularly the jazz and scat singing of "Booze," the gospel number "He Come Down This Morning," and "Man Say," which showed "the influence of the delicate West Indian Islands ballads."[105] Reviewing the national tour, Robert P. Laurence praised the "African Dance," "He Come Down This Morning," and "Measure the Valleys" for being "based directly on the black musical experience," in contrast to the weaker and implicitly whiter "Broadwayish" songs.[106] Critic Richard Philip of the entertainment magazine *After Dark* critiqued "Not Anymore" as a watered-down parody and

how "Broadway's black musicals—as if to appease its upwardly mo-
bile middle-class whites . . . seem to have an obligatory feeling, a sort
of misplaced sense of duty, to include a smattering of minstrelsy."[107]

A few other critics asserted that the music was not black at all.
In *Black Stage*, Judith L. Howell wrote with disappointment, "They
needed Curtis Mayfield, or Marvin Gaye or Jerry Butler, (he's right
there in Chicago; he'll tell you 'bout Southside songs)."[108] Her diction
hails an empathetic insider African American audience and confronts
the white construction of black music. She added, "Leave it to white
folks to write a poor score and then go out and get some baad [*sic*] musicians to try and salvage it," at which point she named Joyce Brown,
the black musical director, and the many black musicians who "really
gigged and try to funk it up as best they could."[109] Howell located authentic black music in black artists. R. H. Gardner of the *Baltimore Sun*
similarly disparaged the score: "[It] is far from being a jazz score. Nor,
despite one number performed in a church, is it gospel, soul or any of
the other idioms associated with the black experience. Indeed, the only
'ethnic' influence apparent in the music—and the same goes for Mr.
Brittan's lyrics and Donald McKayle's choreography—is Broadway."[110]
He deemed *Raisin* "the whitest black production since the beginning
of the black revolution."[111] By "white," he likely meant comfortable, apparently unmarked Tin Pan Alley music as opposed to provocative,
raced, soulful, and improvised. He viewed music in black and white
terms, though Broadway is grounded in black culture. The musical's
"white" aesthetic made him skeptical of the work itself and the audience's standing ovation, which he thought might represent either
"genuine enthusiasm" or "guilt-feelings."[112] He added that he saw only
two other productions at Arena Stage that received standing ovations:
The Great White Hope and *No Place to Be Somebody*. By noting the common theme of blackness between these plays and suggesting that they
earned praise due to "guilt-feelings," Gardner implied that white liberals applauded themselves and *Raisin* for political self-identification
reasons rather than aesthetic ones, as if these can be easily separated.
AP drama critic William Glover replicated this distinction between inauthentic, blacked-up entertainment versus authentic political theatre
with bite: "'Raisin' hasn't quite decided whether to settle into a kind
of blackface period complacency or strive to sustain the satiric bril-
liance of its 'Not Anymore' number."[113] The opposing pictures painted

by these reviews suggest that the musical had to cater to different audiences who had different ways of measuring blackness.

DIVERSIFYING ARENA'S AUDIENCES

The effort to draw black spectators yet hold on to white subscribers formed part of Arena's mission. For instance, for the opening night of the production, Arena invited members of the Congressional Black Caucus. At the same time, Tom Basham remarked in his review: "It is a tribute to the skill of the entire company that this story of a black Chicago family has pulling power for a mostly white audience."[114] Basham implied that white spectators rarely attend black drama and thus given that *Raisin* drew a white audience, the musical had broader appeal. Arena's stage manager reports occasionally noted the presence of black spectators, as if this were an unusual occurrence. The stage manager report for June 10, 1973, said that the house was "only about half full, and half of that black. A good show with very good response from the house, which particularly appreciated the black idiom."[115] On July 21, there was allegedly a "very good audience—lot of Blacks in the audience," while the next day the "audience was all white (mostly) and dull."[116] These reports racialize spectators and their reactions, noting that black audiences were "good," likely meaning enthusiastically responsive, in contrast to quieter white audiences. The results of an Arena audience survey from 1978 do not have racial demographic information, but they do reveal patrons' education levels. The survey noted that 74.5 percent of the audience had more than four years of college, and they were most frequently professional or government workers.[117] Although patronage was still almost entirely white, Washington had developed a large black bourgeoisie, and "by 1970, government employed 57 percent of college-educated black males and 76 percent of college-educated black females."[118] At this time, 71 percent of Washington residents identified as black. At a meeting with other regional theatre leaders in 1974, Zelda Fichandler alleged that 75 percent of the audience for *Raisin* was black.[119] This is surely an exaggeration, but Fichandler's account intimates that the racial mix of the audience for *Raisin* was unusually black for Arena in the 1970s.

The specific clime of DC likely made locals receptive to *Raisin*. Richard L. Coe, the foremost critic because of his position at the *Wash-*

ington Post, praised the musical: "There is an inevitability, a rightness, in the union of this musical and this theater."[120] Although he was referring to the arena space matching the musical, and imagining that the staging would be lost in a Broadway proscenium theatre, he may also have been alluding to the "rightness" of the racial dynamics of Washington. The musical received a warm welcome in New York, where Mayor John Lindsay and *Amsterdam News* editor and publisher Clarence B. Jones cohosted the opening night party. But while *Raisin* was commercially successful at Arena, the musical "grossed under 60% of dollar capacity" during its first year on Broadway.[121] Nemiroff asked the Fichandlers to reduce their 1 percent stake in the profits to 0.75 percent because of poor box office performance due to "resistance" from the city's "white theater-going audience."[122] Dominant narratives of 1970s New York City conflated black shows and patrons with urban decay, as some whites felt afraid to visit Times Square.[123] Zelda Fichandler expressed surprise at the New York response, "since the Washington audience responded so freely and fully to a play that is, is it not?, so universal in its appeal."[124] Yet even after Nemiroff took the musical to 3.5 million people across forty-two cities, he did not recoup the initial investment.

Although *Raisin* ultimately did not turn an economic profit in its commercial runs, it furthered racial integration.[125] For example, when the production played in Los Angeles, it held a benefit performance for the San Fernando Valley Fair Housing Council at which Mayor Tom Bradley proclaimed the event "*Raisin* Day." In his letter to the investors, Nemiroff underscored the production's accomplishments rather than financial losses: "It was part of the theatrical revolution of the '70's— indeed a forerunner that helped to change audience patterns and to bring out new audiences, on Broadway and across the nation."[126]

The press strategy for the tour had advised bifurcated marketing for a general, implicitly white audience as well as a black audience, once again replicating the universal versus specific dynamic that haunted the play and the musical. According to the press materials, the tour should be sold "as a *general entertainment*—a night of fantastic excitement, fun, joy, laughter, and pride for all. And *also* sold—in the Black media and community—for its specific Black qualities."[127] Because of the conviction that black patronage would enhance the communal, emotional responses to the production, the producer literally underlined the importance of black attendance, perhaps having learned from experiences at Arena Stage: "It is important that there be a sizable Black attendance on opening night. This will add an especially appreciative and quite vocal spirit to the occasion—which in turn will help to free the rest of the audience and leave no doubt in the critics' minds as to RAISIN's appeal both to its own first constituency and to the general public."[128] In these comments, black spectators make up the "first constituency" and their emotional, vocal expressiveness would authenticate the production and model appropriate responses for "the general public," which was presumably more reserved white spectators.

CONCLUSION

Raisin followed *The Great White Hope* in transferring to Broadway and in dramatizing African American struggles in ways accessible to white and black audiences. As an unprecedented hit in Arena Stage's twenty-three-year history, *Raisin* signaled the appeal of black musicals with liberal politics. Amid other cultural productions that seemed either too light or too radical, and amid racial, economic, and political upheaval, the production distinguished itself by using the musical form to convey both a serious message and sense of optimism. Its genesis also provoked questions about what constituted authentic blackness.

After *Raisin*, Arena did not produce black musicals for another decade. Personal notes in the early 1970s reveal that Zelda Fichandler had wanted to bring more black narratives to the stage. She created a list of possibilities: "*Les Blancs*, repeat *No Place to Be Somebody*, Ed Bullins, and Glenda Dickerson's stuff."[129] According to meeting minutes in 1977, Thomas Fichandler also wanted to produce black plays: "The theater is continually on the lookout for good black plays but there just aren't many to be found."[130] He made an explicit value judgment about the constitution of Black/black theatre and perceived quality. Arena had focused on international blackness from the 1970s through the 1980s with a few productions by African Americans. During this same period, Ford's Theatre took the lead with black musicals by producing works conceived by Vinnette Carrol in the 1970s, *Black Nativity* by Langston Hughes, the world premiere of *The Amen Corner* based on James Baldwin's novel, and even a revival of a black version of Gilbert and Sullivan's Orientalist operetta titled *The Hot Mikado*.

Starting in the 1980s, when Zelda Fichandler began a dedicated effort to develop African American–centered works, black musicals became an increasingly important part of Arena Stage. She brought in the black vaudeville show *One Mo' Time*, Lee Breuer's *The Gospel at Colonus*, the '60s revue *Beehive*, Sandra Reaves-Phillips's one-woman show *The Late Great Ladies of Blues and Jazz*, and the gospel retelling of Job's narrative *Abyssinia*. Under Doug Wager's artistic leadership in the 1990s, Arena presented the revue *It Ain't Nothin' but the Blues* courtesy of the Denver Center Theatre Company. But it was under Molly Smith, Arena's third artistic director, that black musicals became a core part of the theatre's identity and income, a subject further explored in the following chapter.

The theatre's initial venture with *Raisin* also laid the groundwork for future major productions like the Duke Ellington revue *Sophisticated Ladies* in 2010. The production starred Maurice Hines, who had previously been in Arena's 1999 multiracial version of *Guys and Dolls*, and featured local talent including the Manzari brothers, teenaged tap-dancing African Americans. In addition to emphasizing the black music and performers, the marketing capitalized on the black space of U Street and its special connection to Ellington's career. While the company's home in Southwest DC was under renovation from 2007 through 2010, Arena produced and presented works at the historic Lincoln Theatre on U Street. This area was once known as Black Broadway, where Ellington had launched his career. Wearing elaborate hats and furs, many black patrons treated the *Sophisticated Ladies* production as a red-carpet event. Arena's investment in black capital paid off because *Sophisticated Ladies* broke box office records and attracted substantial black audiences. In the fall of 2010, Arena Stage reopened its glistening complex back on 6th Street and Maine Avenue with a multiracial production of *Oklahoma!*, which surpassed the sales for *Sophisticated Ladies*. Racial diversity, musicals, and American narratives had established a blueprint for the company's success.

(PART THREE)
Nation

CHAPTER FIVE

ARTICULATING AMERICAN VOICES

o inaugurate its fortieth anniversary season in 1990, Arena Stage produced *The Caucasian Chalk Circle*, a play that the company had first staged in 1961 to open its permanent building. Much had changed in the intervening years, including new support for multiculturalism from foundations, corporations, and governmental agencies that facilitated this production of Brecht's play, which complicated "Caucasian" with a multiracial cast led by Tazewell Thompson, an African American artistic associate. Arena's eighteen-member acting company boasted six black actors including Gail Grate, who starred as Grusha in *The Caucasian Chalk Circle* as well as Eliza Doolittle in *Pygmalion* that season.[1] The theatre demonstrated that it would persist in producing Western classics but with people of color in lead roles as representative of an increasingly diverse United States.

When Zelda Fichandler stepped down at the end of the 1990–91 season, this vision of national inclusivity did not end. Doug Wager, who had worked at Arena since the 1970s, took up the artistic reins. This transition entailed both change and continuity in leadership, programming, and branding, as Wager staged more works centered on U.S. American theatre. Increased economic pressures plagued Wager's tenure, and his eclectic repertory created a blurry institutional image, factors that contributed to the appointment of Molly Smith as the new artistic director in 1998. Building on Wager's and Fichandler's cultural diversity policies, but definitively rejecting the internationalism of Fichandler's leadership, Smith rebranded the company as a center for American voices. In particular, she capitalized on black musicals.

This chapter examines the ways in which Arena's approach to representing "Americanness" and racial politics have shifted since the 1990s.

It explores how the period of Wager's and Smith's artistic directorships was marked by struggles over who counts as American, struggles produced by contentious discourses over multiculturalism and greater competition over fewer resources. Key productions—including *Before It Hits Home*, by Cheryl West; *A Community Carol*, by Bill Rauch, Alison Carey, Laurence Maslon, Ed Jones, and the Anacostia community; *House Arrest: First Edition*, by Anna Deavere Smith; and *Crowns*, by Regina Taylor—illustrate the theatre's dedication to black American stories as well as the tensions in that mission. Furthermore, interviews, letters, grant narratives, marketing strategy booklets, and meeting minutes show how Arena navigated changing conceptions of the U.S. and its own institutional identity, especially who comprises its rightful audience. Arena's performances of U.S. American identity are indelibly grounded in racial politics and aspirations for equality. But the theatre, much like the nation, also has limits. Its conception of Americanness concentrates on white men and principally includes black artists and audiences on the condition of their participation in a liberal humanist project. In addition, my experience as Arena's dramaturgy intern in 2009 informs my analysis of how Arena rebranded itself explicitly as "Where American Theater Lives" during President Barack Obama's first term in office.[2] On the one hand, these aesthetic and political shifts signified the racial parity that the theatre espouses and on the other, they pointed to a neoliberal multiculturalism in which circumscribed staged diversity provides visibility for Americans of color but also has the potential to obscure continuing structural material inequality.

BACKDROP TO STAGING U.S. DRAMA

While Arena Stage has often taken for granted an unchanging understanding of what "American" means vis-à-vis diversity and democracy, in fact nations and national identity have to be invented, reworked, and performed. Imprecise and in-process, the nation is what Benedict Anderson famously calls an "imagined community" that forms and legitimizes the bounded, sovereign space through shared, circulated media.[3] Nations come into being because people believe that they belong to them. Even with rapid globalization, recent years have seen reinvigorated nationalism largely on the bases of racial dominance and alleged racial purity. In *Theatre, Society, and Nation* S. E. Wilmer writes, "Notions of national identity are constantly being reformulated, revised, and reasserted in an ongoing battle to assert and maintain a hegemonic notion of the nation. Likewise, subaltern groups have confronted the homogeneous image represented by the dominant group in asserting a more pluralistic or counter-hegemonic identity."[4] His invocation of hegemonic discourse is crucial to understanding the nation as a struggle over the narrative that unites a people, and who has the power to tell this story. Theorizing national identity entails not pinpointing a single, stable meaning but addressing competing claims for communal definition and inclusion. Connecting nation to theatre, Jeffrey D. Mason writes in the introduction to the edited collection *Performing America: Cultural Nationalism in American Theater* that the stage "becomes a site of this struggle, a platform where players and audience may enact conceptions of identity and community, where 'America' becomes both the subject and the consequence of artistic, cultural, and social negotiation."[5] The stage enacts identity, policy, and nation, and the stakes increase when a theatre like Arena Stage markets itself on the basis of national identity and when it resides in the nation's capital.

For Arena, articulating Americanness involves the inclusion of racialized voices but on certain terms; some are amplified, while others are muted. In *Who Sings the Nation-State?* Judith Butler analyzes undocumented Latinx people singing the U.S. national anthem in Spanish as a performative act that enunciated a new, heterogeneous collective belonging.[6] Although the performance extended Americanness beyond racialized and national borders, it occurred on the basis of a patriotic song. American Studies scholar Nikhil Pal Singh argues that "the prevailing common sense of the post–civil rights era is that race is the provenance of an unjust, irrational ascription and prejudice, while nation is the necessary horizon of our hopes for color-blind justice, equality, and fair play."[7] This understanding suggests that the problem is race, not racism, and subtly positions whiteness as beyond race. By acting as if race no longer matters, when in reality U.S. Americans continue to see race and systemically treat people of color worse than they do white people, the hegemonic postrace racial project creates plausible deniability and maintains the unequal status quo. This logic also ignores how white supremacy provides a disturbingly rational system designed to preserve white privilege. Moreover, those who identify as American patriots often overlook that the United States rests on a history of racialized dispossession, genocide, and enslavement that made liberty possible for only certain people.[8]

Arena has wrestled with defining those under the American flag. Playbills from productions in the early 2000s included the following credo by Molly Smith: "Arena Stage has a special focus on VOICES OF THE AMERICAS. I believe these voices are unique to our part of the world and deserve a place to sing from."[9] Although Arena has produced only one play by a Canadian writer and several by Caribbean artists, it has never produced works from the rest of "the Americas"—Mexico, Central America, or South America—on its stages. Even as Arena mobilizes the diversity of Americanness in imagining its mission, repertory, and community, the company's artistic leaders draw borders around who may be part of this representation and under what material conditions.

Performing American inclusion at Arena dates back to Zelda Fichandler's original vision for the company and persists through the present day. The theatre's staff members and recent promotional materials call attention to Arena's beginnings in 1950 as the first professional, resident theatre in Washington to welcome a racially mixed audience. Arena employees also emphasized that the company's in-the-round performance space has always been a democratic one. The seating arrangement cultivates a sense of community as spectators process the performance together. Edgar Dobie, the current executive director of the theatre, averred that the ideas of "everyone being welcome" and experiencing theatre communally are "embedded in the architecture and the actual name of [Arena Stage]."[10] Laurence Maslon, the literary manager under Fichandler in the 1980s and later associate artist to Wager in the 1990s, remarked, "For Zelda, the Arena was, first and forever, an arena: a forum where conflicting ideas could be battled out until the last righteous man or woman remained standing."[11] These arguments link Arena with American ideals of liberal democracy, multiracial inclusion, and equality.

As I have already noted, U.S. American playwrights found a home at this regional theatre, including Elmer Rice, Tennessee Williams, and Arthur Miller. *The Great White Hope* and *Raisin* marked Arena's early commitment to producing new works by American dramatists who engaged explicitly with black-white racial dynamics. Fichandler's innovation with a racially integrated acting ensemble lent new meanings to Western classics and grounded U.S. performance in racial diversity. Arena's 1973 tour of *Our Town* and *Inherit the Wind* behind the Iron Curtain solidified Arena's reputation as a representative of the U.S. state.

When Doug Wager arrived at Arena Stage in 1973, he brought an interest in comedies, European classics, new American work, and progressive politics. He both fit Fichandler's aesthetic and complemented it. He had earned his MFA in directing from Boston University, where he had studied with Fichandler, and he had assisted Alan Schneider, whose productions of Edward Albee, Harold Pinter, and Samuel Beckett's dramas he greatly admired. Wager's work with Schneider led him to intern at Arena: "I went there to stay for ten weeks, and I stayed for twenty-five years."[12] He worked on the running crew, stage managed, read scripts, and directed new works for the series called "In the Process." When the director dropped out of *Gemini* by Albert Innaurato during the 1977–78 season, Wager was invited to direct his first mainstage production. He became the theatre's first literary manager, and he was promoted to associate director. During the 1980s, Wager directed several comedies by George S. Kaufman as well as musicals including *Candide*, *On the Town*, and *Merrily We Roll Along*. By staging popular plays and musicals, Wager brought more levity to the Arena season. He also directed classics such as *Measure for Measure* and *The Taming of the Shrew*. Long before he became artistic director in 1991, Wager had shaped and strengthened Arena Stage's aesthetic for many years. Despite the smooth leadership transition, he would have to negotiate new and intensified difficulties with the budget and the demands of multiculturalism.

MANAGING THE ECONOMICS OF CULTURAL DIVERSITY

From the start of his tenure as artistic director, Wager signaled that he would continue Fichandler's aesthetic and cultural diversity policies. In a letter to subscribers, he described Arena as his home for years and "yours" too, evoking a sense of communal ownership.[13] He added, "I intend to build on our legacy of artistic excellence, providing a rich mix of classics, new works, musicals and culturally diverse offerings."[14]

In addition to producing an eclectic repertory with new work by play-wrights of color, Wager continued the Allen Lee Hughes Fellowship program, which offered season-long training and salaries to budding theatre artists and administrators of color, many of whom have become established dramaturgs and university professors.[15] Wager also tried to sustain Fichandler's multiracial acting ensemble.

Although Wager extended the path formed by Fichandler, the terrain of multiculturalism was uneven and unexplored, and the federal financial climate was increasingly inhospitable to the arts. By the early 1990s, multiculturalism had become a highly contested term and policy, especially in the context of literature taught in universities. The political right bemoaned attacks on the white, male, middle-class, Western canon; attempted to separate arts from politics; and implied that artistic works by women, U.S. people of color, and authors from outside of the U.S. and Europe were of inferior aesthetic quality. The left critiqued the canon for its social reproduction of power and called for new approaches that attended to material inequalities and differences. Finally, the center positioned itself as neutral and advised reforming the canon through the inclusion of some minoritized people whose artistic productions represented ostensible differences but ultimately confirmed shared humanistic and aesthetic values.[16] These arguments played out in the theatre as well, including the *Miss Saigon* protests, the Robert Brustein–August Wilson debate, and other controversies across the nation.[17]

Conflicts over which theatremakers and theatergoers should be funded were part of this larger debate on multiculturalism. During George H. W. Bush's presidency, funders became more averse to supporting art that shocked bourgeois and straight sensibilities. In 1990, John Frohnmayer, head of the NEA, vetoed grants that had been awarded to performance artists Karen Finley, Tim Miller, John Fleck, and Holly Hughes, who became known as the NEA Four. From then on, the NEA no longer distributed grants to individual artists, and the grants included a decency clause. Although most Americans supported at least some federal subsidy for the arts, right-wing politicians and pundits steered the conversation toward protesting that taxpayers' money should not be given to queer, feminist, and purportedly objectionable art.[18] Newt Gingrich and the Republican Revolution of 1994 further decimated the NEA's budget.

Challenges to multiculturalism and to the NEA influenced Arena Stage's artistic programs and financing. Because it is located in Washington, the theatre can draw on governmental support at the federal and city levels, not state. In 1990, Fichandler called for support of the arts in her testimony before the congressional subcommittee on interior appropriations. Arena had recently received a $1 million three-to-one NEA challenge grant, the largest in its history, for its cultural diversity initiatives. That one-time grant covered four years, but it did not appear that other foundations would sustain those initiatives thereafter. The theatre had to make some drastic choices about its priorities. When Wager became artistic director, his first action was to furlough the entire staff for two weeks to balance the budget. This extreme measure became an annual practice during his tenure. Although Arena had an endowment of approximately $6 million, it still reeled from deficits of $450,000 two years in a row in the late 1980s. In 1991, the annual budget was $10 million, and at the financial low point of Wager's directorship, it was $8 million. According to Wager, "We had to compromise our commitments to people in ways that would somehow try to preserve the ethos and the emotional integrity of what we committed to doing without being able to back it up financially."[19] As a result, Arena collaborated with more partners. To associate its corporate branding with cultural diversity, AT&T sponsored productions written and performed by black artists. Arena sought out more coproductions with regional theatres to share costs. The company scaled back on its season and by the end of Wager's tenure, Arena was putting on eight mainstage plays as opposed to the usual nine.

The acting company also suffered because of budget shortages. In 1984, Arena had won a four-year ongoing ensembles grant from the NEA to support twenty salaried actors for entire seasons. By 1992, Arena's resident acting ensemble downsized to eighteen company actors, ten of whom were on full-season contracts. Over time, the theatre could offer only part-season contracts and just a few years later, the acting company no longer existed. Offering full-season contracts and producing large-scale plays were expensive endeavors. According to Wager, the fundraising efforts shifted toward cultural diversity beyond the ongoing ensemble.[20] Moreover, because productions in the Arena and Kreeger spaces overlapped with one another, it was difficult to schedule seasons that used the actors efficiently. Wager attempted to align actors with new play workshops and readings when they were not on the mainstage, but the new play program lacked a predictable timetable. Maslon reflected, "We had a resident ensemble that was skewed older, and they were never terribly psyched about doing new plays."[21] According to Kyle Donnelly, who served as associate artistic director from 1992 to 1998, "Part of the problem I think is that the company hadn't had new blood or been shaken up in a while."[22] Still, Arena's decades-old acting ensemble had distinguished this regional theatre as special. Guy Bergquist, who worked at Arena from 1982 to 2010, fondly recalled how resident actors like "the [Bob] Proskys, the [Richard] Bauers, the Halo Wines, made a living there, and there was a time . . . we had, the children of, let's say four company members working backstage on the show . . . and that just brings you know tears to my eyes, because that's what the resident theatre was about."[23] Indeed, aside from the Oregon Shakespeare Festival's ongoing, large, multiracial acting company, most regional theatres' permanent ensembles have declined or disappeared, from the American Conservatory Theater to the Denver Center Theatre Company.[24]

Wager remained committed to a center-left version of multiculturalism as a strategy to try to hold onto older white subscribers, welcome younger audiences of color, and adhere to cultural diversity grant guidelines. To Wager, cultural diversity was "a resourceful investment in the growth of Arena's artistic mission. Growth, not retrenchment, is critical to our desire to invigorate, deepen and clarify our sense of purpose, especially in light of the current economy and the challenge of creating a new theater for a new America in our nation's capital in the nineties."[25] He believed that multicultural artists would create multicultural stories that would attract multicultural patrons. Using the logic of the 1990s multicultural marketplace, Wager articulated a teleology of racial progress and capitalist economic growth, which Arena needed to welcome for the institution to survive.

CHANGE AND CONTINUITY IN REPERTORY, MARKETING, AND AUDIENCES

The 1991–92 season, Wager's first as artistic director, largely maintained Fichandler's aesthetic, although the slots for Eastern European and Russian plays were filled by new black plays in a reinforced commitment to multiculturalism. In the playbill for *Trinidad Sisters* (1992), Mustapha Matura's Caribbean adaptation of Chekhov's *Three Sisters*, Wager pontificated, "Multiculturalism has, in a sense, become a euphemism for the new America, and yet has America ever truly been anything other than multicultural?"[26] He located diversity as fundamental to the United States. At the same time, he positioned the varying definitions of multiculturalism as "an issue of perception" and wrote, "I willingly accept the role of navigator," identifying multiculturalism as a liberal philosophy that one may choose, interpret, and navigate as a free-willed subject rather than as a structural policy that organizes people and distributes resources.[27] In the company's "Long Range Plan," Wager commented that "eclecticism can be an approach to programmatically achieving the thematic diversification of our mission," subsuming racial diversity as another kind of difference within a generalized eclecticism.[28] In addition to *Trinidad Sisters*, his first season featured *The Time of Your Life*, by William Saroyan; *Yerma*, by Federico García Lorca; *A Wonderful Life*, based on the Frank Capra film with book and lyrics by Sheldon Harnick and music by Joe Raposo; *Jar the Floor*, by Cheryl West; *The School for Wives*, by Molière; *The Father* with *The Stronger*, by August Strindberg; *Mrs. Klein*, by Nicholas Wright; and *The Visit*, by Friedrich Dürrenmatt. This season represented what Wager typically produced during the rest of his tenure: one musical, two black plays, one classic American play, three or four European classics, and one or two new American plays; and of those plays, at least one would be a comedy.

These categories to which I assigned plays crudely distinguish "black" from "American," the latter tacitly denoting "white," but demarcating race, artists, and plays is not that simple. Does a black character make *The Time of Your Life* a black play? Does casting company member Franchelle Dorn, a black actress, as the lead make *The Visit* a black production? The 1994–95 dramaturgy fellow Faedra Chatard Carpenter remarked, "I do think there was a reason why I, [as] the young black dramaturg, was assigned Derek Walcott's *The Odyssey*, because the other play that I got assigned while I was there was Cheryl West's *Holiday Heart*, so another piece written by a Black playwright. But here is the wrench thrown in: I also dramaturged *Long Day's Journey into Night*."[29] Integration happened at the casting level as well as the production team level. Moreover, any play that is in any way off-white, meaning nonwhite Anglo, able-bodied, middle-class, straight, cis-male, is frequently counted as cultural diversity. By this model of multiculturalism, certain artists and stories of color are included if they signify visible difference yet adhere to a preexisting genre rubric rather than calling that rubric into question. For example, because *Yerma* was written by a Spanish playwright and directed by Tazewell Thompson, the play functioned as cultural difference but also as comfortable European contemporary classic.

As a newly appointed artistic associate, Thompson was also responsible for bringing attention to emerging playwrights of color, and he discovered Cheryl West. Before becoming a playwright, she had studied U.S. sociocultural politics and worked as an HIV counselor. In *Before It Hits Home* (1991), she dramatizes the struggles of a bisexual black man with HIV/AIDS and a bourgeois family that largely rejects him. She had difficulty getting the play produced:

> I heard disparaging comments such as, "Our subscribers would be offended by the language"; "We have already done our black play and we don't want to exhaust our black audience." There were even threats of boycotts, outrage that I must be a white woman, because no responsible black woman could have written such a lie—after all, blacks don't get AIDS.[30]

West's reflections diagnose the bourgeois ethos of regional theatre, the custom of holding one "black play slot," and the disavowal of the existence of queer black folks. Writing about West's work, director-producer Gwynn MacDonald links black silence about HIV/AIDS to respectability politics, developed to cope with a classist society and a racist-sexist history of oversexualized images of black people.[31] In this context, audiences sometimes expressed their disapproval of Wendal's romantic relationship with another man by grumbling, hissing, and even yelling.[32] But the professional premiere by Arena Stage also received tremendously positive reviews. Jacqueline Trescott of the *Washington Post* compared the domestic drama to "the social realism of Lorraine Hansberry, Charles Gordone and August Wilson," placing West alongside other African American playwrights whose works Arena had produced.[33] West earned more symbolic capital when *Before It Hits Home* won the Susan Blackburn Prize, the first time a black playwright had ever won this award for women. Wager subsequently produced West's *Jar the Floor* (1991), which deals with four generations of black women and domestic abuse, and her *Holiday Heart* (1995), which explores the coming-of-age of a black girl raised by a drug-addicted mother and a drag queen.

West's rise to prominence exemplified a growing trend in major regional theatres producing new plays by African American artists. The total number of plays written by African American women and produced in regional theatres totaled three in 1989, fifteen per year from 1990 to 1993, and then twenty-five per year from 1993 to 1998. Between 1992 and 2003, the most frequently produced black women playwrights were Cheryl West, Pearl Cleage, Suzan-Lori Parks, Endesha Holland, and Anna Deavere Smith.[34] All five of these black women received productions at Arena Stage in the early 1990s and thereafter. Reflecting on her history with Arena, West praised Fichandler and Thompson, described Arena as a "home" for her work, and emphasized that the theatre took artistic risks in its programming.[35]

Black plays like those by West drew new audiences. When the theatre had conducted demographic research in 1985, it determined that 93 percent of its audience was white.[36] In 1992, the audience was 88 percent white, 7 percent black, 1 percent Latinx, 1 percent Asian, and 3 percent other.[37] Minutes from a marketing meeting circa 1992 indicated that "funders are looking to Arena to achieve an audience comprised of at least 5% people of color," which seems like a low bar that Arena cleared easily, and implies that other regional theatre were lagging even further behind.[38] Research also showed that the company's white patrons were on average much older than black patrons, suggesting that the former were longtime subscribers, while the latter were newer to the theatre.[39] Out of all the tickets purchased by black patrons in the 1991–92 season, half of them were for *Jar the Floor*, and one-fifth of them were for *Trinidad Sisters*.[40] Black patrons tended to be single-ticket buyers rather than full-season subscribers.[41] These data indicate that black consumers were more interested in specific plays written by and about black people than in plays such as *Yerma*, which made up only 5 percent of the black audience ticket sales.[42]

These trends are also the result of marketing directives. While implicitly white stage productions were marketed widely, black plays were marketed to specific minoritized groups, reinforcing the idea that the former were universal, whereas the latter were special interest-oriented. For example, the 1995–96 Communications Plan identified the target audiences for the Leonard Bernstein operetta *Candide* as "Active Theater Goers, Traditionalist, Pop, Family, Student, Tour and Adult Groups. Previous musical, and comedy buyers to Arena. Musical buyers from other arts organizations."[43] Because the marketing team viewed *Candide* as not racialized, they advertised in major newspapers such as the *Washington Post*. Meanwhile, the imagined audiences for *Holiday Heart* were "Pop, Experimental, African American, Group, some crossover with Active Theater Goers. Previous ticket buyers for Cheryl [West]'s plays at Arena."[44] The committee aired concerns about how to market this play because its "plot twists and character of the drag queen are difficult to talk about. Tends to put people off."[45] Consequently, the communications team planned to spend most of its advertising resources on black radio stations and to reach out to black churches, drug rehabilitation groups, and LGBTQ organizations. By producing West's works, Arena fulfilled missions of staging African Americans, diversifying audiences, and connecting with local social justice organizations yet made only a half-hearted attempt to bring this kind of work to the public as a whole.

While Arena's dedication to new black plays appealed to growing black audiences, the theatre lost some of its longtime subscribers, and some of the blame went to the company's investment in blackness. At the end of Wager's first season as artistic director, Arena convened focus groups consisting of white lapsed subscribers. This research was prompted by a "predicted $250,000 shortfall in subscriptions income due to [a] decrease in renewal rate" for the 1992–93 season.[46] Although black works comprised only one-quarter of season programming, 70 percent of nonrenewers expressed concern that "Arena is becoming an African American theater."[47] Arena staff collected letters from former subscribers, circulated them among themselves, and put sticky notes on them with remarks such as, "Did we just lose another racist?"[48] Some letter writers avowed that they were not racist because they enjoyed new plays by African Americans, but they found mixed-race casting in classics to be "disconcerting,"[49] "distracting,"[50] and "contrived."[51] Multiracial casts "interfered with the integrity of many of the plays."[52] In their reasoning, these former subscribers often asserted that Arena would not put white actors into *Fences* or *A Raisin in the Sun*. They made false equivalencies between blackface minstrelsy and casting people of color in implicitly white classics. In an attempt to frame the issue as one of quality, many of them critiqued black artists as less skillful than white ones. Others wanted to separate art from social justice: "Arena may not consider itself a professional theater company but rather a community activist organization which produces plays."[53] Moreover, they resented what appeared to be a prioritizing of black patrons over white patrons, who were positioned as the real and loyal audience: "What is driving this perceived need for increased cultural diversity? If, as one of your personnel indicated to me on the phone, it stems from a desire to meet the 'culturally diverse' needs of the community, then I can only say, based on our years of observation, that this cultural diversity *is not now, nor has it ever been*, reflected in the Arena Stage audience."[54] Another threatened, "Beware that you do not alienate your longest, strongest, and most loyal supporters who will leave Arena and Kreeger in protest over your shoving your latter-day liberalism down their throats."[55] Others were more explicit in their allegiance to white supremacy, such as one patron who returned the 1992–93 subscription brochure and wrote on it, "You must be kidding! Looking through this brochure was such a *sickening* experience—hardly a white person anywhere. No wonder everyone we know has stopped going to Arena."[56] The former subscribers said that they were emphatically not affected by the change in leadership from Fichandler to Wager.[57] Wager was continuing the artistic and political policies of his predecessor, and older white subscribers became aggravated when they discovered that multiculturalism at Arena Stage was to be an institutionalized effort rather than a passing fad.

NEW VOICES FOR A NEW AMERICA

Wager called his chief cultural diversity initiative New Voices for a New America. Although he had acknowledged the long historical presence of people of color in the United States in his musings on multiculturalism, he also wrote in 1992, "A new America is forming on the horizon. It is incumbent upon Arena Stage to recognize that, as Americans, we are citizens of a growing, diverse, global community, and, as a theater, we strive to fulfill our destiny as visionary interpreters of the human experience."[58] Wager argued that Arena's artists and audiences as Americans-cum–world citizens had a responsibility to diversity, framed as global and grounded in humanism. In the context of 1990s Washington, African Americans gained greater representation rather than Asian Americans, Native Americans, or Latinxs.[59]

The centerpiece of New Voices for a New America was PlayQuest, launched in 1993. This program followed in the tradition of Arena's earlier new play development initiatives from the 1970s and '80s.[60] A program to commission, develop, and produce new plays largely by artists of color, PlayQuest was designed to produce works for the theatre's multiracial acting ensemble and increasingly diverse audiences. These new plays would theoretically move up from a barebones staging in the Old Vat Room to the mainstage. The program identified the reality that playwrights of color need dedicated support. Although the grant requests and promotional materials for PlayQuest emphasized the commissions of writers of color including Cheryl West, Silas Jones, Alonzo Lamont Jr., Mustapha Matura, and Carlyle Brown, these materials deemphasized the fact that the program also commissioned white playwrights to write new plays and translations of European classics. However, few of the Old Vat productions transferred to the mainstage, and few of the plays were published. This track record surpassed comparable companies, yet Laurence Maslon lamented, "We never really created what I wanted, which was a kind of battalion of writers out there who could write for our city and write for our company."[61]

As part of New Voices for a New America, Arena Stage collaborated with Cornerstone Theater on *A Community Carol* in 1993. Cofounded by Bill Rauch and Alison Carey, Cornerstone has worked with communities across the U.S. to create and stage performances, often adaptations of classics that resonate with contemporary, local issues. After Wager watched their production of *The Winter's Tale* on the National Mall in 1991, he reached out to Rauch and Carey. Theatre historian and dramaturg Sonja Kuftinec documented the Arena-Cornerstone collaboration adapting Charles Dickens's *A Christmas Carol* with the largely black and working-class Anacostia community in Southeast Washington. This community was and is physically close to Arena Stage but separated by multiple barriers including a river, unaffordable ticket prices, and the appearance of inaccessibility to an elite, white space. According to Kuftinec, Arena and Cornerstone hoped they would mutually benefit, as the former addressed its "concern with diversity," glossed as its desire for black audiences and stories, while the latter could "reach a larger audience" with a "more fully realized production."[62] The companies developed an advisory board and cast ten adults and ten children from the community.

But there were some tensions between Arena, Cornerstone, and the Anacostia participants. For example, Arena had expected the production to be the highest-grossing of the season and regretted the lost income from pay-what-you-can tickets offered to members of the Anacostia community. Kuftinec critiques Arena's liberal humanist approach that celebrated "artistic excellence" and disavowed politics, which manifested in some company members characterizing Cornerstone as amateurish and overly inclusive.[63] Maslon, who worked with Rauch, Carey, and short story writer Ed Jones on the text of *A Community Carol*, remarked that the production was "a little too much of a Christmas pudding. Every possible person, sexual preference and religion was on the stage."[64] But he also said that the experience was "the most gratifying thing I worked on in seven years."[65] Marvin McAllister, the dramaturgy fellow who worked closely with residents of Anacostia to try to incorporate their stories into the production, reflected that receiving an award from them as "Community Dramaturg" was one of his proudest moments.[66] Kuftinec observes that the collaboration ultimately changed little of Arena's hierarchical structure, profit motives, and audience base. But at least Wager was open to expanding Arena and conceptions of the United States to include greater racial and economic diversity. In the program for *A Community Carol*, he wrote, "I pray that all those politically correct buzzwords [i.e., "community" and "outreach"], so helpful to us in our recent past, are quickly rendered obsolete for the sake of our common future."[67] By inviting Arena's artists and audiences to imagine a new American community, Wager posited a utopia based on shared theatre that hurriedly gets over "politically correct buzzwords," without attending to the traction of material inequality. Perhaps because Arena's multicultural repertory had alienated some subscribers, Wager tried to use celebratory diversity-driven productions and meditations on those productions to ease frictions.

Arena's commissioning of Anna Deavere Smith underscores the theatre's desire for cultural productions that imagine multicultural harmony in ways that do not necessarily restructure power dynamics. After Arena had presented Smith's *Fires in the Mirror* in 1993, Wager approached the performance artist to create a new piece about the culture of Washington. By the mid-1990s, Smith had won a MacArthur "genius" grant and gained acclaim for *Fires in the Mirror* and *Twilight: Los Angeles, 1992*, which explored racial tensions in the Crown Heights and Rodney King riots, respectively. Her process involved interviewing an array of people related to her subject of study and then embodying their words, mannerisms, and movements. Performance theorist Xavier Lemoine celebrates how "Smith displaces fixed understandings of identity in her own characters, and potentially in the audience, by mobilizing a hybrid theatricality based on process, difference, and multiplicity."[68] This model of multiculturalism destabilizes identity and offers empathy with minoritized people. But this tactic also has limits. In *Enacting Others*, Cherise Smith problematizes how the performance artist frames the artwork as politically neutral and potentially reifies stereotypes when she plays races other than her own. She contends that Anna Deavere Smith "promulgates a discursive ambivalence that leaves the texts open to radically different interpretations wherein difference matters, or it doesn't."[69] This political project and hybrid aesthetic allows her to accommodate spectators across a right-center-left spectrum where all views appear equally valid and reconcilable. As a light-skinned African American woman, Smith suggests integration in her very embodiment. Critic Nelson Pressley contends that Smith's popularity is "due in no small part to the new critical habitus that routinely greeted her 'document'-based work not as lecturing, hectoring, or propaganda, but as objective, neutral, balanced."[70] It is unsurprising that traditionally white theatre institutions have found her work so compelling.

Beginning in 1994, Smith developed *House Arrest: First Edition* to explore how the press mediates public knowledge about the presidency. During her three-year research process, she conducted five hundred interviews that revealed how the popular narratives that circulate and ideas of what constitutes the truth are in the hands of a few privileged storytellers.[71] She drew attention to U.S. histories of racism from the White House to the prison industrial complex. Unlike her previous productions, *House Arrest* employed a multiracial ensemble to which Smith taught her methodology, thus furthering the theatre's project of cross-identity embodied performance. At nearly $2 million, the project was much more expensive than Arena's typical productions, and meeting minutes indicate anxieties over controlling costs. The company co-produced the play with the Goodman Theatre, Mark Taper Forum, and Intiman Theatre and received hundreds of thousands of dollars from AT&T and from the National Theatre Artist Residency Program funded by the Pew Charitable Trust. Dorinne Kondo, who served as drama-turg, proposed that Smith "may be enjoying mainstream success precisely because many audiences and funding agencies view the work as evidence that 'we can all get along.'"[72] She believed that *House Arrest* resonated with liberal humanism, but it also performed progressive work as "a demystification of power, a revisionist history related by subaltern subjects."[73]

When Arena produced the first version of the play in 1997, it was colored by two major scandals: President Bill Clinton's affair with Monica Lewinsky and the DNA testing results that suggested President Thomas Jefferson raped and had children with enslaved woman Sally Hemings. Smith's work, which was already invested in critiquing white patriarchy and included an interview with Clinton and writings by Jefferson, suddenly took on more immediate relevance yet also quickly became dated. With video, dance, a multiracial ensemble, and a fictional frame of an incarcerated group telling the story and playing with the theme of "arrest," *House Arrest* strayed from Smith's signature solo style. These departures from *Fires* and *Twilight* led to only a work-shop production at the Mark Taper Forum and no productions at the Goodman and Intiman. When the play was published, the prison narrative was removed, and Smith performed the piece solo at the Public Theater in 2000. Only Arena committed to the full realization of this ambitious project. *House Arrest* allowed Smith to experiment, tell a Washington-specific story, shed light on how power shapes the presidency and the press, and teach her methodology to other theatre artists, thanks to Arena's multiculturalist infrastructure.

During Wager's tenure with Arena, he expanded opportunities for African Americans and continued to support African and Caribbean works. In a 1994 communications meeting about *I Am a Man*, a play about the black sanitation workers' strike in Memphis in 1968, audience researcher Mark Shugoll advised "that Arena be careful about emphasizing this show as a black play that might evoke negative feelings about Arena's multicultural efforts."[74] If Arena appeared too black, the company might scare more conservative white patrons who would tolerate only a certain kind and level of multiculturalism. Yet *I Am a Man* earned the second-highest group ticket sales in Arena's history, demonstrating a hunger for black American drama.[75] Mainstage productions by black artists or about black people produced under Wager included *Jar the Floor*, by Cheryl West; *Trinidad Sisters*, by Mustapha Matura ('91–'92); *The African Company Presents "Richard III,"* by Carlyle Brown; *Blood Knot*, by Athol Fugard ('92–'93); *Fires in the Mirror*, by Anna Deavere Smith; *A Small World*, by Mustapha Matura ('93–'94); *The Odyssey*, by Derek Walcott; *I Am a Man*, by OyamO ('94–'95); *Holiday Heart*, by Cheryl West; *Coming of the Hurricane*, by Keith Glover ('95–'96); *Blues for an Alabama Sky*, by Pearl Cleage; *It Ain't Nothin' but the Blues*, by Charles Bevel, Lita Gaithers, Randal Myler, Ron Taylor, and Dan Wheetman ('96–'97); *House Arrest: First Edition*, by Anna Deavere Smith; and *Black No More*, by Syl Jones ('97–'98). Most of these plays were written in realistic modes and engaged either with histories of struggle or pressing contemporary issues.

WAGER'S EXIT

The 1997–98 season marked Wager's last as artistic director due to board pressure to balance the budget, move the theatre to a new space, and refocus institutional branding. In 1996, Wager presented his reinvention initiative: "We must radically reassess how we gather and allocate these resources to overcome the loss of entitlement and become more independent and entrepreneurially responsive to opportunity."[76] These calls for entrepreneurship translated to a plan for more coproductions and book-in productions in the Kreeger proscenium space, while company productions stayed in the Fichandler in-the-round theatre. The board was unmoved by Wager's proposal. Fiscal constraints also affected the size of the plays produced. In 1990–91 (Arena's fortieth anniversary season), the produced plays had boasted a total of 120 characters. That was reduced by two-thirds for the 1995–96 season. When David Savran interviewed leading playwrights in the mid- to late 1990s, nearly all of them from Tony Kushner to Terrence McNally expressed pessimism over the state of the NEA and regional theatre on account of conservative subscriber bases and tightened budgets, both of which led to producing smaller, safer plays.[77] During the second half of the 1990s, many boards pushed out adventurous leaders, including Joanne Akalaitis at the Public Theater, Liviu Ciulei at the Guthrie, and Anne Bogart at the Trinity Repertory Company, who had been chosen to replace founding artistic directors.[78]

Arena's board pushed out Wager, in part because he wanted to keep Arena Stage in its Southwest home, whereas the board wanted to move to a new, smaller space in downtown Washington. In the 1990s, Northwest Washington developed more initiatives directed toward wealthy, white consumers, and the city began an era of gentrification that continues to this day. In 1991, the Metro had opened a station at Waterfront near Arena Stage, finally giving subway access to less privileged audience members and residents. Debating this move from Southwest to Northwest was embedded in institutional identity as reflected in geographic location and the social, economic, and racial connotations of location. According to some staff members, the institutional home was physically disintegrating, though production manager Guy Bergquist contested that claim.[79] He was a key player in keeping Arena on 6th Street and Maine Avenue. The cost to renovate the company's home would have been $50 million, and an additional study determined that Wager would be able to raise only $30 million.[80] Mitigating the riskiness of a move, Arena stayed in Southwest in its in-the-round playing space, while Woolly Mammoth Theatre Company now occupies the targeted space in Northwest.

Arena Stage also suffered from a fuzzy institutional image by the late 1990s. In a 2012 interview, Zelda Fichandler recalled when a board member criticized her theatre for lacking a brand: "We were having a rough time with box office. 'The problem with this theatre is that it doesn't have a brand.' And I said, 'What?' She said, 'You don't have a specialty.' I said, 'My specialty is the human animal. That's my specialty.' And she said, 'Well, the audience doesn't see it that way.' It really hurt me a lot."[81] When Wager became the artistic director, the *New York Times* similarly reported, "Mr. Wager said the Arena has no specific artistic mission. 'Arena just is,' he said, 'but we seem to gravitate to doing or developing plays that speak to the human condition, plays that resonate to what we feel is going on in the world around us.'"[82] In a communications committee meeting, staff members cautioned, "New Voices [for a New America] is an artistic theme, but not a marketing objective" and "To some long-time Arena patrons, the term New Voices implies something young, unheard of, and unfamiliar that may or may not be interesting. People who are used to Arena may or may not feel included or interested by this concept, especially when it has a multicultural emphasis."[83] The communications committee concluded that "Arena could build an institutional focus around a personality. This takes time, especially because Doug's style is so different from other leaders like Zelda."[84] The implication was that Wager did not excel in visionary leadership, although he is a gifted theatre director. An internal study of Arena Stage staff members, managers, and trustees revealed that they found the company to be lacking in excitement and distinction. By 1995, one employee remarked, "Everyone used to call it the flagship. Now, people refer to it as, 'the flagship is sinking.'"[85] The study reported that "Several respondents do not feel Arena Stage has realized its reputation for being the 'multicultural' institution it professes to be" because it ignored the growing Latinx community in Washington, DC.[86] Much like multiculturalism, Arena's aesthetics and politics were difficult to name and to sell in an increasingly competitive theatre market, as the company did not accommodate everyone.

Wager had not had a contract since 1994, and according to his account, the board, led by its president Riley Temple, exhorted him to step down. When the *Washington Post* remarked, "A frequently heard criticism during Wager's regime has been that Arena is 'adrift,'" Wager responded, "In some cases, I think it was a response to our doing more black plays than we 'should' be doing. And we were changing, but not radically, so no one could put a finger on what we were changing into."[87] Committed to black theatre, patrons, and respectability politics, Temple said,

> I would take half of what we do, half of our resources, and say, This is Arena's African American theater company. . . . It's a gamble, but one that has to be taken. Washington is still predominantly an African American city, a wonderful place for blacks who are well educated and thoughtful to reside. And they love and will go to the theater. I can't think of a better home for theater that has some resonance with the African American community than Arena Stage.[88]

Articles reporting Wager's resignation touched on board strife and financial issues, though Wager framed the end of his artistic director-

Douglas Wager, former Arena Stage artistic director, with Molly Smith, current artistic director, at the Mead Center for American Theater Homecoming Grand Opening Celebration, October 23, 2010. Photo by Scott Suchman courtesy of Arena Stage.

ship around his desire to direct more productions. In 2012, Fichandler reflected, "I think Doug is an A-1 artist, and he hit a piece of history where he had to be—I don't think I could have done any better in that period. It was *the* period where everybody suffered."[89] Fichandler had placed a bet on him, and Arena lost Wager. The 1997–98 season was the last of his seven years as artistic director. However, in 1998 and 1999 under the new leadership of Molly Smith, Wager returned to direct several productions. He is now a professor and associate dean of theater, film, and media arts at Temple University.

ENTER MOLLY SMITH AND BRIDGING THE OLD AND NEW ARENA STAGE

As Wager stepped down, the board of trustees searched for a new artistic director and a new identity for Arena Stage. Molly Smith, at forty-five years old, had plenty of leadership experience, having founded Perseverance Theatre, the biggest professional regional theatre in Alaska, in 1979. She already had a connection to Washington because she had studied at American University and Catholic University. Although women have been at the forefront of the regional theatre movement in the U.S., today relatively few leaders of major theatre institutions are women. During the 2013–14 season, Smith was one of fifteen LORT women artistic directors out of seventy-four total.[90]

When Smith met with the Arena board in 1997, she presented two visions for the theatre: all-American or all-international. She argued that concentrating on U.S. American artists took advantage of Arena's positioning in the nation's capital and her history at Perseverance Theatre: "This is a city that expects to have a conversation about our national character. Later I realized that this was a through-line from my work in Alaska. In Alaska, I was searching for Alaskan voices. Our mission statement was by, about Alaskans. So, in a sense, it was the same idea writ large, from a national point of view."[91] In 1950, Arena Stage had been the only professional resident theatre in Washington, and therefore an eclectic sensibility was welcomed. When the Helen Hayes Awards were first given in 1983 to recognize excellence in Washington-area theatre, there were still only twenty professional local theatres. But by 1998, the company competed with approximately seventy local theatres for ticket sales, donations, grants, and awards. Shakespeare Theatre Company appeared to many as the foremost theatre in the nation's capital, and its first-rate productions of classical work rivaled those by Arena Stage. In addition, some leading local theatres such as Woolly Mammoth Theatre Company, Studio Theatre, and Signature Theatre consistently produced new American plays, although none of the companies marketed themselves as American. Smith's pitch to focus on Americanness resonated with board members and her appointment showed their willingness to change in response to the contemporary theatre ecosystem.

Because Smith was an outsider to Arena, she had to find ways to make inroads with the staff members. Smith agreed with executive director Stephen Richard and the board about moving to Northwest Washington, estranging some staff who wanted to remain in Southwest. Staff meeting minutes prior to Smith's arrival suggest some discontent among employees and "the importance of not allowing negativity to go beyond the theater."[92] From the start of her tenure, Smith and the administration concluded that there would be no more annual two-week furloughs—a huge win for the staff. According to Alison

Irvin, who has worked almost continuously at Arena Stage since 1994 and now serves as the leadership office manager, one of Smith's first acts was "hanging giant posters of previous Arena productions. She definitely looked to the future. She did not entirely discard the past, although it is hard to truly move forward without making some big changes."[93]

Smith had to bridge the old and new Arena, particularly its image and repertory. The institution sought to rebrand itself as "An American Original" and as "adventurous, classy and fresh."[94] The "Arena Stage Identity Redesign Creative Brief" emphasized that the theatre would produce American work. It also noted the need to contend with financial hardships: cuts to donations and grants, shrinking subscriber base, and greater competition. The brief discussed the importance of retaining long-standing patrons, bringing the company's legacy into the twenty-first century, and attracting new audiences in order to survive in a system of neoliberal precarity.[95] To balance these concerns, Smith continued to produce a few European plays including *The Misanthrope*, by Molière; *A Man's a Man*, by Bertolt Brecht; and *Noises Off*, by Michael Frayn. In so doing, Smith hoped to retain long-term subscribers by reviving the kinds of plays that Fichandler and Wager had championed. She also produced canonical U.S. playwrights such as Arthur Miller, who had established a relationship with Arena Stage. In 2000, for the theatre's fiftieth anniversary, she revived *The Great White Hope*.

REBRANDING ARENA AS AMERICAN AND RACED

Smith's programming called attention to Arena's foundation in American works and then built on that foundation. She launched her first season in 1998 with Tennessee Williams's *Cat on a Hot Tin Roof*, while the rest of the season consisted mostly of new work. The program for *Cat on a Hot Tin Roof* included an extensive interview in which Smith introduced herself and her vision to Arena's audiences by explaining, "It seemed to me the first play needed to be a great American classic, and for me, Tennessee Williams ranks right up there."[96] In addition to Miller and Williams, the playwrights that she has produced most frequently have been Edward Albee and Eugene O'Neill. These "American Giants," to use the company's parlance, each received their own festivals with mainstage productions and staged readings in 2011 and 2012, respectively. Arena expanded the honor beyond white male playwrights to Lillian Hellman in the 2016–17 season.[97]

Under Smith (as under Wager), playwrights of color contributed at least two mainstage plays, and now sometimes as many as five to each season, which also featured productions of classics with multiracial casts. Smith oversaw diversity-specific new play development initiatives such as Voices of Women and District Views. In bringing back Cheryl West for *Play On!* (2000), *Pullman Porter Blues* (2012), and *Akeelah and the Bee* (2015) and Anna Deavere Smith for *Let Me Down Easy* (2010), Molly Smith continued to produce playwrights who had previously worked at Arena Stage. She provided playwriting and directing opportunities to black artists, including Tazewell Thompson, Charles Randolph-Wright, Kenny Leon, Lydia Diamond, and Daniel Beaty.

Capitalizing on cultural diversity with the production of black playwrights helped to keep Arena Stage afloat. This regional theatre uniquely went beyond the one-slot tokenism common among other companies by producing several writers of color each season, casting actors of color in classics, hiring directors of color, reaching out to audiences of color, training young artistic administrators of color, and working with local communities of color. This antiracist work redistributed resources toward people of color, especially black Americans. But it ultimately gave resources to Arena to maintain itself as a historically white institution. White audiences and artists continued to make up the majority of the theatre, just as the leadership remained white and authorized by the immense success of black productions. Whiteness persisted as the center, with blackness buttressing the apparatus. By promising to include some people of color, Arena could secure diversity funding that otherwise might have gone to culturally specific theatres, which have been on the decline since the 1990s. In 2000, Arena won $1.2 million from the Lila Wallace–Reader's Digest Fund to diversify its audience, of which only 15 percent were people of color.[98] With the closing of the African Continuum Theatre Company in 2015, the remaining small, black-run theatres devoted to black stories in the Washington metro area include Live Garra Theatre, the Essential Theatre, and Restoration Stage. In the zero-sum game of competitive grants, some black-specific theatres lost, while large, white-but-inclusive theatres like Arena won. Productions by artists of color in traditionally white regional theatres offered familiar middlebrow aesthetics, a safe space for the white and black middle class, and the liberal politics of inclusion.

Under Smith's tenure, Arena became the Washington outpost for August Wilson by staging, for example, *Ma Rainey's Black Bottom*, *The Piano Lesson*, and *Gem of the Ocean*. Excluding Shakespeare, Wilson was the most-produced playwright at large regional theatres in the 2000s.[99] Along with many awards, his realistic yet magical, historical, musical, and literary dramaturgy positioned him as the anointed African American playwright with the "black play slot." African American theatre scholar Harry J. Elam Jr. suggests, "Perhaps one of the reasons for Wilson's success with white audiences is that his proposed racial radicalisms do not overtly threaten whites but hide behind the distance of history and the safety of spirituality."[100] Elam further argues the dangers of historically white theatres staging only one story of color per season and pitting people of color against each other: "If the works of artists of color are branded only as different, as other, as outside of the traditional or the normative, then implicitly they reinforce the power of normative Whiteness. Whiteness stays at the center of aesthetic standards and artistic control as artists of color can only fight amongst themselves for the living 'diversity' slots that are open to them."[101] Citing Elmo Terry-Morgan, Wilson scholar Dana A. Williams writes, "As long as the majority of subscription audiences are white, this privileged audience 'holds the seats of [the] theatres hostage to the mediocrity of its tastes, and serves to impede the further development of an audience' that is more likely to be attuned to the aesthetic values of non-white playwrights."[102] Theatre educator Yvonne Shafer has praised and identified Wilson's broad appeal because "his characters break through the barriers of race."[103] However, Jackie M. Roberts asserts that she does not teach Wilson's plays because "they leave students with the feeling that the quest for black equality in America has been fully accomplished."[104]

Expanding on Fichandler's and Wager's cultural diversity policies, Smith concretized Arena Stage as the major nonprofit theatre in Washington that worked to make black patrons feel like they were not mere guests to this theatre but part of its home. She recounted visiting local black churches at the start of her tenure: "There were greeters welcoming people in. I realized we didn't have that at Arena so we now have ushers welcome people as they enter the building. Theatres can be threatening for people—especially coming to a theatre for the first time."[105] Few large regional theatres reach out to black communities the way that Arena does. It is helped in no small part by its location in Washington.

Consider, by contrast, the Guthrie Theater, which produced only one play by a black writer between its founding in Minneapolis in 1963 and 1989.[106] Although both regional theatres shared similar programming in the '60s, their artistic missions have since come into sharper, distinct focus. Under Smith, Arena has committed to producing multiple plays by, about, and for African Americans each season, while under Joe Dowling from 1996 to 2015, the Guthrie typically staged one such work per year. Those productions sometimes came via Penumbra Theatre Company, a separate African American organization invited to present their work on one of the Guthrie's smaller stages.[107] Penumbra nearly closed due to bankruptcy in 2012, suggesting the limited support there is for African American–specific regional theatre.

On the national and local scale, Arena does better than most comparable companies in putting racial diversity rhetoric into practice. From 1998 through 2014, 30 percent of plays produced at Arena were written by playwrights of color, and 26 percent of productions were directed by directors of color.[108] During that same period, the Mark Taper Forum in Los Angeles, another majority-of-color city, had only 19 percent of the repertory come from playwrights of color and 10 percent of productions were directed by directors of color.[109] Even within Washington, Arena has a more diverse audience than other traditionally white companies. In my personal theatergoing experience, I have noticed that local peer institutions such as Signature Theatre and Woolly Mammoth Theatre have paled in comparison, as it were, even when these companies produced the black musical *Dreamgirls* (2012) and Robert O'Hara's political melodrama *Zombie: The American* (2015), respectively. Smith has framed Arena as having four segmented audiences: "Classics, African American Works, Special Projects (generally musicals), and New Plays (the smallest audience)."[110] It seems noteworthy that even in 2012 Smith highlighted the importance of black theatre and patrons, yet segregated the classics, musicals, and new plays as not African American, though these categories overlap, as in classic black musicals.

Smith has staged the blues musical *Thunder Knocking on the Door* (1999), by Keith Glover, Keb' Mo', and Anderson Edwards; the adaptation of *Twelfth Night* titled *Play On!* (2000), conceived and directed by Sheldon Epps, with book by Cheryl West and music by Duke Ellington; *Polk County* (2002), by Zora Neale Hurston, with Dorothy Waring and coadapted by Kyle Donnelly and Cathy Madison; *Crowns* (2003, 2004, 2005, 2009) by Regina Taylor; the Harlem Renaissance revue *Ain't Misbehavin'* (2003); *Hallelujah, Baby!* (2004), with a revised book by Arthur Laurents, music by Jule Styne, and lyrics by Betty Comden and Adolph Green; *3 Mo' Divas!* (2006), by Marion J. Caffey; the Billie Holiday play with music *Lady Day at Emerson's Bar and Grill* (2006) by Lanie Robertson; *The Women of Brewster Place* (2007), by Tim Acito; the Ella Fitzgerald musical *Ella* (2007); Maurice Hines's autobiographical *Tappin' thru Life* (2013); the jukebox musical *Smokey Joe's Café* (2014); *Five Guys Named Moe* (2014), directed by Robert O'Hara; *Born for This: The BeBe Winans Story* (2016), by Charles Randolph-Wright and BeBe Winans; and *Nina Simone: Four Women* (2017), by Christina Ham. Most of these productions have been revues, a particularly pleasurable and safe form that celebrates nostalgia rather than critiquing structures of racial hierarchy. They showcased the history of African American artists in ways that provided uplift for black bourgeois audiences.[111] Charles Randolph-Wright explained that, at Smith's urging, he adapted *Cuttin' Up* about black men in barbershops because stories of middle-class black Americans are rarely told: "I wanted to see seven black men on stage in suits."[112] Arena has also produced classic musicals with black directors and leads. In 1999, Randolph-Wright directed *Guys and Dolls* starring Maurice Hines in a multiracial production that was so successful that it went onto a national tour. Collaborating with the comic-political group Culture Clash, he also directed *Señor Discretion Himself*, an unfinished musical by Frank Loesser.

Crowns offers a useful example of a black musical that drew multiracial support as it was revived repeatedly at Arena between 2003 and 2009. Regina Taylor adapted this gospel musical from the best-selling book *Crowns: Portraits of Black Women in Church Hats* by Michael Cunningham and Craig Marberry. The musical traces the self-discovery of a young African American woman who learns about the different histories, rituals, dances, and most of all the crowns or elaborate hats that give strength to black women when they attend church. For its initial run in 2003, *Crowns* received eight Helen Hayes nominations and won for best director, musical director, and musical among resident productions. Because the first run of *Crowns* was one of the most financially successful productions in Arena's history, the company restaged the piece three additional times. In the first two runs of *Crowns*, the production generated more than $2 million.[113] The uplifting narrative, music, dance, and bourgeois culture celebrated in *Crowns* pleased audiences who wanted to see people like themselves onstage. For black-themed works, Arena's audiences were 59 percent black, matching the demographics of Washington circa 2000.[114] According to Kathy A. Perkins, "From 2003 onward, the dominant [African American women] playwrights have been Lynn Nottage, Regina Taylor, and Dael Orlandersmith . . . but only two women—Nottage and Taylor—accounted for thirty-three of the forty-one produced" during the 2005–6 LORT season.[115] This pattern speaks to Taylor's popularity and suggests that once white institutional gatekeepers accept a particular woman-of-color playwright, the rest of the regional theatres follow suit.

Although Molly Smith defined Americanness in primarily black-and-white terms, she extended mainstage opportunities to some other stories and artists of color, illustrating a richer understanding of the nation. In 2001, she directed *Coyote Builds North America*, a theatre piece with music and dance inspired by Native American creation myths that she had originally produced at Perseverance Theatre. In 2004, Tazewell Thompson directed David Henry Hwang's *M. Butterfly*, the first full-length play by an Asian American to receive a mainstage production at Arena.[116] Smith has been more attentive to Latinx artists, including Nilo Cruz, Karen Zacarías, and Culture Clash. Culture Clash consists of Richard Montoya, Ric Salinas, and Herbert Sigüenza, who perform political, comic plays inspired by specific cities. Arena commissioned them to compose *Anthems: Culture Clash in the District* (2002) based on interviews with locals whose experiences represented the sociopolitics of the nation's capital, reminiscent of the work by Anna Deavere Smith.[117] Theatre historian James M. Harding praised *Anthems* as an avant-garde piece that reminded audiences how 9/11 marked a history of racial terrorism within the United States: "[The play] is remarkable for its refusal to let the call for unity, the call for an anthem, to become a sentimental whitewash that elides a national history full not only of acts of aggression on behalf of corporate interests abroad, but also of acts of terror against the weak, the poor, and the minorities at home."[118] Arena provided a stage for some works by artists of color that challenged hegemonic national narratives of simplified harmony precisely at a time of passionate patriotism and heightened policing of brown bodies.

SOUTHWEST ROOTS

In addition to making the repertoire more racially inclusive, Arena ultimately decided to keep the company in its home in Southwest, build a new structure, renovate the existing theatres, and expand its collaborations with area theatrical partners. According to executive director Stephen Richard, who worked at the theatre from 1991 to 2008, "The board concluded that the deal that was involved in moving downtown contained too much financial risk. And we concluded that we could build what we wanted to build in the current location."[119] In 2001, Arena selected a design by Bing Thom, who had designed other arts centers but never before a theatre. Bergquist, with his decades of experience at Arena, oversaw the construction to ensure that the design met the needs of the theatremakers. Thom's design called for building a glass wall to surround the Fichandler in-the-round stage and Kreeger proscenium theatre and a new oval-shaped theatre called the Kogod Cradle. Tall wooden trunks served as columns to hold up the metallic roof, which, along with the glass, created a contemporary look of natural and artificial materials that brought together the three theatre spaces and their patrons. The building would come to be known as the Mead Center for American Theater, named for Gilbert and Jaylee Mead, who had donated $35 million to the capital campaign, the largest gift in the company's history.

To deepen Arena's roots in Southwest, Smith called for changes in community engagement and education. The theatre had long provided support for Living Stage, an artist-activist group founded by Robert Alexander. Since 1969, Alexander and other teaching artists worked with local public school students, inmates, and people with disabili-

(top) Interior of the Fichandler Stage, Arena Stage at the Mead Center for American Theater. Photo by Nic Lehoux courtesy of Bing Thom Architects. (bottom) Interior of the Kogod Cradle, Arena Stage at the Mead Center for American Theater. Photo by Nic Lehoux courtesy of Bing Thom Architects.

Interior of the Kreeger Theater, Arena Stage at the
Mead Center for American Theater. Photo by Nic Lehoux
courtesy of Bing Thom Architects.

ties, among other marginalized groups, to produce plays that explored subjects such as racism, poverty, and drug abuse. Laura Penn, who worked in the Arena box office in the 1980s, called Living Stage the "conscience" of Arena Stage.[120] In 1995, Alexander passed the leadership to Oren Sandel, who extended programs to Latinx and Asian American groups. Because Living Stage was aesthetically and functionally separate from Arena Stage, Smith decided to end the program and develop new ones more in keeping with her mission and the practices of other major nonprofit theatres. She commissioned Rebecca Rice, who had worked with Living Stage, to create a theatre piece based on the histories and testimonies of people living in Southwest Washington. According to Cathy Madison, who performed extensive research for this project, "The basic idea of the project was to celebrate the developmental arc of the neighborhood over time, culminating in the rebirth of Arena Stage."[121] Having displaced black people in the mid-twentieth century, the Redevelopment Land Agency made space for Arena's permanent home, and the Southwest project unpacked that history while still celebrating the theatre.

Meanwhile, Arena's education department continued some programs from the previous leadership and initiated new ones. Anita Maynard-Losh, the director of community engagement since 2004, explained that Arena had a long-standing initiative through which public school students received study guides and free tickets to Arena Stage productions.[122] Early in Smith's tenure, the theatre launched Voices of Now, originally an after-school program to develop autobiographical performances that has since expanded with the support of the State Department to travel to India, Croatia, and Peru. In 2004, with Rebecca Campana and others, Maynard-Losh launched Camp Arena Stage to raise revenue for other programs and to teach artmaking to economically and racially diverse young people. Stacey Stewart, who had worked in the box office and development department, became the director of education for schools and professional development in 2007. She headed the Student Playwrights Project and worked with the Allen Lee Hughes Fellows. According to Stewart, by the late 2000s, these fellowships were no longer offered solely to artists and administrators of color, in part because one of Arena's lawyers said that, if challenged, the practice probably would not be upheld in court.[123] As a consequence, Arena no longer had a dedicated pipeline for young people of color to move up from the fellowships into full-time jobs.[124] While these community and educational programs helped to anchor Arena as a more traditional nonprofit institution invested in Southwest and Washington and provided much-needed opportunities for locals, they lost the radical equalizing spirit that Living Stage and the Allen Lee Hughes Program had originally wielded.

ENUNCIATING AMERICAN VOICES: ARENA RE-STAGED

Despite Smith's efforts to promote "Americanness," due to producing European works, canonical American plays, and new American artists of color, Arena's U.S. American identity remained imprecise. In 2006, David Dower joined the theatre as an artistic associate to provide additional artistic leadership. He had come from San Francisco, where he cofounded the Z Space, a place to develop original, local work. Dower expressed concern at the lack of clarity in Arena's mission. At a meeting with senior staff, he received pushback for his critiques. Eventually the leadership decided to update the company's website that described Arena as a "Theatre of the Americas" to "American Theatre."[125] Arena decided that its revamped building would be named the Mead Center for American Theater, which provoked greater exigency for a clearer mission. According to Dower, "But at that point, there wasn't any plan for programming this 'Center.' The assumption among the staff was we would move back into the building after it had been opened and do pretty much what we had been doing there before. So that means eight plays a year. But now there was a third theatre, and there was all this other space, and a name that said 'Center for American Theater.'"[126] With an American brand name and three spaces, but the same number of staff members and insufficient funding, Arena had to program differently.

Smith emphasized the viability and diversity of Arena having an all-American repertory, which she found capacious rather than limiting:

Just about anybody, unless you're Native American, is an immigrant. From Africa to Ireland to India—we all come from someplace else. There is a tremendous diversity of voices here, and

I believe part of the vitality of all these American voices in the theatre comes from being a country of immigrants. So I don't think you can really define an American voice. It's more like a cacophony of voices in America.[127]

She located U.S. American identity in indigeneity but mostly in immigration. Instead of Wager's conception of cultural diversity as multipart harmony, she emphasized difference. Although she did not call out the United States as grounded in racial oppression, she at least suggested the richness of diversity and the irreducible tensions therein.

While the Mead Center was being constructed between 2007 and 2010, the company launched "Arena Re-staged," a campaign to rebrand its image, and that came with a price. Arena produced work in two temporary operating spaces, a 460-seat proscenium theatre in Arlington, Virginia, and the historic 1,225-seat Lincoln Theatre on U Street. To save on production costs, the company hosted more coproductions and presentations and developed stronger relationships with commercial producers. Of the shows in the 2008–9 season, *Wishful Drinking* by Carrie Fisher, *Next to Normal* with music by Tom Kitt and book and lyrics by Brian Yorkey, and *Looped* by Matthew Lombardo all moved to Broadway. An informal agreement evolved between Arena and Shakespeare Theatre Company around who would do what in Washington: while Arena focused on U.S. touring and regional productions, Shakespeare Theatre Company would complement them by presenting primarily international productions.[128] Arena staffers who had worked on crafting homegrown productions for decades resented the book-in productions. For instance, Guy Bergquist remarked that "the Mead Center is a presenting house" and "most of us who were there before will say that it's not Arena Stage anymore."[129] While true that Arena increased the number of outside presentations in its mainstage season, book-in productions had been part of the company's tradition since the 1960s when Arena experienced its first budget shortfall and presented the musical revue *Jacques Brel Is Alive and Well and Living in Paris*. Additionally, because of the global fiscal crisis in 2008, the design for the Mead Center changed. Raising contributed income for the capital campaign and paying for the rising costs of materials and construction became increasingly difficult. As a consequence, the income-generating aspects of the building, specifically apartments for actors and a full restaurant for patrons, were eliminated. In the end, the Mead Center cost $135 million to build.

Interested in becoming a hub for research as well as a forum for developing artists, Arena formed the American Voices New Play Institute (AVNPI) in 2009. In part thanks to Dower's expertise in the new play ecosystem and his relationship with the Andrew Mellon Foundation, Arena won a $1.2 million grant to support new play development. The AVNPI included a slew of initiatives, but at the core were five three-year playwriting residencies for Amy Freed, Katori Hall, Lisa Kron, Charles Randolph-Wright, and Karen Zacarías. In selecting these playwrights, Arena addressed gaps in support for mid-career artists, women, and people of color. The residencies included an annual salary of approximately $40,000, health benefits, housing, funding for research and development, and a commitment to produce one play as part of the mainstage season. AVNPI represented an explicitly anticapitalist experiment to see if providing stability and resources, which artists could self-direct, would lead to stronger artwork, rather than the nonprofit theatre model of commissioning plays for $3,000 (and often not actually producing those plays). Arena took a risk in supporting these playwrights and showcasing the possibility of a nonprofit regional theatre providing an artistic home for American voices. Arena hosted convenings on the state of the field, produced white papers, trained new play producing fellows of color, and created an online platform devoted to documenting institutional practices called *HowlRound*. In 2007, Arena also won a major grant from the NEA to administer the New Play Development Program that awarded funding to promising works. These programs positioned Arena as a leader in the field of new plays. By 2018, Arena described its mission as the "production, presentation, development and study of American theater."[130]

The 2010–11 season marked the theatre's sixtieth anniversary and the opening of Arena Stage at the Mead Center for American Theater. By directing a multiracial production of *Oklahoma!* in the Fichandler in-the-round space to inaugurate the new building, Smith sited Arena Stage as a center for American stories, genres, and community formation marked by racial and national politics, unpacked in the final chapter. In the Kreeger Theater, Arena presented Second Stage Theatre's production of *Let Me Down Easy* by Anna Deavere Smith, extending the company's relationship with Smith and its commitment

Exterior of Arena Stage at the Mead Center for American Theater.
Photo by Nic Lehoux courtesy of Bing Thom Architects.

to exploring U.S. current issues, in this case health care. In the new Kogod Cradle, the theatre staged the world premiere of *every tongue confess* by Marcus Gardley, who used Ancient Greek and magical realist devices to dramatize a story about the hundreds of black church burnings in the Deep South in the 1990s. The company also produced Lynn Nottage's *Ruined*, her Pulitzer-winning play about the devastating impact of war on women in the Congo, one of the most produced plays at regional theatres that season.[131] Arena coproduced *The Arabian Nights* by Mary Zimmerman and presented *The Laramie Project* alongside *The Laramie Project: 10 Years Later*, the pre-Broadway tryout of *A Time to Kill* based on the John Grisham novel, and Steppenwolf Theatre Company's *Who's Afraid of Virginia Woolf?*

Finally, Arena produced *At Home at the Zoo* and a festival of all of Edward Albee's plays, highlighting the importance of the U.S. canon and bringing together companies across Washington to stage readings of his work. The repertory that Molly Smith crafted articulated Arena and the nation's capital at the intersections of nonprofit, black, and American identities and demonstrated how those identities are inseparable.

CONCLUSION

Molly Smith was hired based on her unifying vision of Arena as a center for American theatre, a vision that became clearer over time as African Americans became an indelible part of the theatre's identity. Leveraging diversity grants and black musicals, she more successfully capitalized on blackness to subsidize this traditionally white institution. With the renaming of the theatre building as the Mead Center for American Theater, she affirmed Arena as a space for American voices. But the new building also led to more economical season selections, including musicals and collaborations with other regional theatre companies. Under Smith's directorship, Arena carved out a sustainable space in the contemporary theatre ecosystem of Washington by performing a multiracial United States that made white and black Americans feel included.

(CHAPTER SIX)

RECASTING AMERICANS IN A
MULTIRACIAL *OKLAHOMA!*

Over a lunch in 2009, Molly Smith invited the artistic development team to pitch their ideas for which musical Arena Stage should produce to celebrate the company's sixtieth anniversary, cement its American identity, and open its new theatre complex. I was serving as the dramaturgy intern at the time, and I proposed the Gershwins' political satire *Of Thee I Sing*. New play–producing fellow Travis Lemont Ballenger advocated for *The Gospel at Colonus*, the black gospel retelling of *Oedipus at Colonus*. Arena had previously produced both of those musicals, in 1992 and 1984, respectively. But Smith ultimately landed on perhaps the most American of musicals: Richard Rodgers and Oscar Hammerstein's *Oklahoma!*

Smith adopted a multiracial directorial approach to redefine the United States and Arena. But her approach also incited the dangers of colorblindness. Staged in the nation's capital, *Oklahoma!* resonated with the racial triumphalism of Barack Obama's presidency; at the same time, the multiracial casting covered up historic and continuing material inequality. By producing this classic musical with a multiracial cast, Arena articulated the conditions under which a racially integrated group of people could sing their American belonging. The production articulated power dynamics at the crossroads of race and nation, at a time when postracial projects increasingly co-opted representations of interracial harmony to deny the persistence of racial hierarchy and violence. It was a huge hit. Debuting in October 2010, *Oklahoma!* became the highest-grossing single-run production in Arena's history. It won rave reviews and four Helen Hayes Awards, including Best Resident Musical, and it played again during the summer of 2011.

This chapter examines how Arena's multiracial productions stage racial diversity as the core of Americanness. Reviewing this history grounds the context for *Oklahoma!* Promotional materials and interviews with artistic staff members illuminate the marketing and casting of *Oklahoma!*, showing how bodies become variously understood within existing racial projects: multiracial-conscious, whitened, and postracial. Angela Pao's key work on casting, *No Safe Spaces: Re-casting Race, Ethnicity, and Nationality in American Theater,* informs my close readings of specific characters and actors as well as the possibilities and limits to representing U.S. Americans.[1] My identity as a woman of color, as well as my experiences having worked at Arena Stage the season prior and having seen its production of this musical, influence my theorization. Arena staged American inclusiveness, which rested troublingly on the elisions of indigenous genocide, difference, and racial inequality. Both parts of this argument are crucial when many white Americans openly disparaged people of color during Obama's first term, while others both celebrated diversity and denied the depths of systemic racism. The production represented not only a moment of apparent advancement through racial diversity, hope, and change, but also a continuation of the status quo through the avoidance of addressing institutional racism. Finally, critical reviews exemplify how audiences negotiated the multiracial *Oklahoma!*, Arena Stage, and the United States as multiracial, white, and/or postracial. They reveal the struggles for defining and who gets to define race and U.S. American identity.

Often hailed as the first integrated musical, in the sense that the story and the score appeared strongly connected, *Oklahoma!* epitomizes what has been called the Golden Age of American musicals. The musical is based on the play *Green Grow the Lilacs*, written in 1930 by Lynn Riggs, a playwright of Cherokee and European descent who dramatized mixed-race characters and an ambivalent critique of U.S. nationalism and white supremacy. For the musical, which premiered in 1943, Rodgers and Hammerstein turned the narrative into a celebration of nationhood through the union of romantic couples, farmers and cowmen, and the Indian and Oklahoma Territories. The libretto focuses on Laurey's choice between two suitors: cowboy Curly and farmhand Jud.

The Arena production of *Oklahoma!* actively encouraged a multiracial reading of the musical and challenged assumptions about who lived on the frontier and, by implication, who comprised the nation in 2010. This production offers an example of what feminist theatre critic Jill Dolan calls "utopian performatives," when artists ask "what if," allowing "performance a hopeful cast, one that can experiment with the possibilities of the future in ways that shine back usefully on a present that's always, itself, in process."[2] Because Smith and her creative team asked "what if" and wanted the racial makeup of the nation to be reflected in the cast and the new Arena Stage, their *Oklahoma!* featured a racially diverse ensemble and principals. Sensitive to stereotypes, the creative team made these casting choices carefully and provoked spectators to read and reframe the territory folks both racially and temporally. Not quite yet U.S. citizens and not exactly all white, the people of the Indian Territory, *can* be, as Will sings, "all er nuthin'," "in between," and "now and then."[3]

BRANDING AMERICA, ARENA, AND *OKLAHOMA!* AS MULTIRACIAL

As I have previously written, Arena Stage has experimented with multiracial casting in classic plays and musicals since the 1960s, a practice that effectively positioned the company as a laboratory for staging racial integration. In addition to the company's resident acting ensemble of black and white actors formed in 1968, in 1987, Arena hosted the first Non-traditional Casting Symposium to explore race and casting issues at the core of U.S. theatre. In her remarks at the symposium, Fichandler asked, "What if one took nontraditional casting as far as one could think about it?"[4] She stressed the importance of providing specific opportunities for minoritized actors on the basis of not only proven merit but future promise.[5] She further theorized multiracial casting in memos to the Arena Stage staff, newspaper articles, and interviews. For instance, in 1988 in "Casting for a Different Truth" she called for opening our imaginations because we are all human underneath, though this philosophy erases material differences in suggesting that people of color can play nonspecific roles just as whites can play people of color-specific parts.[6] Fichandler enriched Arena with cultural diversity initiatives in the late 1980s, including building a multiracial resident acting ensemble once again. Tazewell Thompson directed an all-black production of *The Glass Menagerie* in 1989 and a multiracial production of *The Caucasian Chalk Circle* in 1990. In the *Arena Arrow*, the theatre's internal cultural diversity newsletter, the editors contextualized Thompson's *Glass Menagerie*. Because some people in the company did not believe Amanda Wingfield as a wealthy southern woman could be black, the newsletter provided historical information on property-owning black Americans and stated emphatically that Thompson "did not want anyone overlooking the actor's blackness."[7]

The practice of casting an array of actors of different races in contemporary and canonical plays continued when Doug Wager became artistic director in 1991. His most controversial production was likely *Our Town*, which included eighteen white actors, seven black actors, and one Latinx actor to represent a multiracial United States.[8] Jonathan Yardley of the *Washington Post* censured this casting on the grounds of inaccuracy and excessive political correctness, which meant (to him) unnecessary racial justice. The cast did not reflect the demographics of New Hampshire, the racial logic of siblings, and the way Doctor Gibbs should sound—not like "Ricky Ricardo."[9] His article prompted rebuttals from Fichandler, Wager, and Arena Stage's patrons that emphasized the U.S. as multiracial, the play as nonrealistic, and the casting as in keeping with Thornton Wilder's note calling for artifice. But other letters from former subscribers revealed that Yardley was far from alone in his objections to multiracial casting. Wager nevertheless upheld his "ongoing commitment to the poetry of pluralism in the performing arts."[10] He argued that he originated the practice of casting multiracially for musicals at Arena.[11]

After her appointment as artistic director in 1998, Smith sustained Arena's history of multiracial casting as part of her U.S. American rebranding, especially for classic musicals. Musicologist Raymond Knapp argues that musicals are American in their production, consumption, and themes of community-building.[12] Smith agrees, considering musicals to be one of the true American art forms: "It's in our bones. It's in our sensibility. The best of the musicals really define the American character."[13] In the 2000s, Arena Stage repeatedly sampled the American songbook, showcasing better-known musicals such as *South Pacific* and less well-known examples such as *Hallelujah, Baby!* that often have explicit racial themes.[14] In addition, the company regularly staged multiracial productions of musicals. According to Smith,

"When one does American work, it is often about race, because race is our underlying tragedy in this country. It's the wound that we are continually trying to heal. So a theatre that focuses on American work, it's always going to be there. So in a profound way, I'm answering that through casting as well as choice of productions."[15]

In 2009, Amanda Dehnert directed the classic musical *The Fantasticks* with a multiracial cast at Arena, and its commercial success suggested the effectiveness of this directorial approach in the age of Obama. Although the theatre leveraged this casting to attract a racially diverse audience, the production seemed to encourage seeing past race. The racial identities of the performers playing the ingénues Matt and Luisa did not match those of their single fathers (which could easily have been accomplished by having the actors playing the fathers switch roles). The casting decision subverted what a realism-primed audience would expect in attempting to make sense of familial racial dynamics. On the other hand, for some spectators, race mattered suddenly and painfully when the script called for Matt to be caged, beaten, and burned. Played by a black actor, Matt conjured up images of slavery that the production team had not intended. Arena's artistic staff learned from this experience to consider how a history of racialized representations would affect marketing, casting, and reception.

When advertising *Oklahoma!* the following season, Arena Stage linked the redefined theatre space, the musical, and the United States past and present. Smith pronounced, "It's a beautiful morning for Arena Stage," implicitly evoking Reagan-esque diction ("It's morning in America") and dawn imagery while explicitly connecting the musical's opening number "Oh, What a Beautiful Mornin'" to the theatre's opening of the Mead Center.[16] The marketing materials stressed the theme of change for Arena, the Territories, and the musical form. The header "GREAT AMERICAN MUSICAL" accompanied *Oklahoma!* in overviews of the season that claimed, "*Oklahoma!* introduced a change in musical theater—the fully developed book musical."[17]

Arena capitalized on the general acceptance of *Oklahoma!* as one of the chief Golden Age musicals that legitimized the genre and embodied U.S. identity. This narrative is fundamental not only to Arena's rebranding but also to Gerald Mast's larger claim that Rodgers and Hammerstein "sought to define exactly what America meant and Americans believed."[18] Academic articles on *Oklahoma!* often argue that the musical invokes positive "American" ideals of inclusiveness, reconciliation, and community.[19] Many scholars locate *Oklahoma!*'s American identity on the frontier, deploying Frederick Turner's influential thesis that encounters between indigenous and pioneering white ethnic peoples along the westward frontier produced a distinctly American character. Accordingly, in one promotional YouTube video, Smith earnestly claimed that *Oklahoma!* represented "the kind of grit, the kind of robustness, that I think America is made of."[20] Some Washington critics connected the frontier spirit of the musical to Smith's former leadership of Perseverance Theatre in Alaska.[21] In the same video, Smith claimed that "the territory" was "completely diverse," at which point a photograph of a Native American man and a white frontiersman standing side by side appeared. Such a claim and the accompanying image intimate a sense of indigenous peoples and American settler colonialism but without pointing out the tensions therein. Nor did Smith explain what she meant by "completely diverse."

To unsettle preconceptions of the frontier as white, Arena used historical documentation to justify its multiracial casting.[22] Extensive dramaturgy in patrons' programs detailed the racial demographics and histories of the Indian and Oklahoma Territories. Dramaturg Janine Sobeck Knighton shed light on ways race and labor were linked to Asian immigrant workers, and how tribes such as the Cherokee enslaved black people. This historical rationalization for casting people of color helped to persuade skeptics and satisfy *Oklahoma!*'s reputation as a more realistic book musical than its predecessors. In the director's note, Smith asserted, "Arena's cast is an American tapestry, with all colors and types. African-Americans, Native Americans and Asian-Americans lived in Oklahoma at [the] beginning of the 20th century. They shared a territory but lived in separate communities. . . . Arena's frontier is a fully cross-cultural one."[23] With romantic imagery of the "tapestry" and "frontier," Smith wove together a rationale for the multiracial cast to represent both the territory folks in 1907 and Americans in 2010.

Because Smith staged *Oklahoma!* in the round, the diverse audience helped form the "tapestry" that was the backdrop to the production. The theatrical space attempted to promote a spirit of U.S. patriotism by hanging dozens of flags along the interior perimeter of the in-the-round theatre. The flags enveloped the spectators, actors, and musicians, encouraging inclusiveness in the "brand-new state" that promises to "treat you great."[24] The multiracial cast mediated the optimistic sense that equality is possible under the star-spangled banner. Yet this banner of nationalism covered up racial material differences, asking U.S. spectators to forget race because, after all, they are all Americans, even as race has always been a constitutive part of defining who counts as a U.S. citizen with full rights. Moreover, the multiracial casting as reflected in Arena's increasingly diverse audience can obscure historical and persistent racial segregation, particularly in the racially fraught DC metropolitan area.

Even as it potentially masks racial oppression, multiracial casting can also inspire social change. The Arena provides a space for people with different identities to sit next to each other, even though they likely live in segregated neighborhoods and attend segregated schools. For audiences of color, seeing performers of color especially in leading roles can provide crucial validation. The affect of joy and hope provoked by witnessing and participating in multiracial harmony can in turn provoke actions to make that harmony a reality outside the theatre. In 2012, reflecting on Smith's production as a "glorious, hopeful representation of a reimagined future," Dolan commended the artistic director for how she "takes the American canon—part of Arena's mandate—and refashions it to speak across identity communities, instead of sequestering it in presumptively white enclaves and preserving it for white people" and urged fans to write to Smith with their support.[25] In the context of a major theatre institution in Washington, and one that politicians often patronize, a multiracial *Oklahoma!* can ring a note of hope and progressive policy that resounds across the capital.

THEORIZING MULTIRACIAL MUSICAL REVIVALS AND CASTING

Musicals offer what Bruce Kirle calls "open texts," ready to be read differently across time and space in productions with new casts and directorial visions.[26] Revivals allow artists and audiences to reconsider the same story within new historical contexts and new racial projects. The prevailing racial project of the U.S. in 2010 was colorblindness, which sociologists of U.S. racial formation Michael Omi and Howard Winant have identified as a reaction to 1960s strides for civil rights.[27]

To end policies like affirmative action and ignore persistent structural inequities, conservatives perverted Martin Luther King Jr.'s call to look beyond skin color and pretend that race has no effect on how people are treated. In the 1990s, liberals had favored policies that would disproportionately benefit people of color such as funding for urban public schools but without naming race. The term "postrace" gained more currency during the Obama presidency, at once signaling a belief that Americans no longer noticed race and, at the same time, contradictorily *did* notice the remarkable achievement of electing a black president. Staging a multiracial *Oklahoma!* in 2010 put forth competing visions of race that resonated with Obama's presidency, since it depicted some cultivating symbols of racial equality and others adamantly preserving white privilege. Arena's artists and patrons navigated the racial projects and overdetermined texts of *Oklahoma!*, its marketing, and its casting to make sense of race and U.S. identity in this production and in that particular moment.

Historicizing race relations and theorizing spectatorship are messy, multifaceted endeavors. Naming racial identities should not be taken as ahistorical, essentialized, and knowable, as if they have only one way of being that transcends context. Yet naming race may be necessary, even as such naming troublingly reifies race as if it were fixed or natural, rather than unstable or manufactured. The words that people choose to discuss race have a material impact on how they address racism. To underscore and examine race, I argue that the term I have used throughout the text—"multiracial" casting—makes more sense here than "colorblind" or "nontraditional" casting. Calls for theatrical "colorblindness" often come from white men and presume that people do not or should not see race, as if race rather than systemic racism is the impediment.[28] Even though theatre conjures a make-believe world, U.S. Americans do see color, and disavowing that perception erases the realities of how racial hierarchy shapes individuals' identities, communities, social relations, and actual lifespans. The erasure preserves current inequalities by rationalizing that if they are not seen, then they must not exist. In *The Problem of the Color[blind]*, Brandi Wilkins Catanese shows the ironies of colorblindness: "a heightened and sublimated awareness of race" that can lead to tokenistic casting of nonwhite actors "to prove that they no longer face specific barriers" and mark "the triumph of racial transcendence."[29] The inclusion of a single person of color, on the basis of race, paradoxically mitigates the appearance of white supremacy and the salience of race. The 1988 Non-traditional Casting Project framed "nontraditional" casting as a social justice project to give more roles to minoritized performers. The project took into consideration the uneven distribution of parts based on privileges.[30] But what constitutes "traditional" casting, and for how long has that been common practice? Director and educator Daniel Banks offers "integrated" in lieu of "nontraditional," and playwright Dominique Morisseau proposes "color-consciousness," the latter being a term that Arena staff members use themselves.[31] "Multiracial" avoids the not-so-blind spots of "colorblindness" and the false binary of "nontraditional," while still leaving room for dynamic interpretations. "Multiracial casting" can encompass Banks's and Morisseau's critiques of whiteness as the apparently neutral, unmarked default, and specifically address productions with intentionally racially diverse casts, not theoretically color-conscious, all-white productions.

Understanding the casting of territory folks in *Oklahoma!* in the age of Obama falls into three primary modes: (1) multiracial-conscious, (2) whitened, and (3) postracial. In the multiracial-conscious mode, producers and spectators could make the bodily equation of actor and character, using the logic of racial legibility. Angela Pao stresses the dominance of realism in U.S. media so that audiences perceive the racialized body of an actor in relation to their character, and consciousness of this process develops especially when people of color portray implicitly or explicitly white characters.[32] In *Oklahoma!* a race- and body-conscious lens would present a multiracial utopia of black, Latinx, Asian, Native American, white, and mixed-race actors singing and dancing together as black, Latinx, Asian, Native American, white, and mixed-race characters. In the whitened mode, producers and spectators could whitewash the roles. They could register the various races of the actors and then assume that they were for the most part playing white characters. For example, the black actresses who portrayed Laurey and Aunt Eller could appear white in order to conform to typically all-white productions of *Oklahoma!* and hegemonic narratives of the state's history. In *Whiting Up*, Marvin McAllister calls this practice "Stage Europeans," with "black actors exploring whiteness through conventional white dramatic characters."[33] In the postracial mode, producers and spectators could perceive the cast and characters as transcending race. They could have comprehended the cast in the allegedly colorblind world of Obama's presidency where racism does not exist. For instance, this view permits the disavowal of any racial meaning in Jud, played by a white actor, breaking up the romance of Laurey and Curly, played by actors of color. Here Jud may be just a jealous lover. The multiracial, whitened, and postracial modes of understanding bodies as performing racial projects are not static but dynamic, and they are not necessarily discrete. They can be contradictory within and between modes. They have different political valences in affirming, challenging, and changing race and institutional racism.

Audiences have different horizons of expectations with respect to *Oklahoma!*, Arena Stage, and other multiracial productions, as well as different processes for understanding race in the United States. In *Signifying without Specifying: Racial Discourse in the Age of Obama*, Stephanie Li observes, "In the absence of specifically racialized language, individuals interpret codes and behaviors in multiple and even contradictory ways. 'Race-specific, race-free language' performs a form of double consciousness by making race apparent only to the discerning reader."[34] Multiracial casting can trigger numerous questions, especially because U.S. American spectators versed in realism tend to read the body of an actor into the character and try to make sense of that character in context. In Arena's production of *Oklahoma!* the context could be one or more of several multiracial, whitened, and/or postracial frames with which the audience could measure "reality": the Oklahoma and Indian Territories in the early 1900s, the time of the debut of the musical in 1943, and/or the time of Arena's production in 2010. But all three modes contribute to the oppressive premises of *Oklahoma!*'s narrative. Having a multiracial cast without significant indigenous presence that is read as multiracial, white, or postracial erases Native Americans and makes racial egalitarianism appear effortless.

White and Native American playwright Lynn Riggs was far more attentive to racial specificity and history in *Green Grow the Lilacs*, which has a different ending from the musical version of the story. In the play, after Curly and Jud fight and Jud dies by falling on his own knife, Curly goes to federal prison to await a formal trial. When the territory folks catch him escaping from prison, Aunt Eller persuades everyone to allow him to spend his wedding night with Laurey. She admonishes them, "Why, the way you're sidin' with the federal marshal, you'd think us people out here lived in the United States!" to which they reply, "Now, Aunt Eller, we hain't furriners. My pappy and mammy was *both* borned in Indian Territory! Why, I'm jist plumb full of Indian blood myself."[35] Citing blood, which reduces race to biological essence, they claim to be part Indian, and they identify as Indian Territory folks, not as U.S. Americans, so they are willing to flout U.S. federal law. To Americanize the musical, Hammerstein erased this indigenous complexity and celebrated only the United States. In the musical, Curly does not go to prison; instead, the ensemble immediately stages an informal trial and exonerates him, and they gleefully sing about the territory becoming a state. The musical ultimately celebrates settler colonialism.

Seen through the postracial mode, Arena's multiracial casting and the celebratory ending have the potential to elide *Oklahoma!*'s material differences, as if territory folks are all the same and have always harmonized. Audience members may enter and leave the theatre believing that racial parity has already been achieved and therefore race does not matter. As sociologist Eduardo Bonilla-Silva has illustrated in *Racism without Racists*, the vast majority of white Americans refute the existence of white privilege and trip over their tongues when pressed to discuss race.[36] They deny systemic white supremacy and their implication therein, typically using a frame of abstract liberalism that champions equal opportunity and assumes an already-level playing field, while it obscures and justifies racial material inequality. They downplay vast racial disparities in income, housing, education, hiring, media representation, life expectancy, policing, and sentencing of those convicted of crimes.[37] Although Arena Stage's casting decisions productively redefined the borders of the United States to include multiracial territory folks, those same decisions excluded and flattened others. The result largely maintained structural racism because of what American Studies scholar Jodi Melamed calls neoliberal multiculturalism, which mobilizes images of diversity to drown out radical articulations of race and nation and equitable redistribution of power.[38]

When casting the musical, Arena's creative team was sensitive to the storytelling aspect of having certain characters played by actors of certain races because of histories of racial representations. They anticipated that spectators would pay attention to bodily racial legibility and then map the race of the actors onto the race of their respective characters. As a consequence, they decided that the comic couple Will Parker and Ado Annie should not be played by black actors for fear of recalling blackface minstrelsy, and that Jud should not be played by a black or Native American actor in order to avoid stereotypes of drunken, sexually threatening, working-class, male villains of color. The creative team briefly considered casting a Native American actor as Jud because his outsider status and death would resonate with the violent treatment of indigenous peoples by the U.S. state. But they claimed that they did not find a suitable singing actor, and they expressed concerns about offending audiences who might misinterpret their intention with such a portrayal.[39] White actors were cast in these three parts, suggesting that whiteness appears unmarked, unburdened with racial baggage, so that it can be safely laughed at or villainized.

To avoid simple tokenism, the creative team cast the rest of the principals, not just a few ensemble members, with actors of color. For Aunt Eller, the creative team reached out to the African American actress E. Faye Butler. Although she regularly performs at Arena, she initially did not think the offer was serious because the idea of a multiracial production of Oklahoma! felt so farfetched; her response suggested that multiracial stagings of Golden Age musicals are rarities.[40] Once she accepted, Arena Stage cast another black actress as Laurey: Valisia LeKae. When LeKae left the production shortly before the opening, Arena hired another black actress, Eleasha Gamble, instead of turning to the white understudy. Because the creative team wanted Curly to be of a different race from Laurey, they cast a mixed white, Latino, and Native American actor, Nicholas Rodriguez. Ali Hakim, a Persian peddler, was originally played on Broadway by a white Jewish actor, and white actors often continue to play this role in contemporary productions. Casting director Dan Pruksarnukul, however, determined that the role had to be considered "ethnically 'Persian' from the outset."[41] Illustrating sensitivity to a history of brownface, he cast a South Asian

American–identified actor, Nehal Joshi. Finally, the ensemble boasted black, Latinx, Asian, Native American, white, and mixed-race performers, resulting in an *Oklahoma!* where almost half the performers were people of color.

Arena Stage's multiracial casting practices are unusual and laudable. At the nearby Shakespeare Theatre Company during the same 2010–11 season, actors of color received 8 percent of the season's roles (9 out of 114), although nearly all of the roles lacked racial specificity. Signature Theatre cast only three actors of color during its 2010 season, one of them being Eleasha Gamble. Far from being a local anomaly, these statistics parallel those of New York City. The Asian American Performers Action Coalition (AAPAC) found that from 2006 to 2011, white actors made up four-fifths of roles on and off Broadway.[42] Actors of color played parts that correlated with their racial identity, rather than nonspecific roles, nine out of ten times.[43] According to the 2010 census, Washington residents were 51 percent black, 39 percent white, 9 percent Latinx, and 4 percent Asian.[44] Faring better than the average New York professional production, Arena's multiracial production of *Oklahoma!* more accurately reflected DC demographics and provided greater opportunities for performers of color.

Spectators may not have known the specific rationales for the casting of each character, yet the marketing probably prepared many of them. The subscription brochure avowed that the production was "not your mother's *Oklahoma!*"[45] Although the phrase hinted at a kind of daring progressiveness to make the production up to date like Kansas City, it also presumed a universalized ownership of this musical. At the top of the performance, Curly, performed by Nicholas Rodriguez, played "Oh What a Beautiful Mornin'" on his harmonica as he walked through the audience to reach the stage and Aunt Eller, performed by E. Faye Butler. Registering racial difference in the actors and audience around the Arena, spectators could actively think about the performativity and legibility of race. According to casting director Pruksarnukul, "Initially an audience reaction could be wondering, 'Why are people of a certain race?' But . . . eventually our hope was that that would be such a seamless, integrated, and well-balanced production and cast composition that it would no longer become a thought."[46] His remark resonates with Harvey Young's observation on multiracial productions: "As the play progresses, spectators become less conscious of an individual actor's race as the performer melds into her role and the audience becomes absorbed into the world of the play."[47] Pruksarnukul and Young both touch on contradictions between modes of reading productions as multiracial, whitened, and postracial. Arena's artists wanted to ground the multiracial cast in historical and contemporary demographics and redefine how the United States and Arena are racialized; at the same time, they wanted patrons to forget race. These desires reveal the intricacies of racial formation, intention, and reception. Although the creative team cast the production with progressive politics and a multiracial-conscious lens, the production could also serve more conservative ends when spectators viewed it through different lenses that whitened the characters or rendered race and structural racism invisible. Casting actors of color in white canonical works gives the appearance of inclusivity, but as August Wilson famously warned, that is also a form of cultural imperialism.[48]

WHITENING AND ERASING RACE

Because of a history of racial inequality and whitewashed productions, a multiracial version of *Oklahoma!* and the musical itself lend themselves to whitened readings. Marvin Carlson's concept of haunting is useful for thinking through how white actors in earlier productions of *Oklahoma!* and histories of Oklahoma itself influence audience's expectations of revivals.[49] Spectators may use the original Broadway production, white community or school productions, or the 1955 film version as authoritative texts that position the territory folks as white and that haunt contemporary productions.[50] The commonly accepted demographics of early twentieth-century frontier pioneers as white may also paint a white picture. To justify the equal treatment of all the characters in a multiracial revival, some spectators may consider the characters white, thereby putting them on a level playing field. The sole explicit dialogue engagement with race is the naming of Ali Hakim as Persian, leading to a presumption of whiteness for the other characters. Given the whitened preconceptions of *Oklahoma!*, spectators may reshape their understanding of the multiracial production to fit the white mold.

This whitened view particularly invisibilizes Native Americans, socially reproducing genocide.[51] The history of Oklahoma Territory and

Indian Territory is bound up with the United States' violent resettlement and containment of indigenous people. In the nineteenth century, the federal government forcibly removed many tribes to what became known as Indian Territory. Land runs by settlers from nearby states then resulted in parceling the area into Indian and Oklahoma Territories. While an attempt to turn Indian Territory into a state failed, the union of the territories made Oklahoma a state in 1907. Knapp argues that the musical silences this narrative because Rodgers and Hammerstein whitened and Americanized the characters of the original play *Green Grow the Lilacs*.[52] The musical demands a narrative in which implicitly or explicitly white characters stand for all the territory folks, and U.S. Americans revel in the ongoing project of settler colonialism.

Another portion of the audience may subscribe to the postracial project, using erasure to maintain unmarked and unremarked whiteness and its attendant privileges. Unlike the whitened view, the postracial view denies the significance of whiteness. This view argues that race no longer matters because racial equality has been achieved. McAllister observes, "There is a significant difference between racially transcendent and racially deconstructive whiting up, between stage Europeans who seek to 'get beyond' race and whiteface minstrels and stage Europeans who directly address racial representation onstage and identity construction offstage."[53] Seeing people of color play white characters, spectators may recognize race but then disavow it, because somehow by singing, by dancing, and by casting actors of color, white supremacy has been overcome. On seeing a multiracial production of a musical, they may conclude that there is no need to unpack the racial dynamics of the production because Americans are beyond race. The very existence of a multiracial cast, or a black president, provided proof that structural racism no longer existed. When spectators see representations of people of color, they often conclude that political and economic equality have also been achieved off the stage. Even as people of color become included on the stage, the terms of that inclusion rest on denying the solidity of continuing racial barriers.[54] Addressing this contradiction, Pao describes understandings of multiracial casting in plays by canonical white writers as both "a bold way for nonwhite actors to actively redefine national identity not only as individual artists but as representatives of their respective communities" and "a broad move [that] reinstates rather than destabilizes whiteness as the racial and cultural norm by reinforcing the illusion that white experiences, attitudes, and behavior exist outside history."[55] By casting actors of color in what is essentially a white version of Oklahoma history, the production to some extent legitimized that narrative as timeless and universal. Through Rodgers and Hammerstein's avoidance of naming race, the musical suggests that it does not exist as lived experience. Thus some spectators could subsequently slip into the postrace belief that race is merely a mask that can be put on and taken off at will. Josephine Lee, a scholar of Critical Race Studies and theatre, makes this critique of "colorblind" casting: the "paradox of seeing and not seeing race—where visible difference is important only to suggest that ultimately 'color doesn't really matter.'"[56] Because the characters in *Oklahoma!* were cast racially in ways to limit potential offense, some spectators could more easily erase color as well. For example, casting a white actor rather than a black or Native American actor as Jud reduces spectator fixation on racial stereotypes and violence performed on the bodies of men of color. In the world beyond the theatre, there are political consequences for cultural producers perpetuating the widespread belief of equality as already having been accomplished, when that was far from the case during and after Obama's presidency.

READING RACIALIZED ACTORS/CHARACTERS

Interpretations of Arena's 2010 *Oklahoma!* as multiracial-conscious, white, and/or postracial became more concrete yet also more complex when audiences engaged with racialized bodies onstage. The principal actors and characters raised different issues for racial legibility and relations between one another. For example, as an actor of mixed heritage, Nicholas Rodriguez presented opportunities for multiple readings of Curly. Regular theatre patrons of Arena Stage might have remembered him as Fabrizio the Italian in the musical *The Light in the Piazza* the previous season, casting that suggests the actor could convincingly play "ethnic" whites. Curly's dream ballet double in *Oklahoma!* was, interestingly, played by a white dancer, as spectators made the connection between these actors as the same character. Meanwhile, Rodriguez's recurring role as a gay Latino character on the soap opera *One Life to Live* in 2009 also haunted the actor, encouraging audiences to draw comparisons between these different performances. Reviewers called the actor either Hispanic or Latino, likely because of his last name, resulting in an erasure of his mixed background (Rodriguez identifies as Mexican American, Welsh, and Cherokee). Often racially illegible, mixed-race people exceed the boundaries of boxes, be they on census forms or onstage. Difficulty categorizing an actor's race and consequently a character's race can cause discomfort, self-consciousness, and critical thinking about the performativity of race. Through a multiracial lens, spectators could see Rodriguez and Curly as Latino, Native American, and/or mixed race. But because the actor also read as white and the character did not name race, both may be whitened or read as postracial.[57] In an interview, Rodriguez underlined, "I'm not playing Curly as a Latino; I'm just Curly."[58] Making a postracial move, he wanted to transcend race and asserted that "just" playing Curly was distinct and unmarked as opposed to "playing Curly as a Latino."

Aunt Eller as portrayed by E. Faye Butler also mediated racial signifiers and tensions. With her flirtations, shrewd remarks, and hands on hips, she resembled both the sassy black woman and the old, wise, black matron; these racialized and gendered stereotypes can be read as empowering, if clichéd. For the spectator using a multiracial reading of the production, her interactions with Curly took on different racial charges. When Curly said to her, "I wouldn't marry you ner none of yer kinfolks, I could he'p it," the playful line became striking because he could seem to be demonstrating antiblack and antimiscegenation views.[59] Curly *would* marry Aunt Eller's kinfolk, and he soon asked for Laurey, portrayed by Eleasha Gamble. Because Butler and Gamble, two black actresses, played family members, the casting implied that their characters are also black, a choice Smith often makes as a director[60] since discrepancies in the racial makeup of actors portraying relatives often disturb audience members expecting realism and biological "logic" to race.[61] Such thinking reveals the mode of equating an actor's race with their character's race rather than erasing race altogether.

Some spectators at the 2010 production opposed actors of different races playing romantic couples. Arena Stage received criticism from patrons who objected to Laurey being black, or being played by a black actress, or being involved with an apparently white actor/character.

Eleasha Gamble as Laurey and Nicholas Rodriguez as Curly in the Arena Stage at the Mead Center for American Theater 2010 production of Rodgers and Hammerstein's *Oklahoma!* Photo by Carol Rosegg courtesy of Arena Stage.

The slipperiness in their responses relays racial anxieties as well as uncertainties over the meaning of race in this context. A black actress in the role of Laurey has the potential to trouble notions of innocent, white femininity, mainly for spectators ghosted by Shirley Jones in the film version of *Oklahoma!*, among other productions. According to former literary manager Amrita Ramanan, some patrons complained that the production was "taking away their nostalgic impression of what this musical was meant to look like."[62] However, she added that the casting inclusive of actors who self-identified as black, Latinx, Asian, and Native American gave local public school students who attended the production "a new sense of inspiration" and "connected to the DC cultural zeitgeist at the time."[63] These mixed responses demonstrate that audiences cannot be assumed to perceive, withhold, and/or express the same beliefs about race and systemic racism. Both explicit racism and racial progressiveness are vibrant, resonating with Americans' ambivalence toward Obama's performance as president, another black actor in a typically white role.

White actors played Will, Ado Annie, and Jud, but such casting, expected in white versions of *Oklahoma!*, does not necessarily simplify their racial interpretations and positions in Arena's multiracial production. Many scholars have written on why Jud does not sing or dance with the community, contending that his exclusion rests largely on his racialization as nonwhite. In *Making Americans: Jews and the Broadway Musical*, Andrea Most asserts that Jud reads as black or at least "racial otherness."[64] She points to the smokehouse in which he lives, the resonances of lynching, and the stage direction in which Jud sings "like a Negro at a revivalist meeting." The 2010 edition of the libretto states, "Repeats reverently as if at a revivalist meeting," revealing a contemporary discomfort at bluntly characterizing Jud as "like a Negro."[65] Expanding on Most, Kirle and Knapp contend that the character can be read as Native American, whereas U.S. theatre scholar Derek Miller adds that he might be seen as Jewish.[66] These readings gain greater legibility on the bodies of nonwhite actors, and another multiracial production of *Oklahoma!* that followed Arena's provides an example.

In February 2012, the 5th Avenue Theatre in Seattle produced *Oklahoma!* with a black actor as Jud among white principals and a multiracial ensemble from Spectrum Dance Theater. This significant regional theatre is devoted to presenting and producing musicals, some of which have transferred to Broadway. Many critics cited its casting of a black actor as Jud as "problematic" or "provocative," pointing to when Curly, played by a white actor, encouraged Jud to hang himself and when Curly was acquitted for Jud's death.[67] The theatre company apparently did not anticipate such an uproar, since it subsequently scheduled panels to discuss the casting. These reactions suggest that some spectators saw the production in a multiracial mode, translating the race of the actors to their respective characters. The theatre company saw its *Oklahoma!* as multiracial, yet, in a postracial turn, saw beyond race when censured for the casting of Jud, ultimately disavowing its complicity with black stereotypes and continuing racial inequality.

The 5th Avenue Theatre production throws the Arena Stage production into relief because, for the latter, Jud was cast as white amid a racially diverse cast of principals and ensemble.[68] When he tried to break up Curly and Laurey's wedding, he could be seen as the white who refuses to integrate, so his whiteness amplified rather than neutralized his villainy. In this light, his behavior could bring to mind racial tensions on the frontier in 1907 but also 2010, when many white Americans feared losing their demographic majority, a fear that has intensified in the present. In the multiracial mode, Jud stood for the outlier of the imagined diverse society in Arena's *Oklahoma!* and in the United States. For those communities to thrive, Jud must be removed. Yet Smith directed Jud as a possible romantic partner for Laurey, played by a black actress. To cultivate sympathy for Jud, she created a long, tense pause after Curly emerged from the knife fight alive. As a consequence, Jud could be read as a white ally who deserves to be mourned. To reconcile the complexities of his outsider status, desire for Laurey, and death, spectators could relinquish racial meanings for a postracial understanding. The move toward colorblindness can be seductive because it glosses over the complexities of racial power dynamics in order to make sense of the dramaturgy on- and offstage and, in this case, it can exempt whites' responsibility in dismantling racial structures.

Scholars' arguments about Jud as outsider frequently involve Ali Hakim as his counterpart and assimilated other, yet reading his race proves another complicated process. Most offers a compelling case for the character's implicit Jewishness because of his coded mannerisms and dialogue.[69] Ali Hakim was initially Armenian in honor of the musi-

The company of the Arena Stage at the Mead Center for American Theater 2010 production of Rodgers and Hammerstein's *Oklahoma!* Photo by Carol Rosegg courtesy of Arena Stage.

cal's original director, Rouben Mamoulian, and later became a Persian played by a Jewish actor.[70] When Nehal Joshi played Ali Hakim, his South Asian identity related to the rest of the cast in various ways. If the races of the other actors were meant to be reproduced in their characters, as in the multiracial mode, then Ali Hakim was part of that diverse community, and he would be subsequently welcomed by Ado Annie, her father, and finally his betrothed Gertie Cummings. But such an interpretation disrupts how his character is meant to be racially distinct from the other territory folks. Joshi used a different accent from the rest of the actors, inviting spectators to take his actor-character race literally, while the accents of the other characters were whitened.

Ultimately, *Oklahoma!* the musical celebrates community, and the multiracial production encouraged a multiracial reading of U.S. nationhood. In lyrics that resonate with class, race, and gender equality, Aunt Eller teaches the farmers and cowmen, both played by actors of multiple races, to sing together, "I don't say I'm no better than anybody else, / But I'll be damned if I ain't jist as good!"[71] The choreography for this number mediated her sentiment with grounded footwork and athletic moves that the multiracial ensemble performed

NATION

in sync as if to say that all were strongly and equally capable. Spread out across the stage with their toes turned out and arms akimbo, the actors took up equal shares of space. Finally, after Jud and Ali Hakim leave the stage, the company sings the rousing titular song to proclaim their rightful place in a multiracial United States: "We know we belong to the land."[72] In the final scene, the black, Latinx, Asian, Native American, white, and mixed-race performers, led by the white Latino–Native American actor playing Curly, formed a circle around a float, an oil rig bedecked with Americana, and faced the audience on all four sides of the arena. The performers and characters staked a claim to what constituted American identity historically, in 2010, and in the future as a multiracial, equal collective. This claim was exceedingly important in 2010, a time when Oklahoma, which means "the Land of the Red People" in Choctaw, remained one of the most conservative states in the union—red in an entirely different way. Musical harmony suggested the possibility of national harmony.

When watching this number from the audience in 2010, I felt brief hope. A child of immigrants, I belong here. I looked at the multiracial performers below and the audience members around me. I thought about my queer and of-color coworkers at Arena Stage. I considered Barack Obama sitting in the Oval Office just a few miles away. My eyes welled with the tears of optimism. I experienced the affect of Dolan's utopian performative "that beyond this 'now' of material oppression and unequal power relations lives a future that might be different, one whose potential we can feel as we're seared by the promise of a present that gestures toward a better later."[73] Yes, if only this nation could be like this production of *Oklahoma!*

Yet after leaving the theatre, I was "seared" by the discrepancy between representation and reality. Bonilla-Silva uses an apt musical metaphor to diagnose post–civil rights–era colorblind racism: "Its 'we are beyond race' lyrics and color-blind music will drown the voices of those fighting for racial equality ('Why continue talking about race and racism when we are all Americans?') and may even eclipse the space for talking about race altogether."[74] Privileging Americanness forms an imagined community of settler colonists who share nationhood at the expense of Native Americans as well as racial, gender, class, sexuality, and ability differences and discourses. Moreover, images of racial diversity potentially frame debates over resources as only debates over representation. Multiracial casts in musical revivals may be pleasing and inspire utopian performatives, but they do not solely, directly, and necessarily counter hegemony; indeed, they can be deployed to maintain power structures. When the multiracial ensemble sings, "Oklahoma / OK!," a largely middle-class, white audience can come away with the message that that state of the union is "OK!," thereby sustaining the status quo of material inequality and belief that racism is no longer salient. To the extent that white Americans do believe that systemic racial discrimination exists, they think that antiwhite bias surpasses antiblack bias.[75] As Pruksarnukul and Young suggest, audiences may begin by viewing multiracial actors as multiracial characters, but as the performance progresses, they may see the characters as white or the world as postracial. When people of color deal with systemic violence daily, and when many with white privilege see U.S. institutions as fair, multiracial musicals can both offer hope and do damage.

CRITICAL GAZES

Reviews of the 2010 Arena production represent a range of spectatorship experiences in the modes of multiracial-conscious, whitened, and/or postracial. For the most part, critics were extremely enthusiastic. Several of them cited the multiracial casting as the fresh element that justified the production of such a "chestnut" as *Oklahoma!*[76] The reviewers tended to detail the races of the actors playing Curly, Laurey, and Aunt Eller but never discussed those of Jud, Will, Ado Annie, and Ali Hakim. This implies that performers of color in typically white roles must be named, while whiteness need not be identified because it is presumed. Meanwhile, the silence about Ali Hakim suggests that Joshi's South Asian background was normal or expected, despite a history of casting white actors in that role. These critics celebrated the racial diversity of the U.S. both in the present and in the past, registering surprise because of the historical information regarding Oklahoma's frontier diversity in their theatre programs.[77]

Other critics adopted more ambivalent views that gestured toward the multiracial mode but concluded with normative whiteness and disavowals of race. Terry Teachout of the *Wall Street Journal* asserted, "Ms. Smith's 'Oklahoma!' is a perfectly, almost baldly straightforward production that deviates from the norm in only two ways: It is performed in the round by a multicultural cast whose members include a Latino Curly (Nicholas Rodriguez) and a black Laurey (Eleasha Gamble). Otherwise, this is much the same 'Oklahoma!' that your grandfolks loved."[78] Leslie Milk of the *Washingtonian* wrote, "Smith has assembled a multicultural cast, but to be honest, you hardly notice."[79] These reviews work against Arena's marketing and further reveal how the identity of "your grandfolks" and "you" shape conceptions of race, in this case, among privileged white critics who work for bourgeois newspapers and presume that "you" identify the same way. Claiming that the multiracial production resembles earlier productions and that race is hardly noticeable depoliticizes and ahistoricizes race. Furthermore, Teachout and Milk used the term "multicultural" instead of "multiracial" to downplay race, even though the former referred to the characters as "Latino Curly" and "black Laurey." A few reviewers never mentioned the multiracial casting, perhaps not wanting to show that they see race in the first place or, again, not seeing it as significant. Not naming race could also be because production stills accompanied the reviews, allowing the reader to interpret the visual, bodily "evidence" of the actors. Through these reviews, the critics, like Arena Stage, took part in redefining race and the United States when making sense of the multiracial production.

The review by Peter Marks, chief critic of the *Washington Post*, was noteworthy because he is at present the most powerful critic in the nation's capital. His review negotiated several positions but primarily that of postrace. He remarked that the production had a "cast whose faces reflect the America of this moment. [Molly Smith's] exciting take . . . touches on the uplift you feel merely walking into Arena's newly glittering complex, itself a representation of the nation's optimistic impulse for reinvention."[80] Like Smith, Marks connected racial diversity with the U.S., Arena Stage, and the company's new theatre building, using a positive, bootstraps outlook of "reinvention." After identifying the lead actors' ethnicities, he stated, "But not only is there some historical support for these choices, it's also a fact that each of them sings like a dream. In the benevolent land of opportunity that is conjured here, they've earned these jobs, on merit."[81] He highlighted the historical justification for the multiracial cast, implying that he was skeptical before reading the dramaturg's and director's notes. In his praise of the performers, Marks randomly criticized affirmative action, suggesting that not all people of color have gotten their jobs "on merit."[82] He performed a dubious move here, as if people of color, not white people, are the ones who profit from systemic advantages. Marks also praised *Oklahoma!* in contrast with Smith's prior direction of Golden Age musicals such as *Damn Yankees!* and *Cabaret*, which "too often seemed to feel the need for intrusive statementmaking and stagy embellishment."[83] In so doing, he intimated that the multiracial cast in *Oklahoma!* was *not* "intrusive statementmaking and stagy embellishment," tempering the profound racial dynamics of the production. For Marks, the key theme of the musical is "American resilience" in an unmarked way, although he began by remarking on the "faces" of the actors and ended by saying, "That beleaguered-looking guy in the White House might want to swing by one night soon."[84] His contradictory understanding of this multiracial *Oklahoma!* in seeming to recognize race yet refuse to recognize racial, material disparity emblematizes the complexity of spectatorship and race. Marks's review indexes the Obama presidency's hegemonic racial project of postrace, which is paradoxically race-conscious. His review likely primed some spectators before they visited *Oklahoma!*, signifying the power of reshaping and reproducing hegemonic racial and national identity formations. However, his review does not foreclose resistant readings that acknowledge the salience of race and systemic racism and imagine a radically equal, multiracial community.

CONCLUSION

Since Arena opened the Mead Center for American Theater building in 2010, it has continued to stage multiracial productions of Golden Age musicals. In 2012, Smith directed *My Fair Lady* featuring Manna Nichols, an Asian/white/Native American actress, as Eliza Doolittle, an Asian American actor as her father, white actors as Henry Higgins and Colonel Pickering, Nicholas Rodriguez as Freddy, and a multiracial ensemble. Through a multiracial reading, the casting provoked considerations of imperialism and the performance of race as intersecting with class. Similar to the treatment of *Oklahoma!*, the marketing and dramaturgy cited historical demographics of Asian immigrants in England to justify the casting. But audiences could also whiten the characters to conform to expectations of *My Fair Lady*, *Pygmalion*, and

England, or they could rationalize race as irrelevant in this allegedly postrace world. In 2016, Arena staged another multiracial production of a Rodgers and Hammerstein musical, *Carousel*, with Nicholas Rodriguez and E. Faye Butler once again in principal roles. The theatre has come to rely on its annual musical during the winter holidays to help bankroll the institution.[85]

Multiracial musical revivals are a major part of Arena's branding as the largest regional theatre devoted to American voices, and their modes of production and consumption mediate contemporary racial politics. Cara Mazzie, an actress in *Oklahoma!*, said that she thought that the 2010 production was successful because it reflected the diversity of the United States, Obama's administration, and larger social change.[86] That final, hopeful word, "change," gestures to how the multiracial production of this particular musical staged a utopian performative and keyed into the age of a black president sitting in the White House in the same city; it signaled a step forward in representation but also a continuation in structure. Although Arena Stage's multiracial casting decisions reinforced troubling visions that occlude Native Americans, material difference, and ongoing fights for equality, the casting also troubled visions of territory folks as only white farmers and cowmen. Arena staged Americans as multiracial territory folks who ought to stick together.

EPILOGUE

n 2011, Zelda Fichandler pronounced, "a theatre institution, in and of itself, is an artwork."[1] As the founding producing director of Arena Stage, she crafted the company by both satisfying and expanding what the field of cultural production could bear, and she created the template for Doug Wager and Molly Smith. Arena Stage's legacy encompasses inventing nonprofit theatre status to representing both blackness and Americanness in the round. Although Arena's aesthetic has changed from eclectically global to definitively U.S. American, one through-line of Fichandler's, Wager's, and Smith's tenures has been a commitment to cultivating black artists, audiences, and stories. This commitment came from not only a sense of social justice to offer more diverse U.S. representation and give greater access amid a majority-black population in Washington, but also an economic imperative to attract new audiences and win grants. A reformist move, the gradual inclusion of blackness performs progressive work, yet the time for justice is now. For nearly seventy years, Arena has thrived critically and commercially by celebrating racial liberalism, from its onstage productions and audience development to its symbolic location and narrative of inclusivity in its institutional identity.

The first professional resident company in the nation's capital, Arena now competes with more than ninety local companies, though it remains the second largest after the Kennedy Center. Only New York City has more theatre productions each year than Washington does.[2] Arena's annual budget has grown to almost $20 million to support its new facilities, plays, and community of multiracial American artists and audiences.

Initially, Arena struggled with generating income following the opening of the Mead Center in 2010. Paying for and maintaining the building created a huge financial burden that influenced programming decisions. According to former artistic associate David Dower, after the economic recession in 2008, "we hit a kind of perfect storm: the financing fell apart, fundraising stalled, and then the audiences didn't materialize in Crystal City for the years that we were out of the building."[3] Jamie Gahlon, who cofounded and codirected the American Voices New Play Institute (AVNPI) and who had worked in the human resources and business departments, added, "as soon as the doors opened, people thought, 'Oh, it's all raised, right?' But that wasn't the case."[4] Dower argued that "the building really distorted the ambition and aspiration," leading the company to produce known commodities rather than take risks.[5] The artistic development team needed time to figure out how to operate effectively in the new building, but they could not afford that time. In 2012, Nelson Pressley of the *Washington Post* critiqued Arena for producing few world premieres in the Cradle, which had been designated as the space to "cradle" challenging new work.[6] At the same time, Arena alienated some theatre organizations by calling its glistening complex a "Center for American Theater," a move which seemed to claim ownership of that title.

The organization's structure changed significantly in 2012. Dower and Gahlon, along with AVNPI staff members Vijay Prashad and P. Carl, moved HowlRound, Arena's hub for studying contemporary U.S. theatre, to Emerson College, shifting the location to a formal educational institution. Since then, the AVNPI has been reduced considerably, leaving behind some playwright residencies and commissions.

Arena has not been alone in its struggle to survive after the 2008 recession. The Guthrie Theater, which has hewed to classics but has also presented new Broadway musicals, furloughed most of its full-time employees for one week in January 2014.[7] Later that year, Signature Theatre, just outside of Washington, was saved from disaster by a multimillion-dollar loan and generous debt forgiveness.[8] Some critics have blamed the deficits on the exorbitant cost of the theatres' new buildings.

To help justify their existence, nonprofit theatres often point to the economic benefit that they bring to their communities via dollars spent on local restaurants. A 2009 study of Signature and Arena, when the company operated in Arlington, Virginia, found that theatre attendance generated approximately $4 million in restaurant and retail sales annually.[9] But this argument reduces the value of performance to monetary accumulation within the terms of capitalism. In his study of arts policy in an increasingly competitive ecosystem of entrepreneurship, Paul Bonin-Rodriguez encourages measurements of success beyond economic capital, as he traces tensions and collaborations between funding agencies and artist-producers.[10] Others studies, such as *Counting New Beans*, attempt to quantify the intrinsic impact of theatre in order to move the central value away from money and toward affective experiences.[11] Some critics continue to lament the state of the art as having gone commercial, while they romanticize the purer motives and ideals of theatre companies and leaders of the past. Such was the common complaint during a convening of theatre professionals in 2011 hosted by HowlRound.[12] However, in her speech launching the first Zelda Fichandler Award given by the Stage Directors and Choreographers Society in 2009, Fichandler reminded the audience that producing regional theatre had not been any easier in the past.[13]

Still, it is true that there are more tangled relations between nonprofit and for-profit theatre now than when Fichandler first launched Arena. In "Puttin' the Profit in Nonprofit Broadway Theatre Companies," Dean Adams expresses concern for the legal classification and purpose of nonprofit companies: "Blurring the distinctions, bringing profits to nonprofits, can be hazardous to a nonprofit's mission (or definition), even as these new financial arrangements provide nonprofits with an infusion of funds, a company's lifeblood, to help ensure survival."[14] Commercial producers increasingly give nonprofit theatres enhancement money. They cover a significant percentage of production costs to test new shows with subscription audiences before transferring the productions to commercial runs. In exchange, nonprofit companies receive subsidy and the sheen of a pre-Broadway tryout. This is the new "nonprofit yet for-profit" model. Since the Mead Center opened, Arena has presented more productions and accepted enhancement money from commercial producers to stage Broadway-bound plays including *A Time to Kill*, *One Night with Janis Joplin*, and *The Velocity of Autumn*. In 2018, the company produced the world premiere of the political comedy *Dave*, a musical adaptation of the Warner Brothers film, which the *Washington Post* called "Arena's most decidedly corporate alliance yet, as a major film studio is a principal backer."[15]

Molly Smith's Broadway directing debut, *The Velocity of Autumn*, exemplifies Arena's continuing anxieties about accumulating economic and symbolic capital. Written by Eric Coble, the play premiered at Arena in 2013 and played for five weeks on Broadway in 2014. A small play, in contrast with *The Great White Hope*, it featured a single set designed by Eugene Lee and only two characters, played by theatre actors Estelle Parsons and Stephen Spinella. Engaging with themes of property, queer identity, and support for elderly parents, *The Velocity of Autumn* focuses on an old white woman who threatens to blow up her apartment if her son forces her to leave. In New York, the production earned a Tony nomination for Parsons, little critical praise, and low ticket sales. The Broadway playbill included an insert with a biography for Arena, suggesting that the company's role in the production had been forgotten in the original publication. The description emphasizes Arena's American identity ("national center dedicated to American voices and artists"), new work ("committed to commissioning and developing new plays"), huge size ("annual audience of more than 300,000"), diversity ("presents diverse and ground-breaking work"), and educational initiatives ("impacts the lives of more than 20,000 students annually") in order to distinguish Arena and its programs made possible by nonprofit classification.[16] Nowhere does the biography locate the theatre in Washington. This absence indicates Arena's move to position itself as a "national center" rather than simply a regional theatre, just as the move to Broadway boosts the company's status. As of this writing, Arena has staged twenty-two productions that went on to Broadway.[17] During the 2016–17 season, the company found immense success with the musical *Dear Evan Hansen* by Benj Pasek and Justin Paul and the play *Sweat* by Lynn Nottage, both of which transferred to Broadway and garnered significant awards including Nottage's second Pulitzer Prize.

As it did from Arena's earliest days, national success allowed the company to continue its layered performance of U.S. racial and national identities by commissioning new locally based works and world premieres. In 2014, inspired in part by Baltimore-based Center Stage's My America project, Smith commissioned twenty-five U.S. playwrights to pen short monologues or scenes for *Our War*, directed by Anita Maynard-Losh.[18] The project unpacks the legacy of the Civil War through not only black and white perspectives but other marginalized voices bound up in histories of U.S. material inequality. The invited playwrights included artists who have ongoing relationships with Arena and span different racial, gender, and queer identities, from Lydia Diamond and Robert O'Hara to Tanya Saracho and Taylor Mac. The ensemble of actors was multiracial, and each performance featured a monologue delivered by an important local figure such as Supreme Court Justice Ruth Bader Ginsburg or Washington Delegate to the House of Representatives Eleanor Holmes Norton. According to actress Kelly Renee Armstrong, audiences responded to *Our War* with affirmations: "One performance house night had some audience members like me. That is to say, they respond to theatre in a vocal way that everyone can hear. It was an 'amen corner' type experience, and we just had fun."[19] Armstrong recounted that audiences often pondered the future life of *Our War*, even as they noted its aptness for Washington and Arena Stage. The production illustrates the generative possibilities for a nonprofit theatre staging multifaceted, multiracial understandings of representation in the United States, and the queries concerning which city the production might appear in next hint at the national economies of regional and New York theatres.

More than fifty years after the construction of Arena's permanent home, Southwest DC is experiencing the development that urban planners had long desired. In 2013, during the run of David Lindsay-Abaire's *Good People*, which deals with classism, Arena hosted a job fair for nontheatre people, now a regular affair. In addition, the theatre permits community members to use a library named Molly's Study as a meeting space. Such endeavors symbolize Arena's commitment to its community, bound up with capitalist urban development and gentrification. Since the 2010 census, the black population of Washington has dipped to under 50 percent for the first time in decades. The city has become increasingly white, wealthy, and educated. In 2010, the average Arena Stage patron had a household income of $105,800 and a graduate degree, while the median income in the nation's capital was $62,009.[20] In 2015, Arena's executive director Edgar Dobie remarked enthusiastically, "Everything's demolished across the street. They're building three new hotels. And eventually 1,200 new condos, a 6,000-capacity music hall, at least two dozen restaurants. It's really, really an exciting place to be. We discovered our architecture was truly embraced by its neighbors old and new."[21]

Even as the nation's capital becomes whiter, Smith has remained committed to a vision of U.S. identity focused on black Americans. Aside from Edward Albee and Eugene O'Neill, who have had festivals devoted to them, the most produced playwrights at Arena from 1990 to 2018 have been Cheryl West and August Wilson. The six mainstage productions of West's and Wilson's works represent the company's strong support of their voices and stories about African Americans. In the same 2013–14 season that Smith directed *The Velocity of Autumn*, she produced *Love in Afghanistan*, by Charles Randolph-Wright; *Guess Who's Coming to Dinner*, by Todd Kreidler; *Tappin' thru Life*, by Maurice Hines; *Smokey Joe's Café*, by Jerry Leiber and Mike Stoller; and *The Tallest Tree in the Forest*, by Daniel Beaty. In this repertory, she offered dramas of interracial relationships, feel-good black musicals, and a history of performer-activist Paul Robeson.

Performing American stories in the nation's capital, Arena provides sounding boards for voices that are often silenced and spaces for American audiences to assemble and think critically about national history and identity. Shortly after the presidential election in 2016, Arena announced Power Plays, an ambitious initiative to commission and develop twenty-five plays that grapple with U.S. politics from 1776 to the present with one play per decade. Speaking to this reactionary political moment, Smith asserted, "D.C. audiences are hungry for these stories, and there is no other place in the country where these plays could have such an impact. There is no better time to launch this massive commissioning cycle, the largest in Arena's history. The more we understand our American stories of politics and power, the more informed we become as a democracy."[22]

Even as nonprofit organizations provide the potential for groundbreaking, antiracist work, racially liberal theatre remains implicated in and largely upholds systems of power. The profit motive influences the selection of repertory so as to be not too radical and discomfiting for privileged patrons and critics. Arena certainly deserves recognition as one of the first U.S. companies to attempt a sustained commitment to multiracial casting in classic stage productions.[23] The company took risks and told critical U.S. American stories, pushing at the boundaries of what can be financially viable and nationally inclusive. But the company needed these black stories and patrons to survive. Epic histories, uplifting musicals, and adaptations of Western classics with people of color grappling with systemic racism give much-needed attention to minoritized people and their struggles. What is more, these are popular productions, suggesting a hunger for these narratives. They mobilize the framework of the United States to include others, but only with certain profitable, safer representations. They do not radically dismantle structures of capitalist accumulation, white supremacy, and patriotism; they foster inclusion on the basis of profit and under the U.S. flag. By producing racially liberal dramas, Arena generates different kinds of capital, diversifies Americanness, and stabilizes the institutions that are the theatre and the nation.

Arena Stage is by no means a perfect theatre, nor is the United States a perfect union magically free from socially reproducing capitalism, racism, and nationalism. But the company's unique history among regional theatres and deliberate incorporation of black bourgeois aesthetics and audiences deserve attention and, more than that, critical analysis. Nonprofit status, blackness, and an inclusive definition of Americanness provide the conditions of possibility for this traditionally white flagship to stay afloat. Even as the theatre capitalizes on the minoritized, Arena stages glimpses of equity in the round.

NOTES

INTRODUCTION

1. Zora Neale Hurston and Dorothy Waring, *Polk County*, adapted by Cathy Madison and Kyle Donnelly, p. 42, box 272, fol. 3, Arena Stage Administrative Records, Special Collections Research Center, George Mason University Library (hereafter cited as GMUL), Fairfax, VA.

2. For a close reading of the black feminist politics of *Polk County*, see Eric M. Glover, "By and About: An Antiracist History of the Musicals and the Antimusicals of Langston Hughes and Zora Neale Hurston" (PhD diss., Princeton University, 2017).

3. Playbill of *Polk County*, December 11–12, 2000, p. 2, box 51, fol. 4, Arena Stage Printed Materials, GMUL.

4. Anthea Kraut, *Choreographing the Folk: The Dance Stagings of Zora Neale Hurston* (Minneapolis: University of Minnesota Press, 2008), 4.

5. Cathy Madison and Kyle Donnelly's adaptation removes the word "Negro," perhaps due to a contemporary discomfort with this term.

6. E. Patrick Johnson, *Appropriating Blackness: Performance and the Politics of Authenticity* (Durham, NC: Duke University Press, 2003), 3.

7. John Lowe, "Hurston, Toomer, and the Dream of a Negro Theatre," in *"The Inside Light": New Critical Essays on Zora Neale Hurston*, ed. Deborah G. Plant (Santa Barbara: Praeger, 2010), 84.

8. Lynda Marion Hill, *Social Rituals and the Verbal Art of Zora Neale Hurston* (Washington: Howard University Press, 1996), 187.

9. For a theorization of Dorothy Waring's contributions to *Polk County*, see Keith L. Huneycutt, "'The Profound Silence of the Initiated': Zora Neale Hurston's *Polk County*, Dorothy Waring, and Stage Voodoo," in *Florida Studies: Proceedings of the 2009 Annual Meeting of the Florida College English Association*, ed. Claudia Slate and Carole Policy (Newcastle upon Tyne, UK: Cambridge Scholars, 2010), 39–49.

10. Robert E. Hemenway, *Zora Neale Hurston: A Literary Biography* (Urbana: University of Illinois Press, 1980), 298.

11. Pamela Bordelon, "New Tracks on *Dust Tracks*: Toward a Reassessment of the Life of Zora Neale Hurston," *African American Review* 31, no. 1 (1997): 9.

12. Cathy Madison, in discussion with the author, December 2014.

13. Kyle Donnelly, in discussion with the author, March 2015.

14. Cathy Madison, in discussion with the author, December 2014.

15. Mark Joseph Stern, "Scalia Fan Fiction," *Slate*, March 27, 2015, http://www

.slate.com/articles/news_and_politics/jurisprudence/2015/03/the_origin
alist_the_new_play_about_antonin_scalia_and_his_lesbian_law_clerk.html.

16. "'The Originalist' extends its hand across the aisle and finds the humanity in our civil discourse." http://ow.ly/1Rob3oclobf," tweet by @arenastage (Arena Stage), June 5, 2017, 3:00 p.m., https://twitter.com/arenastage/status/871849 184638488576.

17. David Román, *Performance in America: Contemporary U.S. Culture and the Performing Arts* (Durham, NC: Duke University Press, 2005), 36.

18. For data on U.S. faculty in general, see "Race/Ethnicity of College Faculty," National Center for Education Statistics, https://nces.ed.gov/fastfacts/display .asp?id=61. The only recent theatre-specific data with which I am familiar come from the American Society for Theatre Research and Association for Theatre in Higher Education's study of adjunct faculty: 81.1 percent self-identified as "Euro American," 5.4 percent declined to identify, and 4.5 percent identified as international, a category that includes white dominant countries. I should also note that there tends to be a lower percentage of people of color among full-time than adjunct faculty. "ASTR/ATHE Adjunct Survey Data," *News and Press: ATHE News*, August 25, 2016, http://www.athe .org/news/305136/ASTRATHE-Adjunct-Survey-Data.htm.

19. Hillary Miller, *Drop Dead: Performance in Crisis, 1970s New York* (Evanston, IL: Northwestern University Press, 2016), 44.

20. James M. Harding and Cindy Rosenthal, eds., *The Sixties, Center Stage: Mainstream and Popular Performances in a Turbulent Decade* (Ann Arbor: University of Michigan Press, 2017), 3–23.

21. Joseph Wesley Zeigler, *Regional Theatre: The Revolutionary Stage* (Minneapolis: University of Minnesota, 1973).

22. For examples of recently published histories of U.S. regional theatres, see Richard Christiansen, *Theater of Our Own: A History and a Memoir of 1,001 Nights in Chicago* (Evanston, IL: Northwestern University Press, 2004); Andrew Davis, *America's Longest Run: A History of the Walnut Street Theatre* (University Park: Penn State University Press, 2010); Yuko Kurahashi, *Asian American Culture on Stage: The History of the East West Players* (London: Routledge, 1999); Macelle Mahala, *Penumbra: The Premier Stage for African American Drama* (Minneapolis: University of Minnesota Press, 2013); John Mayer, *Steppenwolf Theatre Company of Chicago: In Their Own Words* (London: Bloomsbury, 2016); Claudia Orenstein, *Festive Revolutions: The Politics of Popular Theater and the San Francisco Mime Troupe* (Jackson: University Press of Mississippi, 1998); Jeffrey Ullom, *The Humana Festival: The History of New Plays at the Actors Theatre of Louisville* (Carbondale: Southern Illinois University Press, 2008) and *America's First Regional Theatre: The Cleveland Play House and Its Search for a Home* (New York: Palgrave Macmillan, 2014);

and Harvey Young and Queen Meccasia Zabriskie, *Black Theater Is Black Life: An Oral History of Chicago Theater and Dance, 1970–2010* (Evanston, IL: Northwestern University Press, 2013).

23. Laurence Maslon, *The Arena Adventure: The First 40 Years* (Washington: Arena Stage, 1990).

24. David Savran, *A Queer Sort of Materialism: Recontextualizing American Theater* (Ann Arbor: University of Michigan Press, 2003), 10.

25. For more on the distinction between highbrow and lowbrow culture in the United States, see Lawrence Levine, *Highbrow/Lowbrow: The Emergence of Cultural Hierarchy in America* (Cambridge, MA: Harvard University Press, 1988) and Michael Kammen, *American Culture, American Tastes* (New York: Alfred A. Knopf, 1999).

26. Savran, *A Queer Sort of Materialism*, 22–23.

27. Christopher B. Balme, *The Theatrical Public Sphere* (Cambridge: Cambridge University Press, 2014), 43.

28. Savran, *A Queer Sort of Materialism*, 100.

29. Frank Rizzo, "Yale Rep Celebrates Its 50th Amid Nostalgia (and a Few Worries)," *New York Times*, October 10, 2016, http://www.nytimes.com/2016/10/11/theater/yale-rep-celebrates-its-50th-amid-nostalgia-and-a-few-worries.html?_r=0. Brustein aided this commercialization process in 1984 when he produced the musical *Big River* at American Repertory Theatre at the behest of producer, future NEA head, and former student Rocco Landesman, and the musical subsequently transferred to Broadway.

30. Pierre Bourdieu, *The Field of Cultural Production* (New York: Columbia University Press, 1993).

31. Zelda Fichandler, "Whither (or Wither) Art?," *American Theatre* (May/June 2003): 30.

32. Charles W. Mills, *Black Rights / White Wrongs: The Critique of Racial Liberalism* (New York: Oxford University Press, 2017), 31.

33. Walter A. Jackson, *Gunnar Myrdal and America's Conscience: Social Engineering and Racial Liberalism, 1938–1987* (Chapel Hill: University of North Carolina Press, 1990), 240.

34. Cathy Irwin and Sean Metzger, "Keeping Up Appearances: Ethnic Alien-Nation in Female Solo Performance," in *Mixing It Up: Multiracial Subjects*, ed. SanSan Kwan and Kenneth Speirs (Austin: University of Texas Press, 2004), 178.

35. Harvey Young, *Theatre and Race* (New York: Palgrave Macmillan, 2013), 8.

36. Michael Omi and Howard Winant, *Racial Formation in the United States from the 1960s to the 1990s*, 2nd ed. (New York: Routledge, 1994), 56.

37. Ruth Ann Gilmore, *Golden Gulag: Prisons, Surplus, Crisis, and Opposition in Globalizing California* (Berkeley: University of California Press, 2007), 28.

38. Cedric J. Robinson, *Black Marxism: The Making of the Black Radical Tradition*, 2nd ed. (Chapel Hill: University of North Carolina Press, 2000).

39. Eduardo Bonilla-Silva, *Racism without Racists: Color-Blind Racism and the Persistence of Racial Inequality in America*, 4th ed. (Lanham, MD: Rowman & Littlefield, 2014), 9. Italics in the original.

40. David R. Roediger, *The Wages of Whiteness: Race and the Making of the American Working Class* (Brooklyn: Verso, 2007).

41. Cedric J. Robinson, *Forgeries of Memory and Meaning: Blacks and the Regimes of Race in American Theater and Film before World War II* (Chapel Hill: University of North Carolina, 2007).

42. Stephanie Batiste, *Darkening Mirrors: Imperial Representation in Depression-Era African American Performance* (Durham, NC: Duke University Press, 2012).

43. Adrienne Macki Braconi, *Harlem's Theaters: A Staging Ground for Community, Class, and Contradiction, 1923–1939* (Evanston, IL: Northwestern University Press, 2015).

44. U.S. Census Bureau, "District of Columbia—Race and Hispanic Origin: 1800 to 1990," U.S. Census Bureau, September 13, 2002, https://web.archive.org/web/20080726045433/http://www.census.gov/population/www/documentation/twps0056/tab23.pdf.

45. Sabrina Tavernise, "A Population Changes, Uneasily," *New York Times*, July 17, 2011, http://www.nytimes.com/2011/07/18/us/18dc.html.

46. Bernard Rosenberg and Ernest Harburg, "Prime City Box Office Totals," in *The Broadway Musical: Collaboration in Commerce and Art* (New York: New York University Press, 1993), 292–93.

47. Peter Marks, "The State of D.C. Theatre," *Washington Post*, January 6, 2012, http://www.washingtonpost.com/entertainment/theater-dance/the-state-of-dc-theater/2012/01/03/gIQADvwIfP_story.html.

48. Marvin Carlson, "National Theatres: Then and Now," in *National Theatres in a Changing Europe*, ed. S. E. Wilmer (Houndmills, UK: Palgrave Macmillan, 2008), 21.

49. Arena Stage, "About Arena Stage," http://www.arenastage.org/about/ (accessed May 7, 2012).

50. Arena Stage, "Mission, Vision and Values," https://www.arenastage.org/about-us/mission-vision-and-values/ (accessed July 31, 2018).

51. For more on imagined and invented nations, see Benedict Anderson, *Imagined Communities: Reflections on the Origin and Spread of Nationalism* (London: Verso, 1983); Eric Hobsbawm, *Nations and Nationalism since 1780: Programme, Myth, Reality*, 2nd ed. (New York: Cambridge University Press, 1992).

52. For more on the nation and intersectional identities, see Robert John Ackermann, *Heterogeneities: Race, Gender, Class, Nation, and State* (Amherst: Uni-

Notes to Pages 10–14

versity of Massachusetts Press, 1996); Étienne Balibar and Immanuel Waller-stein, *Race, Nation, Class: Ambiguous Identities*, 2nd ed. (London: Verso, 2011). For more on affect and the nation, see Sara Ahmed, *The Cultural Politics of Emotions* (New York: Routledge, 2004). For a queer-of-color critique on the relationship between state violence and national identity, see Chandan Reddy, *Freedom with Violence: Race, Sexuality, and the US State* (Durham, NC: Duke University Press, 2011).

53. Although using "America" and "American" can replicate global hierarchies, I use the same terminology as Arena Stage does for the sake of clarity and critical assessment. A simple substitution in terminology might do another kind of symbolic violence by ignoring the United States' historic and continuing imperialist projects, whereas "America" and "American" gesture toward empire and technologies of power.

54. Arena Stage, "Mission, Vision and Values," https://www.arenastage.org/about -us/mission-vision-and-values/ (accessed July 31, 2018).

55. Donatella Galella, "Diversity in Theatre and Higher Education," in "Archiving ATHE's Thirtieth Anniversary Conference Plenaries," ed. Kelly Howe, *Theatre Topics* 27, no. 1 (2017): 5–6. See also Sara Ahmed, *On Being Included: Racism and Diversity in Institutional Life* (Durham, NC: Duke University Press, 2012).

56. I use "[*sic*]" for gender inclusivity, and because regional theatre patrons tend to be women, though Fichandler referred to spectators using the pronoun "he."

57. Zelda Fichandler, "Introductory Remarks at a Panel on The Open Stage," given at the International Theatre Institute Conference in New York City, June 1967, reproduced in "Remembering Zelda: The Words of a Visionary," p. 98, http://arenastage.net/zelda/images/All%20Speeches.pdf?ignoremobile=y.

CHAPTER ONE

1. Martin Gottfried, *A Theater Divided: The Postwar American Stage* (Boston: Little, Brown, 1967), 6. Italics in the original.

2. Ibid., 4.

3. Ibid., 7.

4. See for instance Richard Schechner, "Blau and Irving at Lincoln Center," *Tulane Drama Review* 9, no. 4 (Summer 1965): 15–18.

5. Pierre Bourdieu, *The Field of Cultural Production* (New York: Columbia University Press, 1993).

6. Vincent Landro, "The Mythologizing of American Regional Theatre," *Journal of American Drama and Theatre* 10 (Winter 1998): 82.

7. I avoid the terms "unearned income," denoting money from donations and grants, and "earned income," denoting money from ticket sales, rentals, and the like, because both are earned or generated by labor.

8. Bourdieu, *The Field of Cultural Production*, 78.

9. Ibid., 51.

10. Dorothy Chansky, *Composing Ourselves: The Little Theatre Movement and the American Audience* (Carbondale: Southern Illinois University Press, 2004).

11. Paul DiMaggio, "Cultural Boundaries and Structural Change: The Extension of the High Culture Model to Theater, Opera, and the Dance, 1900–1940," in *Cultivating Differences: Symbolic Boundaries and the Making of Inequality*, ed. Michele Lamont and Marcel Fournier (Chicago: University of Chicago Press, 1992), 21–57.

12. See Elizabeth A. Osborne, *Staging the People: Community and Identity in the Federal Theatre Project* (New York: Palgrave Macmillan, 2011).

13. For more on Margo Jones, see Helen Sheehy, *Margo: The Life and Theatre of Margo Jones* (Dallas: Southern Methodist University Press, 1989).

14. Margo Jones, *Theatre-in-the-Round* (New York: Rinehart & Company, 1951), 67–68.

15. Kelsey Matthew, "How Helen Hayes Helped Desegregate the National Theatre," *Boundary Stones*, WETA's Local History Blog, June 22, 2016, http://blogs.weta.org/boundarystones/2016/06/22/how-helen-hayes-helped-desegregate-national-theatre.

16. Qtd. in Bernard Coyne, "A History of Arena Stage, Washington, D.C." (PhD diss., Tulane University, 1964), 14.

17. John DeFerrari, "Lost Washington: The Gayety Theater," *Greater Greater Washington* (blog), January 26, 2011, https://ggwash.org/view/8040/lost-washington-the-gayety-theater.

18. See for example Laurence Maslon, *The Arena Adventure: The First 40 Years* (Washington, DC: Arena Stage, 1990), 9.

19. Natka Bianchini, *Samuel Beckett's Theatre in America: The Legacy of Alan Schneider as Beckett's American Director* (New York: Palgrave Macmillan, 2015), 116.

20. Zelda Fichandler, "Report to the Stockholders of Arena Stage, Inc.," June 8, 1955, p. 1, box 1, fol. 32, Arena Stage Historical Documents 1950–1998, GMUL.

21. Zelda Fichandler, in discussion with the author, December 2012.

22. Qtd. in Bob Mondello, "Remembering Zelda Fichandler, Matriarch of American Regional Theater," *NPR*, August 4, 2016, http://www.npr.org/2016/08/04/488710159/remembering-zelda-fichandler-matriarch-of-american-regional-theater. Italics in the original.

23. Zelda Fichandler, "Report to the Stockholders of Arena Stage, Inc.," June 8, 1955, p. 5.

24. Zelda Fichandler, in discussion with the author, December 2012. For more on the politics of popular U.S. plays in this period, see Bruce McConachie,

American Theater in the Culture of the Cold War: Producing and Contesting Containment, 1947–1962 (Iowa City: University of Iowa Press, 2003).

25. Minutes of a Meeting of the Board of Directors of Arena Enterprises, May 8, 1958, p. 1, box 30, fol. 1, Thomas C. Fichandler Papers 1950–1997, GMUL.

26. Minutes of a Meeting of the Board of Directors of Arena Enterprises, June 29, 1959, p. 1, box 30, fol. 1, Thomas C. Fichandler Papers.

27. Zelda Fichandler, "A Permanent Classical Repertory Theatre in the Nation's Capital," p. 27, box 2, fol. 11, J. Burke Knapp Papers 1960s, GMUL.

28. Howard Taubman, "In Culture, Is Washington a Hick Town?," *Washington Post*, December 27, 1959, http://ezproxy.gc.cuny.edu/login?url=http://search .proquest.com.ezproxy.gc.cuny.edu/docview/114634140?accountid=7287 (accessed January 20, 2014).

29. Zelda Fichandler, "June 10, 1960 Meeting, Washington Drama Society," p. 10, box 107, fol. 22, Zelda Fichandler Papers 1950–2000, GMUL.

30. For more on the influence of critics, see John E. Booth, *The Critic, Power, and the Performing Arts* (New York: Columbia University Press, 1991), especially 44–45 for a study completed by the Kennedy Center.

31. Zelda Fichandler, "Arena Stage," May 11, 1963, p. 10, box 108, fol. 13, Zelda Fichandler Papers.

32. Zelda Fichandler, remarks at the meeting of the Washington Drama Society, June 7, 1961, p. 10, box 108, fol. 1, Zelda Fichandler Papers.

33. Ibid.

34. Ibid., p. 4.

35. Minutes of the First General Membership Meeting of the Washington Drama Society, Friday, June 10, 1960, p. 1, box 30, fol. 2, Thomas C. Fichandler Papers.

36. Zelda Fichandler, in discussion with the author, December 2012.

37. Zelda Fichandler, "Address to the Stage Directors and Choreographers Society in Celebration of the Third Annual Zelda Fichandler Award," *Howl-Round*, November 13, 2011, http://howlround.com/address-to-the-stage -directors-and-choreographers-society-in-celebration-of-the-third-annual -zelda.

38. "The Early Years," Historical Landmark Application, 1981, p. 15, box 2, fol. 4, Arena Stage Historical Documents 1950–1998.

39. Howard Gillette Jr., *Between Justice and Beauty: Race, Planning, and the Failure of Urban Policy in Washington, D.C.* (Philadelphia: University of Pennsylvania Press, 2006).

40. U.S. Department of Commerce, "1950 Census of Population," October 15, 1950, https://www2.census.gov/library/publications/decennial/1950/pc-02 /pc-2-49.pdf.

41. Matthew B. Gilmore, "District of Columbia Population History," *Washing-*

ton DC History Resources (blog), 2014, https://matthewbgilmore.wordpress.com/district-of-columbia-population-history/.

42. Harry S. Jaffe and Tom Sherwood, *Dream City: Race, Power, and the Decline of Washington, D.C.* (New York: Simon & Schuster, 1994), 24.

43. Gillette, *Between Justice and Beauty*, 155.

44. Spencer R. Crew, "Melding the Old and the New: The Modern African American Community, 1930–1960," in *Urban Odyssey: A Multicultural History of Washington, D.C.*, ed. Francine Curro Cary (Washington: Smithsonian Institution Press, 1996), 214.

45. Margaret E. Farrar, *Building the Body Politic: Power and Urban Space in Washington, D.C.* (Urbana: University of Illinois Press, 2008), 84.

46. Ibid., 161–65.

47. Jaffe and Sherwood, *Dream City*, 29.

48. George Lipsitz, *How Racism Takes Place* (Philadelphia: Temple University Press, 2012).

49. Dorothy B. Magnus, "Matriarchs of the Regional Theatre," in *Women in American Theatre*, 3rd ed., ed. Helen Krich Chinoy and Linda Walsh Jenkins (New York: Theatre Communications Group, 2006), 208.

50. Minutes of a Meeting of the Board of Trustees, Washington Drama Society, June 24, 1962, p. 1, box 30, fol. 3, Thomas C. Fichandler Papers.

51. Joseph Wesley Zeigler, *Regional Theatre: The Revolutionary Stage* (Minneapolis: University of Minnesota, 1973), 185.

52. John Lahoud, "Theatre Reawakening: A Report on Ford Foundation Assistance to American Drama" (New York: Ford Foundation, 1977).

53. For more on the Ford Foundation in this period, see Richard Magat, *The Ford Foundation at Work: Philanthropic Choices, Methods, and Styles* (New York: Plenum Press, 1979).

54. Ruth Wilson Gilmore, "In the Shadow of the Shadow State," in *The Revolution Will Not Be Funded: Beyond the Non-profit Industrial Complex*, ed. IN-CITE! (Durham, NC: Duke University Press, 2017), 46.

55. Christine E. Ahn, "Democratizing American Philanthropy," in INCITE!, *The Revolution Will Not Be Funded*, 68.

56. Sheila McNerney Anderson, "The Founding of Theater Arts Philanthropy in America: W. McNeil Lowry and the Ford Foundation, 1957–65," in *Angels in the American Theater: Patrons, Patronage, and Philanthropy*, ed. Robert A. Shanke (Carbondale: Southern Illinois University Press, 2007), 176.

57. Ibid., 180–83.

58. Zelda Fichandler, in discussion with the author, December 2012.

59. Qtd. in Maslon, *The Arena Adventure*, 19.

60. Zelda Fichandler, introduction to Maslon, *The Arena Adventure*, 6.

61. Zelda Fichandler to Mac Lowry, March 30, 1962, box 154, Zelda Fichandler Papers.

62. Box Office Receipts, 1961–62 and Subsequent Seasons, p. 1, box 82, fol. 2, Zelda Fichandler Papers.

63. Minutes of a Meeting of the Board of Trustees, Washington Drama Society, February 28, 1963, p. 1, box 30, fol. 3, Thomas C. Fichandler Papers.

64. Zelda Fichandler, in discussion with the author, December 2012.

65. "Case History of the Economic Workings of Arena Stage," p. 6, box 12, fol. 3, Arena Stage Financial Documents, GMUL.

66. Susan Powers, Press Release, January 20, 1964, Arena Stage Records, GMUL.

67. Siegfried Mews, "'Brecht, Motherhood, and Justice': The Reception of *The Caucasian Chalk Circle* in the United States," in *The Fortunes of German Writers in America: Studies in Literary Reception*, ed. James Wolfgang Elfe, James Harding, and Gunther Holst (Columbia: University of South Carolina Press, 1992), 246.

68. Martin Esslin, "Brecht at Seventy," *TDR* 12, no. 1 (1967–68): 36.

69. Tomoko Aono, "The Foundations of American Regional Theatre" (PhD diss., CUNY Graduate Center, 2010), 27. Aono compiled the data using *The Best Plays*, local newspapers, and theatres' commemorative publications and internal records.

70. Zelda Fichandler, "The Future of the Resident Professional Theatre in America," August 22, 1967, p. 6, box 108, fol. 24, Zelda Fichandler Papers.

71. Aono, "The Foundations of American Regional Theatre," 27.

72. Maslon, *The Arena Adventure*, 36.

73. Staff Meeting Minutes, March 4, 1966, p. 1, box 25, fol. 15, Thomas Fichandler Papers.

74. Geoffrey A. Wolff, "Stark and Brutal Theme Is Found in 'Sergeant Musgrave's Dance,'" *Washington Post*, March 19, 1966, http://search.proquest.com.ezproxy.cul.columbia.edu/docview/142698928?accountid=10226 (accessed April 14, 2012).

75. Minutes of the Fourth General Membership Meeting of the Washington Drama Society, June 23, 1963, p. 1, box 30, fol. 3, Thomas C. Fichandler Papers.

76. Fichandler, "The Future of the Resident Professional Theatre in America," pp. 5–6.

77. Maslon, *The Arena Adventure*, 24.

78. Yael Zarhy-Levo, *The Making of Theatrical Reputations: Studies from the Modern London Theatre* (Iowa City: University of Iowa Press, 2008), 63–160.

79. "Arena Stage: Attendance and Box Office Income, 1961–62 through 1970–71 Seasons," box 24, fol. 5, Thomas C. Fichandler Papers.

80. Aono, "The Foundations of American Regional Theatre," 27.

81. Box Office Receipts, 1961–62 and Subsequent Seasons, box 82, fol. 2, Zelda Fichandler Papers.

82. Fichandler, "The Future of the Resident Professional Theatre in America," pp. 7–8.

83. Ibid.

84. Zelda Fichandler, "Whither (or Wither) Art?," *American Theatre* (May/June 2003): 31.

85. See, among others, "What Future for Lincoln Center Repertory?," *New York Times*, December 10, 1967, http://search.proquest.com/docview/118133144?accountid=7287, in which critic Michael Smith writes, "From the start the Repertory Theater has been burdened with too much advice. Mr. Irving is responsible to a board of directors concerned more with financing culture than creating theater."

86. Zeigler, *Regional Theatre*, 35.

87. Zelda Fichandler, "Theatres or Institutions?," *Theatre* 3 (September 1970): 105–16.

88. "Case History of the Economic Workings of Arena Stage," pp. 9–10, box 12, fol. 3, Arena Stage Financial Documents.

89. Dick Netzer, *The Subsidized Muse: Public Support for the Arts in the United States* (Cambridge: Cambridge University Press, 1978), 126–31.

90. Rockefeller Panel Study, *The Performing Arts: Problems and Prospects* (New York: McGraw-Hill, 1965), 38.

91. For more on 1960s regional theatre in Minneapolis, see Susannah Engstrom, "Twin Cities Theater in the 1960s: Negotiating the Commercial/Experimental Divide," in *The Sixties, Center Stage: Mainstream and Popular Performances in a Turbulent Decade*, ed. James M. Harding and Cindy Rosenthal (Ann Arbor: University of Michigan Press, 2017), 251–72.

92. Zelda Fichandler, "Arena Stage," May 11, 1963, p. 3, box 108, fol. 13, Zelda Fichandler Papers.

93. Rockefeller Panel Study, *The Performing Arts*, 62.

94. Ibid., 54.

95. William J. Baumol and William G. Bowen, *Performing Arts: The Economic Dilemma* (Cambridge, MA: MIT Press, 1966), 35–70, 161–302.

96. "Analysis of the Income Gap 1966–67 Season," p. 1, box 26, fol. 20, Thomas Fichandler Papers.

97. Ibid.

98. Joseph Zeigler, "Statistics for Eighteen Professional Resident Theatres, Seasons of 1966–67 through 1969–70," with accompanying letter to Thomas Fichandler, October 23, 1970, p. 1, box 26, fol. 20, Thomas Fichandler Papers.

99. Aono, "The Foundations of American Regional Theatre," 137–42.

100. Zeigler, *Regional Theatre*, 35.

101. Zelda Fichandler, in discussion with the author, December 2012.

102. For more on Living Stage, see Susan C. Haedicke, "Theater for the New Generation: The Living Stage Theatre Company's Program for Teen Mothers," in *Performing Democracy: International Perspectives on Urban Community-Based Performance*, ed. Susan C. Haedicke and Tobin Nellhaus (Ann Arbor: University of Michigan Press, 2001), 269–80.

103. Zeigler, *Regional Theatre*, 4.

104. For more on the establishment of the NEA, see Donna M. Binkiewicz, *Federalizing the Muse: United States Arts Policy and the National Endowment for the Arts, 1965–1980* (Chapel Hill: University of North Carolina Press, 2004); Gary O. Larson, *The Reluctant Patron: The United States Government and the Arts, 1943–1965* (Philadelphia: University of Pennsylvania Press, 1983); and Joseph Wesley Zeigler, *Arts in Crisis: The National Endowment for the Arts versus America* (Chicago: A Cappella Books, 1994).

105. Zelda Fichandler, "Toward a Deepening Aesthetic," p. 23, box 108, fol. 27, Zelda Fichandler Papers.

106. Zeigler, *Regional Theatre*, 196.

107. Martin Gottfried, "What Shall It Profit a Theatre If . . . ?," *New York Times*, August 23, 1970, http://search.proquest.com.ezproxy.gc.cuny.edu/docview/117965802?accountid=7287 (accessed April 15, 2012).

108. Julius Novick, *Beyond Broadway: The Quest for Permanent Theatres* (New York: Hill and Wang, 1968), 50.

109. Minutes of a Meeting of the Board of Trustees, Washington Drama Society, May 21, 1969, p. 1, box 30, fol. 7, Thomas Fichandler Papers.

110. For histories of nineteenth-century yellowface onstage, see Josephine Lee, *The Japan of Pure Invention: Gilbert and Sullivan's "The Mikado"* (Minneapolis: University of Minnesota Press, 2010); Krystyn R. Moon, *Yellowface: Creating the Chinese in American Popular Music and Performance, 1850s–1920s* (New Brunswick, NJ: Rutgers University Press, 2004); and Sean Metzger, "Charles Parsloe's Chinese Fetish: An Example of Yellowface Performance in Nineteenth-Century American Melodrama," *Theatre Journal* 56, no. 4 (2004): 627–51.

111. Zelda Fichandler, "Arena to Create a New Inter-Racial Stage Force," *Washington Star*, June 30, 1968, D-1.

112. Zelda Fichandler, "Toward a Deepening Aesthetic," p. 15, box 108, fol. 27, Zelda Fichandler Papers.

113. Ibid., i.

114. Ibid., 13.

115. Ibid., i.

116. Dylan Rodríguez, "The Political Logic of the Non-profit Industrial Complex," in INCITE!, *The Revolution Will Not Be Funded*, 29. Italics in the original.

117. See Karen Ferguson, *Top Down: The Ford Foundation, Black Power, and the Reinvention of Racial Liberalism* (Philadelphia: University of Pennsylvania Press, 2013).

118. Fichandler, "Toward a Deepening Aesthetic," 25.

119. Richard L. Coe, "'Threepenny Opera' Opens Arena Stage," *Washington Post*, November 28, 1968, http://search.proquest.com.ezproxy.cul.columbia.edu/docview/143394613?accountid=10226 (accessed April 19, 2012); Richard L. Coe, "Arena Puts New Note into Pirandello," *Washington Post*, November 29, 1968, http://search.proquest.com.ezproxy.cul.columbia.edu/docview/143243006?accountid=10226 (accessed April 19, 2012).

120. Richard L. Coe, "Impulses," *Washington Post*, January 23, 1969, http://search.proquest.com.ezproxy.cul.columbia.edu/docview/147723744?accountid=10226 (accessed April 19, 2012).

121. Letter from Peter Weidenbruch Jr. to Arena Stage, June 9, 1969, box 19, fol. 12, Arena Stage Financial Documents and Projects.

122. Zelda Fichandler to Mac Lowry, July 8, 1969, box 154, Zelda Fichandler Papers.

123. Minutes of a Meeting of the Board of Trustees, Washington Drama Society, April 22, 1968, p. 1, box 30, fol. 7, Thomas Fichandler Papers.

124. Minutes of the Annual Meeting of the Membership of the Washington Drama Society, November 10, 1969, Thomas C. Fichandler Papers.

125. Zelda Fichandler, in discussion with the author, December 2012.

126. Minutes of a Meeting of the Board of Trustees, Washington Drama Society, February 9, 1967, p. 2, box 30, fol. 3, Thomas C. Fichandler Papers.

127. Dorothy Chansky, "Alphabet Soup: The Acronymization of the American Theater," in Harding and Rosenthal, *The Sixties, Center Stage*, 231–50.

128. Margaret M. Knapp, "Narrative Strategies in Selected Studies of American Theatre Economics," in *The American Stage: Social and Economic Issues from the Colonial Period to the Present*, ed. Ron Engle and Tice L. Miller (Cambridge: Cambridge University Press, 1993), 276.

129. Jack Poggi, *Theater in America: The Impact of Economic Forces 1870–1967* (Ithaca, NY: Cornell University Press, 1968), 235.

130. Fichandler, "Theatres or Institutions?," 110.

131. Ibid.

132. Ibid., 108, 111.

CHAPTER TWO

1. Steve Samuels, "Pioneering: 50 Years of Arena Stage," *The Great White Hope Program Book*, fall 2000, 21–28, Washingtoniana Division, Martin Luther King Jr. Memorial Library, Washington, DC.

2. Qtd. in Maggie Boland, "Q&A with Artistic Director Molly Smith," ibid., 16.

3. To distinguish the fictional character Jack Jefferson from the real boxer Jack Johnson, I will refer to the former as "Jack" and the latter as "Johnson."

4. In addition to *The Great White Hope*, there have been several plays inspired by Jack Johnson's life, including *The Royale* by Marco Ramirez (2015) and *Dare to Be Black* by Tommie J. Moore (2016).

5. Joseph Wesley Zeigler, *Regional Theatre: The Revolutionary Stage* (Minneapolis: University of Minnesota Press, 1973), 193.

6. Harvey Young, *Embodying Black Experience: Stillness, Critical Memory, and the Black Body* (Ann Arbor: University of Michigan Press, 2010).

7. David Krasner, *A Beautiful Pageant: African American Theatre, Drama, and Performance in the Harlem Renaissance, 1910–1927* (New York: Palgrave Macmillan, 2002).

8. Theresa Runstedtler, *Jack Johnson, Rebel Sojourner: Boxing in the Shadow of the Global Color Line* (Oakland: University of California Press, 2012).

9. Pierre Bourdieu, *The Field of Cultural Production* (New York: Columbia University Press, 1993).

10. Henry Louis Gates Jr., *The Signifying Monkey: A Theory of African-American Literary Criticism* (New York: Oxford University Press, 1988). Gates theorizes how African American literature signifies on or repeats and revises earlier texts.

11. Young, *Embodying Black Experience*, 20.

12. Ibid.

13. In 1964, Ali changed his name, which was formerly Cassius Clay.

14. Young, *Embodying Black Experience*, 109.

15. For more on the distinctions between highbrow, lowbrow, and middlebrow, see David Savran, *Highbrow/Lowdown: Theater, Jazz, and the Making of the New Middle Class* (Ann Arbor: University of Michigan Press, 2009), especially 47. For more on the racialization of science and liberal philosophy, see Denise Ferreira da Silva, *Toward a Global Idea of Race* (Minneapolis: University of Minnesota, 2007).

16. Bourdieu, *The Field of Cultural Production*, 42.

17. David Savran, *A Queer Sort of Materialism: Recontextualizing American Theater* (Ann Arbor: University of Michigan Press, 2003), 18.

18. Ibid., 24–46.

19. Letter from Zelda Fichandler to Howard Sackler, c. December 21 or 22, 1966, box 136, fol. 9, Zelda Fichandler Papers.

20. Cecil Smith, "Stage: 'Great White Hope' a New Champion on Broadway," *Los Angeles Times*, November 17, 1968, D30, ProQuest Historical Newspapers.

21. Todd London, Ben Pesner, and Zannie Giraud Voss, *Outrageous Fortune: The Life and Times of the New American Play* (New York: Theatre Development Fund, 2009), 58.

22. Qtd. in Sam Zolotow, "Arena Stage Fails in 'White Hope' Bid," *New York Times*, October 11, 1968, 38, clipping from box 3, Arena Stage Production Files, GMUL. Unless otherwise noted, all newspaper articles and reviews published in the late 1960s are in this same box.

23. Larry Michie, "D.C. Arena Stage Heads Decry Lack of 'White Hope' Payment or Billing; Regional Group Drafts New Terms," *Variety*, November 6, 1968.

24. Ibid.

25. Zolotow, "Arena Stage Fails in 'White Hope' Bid."

26. Howard Taubman, "Forges for Playwrights," *New York Times*, January 5, 1968.

27. Letter from Zelda Fichandler to Herman Levin, August 27, 1968, box 136, fol.14, Zelda Fichandler Papers 1950–2000, GMUL.

28. See Faedra Chatard Carpenter, "Activating the Asterisk: The Dramaturgy of Intentionality," *Journal of Dramatic Theory and Criticism* 32, no. 2 (Spring 2018): 129–40.

29. Howard Sackler, *The Great White Hope* (New York: Samuel French, 1968), 15.

30. Ibid., 41–42.

31. Krasner, *A Beautiful Pageant*, 30.

32. For an excellent documentary on Jack Johnson that does show film of the boxing matches, see Ken Burns, *Unforgivable Blackness: The Rise and Fall of Jack Johnson* (WETA, 2005), based on the book of the same name by Geoffrey C. Ward.

33. James Burns and Abel Bartley, *"The Great White Hope*: A Forgotten Biopic?," *a/b: AutoBiography Studies* 26, no. 1 (Summer 2011): 57.

34. Young meanwhile highlights incidents of Johnson wearing pink pajamas and wrapping his penis in gauze bandages, shaping the perception of his body. Young, *Embodying Black Experience*, 91.

35. Carol Bunch Davis, *Prefiguring Postblackness: Cultural Memory, Drama, and the African American Freedom Struggle of the 1960s* (Jackson: University of Mississippi Press, 2016).

36. Erica Edwards, *Charisma and the Fictions of Black Leadership* (Minneapolis: University of Minnesota Press, 2012).

37. Shane Vogel, *The Scene of Harlem Cabaret: Race, Sexuality, Performance* (Chicago: University of Chicago Press, 2009).

38. Cathy J. Cohen, "Punks, Bulldaggers, and Welfare Queens: The Radical Potential of Queer Politics?," *GLQ: A Journal of Lesbian and Gay Studies* 3 (1997): 438.

39. Jayna Brown, *Babylon Girls: Black Women Performers and the Shaping of the Modern* (Durham, NC: Duke University Press, 2009).

40. Daphne Brooks, *Bodies in Dissent: Spectacular Performances of Race and Freedom, 1850–1910* (Durham, NC: Duke University Press, 2006).

41. Soyica Diggs Colbert, *Black Movements: Performance and Cultural Politics* (New Brunswick, NJ: Rutgers University Press, 2017).

42. Sackler, *The Great White Hope*, 12.

43. Ibid., 94.

44. Richard Coe, "'Hope' Dashed by Too Much," *Washington Post*, December 14, 1967.

45. Sackler, *The Great White Hope*, 67.

46. Ibid., 22.

47. Diana Rebekkah Paulin, *Imperfect Unions: Staging Miscegenation in U.S. Drama and Fiction* (Minneapolis: University of Minnesota Press, 2012), 26–27.

48. Some cultural critics point to an episode of *Star Trek*, having aired four months earlier, as boasting the first interracial kiss, because Captain Kirk and Lieutenant Uhura lock lips. But as film scholar Daniel Bernardi notes, that kiss was controlled by evil on-looking aliens, and *Star Trek*'s liberal humanism continually centers on whiteness. Daniel Bernardi, *Star Trek and History: Race-ing toward a White Future* (Rutgers: Rutgers University Press, 1998).

49. *Preserving the Legacy: Voices of the American Theatre*, vol. 1, 2003, DVD, Theatre Communications Group.

50. Peter Wallenstein, "Interracial Marriage on Trial: *Loving v. Virginia*," in *Race on Trial: Law and Justice in American History*, ed. Annette Gordon-Reed (New York: Oxford University Press, 2002), 183.

51. Aliyyah Abdur-Rahman, *Against the Closet: Identity, Political Longing, and Black Figuration* (Durham, NC: Duke University Press, 2012), 83.

52. Celia R. Daileader, *Racism, Misogyny, and the "Othello" Myth: Inter-racial Couples from Shakespeare to Spike Lee* (Cambridge: Cambridge University Press, 2005).

53. Sackler, *The Great White Hope*, 113.

54. Ibid., 115. Italics in the original.

55. Nelson Pressley, "The Good Fight," *American Theatre* (October 2000): 31.

56. Lewis Funke, "Jane Alexander Tells of 'White Hope' Challenge," *New York Times*, October 29, 1968, 54, ProQuest Historical Newspapers.

57. Pressley, "The Good Fight," 31.

58. Richard F. Shepard, "Author of 'Great White Hope' Wins Purse, Crown," *New York Times*, May 6, 1969, C 35.

59. Ibid.

60. Ibid.

61. Lewis Funke, *Playwrights Talk about Writing: 12 Interviews with Lewis Funke* (Chicago: Dramatic Pub. Co., 1975), 45.

62. "In This Corner, the New Champion," *New York Times*, October 13, 1968.

63. Ibid.

64. Pressley, "The Good Fight," 30.

65. Ibid.

66. Soyica Diggs Colbert, *The African American Theatrical Body: Reception, Performance, and the Stage* (Cambridge: Cambridge University Press, 2011).

67. "In This Corner, the New Champion."

68. Nancy Goldberg, "An Actor Who Must Be Involved Finds a Spark in 'Great White Hope,'" *Daily News Record*, December 22, 1967.

69. Ibid.

70. "In This Corner, the New Champion."

71. Martin Gottfried, "Theatre," *Women's Wear Daily*, December 14, 1967.

72. Thomas Shales, "Great Hopes for 'The Great White Hope,'" *Washington DC Examiner*, December 21, 1967.

73. Martin Gottfried, "Theatre," *Women's Wear Daily*, December 15, 1967.

74. Peter Altman, "'Great White Hope' Could Be Knockout," *Minneapolis Star*, n.d.

75. Don Rubin, "Vigorous Theater Adds Luster to Capital Life," *New Haven Register*, December 17, 1969, 1, 7.

76. Ibid.

77. Russell Shaw, "'White Hope' Is Powerful Play," *St. Louis Review*, January 12, 1968.

78. William J. Eaton, "Premiere of a Significant Play," *Chicago Daily News*, December 9, 1967.

79. Martin Gottfried, "Theatre," *Women's Wear Daily*, December 15, 1967.

80. Martin Gottfried, "Is All Black Theater Beautiful? No," *New York Times*, June 7, 1970, 89, ProQuest Historical Newspapers.

81. Ibid.

82. Shaw, "'White Hope' Is Powerful Play."

83. Eaton, "Premiere of a Significant Play."

84. Samuel Hirsch, "'Great White Hope' Lights Theater with Flaming Zeal," *Boston Herald*, December 5, 1967.

85. Shaw, "'White Hope' Is Powerful Play."

86. Shales, "Great Hopes for 'The Great White Hope.'"

87. Kevin Kelly, "'The Great White Hope,' Jack Johnson's Life a Two-Fisted Drama," *Boston Globe*, December 24, 1967.

88. Harry MacArthur, "Long Search for a White Hope," *Washington Star*, n.d.

89. Tom Donnelly, *Washington Daily News*, December 14, 1967.

90. See for instance Bruce Weber, "Critic's Notebook: Power, Pitfalls and 'The Great White Hope'; A Washington Company Revisits a Shining Moment from a Decidedly Different Era," *New York Times*, September 14, 2000, E1, Lexis-

Nexis: "The rhetoric of the early 20th century is so blatantly and viciously un-complicated that many of the white characters sound clownishly villainous, the black ones embarrassingly defeated."

91. Jules Novick, "Tragic Cakewalk," *Nation*, January 15, 1968. Novick repro-duced his review of *The Great White Hope* nearly verbatim in his book *Beyond Broadway: The Quest for Permanent Theatres* (New York: Hill and Wang, 1968), 50.

92. Novick, *Beyond Broadway*, 13.

93. Clive Barnes, "'The Great White Hope,' a Chronicle of a Modern Othello, Opens in Washington," *New York Times*, December 14, 1967.

94. Martin Gottfried, "Theatre," *Women's Wear Daily*, December 14, 1967.

95. Altman, "'Great White Hope' Could Be Knockout."

96. Davis, *Prefiguring Postblackness*, 103.

97. bell hooks, *Ain't I a Woman: Black Women and Feminism* (Cambridge, MA: South End Press, 2007), 63.

98. Indicating the continued popularity of this narrative, in 2013, Arena staged *Guess Who's Coming to Dinner* adapted by white playwright Todd Kreidler and starring *Cosby Show* actor Malcolm-Jamal Warner.

99. Toni Cade Bambara, *The Black Woman: An Anthology* (New York: Washing-ton Square Press, 1970), 309.

100. Earl Plater, "Curtain Call: A Glance at Broadway," *Washington Informer*, January 23–29, 1969.

101. Bambara, *The Black Woman*, 310.

102. Ibid., 309.

103. Dan Sullivan, "'White Hope' Drama of a Fallen Champ: 'Great White Hope' at the Ahmanson," *Los Angeles Times*, December 4, 1969, C1, ProQuest His-torical Newspapers.

104. Clive Barnes, "Theater: Howard Sackler's 'Great White Hope,'" *New York Times*, October 4, 1968, 40, ProQuest Historical Newspapers.

105. Mildred Pitts Walter, "Black Woman Examines Two Plays by White Men," *Los Angeles Times*, February 15, 1970, Q12, Proquest Historical Newspapers.

106. Ibid.

107. Ibid.

108. Walter Kerr, "To Make You Feel, Not Just Watch," *New York Times*, December 24, 1967.

109. R. H. Gardner, "New Play at Arena Stage," *Baltimore Sun*, December 15, 1967.

110. See for instance Samuel Hirsch, "'Great White Hope' Lights Theater with Flaming Zeal." See also David Savran, "The Canonization of Eugene O'Neill," in *Highbrow/Lowdown*, 221–64.

111. See for example Martin Gottfried, "Theatre," *Women's Wear Daily*, Decem-ber 29, 1967, 29.

112. Savran, *A Queer Sort of Materialism*, 25.

113. Sam Zolotow, "Fund to Support 2 Incoming Plays," *New York Times*, September 12, 1968, 55, ProQuest Historical Newspapers.

114. Richard Coe, "It's Time the Pulitzer People Woke Up," *Washington Post*, May 11, 1969.

115. "Around Town," *Washington Post*, April 23, 1969, A16.

116. "The 23rd Annual Tony Awards," New York, 1969, DVD, Theatre on Film and Tape Archive, Performing Arts Library, New York, NY.

CHAPTER THREE

1. Zelda Fichandler and Edwin Wilson, "Interview with Zelda Fichandler," *CUNY Spotlight*, 1991, VHS, Theatre on Film and Tape Archive, Performing Arts Library, New York, NY.

2. Ibid.

3. Jodi Melamed, "The Spirit of Neoliberalism: From Racial Liberalism to Neoliberal Multiculturalism," *Social Text* 24, no. 4 (Winter 2006): 4.

4. Bruce McConachie, *American Theater in the Culture of the Cold War: Producing and Contesting Containment, 1947–1962* (Iowa City: University of Iowa Press, 2003).

5. Brent Hayes Edwards, *The Practice of Diaspora: Literature, Translation, and the Rise of Black Internationalism* (Cambridge, MA: Harvard University Press, 2003), 11.

6. Sandra Richards, "African Diaspora Drama," in *The Cambridge Companion to African American Theatre*, ed. Harvey Young (Cambridge: Cambridge University Press, 2012), 232–33.

7. Charlotte Canning, *On the Performance Front: US Theatre and Internationalism* (Houndmills, UK: Palgrave Macmillan, 2015), 134, 152.

8. See Mary L. Dudziak, *Cold War Civil Rights: Race and the Image of American Democracy*, 2nd ed. (Princeton, NJ: Princeton University Press, 2011).

9. Penny von Eschen, *Satchmo Blows Up the World* (Cambridge, MA: Harvard University Press, 2004), 256. For more on the *Porgy and Bess* tour, see Canning, *On the Performance Front*, 186–222.

10. Canning, *On the Performance Front*, 15.

11. Ibid., 236–41.

12. For more on Arena's tour in the USSR, specifically from Alan Schneider's perspective, see Jeffrey Stephens, "Negotiations and Exchanges: Alan Schneider, *Our Town*, and Theatrical Détente," *Journal of American Drama and Theatre* 23, no. 1 (Winter 2011): 43–65.

13. Letter from Mark B. Lewis to Thomas Fichandler, June 7, 1973, box 7, fol. 14, Thomas Fichandler Papers, GMUL.

14. Department of State, "Arena Stage to Tour U.S.S.R.," March 28, 1973, box 7, fol. 14, Thomas Fichandler Papers.

15. Zelda Fichandler, in discussion with the author, December 2012.

16. Gad Guterman, "Field Tripping: The Power of *Inherit the Wind*," *Theatre Journal* 60, no. 4 (December 2008): 563–83.

17. Department of State, "Arena Stage to Tour U.S.S.R."

18. For more on the reception of Arena Stage in Russia, see Marissa Dever, "Thawing the Cold War with Theatre," *Boundary Stones*, WETA's Local History Blog, February 2, 2017, http://blogs.weta.org/boundarystones/2017/02/02/thawing-cold-war-theatre.

19. "Congressional Record—House," October 17, 1973, box 17, fol. 1976–82, Thomas Fichandler Papers.

20. Ibid.

21. "Staff Meeting," March 10, 1976, box 13, fol. 3, Arena Stage Production Correspondence, GMUL.

22. "Holland Festival June 10–15, 1976," box 2, fol. 54, Thomas Fichandler Papers.

23. Laurence Maslon, *The Arena Adventure: The First 40 Years* (Washington, DC: Arena Stage, 1990), 66–67.

24. Ibid., 56.

25. *Preserving the Legacy: Voices of the American Theatre*, vol. 1, 2003, DVD, Theatre Communications Group.

26. Stephens, "Negotiations and Exchanges," 64.

27. "Staff Meeting," March 10, 1976, box 13, fol. 3, Arena Stage Production Correspondence.

28. Minutes of a Meeting of the Board of Trustees, March 25, 1976, box 30, fol. 5, Thomas Fichandler Papers.

29. "The Arena Stage Story," p. ii, box 17, fol. 1976–82, Arena Stage Printed Materials, GMUL.

30. Arena Stage mailer, c. 1973, Washingtoniana Division, Martin Luther King Jr. Library, Washington, DC.

31. Subscription mailer, c. 1981, box 11, fol. 1981–82, Arena Stage Printed Materials.

32. Maslon, *The Arena Adventure*, 44.

33. In apartheid South Africa, "coloured" denoted mixed-race South Africans and certain other ethnic groups, and American theatregoers may not have been familiar with this distinct racial category. My thanks to Kellen L. Hoxworth for clarifying my wording and understanding.

34. Letter from Thomas Fichandler to Arena Stage Subscriber, December 15, 1967, box 17, fol. 1967–68, Arena Stage Printed Materials.

35. "Staff Meeting," October 2, 1970, box 13, fol. 2, Arena Stage Production Correspondence.

36. Zelda Fichandler, in discussion with the author, December 2012.

37. Letter from Zelda Fichandler to Subscriber, April 7, 1975, box 13, fol. 1, Arena Stage Production Correspondence.

38. Catherine M. Cole, "When Is African Theater 'Black'?," in *Black Cultural Traffic: Crossroads in Global Performance and Popular Culture*, ed. Harry J. Elam Jr. and Kennell Jackson (Ann Arbor: University of Michigan Press, 2005), 45.

39. "Famed Nigerian Dance and Theater Company at Arena Stage," December 20, 1974, box 2, fol. 20, Arena Stage Production Correspondence.

40. "3:30 Friday Meeting," March 7, 1975, box 13, fol. 3, Arena Stage Production Correspondence.

41. Richard Lebherz, "The River Niger Flows Straight into the Kreeger, Shells and All," *Frederick News-Post*, February 21, 1975, clipping from box 63, fol. 6, Arena Stage Printed Materials.

42. "Staff Meeting," December 10, 1974, box 13, fol. 1, Arena Stage Printed Materials.

43. Richard L. Coe, "London Acclaim for 'Texas Trilogy,'" *Washington Post*, February 24, 1977, https://www.washingtonpost.com/archive/lifestyle/1977/02/24/london-acclaim-for-texas-trilogy/ac8f2e03-2221-4b63-b256-11170cc32bae/?utm_term=.b74a1e4dd5ba.

44. "Tony Winners," July 3, 1975, box 17, fol. 1974–75, Arena Stage Printed Materials.

45. David Richards, "A Play Bruising Yet Uplifting," *Washington Star*, July 17, 1975, clipping from box 74, fol. 12, Arena Stage Printed Materials.

46. Letter from Linda Platshon to Zelda Fichandler, August 15, 1975; letter from Thomas Fichandler to Linda Platshon, August 18, 1975, box 99, fol. 2, Zelda Fichandler Papers 1950–2000, GMUL.

47. Playbill of *The Blood Knot*, "Perspectives from the Artistic Director," December 11, 1992, p. 7, box 30, fol. 6, Arena Stage Dramaturgical Files, GMUL.

48. Doug Wager, in discussion with the author, October 2014.

49. Athol Fugard, John Kani, and Winston Ntshona, *Sizwe Banzi Is Dead*, in *Township Plays* (New York: Oxford University Press, 1993), 154.

50. Minutes of a Meeting of the Board of Trustees, October 27, 1976, box 30, fol. 5, Thomas Fichandler Papers.

51. Jeanne Colleran, "Athol Fugard and the Problematics of the Liberal Critique," *Modern Drama* 38, no. 3 (Fall 1995): 389–407, n. 6.

52. Letter from Richard Bryant to "Associate," August 17, 1984, box 29, fol. 6, Arena Stage Printed Materials.

53. David Richards, "In the World of 'Woza Albert!,'" *Washington Post*, September 7, 1984, B1, B12, clipping from box 35, fol. 9, Arena Stage Printed Materials.

54. Consider for example the edited collection *Township Plays*, whose front cover and title page make it seem as if Fugard was the sole author of not

only *No-Good Friday, Nongogo,* and *The Coat* but also *Sizwe Banzi Is Dead* and *The Island.* Athol Fugard, *Townships Plays* (New York: Oxford University Press, 2000). For more on contested authorship and the history of *Sizwe Banzi Is Dead,* see Gibson Cima, "Resurrecting *Sizwe Banzi Is Dead* (1972–2008): John Kani, Winston Ntshona, Athol Fugard, and Postapartheid South Africa," *Theatre Survey* 50, no. 1 (May 2009): 91–118.

55. Colleran, "Athol Fugard and the Problematics of the Liberal Critique."
56. Russell Vandenbroucke, *Truths the Hand Can Touch: The Theatre of Athol Fugard* (New York: Theatre Communications Group, 1985), 124–25.
57. Ibid., xx.
58. Albert Wertheim, *The Dramatic Art of Athol Fugard* (Bloomington: Indiana University Press, 2000), xi.
59. Mel Gussow, "Profiles: Witness," *New Yorker,* December 20, 1982, 48.
60. Doug Wager, in discussion with the author, October 2014.
61. Rita Barnard, *Apartheid and Beyond: South African Writers and the Politics of Place* (New York: Oxford University Press, 2007), 96, 106.
62. Edward Merritt, "A Lesson from Aloes," *WAMU Public Radio,* 88.5 FM, November 11, 1981, clipping from box 79, fol. 4, Arena Stage Printed Materials.
63. Wertheim, *The Dramatic Art of Athol Fugard,* 185.
64. Colleran, "Athol Fugard and the Problematics of Liberal Critique," 394, 397.
65. Shakespeare (thirteen productions)—*Twelfth Night* ('71–'72), *Julius Caesar* ('74–'75), *Hamlet* ('77–'78), *The Winter's Tale* ('79–'80), *A Midsummer Night's Dream* ('81–'82), *Cymbeline* ('82–'83), *As You Like It* ('83–'84), *The Tempest* ('84–'85), *The Taming of the Shrew* ('85–'86), *Measure for Measure* ('86–'87), *The Tale of Lear* (adapted by Tadashi Suzuki, '88–'89), *A Midsummer Night's Dream* ('89–'90), *Two Gentlemen of Verona* ('90–'91); Brecht (seven productions)—*Mother Courage and Her Children* ('70–'71), *The Resistible Rise of Arturo Ui* ('73–'74), *The Caucasian Chalk Circle* ('77–'78), *Galileo* ('80–'81), *Happy End* (with Kurt Weill, '83–'84), *The Good Person of Setzuan* ('85–'86), *The Caucasian Chalk Circle* ('90–'91); Shaw (six productions)—*Heartbreak House* ('75–'76), *Saint Joan* ('76–'77), *Major Barbara* ('81–'82), *Man and Superman* ('84–'85), *Heartbreak House* ('86–'87), *Pygmalion* ('90–'91); Beckett (four productions)—*Jack MacGowran in the Works of Samuel Beckett* ('70–'71), *Two by Samuel Beckett: Krapp's Last Tape and Not I* ('73–'74), *Waiting for Godot* ('75–'76), *Play/That Time/Footfalls* ('76–'77); Fugard (four productions)—*Sizwe Banzi Is Dead* and *The Island* ('74–'75), *A Lesson from Aloes* ('81–'82), *My Children! My Africa!* ('90–'91); Molière (four productions)—*Tricks* (based on *Scapin,* '71–'72), *Don Juan* ('78–'79), *The Imaginary Invalid* ('82–'83), *Tartuffe* ('84–'85); Chekhov (three productions)—*The Three Sisters* ('83–'84), *The Cherry Orchard* ('87–'88), *The Seagull* ('90–'91); Durang (three productions)—*A History of the American Film* ('76–'77), *Beyond Ther-*

apy ('83–'84), *The Marriage of Bette and Boo* ('86–'87); Hansberry (three productions)—*The Sign in Sidney Brustein's Window* ('70–'71), *Raisin* (based on *A Raisin in the Sun*, '72–'73), *Les Blancs* ('87–'88); Miller (three productions)—*Death of a Salesman* ('74–'75, '75–'76), *After the Fall* ('79–'80), *The Crucible* ('86–'87); Örkény (three productions)—*The Tot Family* ('75–'76), *Catsplay* ('76–'77), *Screenplay* ('82–'83); Shepard (three productions)—*Curse of the Starving Class* ('78–'79), *Buried Child* ('82–'83), *A Lie of the Mind* ('88–'89). Nearly all of these were mainstage productions.

66. Qtd. in Bruce King, *Derek Walcott and West Indian Drama: "Not Only a Playwright but a Company." The Trinidad Theatre Workshop 1959–1993* (Oxford: Clarendon Press, 1995), 142.

67. Ibid., 24.

68. Qtd. ibid., 295.

69. James Lardner, "Troubled Island: Arena's 'Pantomime' Misses Its Mark," *Washington Post*, May 21, 1981, clipping from box 48, fol. 6, Arena Stage Printed Materials.

70. "Mini-Staff Meeting," August 25, 1972, box 13, fol. 1, Arena Stage Production Correspondence.

71. My estimate of 150 is based on a table with information about the 1981–82 season, which lists 58 full-time and 134 part-time employees, "Number of Administrative and Non-Acting Artistic Employees," box 3, fol. 2, Zelda Fichandler Papers.

72. Minutes of a Meeting of the Board of Trustees, April 14, 1977, p. 3, box 30, fol. 5, Thomas Fichandler Papers.

73. Ibid.

74. Joan Saudler, ed., *Black Theater: A Resource Directory* (New York: Black Theatre Alliance, 1973), box 53, fol. 17, Zelda Fichandler Papers.

75. See for example the meeting minutes for Washington, DC, theatre leaders discussing the Non-traditional Casting Project and concluding, "The problem is a lack of minority participation in theater in Washington." Minutes of the Meeting—Non-traditional Casting Project, March 30, 1987, box 5, fol. 1, Arena Stage Printed Materials.

76. Thomas O'Connor, *1978 Audience Survey*, p. 1; *1980 Audience Survey*, pp. 3–4, box 17, fol. 3 Thomas Fichandler Papers.

77. Abramson Research, *Attitudes of the Arena Stage Audience*, 1984–85, p. 5, box 17, fol. 3, Thomas Fichandler Papers.

78. Todd London, *The Artistic Home: Discussions with Artistic Directors of America's Institutional Theatres* (New York: Theatre Communications Group, 1988), 47.

79. "The Arena Stage Story," p. 3, box 17, fol. 1976–82, Arena Stage Printed Materials.

80. Ibid.

81. "Summary of Conference of Four Resident Professional Theatres," 1974, Spring Hill Conference Center, p. 14, box 24, fol. 38, Thomas Fichandler Papers.

82. Ibid, p. 20.

83. In the stage manager's reports, I identified only one comment racializing the audience during the run of *No Place to Be Somebody*: "Good performance. Audience was more black than we're used to." "Stage Manager's Report," July 4, 1970, box 5, fol. 34, Arena Stage Stage Manager's Reports, GMUL.

84. Danny Newman, *Subscribe Now! Building Art Audiences through Dynamic Subscription Promotion* (New York: Theatre Communications Group, 1977), 181.

85. "Friday Meeting," May 4, 1979, box 13, fol. 4, Arena Stage Printed Materials.

86. Ibid.

87. "Weekly Staff Meeting," May 18, 1979, box 13, fol. 4, Arena Stage Printed Materials.

88. Ibid.

89. Ibid.

90. Benny Sato Ambush, in discussion with the author, April 2016.

91. Letter from Benny Sato Ambush to David Chambers, February 14, 1979, pp. 3-4, box 1, fol. 5, Zelda Fichandler Papers.

92. David Chambers, in discussion with the author, May 2016.

93. Chris Myers Asch and George Derek Musgrove, *Chocolate City: A History of Race and Democracy in the Nation's Capital* (Chapel Hill: University of North Carolina Press, 2017), 119-54.

94. E. Franklin Frazier, *Black Bourgeoisie: The Rise of a New Middle Class in the United States* (New York: Free Press, 1957), 197-98.

95. Soyica Diggs Colbert, "Drama in the Harlem Renaissance," in Young, *The Cambridge Companion to African American Theatre*, 86.

96. Natalie Hopkinson, *Go-Go Live: The Musical Life and Death of a Chocolate City* (Durham, NC: Duke University Press, 2012).

97. Bart Landry, *The New Black Middle Class* (Berkeley: University of California Press, 1987).

98. Mark Anthony Neal, *What the Music Said: Black Popular Music and Black Public Culture* (New York: Routledge, 1998), 103-4.

99. Karyn R. Lacy, *Blue-Chip Black: Race, Class, and Status in the Black Middle Class* (Berkeley: University of California Press, 2007), 47.

100. Ibid., 75.

101. Bryant Keith Alexander, "'Boojie!': A Question of Authenticity," in *From Bourgeois to Boojie: Black Middle-Class Performance*, ed. Vershawn Ashanti

Young with Bridget Harris Tsemo (Detroit: Wayne State University Press, 2011), 311.

102. Landry, *The New Black Middle Class*, 188.

103. Bereket H. Selassie, "Washington's New African Immigrants," in *Urban Odyssey: A Multicultural History of Washington, D.C.*, ed. Francine Curro Cary (Washington: Smithsonian Institution Press, 1996), 264.

104. Ibid., 265.

105. Keith Q. Warner, "From 'Down the Way Where Nights Are Gay': Caribbean Immigration and the Bridging of Cultures," in Cary, *Urban Odyssey*, 250–63.

106. Doug Wager, in discussion with the author, October 2014.

107. "Re: Arena Stage Equal Employment Opportunity Policy," February 1986, box 12, fol. 3, Arena Stage Production Correspondence.

108. "Cultural Diversity Committee Meeting," March 6, 1989, box 5, fol. 1, Arena Stage Printed Materials.

109. "Arena Stage: 1987–88, Toward Cultural Diversity," c. 1987, box 5, fol. 1, Arena Stage Printed Materials.

110. Qtd. in Janice Arkatov, "Ron Milner's 'Checkmates' at Inner City Center," *LA Times*, May 31, 1987, http://articles.latimes.com/1987-05-31/entertainment/ca-9156_1_ron-milner.

111. Glenn A. Ray, *A Basic Guide to Audience Diversity* (Richmond: Virginia Commission for the Arts, 1988). Copy found in box 5, fol. 1, Arena Stage Printed Materials.

112. "Zelda Fichandler Public Memorial Service at Arena Stage, Washington DC—HowlRound TV," YouTube video, 2:11:00, posted by HowlRound, October 25, 2016, https://www.youtube.com/watch?v=-oS1v56v69U.

113. Elizabeth Kastor, "Arena's Other Worlds on Stage: With 'Playboy,' a Disputed Step toward 'Cultural Diversity,'" *Washington Post*, January 12, 1989, C1 and C4, clipping from box 21, fol. 6, Arena Stage Printed Materials.

114. Ibid.

115. Ibid.

116. David Richards, "'Playboy,' Transported: A Clever Caribbean Twist on the Synge Classic," *Washington Post*, December 9, 1988, clipping from box 21, fol. 6, Arena Stage Printed Materials.

117. "Wild West," *Washington City Paper*, December 16, 1988, clipping from box 48, fol. 10, Arena Stage Printed Materials.

118. Hedy Weiss, "Mustapha Matura," *America's Arena*, c. 1988, excerpted from an article published in the *Chicago Sun-Times*, box 21, fol. 6, Arena Stage Printed Materials.

119. Elizabeth Kastor, "Matura and the Muse," *Washington Post*, January 12, 1989, clipping from box 21, fol. 6, Arena Stage Printed Materials.

120. Mustapha Matura, email to author, October 9, 2014.

121. Teagle F. Bougere, in discussion with the author, March 2016.

122. Guy Bergquist, in discussion with the author, January 2015.

123. "Action Items Relating to Cultural Diversity," February 16, 1990, box 8, fol. 2, Arena Stage Printed Materials.

124. Letter from Joseph C. Dixon to Frank Kirby, February 8, 1971, box 37, fol. 2, Zelda Fichandler Papers.

125. "Life Shouldn't Be All Work and No Plays," Arena Stage subscription mailer, 1988, box 93, fol. 1, Zelda Fichandler Papers.

126. Letter from Norman I. Gelman to Zelda Fichandler, May 11, 1987, box 93, fol. 1, Zelda Fichandler Papers.

127. Letter from W. E. Dugger to William Stewart, August 3, 1988, box 93, fol. 1, Zelda Fichandler Papers.

128. Letter from Leroy D. Clark to Persons, n.d., box 93, fol. 1, Zelda Fichandler Papers.

129. "% Capacity by Season 1974–75 thru 1987–88," November 18, 1988, box 132, fol. 1, Zelda Fichandler Papers.

130. Letter from Elspeth Udvarhelyi to David O. Maxwell, November 9, 1988, box 7, fol. 1, Thomas Fichandler Papers.

131. Zelda Fichandler, "Remarks to the Finance Committee," February 25, 1987, p. 4, box 8, fol. 1, Thomas Fichandler Papers.

132. Zelda Fichandler, "Remarks by Zelda Fichandler at Ford Foundation," February 8, 1989, p. 11, box 37, fol. 9, Zelda Fichandler Papers.

133. Ibid., pp. 6, 3.

134. Letter from Elspeth Udvarhelyi to Jeanne Hodges, December 8, 1988, pp. 1–2, box 37, fol. 9, Zelda Fichandler Papers.

135. Ibid., p. 2.

136. Barbara Gamarekian, "The Arena Theater in Washington Gets Ready for a Change of Cast," *New York Times*, September 2, 1990, http://www.nytimes .com/1990/09/02/theater/the-arena-theater-in-washington-gets-ready-for -a-change-of-cast.html?pagewanted=all.

137. BWW News Desk, "Arena Stage Celebrates 25 Years of Allen Lee Hughes Fellowship Program," *BroadwayWorld*, March 4, 2016, https://www.broadway world.com/washington-dc/article/Arena-Stage-Celebrates-25-Years-of -Allen-Lee-Hughes-Fellowship-Program-20160304.

138. Zelda Fichandler, "Thoughts at 40: Arena Stage 1950–1990," box 37, fol. 1, Zelda Fichandler Papers.

139. London, *The Artistic Home*, 43.

140. Ibid.

141. Ibid., 50–51.

142. Zelda Fichandler, in discussion with the author, December 2012.

143. Doug Wager, in discussion with the author, October 2014.

1. I put "Golden Age" in quotes to show that I do not agree with the implicitly positive value judgment that this term evokes; instead, I use the term to mark book musicals with popular scores from the 1940s through the mid-1960s.

2. For more on *Raisin*, the musical relative to *A Raisin in the Sun*, with consideration of cultural hierarchy and popularity, see Donatella Galella, "*Playing in the Dark/Musicalizing 'A Raisin in the Sun,'*" *Continuum: The Journal of African Diaspora Drama, Theatre, and Performance* 1, no. 2 (2015): http://continuumjournal.org/index.php/component/content/article/33 -volumes/issues/vol-1-no-2-amiri-baraka-revaluation-and-appreciation /vol-1-no-2-content/ysc-1-2/95-playing-in-the-dark-musicalizing-a-raisin -in-the-sun.

3. Laurence Maslon, *The Arena Adventure: The First 40 Years* (Washington, DC: Arena Stage, 1990), 50.

4. Zelda Fichandler, in discussion with the author, December 2012.

5. See for instance Harvey Young, ed., *The Cambridge Companion to African American Theatre* (Cambridge: Cambridge University Press, 2012).

6. Koritha Mitchell, *Living with Lynching: African American Lynching Plays, Performance, and Citizenship, 1890–1930* (Urbana: University of Illinois Press, 2011), 45.

7. Allen Woll, *Black Musical Theatre: From "Coontown" to "Dreamgirls"* (Baton Rouge: Louisiana State University Press, 1989), xiii.

8. Sam O'Connell, "Fragmented Musicals and 1970s Soul Aesthetic," in Young, *The Cambridge Companion to African American Theatre*, 155–73. O'Connell has since revised his interpretation of *The Wiz* as political in "*The Wiz* and the African Diaspora Musical: Rethinking the Research Questions in Black Musical Historiography," paper delivered at the Association for Theatre in Higher Education conference, Montreal, Canada, August 2, 2015.

9. Portia K. Maultsby, "Africanisms in African-American Music," in *Africanisms in American Culture*, ed. Joseph E. Holloway (Bloomington: Indiana University Press, 1990), 185–210.

10. Michael Omi and Howard Winant, *Racial Formation in the United States from the 1960s to the 1990s*, 2nd ed. (New York: Routledge, 1994).

11. Suzan-Lori Parks, "New Black Math," *Theatre Journal* 57, no. 4 (December 2005): 560.

12. For more on blackness in Tennessee Williams's works, see Paige A. McGinley, "Reconsidering 'the American Style': Black Performers and Black Music in *Streetcar* and *Cat*," *Theatre Journal* 68, no. 1 (March 2016): 1–16.

13. Eric M. Glover, "What Is This 'Black' in Black [Musical Theater]?," paper de-

livered at the Association for Theatre in Higher Education, August 12, 2016, Chicago, 2, 8.

14. Kathryn Edney, "Tapping the Ivories: Jazz and Tap Dance in *Jelly's Last Jam* (1992)," in *Gestures of Music Theater: The Performativity of Song and Dance*, ed. Dominic Symonds and Millie Taylor (New York: Oxford University Press, 2014), 113.

15. For more on this trajectory of art and scholarship, see Carol Bunch Davis, *Prefiguring Postblackness: Cultural Memory, Drama, and the African American Freedom Struggle of the 1960s* (Jackson: University of Mississippi Press, 2016).

16. Thelma Golden, *Freestyle* (New York: Studio Museum in Harlem, 2001), 14.

17. Harry J. Elam Jr., "Black Theatre in the Age of Obama," in Young, *The Cambridge Companion to African American Theatre*, 255–78, and Harry J. Elam Jr. and Douglas A. Jones Jr., ed., *The Methuen Drama Book of Post-Black Plays* (London: Methuen Drama, 2012).

18. See for example Toni Morrison, *Playing in the Dark: Whiteness and the Literary Imagination* (New York: Vintage Books, 1992).

19. Saidiya V. Hartman, *Scenes of Subjection: Terror, Slavery, and Self-Making in Nineteenth-Century America* (New York: Oxford University Press, 1997), 57.

20. E. Patrick Johnson, *Appropriating Blackness: Performance and the Politics of Authenticity* (Durham, NC: Duke University Press, 2003), 2.

21. Ibid., 3.

22. In *Appropriating Blackness*, E. Patrick Johnson analyzes Marlon Riggs's documentary *Black Is . . . Black Ain't*, whose title cites Ralph Ellison's novel *Invisible Man*.

23. Letter from Zelda Fichandler to Thomas Fichandler, Alan Schneider, and Hugh Lester, c. 1973, box 196, fol. 1, Zelda Fichandler Papers 1950–2000, GMUL.

24. Letter from Robert Nemiroff to *Raisin* Cast and Company, "RE: Background Information for Interviews," May 1976, p. 3, box 85, fol. 7, Lorraine Hansberry Papers, Schomburg Center for Research in Black Culture, New York, New York. Emphasis in the original.

25. Robin Bernstein, "Inventing a Fish Bowl: White Supremacy and the Critical Reception of Lorraine Hansberry's *A Raisin in the Sun*," *Modern Drama* 42, no. 1 (Spring 1999): 18.

26. Tricia Rose, "Hansberry's *A Raisin in the Sun* and the 'Illegible' Politics of (Inter)personal Justice," *Kalfou* 1, no. 1 (Spring 2014): 38.

27. Harvey Young, "The Long Shadow of *A Raisin in the Sun*," in *The Sixties, Center Stage: Mainstream and Popular Performances in a Turbulent Decade*, ed. James M. Harding and Cindy Rosenthal (Ann Arbor: University of Michigan Press, 2017), 64.

28. Harilaos Stecopoulos, "Melodrama of the Movement: Lorraine Hansberry's *A Raisin in the Sun*," in *From Bourgeois to Boojie: Black Middle-Class Performance*, ed. Vershawn Ashanti Young with Bridget Harris Tsemo (Detroit: Wayne State University Press, 2011), 210.

29. Aaron C. Thomas, "Watching *A Raisin in the Sun* and Seeing Red," *Modern Drama* 58, no. 4 (Winter 2015): 461–81.

30. See for example Lawrence P. Jackson, *The Indignant Generation: A Narrative History of African American Writers and Critics, 1934–1960* (Princeton, NJ: Princeton University Press, 2010).

31. For a critique of Nemiroff's handling of Hansberry's plays, see Woodie King Jr., "The Restructuring of Lorraine Hansberry's 'A Raisin in the Sun,'" in *The Impact of Race* (New York: Applause Theatre and Cinema Books, 2003), 117–23.

32. Maslon, *The Arena Adventure*, 50.

33. Woll, *Black Musical Theatre*, 193–273.

34. Elizabeth Wollman, *The Theatre Will Rock: A History of the Rock Musical from "Hair" to "Hedwig"* (Ann Arbor: University of Michigan Press, 2006), 111.

35. Yvonne Shinhoster Lamb, "Arts Administrator, Playwright Vantile Whitfield Dies," *Washington Post*, January 23, 2005, http://www.washingtonpost.com/wp-dyn/articles/A29685-2005Jan22.html.

36. Donald McKayle, *Transcending Boundaries: My Dancing Life* (London: Routledge, 2002), 217.

37. Letter from Elliot Axelrod to Thomas Fichandler, December 7, 1972, box 27, fol. 23, Arena Stage Financial Documents and Projects 1980s–1990s, GMUL.

38. For more on musical theatre producers, see Laura MacDonald and William Everett, eds., *The Palgrave Handbook of Musical Theatre Producers* (New York: Palgrave Macmillan, 2017).

39. Letter from Thomas Fichandler to Floria Lasky, February 22, 1973, p. 2, Arena Stage Financial Documents and Projects 1980s–1990s.

40. *Raisin* playbill, July 1973, p. 6, box 99, fol. 1, Arena Stage Production Notebooks and Programs 1950–1991, GMUL.

41. Memo from Robert Nemiroff to Zelda Fichandler, November 4, 1972, p. 1, box 44, fol. 1, Zelda Fichandler Papers.

42. Memo from Zelda Fichandler to Robert Nemiroff, December 13, 1972, p. 5, box 44, fol. 1, Zelda Fichandler Papers.

43. Ibid., pp. 2–3.

44. Steven R. Carter, *Hansberry's Drama: Commitment and Complexity* (Urbana: University of Illinois Press, 1991), 79.

45. Robert Nemiroff and Robert Brittan, *A Long Time Comin'*, n.d. p. 1-1-13-1-1-16, box 83, fol. 3, Lorraine Hansberry Papers.

46. Ibid., p. 2-3-7.

47. Robert Nemiroff, Charlotte Zaltzberg, and Robert Brittan, *Raisin*, n.d., p. 1-5-4, box 83, fol. 5, Lorraine Hansberry Papers.

48. Robert Nemiroff, Charlotte Zaltzberg, and Robert Brittan, *Raisin*, April/May 1973, Nemiroff's annotated copy, folder labeled "Final Arena Product," p. 1-2-17, box 84, fol. 3, Lorraine Hansberry Papers.

49. McKayle, *Transcending Boundaries*, 219.

50. Robert Nemiroff, Charlotte Zaltzberg, and Robert Brittan, *Raisin* (New York: Samuel French, 1978), 13. All citations from the play will be from the published edition for the remainder of this chapter.

51. Ibid., 18–19.

52. See for example Gary Wiener, ed., *Gender in Lorraine Hansberry's "A Raisin in the Sun"* (Detroit: Greenhaven Press, 2011).

53. Julie M. Burrell, "To Be a Man: A Re-assessment of Black Masculinity in Lorraine Hansberry's *A Raisin in the Sun* and *Les Blancs*," *Continuum* 1, no. 1 (June 2014): http://continuumjournal.org/index.php/incession-content/26 -volumes/issues/vol-1-no-1-inception/vol-1-no-1-content/articles/58-to-be -a-man-a-re-assessment-of-black-masculinity-in-lorraine-hansberry-s-a -raisin-in-the-sun-and-les-blancs2.

54. Johnson, *Appropriating Blackness*, 22.

55. Kimberlé Crenshaw, "Mapping the Margins: Intersectionality, Identity Politics, and Violence against Women of Color," *Stanford Law Review* 43, no. 6 (July 1991): 1241–99.

56. Roderick A. Ferguson, *Aberrations in Black: Toward a Queer of Color Critique* (Minneapolis: University of Minnesota Press, 2003).

57. Nemiroff, Zaltzberg, and Brittan, *Raisin*, 96.

58. See Henry Louis Gates Jr., "The Chitlin Circuit," in *African American Performance and Theater*, ed. Harry J. Elam Jr. and David Krasner (Oxford: Oxford University Press, 2001), 132–48.

59. Rashida Z. Shaw in *Black Theater Is Black Life: An Oral History of Chicago Theater and Dance, 1970–2010*, ed. Harvey Young and Queen Meccasia Zabriskie (Evanston, IL: Northwestern University Press, 2014), 161.

60. Kathy A. Perkins qtd. ibid., 134.

61. Nemiroff, Zaltzberg, and Brittan, *Raisin*, 46–47.

62. Ibid., 76. Italics in original.

63. Donald McKayle, in conversation with the author, August 2016.

64. Allen Lewis, "'Raisin in the Sun' a Mighty Musical," *New Haven Register*, n.d., clipping from box 85, fol. 9, Lorraine Hansberry Papers.

65. Cecil Smith and Glenn Litton, *Musical Comedy in America: From "The Black Crook" to "South Pacific," From "The King and I" to "Sweeney Todd"* (New York: Routledge, 1981), 328.

66. After I presented some of my work on *Raisin* at the Black Theatre Network

conference in New York City in 2014, Michael Dinwiddie, the president of the Black Theatre Network at that time, told me that he remembered seeing this commercial of "fauna dancing Africans" and decided not to see the musical as a consequence.

67. Nemiroff, Zaltzberg, and Brittan, *Raisin*, 56.

68. For more on the allegedly feminized, queer, and inauthentic nature of musicals as opposed to other genres, specifically rock, see Wollman, *The Theatre Will Rock.*

69. Paul Gilroy, *The Black Atlantic: Modernity and Double Consciousness* (Cambridge, MA: Harvard University Press, 1993), 34.

70. Joy Chong-Stannard, *Donald McKayle: Heartbeats of a Dancemaker*, DVD, 57 min. (Hightstown, NJ: Dance Pioneers and PBS Hawaii, Dance Horizons Video, 2002).

71. "Joyce Brown," Internet Broadway Database, http://ibdb.com/person.php ?id=79156.

72. Letter from Maurice Kogan and Jack Holmes to local contractors, n.d., p. 2, box 85, fol. 7, Lorraine Hansberry Papers.

73. Nemiroff, Zaltzberg, and Brittan, *Raisin*, 80. Italics in the original.

74. Memo from Robert Nemiroff to Zelda Fichandler, November 4, 1972, p. 1.

75. Faedra Chatard Carpenter, *Coloring Whiteness: Acts of Critique in Black Performance* (Ann Arbor: University of Michigan Press, 2014), 214.

76. Nemiroff, Zaltzberg, and Brittan, *Raisin*, 83. Italics in the original.

77. Ibid., 85.

78. Ibid., 65, 98–100.

79. Wollman, *The Theater Will Rock*, 111.

80. Playbill of *Raisin*, July 1973, 15. Donald McKayle's note was originally published in the *New Amsterdam News* alongside a huge rave anticipating the musical and celebrating Hansberry entitled "Lord Have Mercy. *Raisin* Is Back."

81. Mike Heid, "Raisin," *CBS Radio*, n.d. B 35, clipping from box 49, fol. 10, Arena Stage Printed Materials 1950–2000, GMUL. Unless otherwise noted from this point forward, all newspaper articles, reviews, and playbills published in the early 1970s are in this same box and folder.

82. Clive Barnes, "'Raisin' in Musical Form," *New York Times*, October 19, 1973, 59.

83. David Richards, "'Raisin' Gives Cause to Stand and Cheer," *Washington Star*, June 3, 1973.

84. David Richards, "'Raisin': Season's Best Musical," *Washington Star*, May 31, 1973.

85. Bernstein, "Inventing a Fish Bowl," 16–27.

86. Clifford A. Ridley, "Two for the Road: On Stage, Talent Beats Tinkering," *National Observer*, June 23, 1973.

87. Tom Basham, "Arena Presents Warm, Believable *Raisin*," *Performance*, June 7, 1973, 8.

88. Charles B. Jones, "Perspective on the Black Family: The Black Artistic Legacy," *Amsterdam News*, n.d.

89. Ernest Schier, "A 'Raisin' with Fantastic Potential," *Philadelphia Bulletin*, June 1, 1973.

90. Gerard A. Perseghin, "When Black Is Right," *Catholic Review*, June 8, 1973.

91. Richards, "'Raisin': Season's Best Musical."

92. Philip F. Crosland, "Stage Lights," *Wilmington Evening Journal*, June 9, 1973.

93. Elliot Norton, "Broadway Gets First Big One," *Boston Herald*, n.d., box 85, fol. 9, Lorraine Hansberry Papers.

94. Roy Meachum, no title, *Metromedia News*, n.d., clipping from box 20, fol. 40, Donald McKayle Papers, Special Collections and Archives, University of California, Irvine.

95. Richards, "'Raisin' Gives Cause to Stand and Cheer."

96. Leonard Probst, "Raisin," NBC Radio, n.d., box 85, fol. 9, Lorraine Hansberry Papers.

97. Lewis, "'Raisin in the Sun' a Mighty Musical."

98. Perseghin, "When Black Is Right."

99. *Raisin* Broadway souvenir program, Robert Nemiroff, "A Personal Note from the Producer," n.d., p. 11, box 85, fol. 4, Lorraine Hansberry Papers.

100. Emory Lewis, "Hansberry Drama a Musical: 'Raisin' Is Superb," *Bergen Record*, October 19, 1973, B-1-2, clipping from box 20, fol. 40, Donald McKayle Papers.

101. "The 28th Annual Tony Awards," New York, 1974, DVD, Theatre on Film and Tape Archive, Performing Arts Library, New York, NY.

102. Richard Lebherz, "Another Dazzling Arena Production," *Frederick News-Post*, June 4, 1973.

103. Charles Farrow, "'Raisin' a Great Musical; 2-Handkerchief Sniffler," *Washington Afro-American*, June 9, 1973.

104. Ibid.

105. Perseghin, "When Black Is Right."

106. Robert P. Laurence, "'Raisin' Musical Shows Emotion," *San Diego Union*, April 6, 1977, D-1, D-6, clipping from box 20, fol. 40, Donald McKayle Papers.

107. Richard Philip, "Raisin," *After Dark*, January 1974, 67, clipping from box 20, fol. 40, Donald McKayle Papers.

108. Judith L. Howell, "Raisin," *Black Stage* 1, no. 7 (August 1973): 16.

109. Ibid., 22.

110. R. H. Gardner, "New Musical Has World Premiere in Washington," *Baltimore Sun*, June 3, 1973.

111. Ibid.

112. Ibid.

113. William Glover, "Raisin Romps on Broadway," *Dallas Times Herald, AP*, n.d., box 85, fol. 9, Lorraine Hansberry Papers.

114. Tom Basham, "Arena Presents Warm, Believable *Raisin*."

115. Elizabeth Darr, Stage Manager's Report, June 10, 1973, box 4, fol. 6, Arena Stage Stage Manager Reports 1950–2000, GMUL.

116. Helaine Head, Stage Manager's Reports, July 21, 1973, and July 22, 1973, box 4, fol. 6, Arena Stage Stage Manager Reports.

117. Audience Survey, 1978, p. 1, box 68, fol. 8, Zelda Fichandler Papers.

118. Ferguson, *Aberrations in Black*, 145.

119. "Summary of Conference of Four Resident Professional Theatres," 1974, Spring Hill Conference Center, p. 20, box 24, fol. 38, Thomas Fichandler Papers 1950–1997, GMUL.

120. Richard Coe, "'Raisin' at Arena: A Union of Rightness," *Washington Post*, June 10, 1973, E 14.

121. Letter from Robert Nemiroff to "Partner," September 8, 1977, p. 1, box 192, fol. 3, Zelda Fichandler Papers.

122. Letter from Zelda Fichandler to Robert Nemiroff, December 18, 1973, box 44, fol. 3, Zelda Fichandler Papers.

123. Hillary Miller, *Drop Dead: Performance in Crisis, 1970s New York* (Evanston, IL: Northwestern University Press, 2016), 55–76.

124. Letter from Zelda Fichandler to Robert Nemiroff, December 18, 1973.

125. From Broadway previews in October 1973 to national tour performances ending on May 1, 1977, the production grossed approximately $12.5 million. "Raisin Gross," scrap of paper, n.d., box 85, fol. 8, Lorraine Hansberry Papers.

126. Letter from Robert Nemiroff to "Partner," September 8, 1977, p. 2.

127. "Press," c. 1975–1977, p. 14, box 85, fol. 7, Lorraine Hansberry Papers.

128. Ibid.

129. Zelda Fichandler, "For Season after Next," c. 1973, box 196, fol. 1, Zelda Fichandler Papers.

130. Minutes of a Meeting of the Board of Trustees, April 14, 1977, p. 3, box 30, fol. 5, Thomas Fichandler Papers.

CHAPTER FIVE

1. Barbara Gamarekian, "The Arena Theater in Washington Gets Ready for a Change of Cast," *New York Times*, September 2, 1990, http://www.nytimes.com/1990/09/02/theater/the-arena-theater-in-washington-gets-ready-for-a-change-of-cast.html?pagewanted=all.

2. Arena Stage, "Our History," http://www.arenastage.org/about/history/ (accessed February 25, 2015).

3. Benedict Anderson, *Imagined Communities: Reflections on the Origin and Spread of Nationalism* (London: Verso, 1983).

4. S. E. Wilmer, *Theatre, Society, and the Nation: Staging American Identities* (Cambridge: Cambridge University Press, 2002), 3.

5. Jeffrey D. Mason and J. Ellen Gainor, eds., *Performing America: Cultural Nationalism in American Theater* (Ann Arbor: University of Michigan Press, 1999), 4. I am skeptical of Mason's use of "America" versus America without scare quotes, as if the former is the invented nation whereas the latter is the real one.

6. Judith Butler and Gayatri Chakravorty Spivak, *Who Sings the Nation-State? Language, Politics, Belonging* (London: Seagull Books, 2007).

7. Nikhil Pal Singh, *Black Is a Country: Race and the Unfinished Struggle for Democracy* (Cambridge, MA: Harvard University Press, 2004), 11.

8. For a classic history, see Edmund S. Morgan, *American Slavery, American Freedom* (New York: W. W. Norton, 1975).

9. *Polk County* program, 2000, p. 2, 5, box 89, fol. 6, Arena Stage Dramaturgical Files, GMUL.

10. Edgar Dobie, in discussion with the author, January 2015.

11. Laurence Maslon et al., "Zelda Fichandler, Valiant Striver in the Arena," *American Theatre*, August 5, 2016, http://www.americantheatre.org/2016/08/05/zelda-fichandler-valiant-striver-in-the-arena/.

12. Doug Wager, in discussion with the author, October 2014.

13. "Arena Stage 1991–1992 Season: Expect the Unexpected," c. 1990, box 5, fol. 1, Arena Stage Printed Materials 1950–2000, GMUL.

14. Ibid.

15. During Wager's tenure, the literary fellows included Marvin McAllister, Faedra Chatard Carpenter, and Yuko Kurahashi.

16. For staking out different positions around multiculturalism, see Avery F. Gordon and Christopher Newfield, eds., *Mapping Multiculturalism* (Minneapolis: University of Minnesota Press, 1996). For liberal humanist arguments, see Amy Gutmann, ed., *Multiculturalism: Examining the Politics of Recognition* (Princeton, NJ: Princeton University Press, 1994). For critical multiculturalism, see David Palumbo-Liu, ed., *The Ethnic Canon: Histories Institutions and Interventions* (Minneapolis: University of Minnesota Press, 1995). For theatre-specific discourse on multiculturalism, see Roberta Uno with Lucy Mae San Pablo Burns, eds., *The Color of Theater: Race, Culture, and Contemporary Performance* (London: Continuum, 2002).

17. Artists, critics, activists, and Actors' Equity Association contested whether white actor Jonathan Pryce should play a Eurasian character. For more on

Miss Saigon, see Karen Shimakawa, *National Abjection: The Asian American Body on Stage* (Durham, NC: Duke University Press, 2002); Esther Kim Lee, *A History of Asian American Theatre* (Cambridge: Cambridge University Press, 2006); and Celine Shimizu, *The Hypersexuality of Race: Performing Asian/American Women on Screen and Scene* (Durham, NC: Duke University Press, 2007). Robert Brustein railed against culturally specific theatre as segregationist, while August Wilson advocated for more resources to be given to black artists to develop black plays. For more on the Brustein-Wilson debates, see Angela Pao, *No Safe Spaces: Re-casting Race, Ethnicity, and Nationality in American Theater* (Ann Arbor: University of Michigan Press, 2010), and Brandi Wilkins Catanese, *The Problem of the Color[blind]: Racial Transgression and the Politics of Black Performance* (Ann Arbor: University of Michigan Press, 2011).

18. For more on how reactionary politics influenced the NEA, see Joseph Wesley Zeigler, *Arts in Crisis: The National Endowment for the Arts versus America* (Chicago: A Cappella Books, 1994).

19. Doug Wager, in discussion with the author, October 2014.

20. Ibid.

21. Laurence Maslon, in discussion with the author, September 2011.

22. Kyle Donnelly, in discussion with the author, March 2015.

23. Guy Bergquist, in discussion with the author, January 2015.

24. Corey H. Jones, "Why Regional Theater Companies Are Forsaking Their Once-Mighty Resident Acting Ensembles," *Colorado Public Radio*, June 6, 2014, http://www.cpr.org/news/story/why-regional-theater-companies-are -forsaking-their-once-mighty-resident-acting-ensembles.

25. "Arena Stage Announces New Voices for a New America, a Comprehensive New Play Research and Development Program," press release, November 12, 1992, box 40, fol. 19, Arena Stage Historical Documents, GMUL.

26. Doug Wager, "Perspectives from the Artistic Director," *Trinidad Sisters* playbill, 1992, p. 3, box 103, fol. 3, Arena Stage Production Books 1950–2000, GMUL.

27. Ibid.

28. "Long Range Plan," October 5, 1994, p. 4, box 3, fol. 33, Arena Stage Miscellaneous, GMUL.

29. Faedra Chatard Carpenter, in discussion with the author, November 2014. Amended by Carpenter via email, January 2018.

30. Cheryl West, "Remarks from the Susan Smith Blackburn Prize Award Ceremonies," in *Women Writing Plays: Three Decades of the Susan Smith Blackburn Prize*, ed. Alexis Greene (Austin: University of Texas Press, 2006), 71.

31. Gwynn MacDonald, "Engaging Social Issues, Expressing a Political Outlook," in Greene, *Women Writing Plays*, 104–14.

32. Cathy Madison, "West Probes Traumas—with No Flinching," *American Theatre* (March 1999): 46.

33. Jacqueline Trescott, "Cheryl West's Play for Compassion," *Washington Post*, January 28, 1991, clipping from box 73, fol. 9, Arena Stage Production Books.

34. Kathy A. Perkins and Sandra L. Richards, "Black Women Playwrights in American Theatre," *Theatre Journal* 62, no. 4 (December 2010): 542.

35. Cheryl West, in discussion with the author, March 2015.

36. Abramson Research, Attitudes of the Arena Stage Audience, 1984–85, p. 5, box 17, fol. 3, Thomas Fichandler Papers, GMUL.

37. "What Is Your Ethnicity?," c. 1992, box 121, fol. 22, Arena Stage Production Books.

38. "Long Range Plan 1992–1997," "Membership," p. 32, box 122, fol. 14, Arena Stage Production Books.

39. "Age Ranges, by Ethnicity," c. 1992, box 121, fol. 22, Arena Stage Production Books.

40. "Show Distribution and Breakdown by Ethnicity," ibid.

41. "Subscriber Distribution by Ethnicity," ibid.

42. "Show Distribution and Breakdown by Ethnicity," ibid.

43. "Candide," "Growth through Innovation: The 1995-96 Communications Plan," box 122, fol. 13, Arena Stage Production Books.

44. "Holiday Heart," ibid.

45. Ibid.

46. Minutes of the Arena Stage Communications Committee Meeting, September 14, 1993, p. 4, box 122, fol. 18, Arena Stage Production Books.

47. Ibid.

48. Unsigned letter to Doug Wager, April 28, 1992, with sticky note likely written by Wager, box 18, fol. 13, Arena Stage Correspondence, GMUL. Next eight letters in the same box.

49. Letter from Mari Noster to Director, July 16, 1991.

50. Letter from Martin A. Davis to Doug Wager, March 2, 1991.

51. Letter from Judith and Jerry Fried to Arena Stage, March 23, 1992.

52. Letter from Gerald and Florence Berman to Doug Wager, May 5, 1991.

53. Letter from Mari Noster to Director, July 16, 1991.

54. Letter from Ky L. Thompson to Sam Rossi, May 22, 1991.

55. Unsigned letter to Doug Wager, n.d.

56. "Give the Gift of Theatre," 1992–93 season brochure.

57. Mark Shugoll, "Focus Group Study with Long-Term and Short-Term Subscribers," December 1993, pp. 3-4, box 123, fol. 1, Arena Stage Production Books.

58. Doug Wager, "New Voices for a New America," box 40, fol. 19, Arena Stage Historical Records.

59. The only Asian play produced at Arena Stage was *Lady Precious Stream* by S. I. Hsiung in 1952. The staff of the Chinese embassy attended the production, and the U.S. State Department took photographs for its publication in Hong Kong. In 2012, Zelda Fichandler told me that one of her regrets is not having staged more Asian works at Arena. Zelda Fichandler, in discussion with the author, December 2012.

60. See, for example, "Arena Stage New Works Statement of Purpose," box 4, fol. 13, Arena Stage Production Notebooks.

61. Laurence Maslon, in discussion with the author, September 2011.

62. Sonja Kuftinec, *Staging America: Cornerstone and Community-Based Theater* (Carbondale: Southern Illinois University Press, 2003), 147.

63. Ibid., 145.

64. Qtd. ibid., 162.

65. Qtd. ibid., 181.

66. Marvin McAllister, in discussion with the author, November 2014.

67. Doug Wager, "Perspectives from the Artistic Director," 1993, p. 5, box 28, fol. 4, Arena Stage Production Books. Brackets in the original.

68. Xavier Lemoine, "Embodying Hybridity: Anna Deavere Smith's Identity Cross-Overs," in *Understanding Blackness through Performance: Contemporary Arts and the Representation of Identity*, ed. Anne Cremieux, Xavier Lemoine, and Jean-Paul Rocchi (New York: Palgrave, 2013), 257.

69. Cherise Smith, *Enacting Others: Politics of Identity in Eleanor Antin, Nikki S. Lee, Adrian Piper, and Anna Deavere Smith* (Durham, NC: Duke University Press, 2011), 188.

70. Nelson Pressley, *American Playwriting and the Anti-theatrical Prejudice: Twentieth- and Twenty-First Century Perspectives* (New York: Palgrave Macmillan, 2014), 152.

71. Anna Deavere Smith, *Talk to Me: Listening between the Lines* (New York: Random House, 2000), 72.

72. Dorinne K. Kondo, "(Re)Visions of Race: Contemporary Race Theory and the Cultural Politics of Racial Crossover in Documentary Theatre," *Theatre Journal* 52, no. 1 (March 2000): 107.

73. Ibid., 89.

74. Minutes of the Arena Stage Communications Committee Meeting, April 28, 1994, p. 5, box 123, fol. 22, Arena Stage Production Books.

75. Communications Department Staff Meeting Minutes, April 3, 1995, box 121, fol. 20, Arena Stage Production Books; "Sales Information: 1987–88 to 1994–95 by Total Income," box 123, fol. 6, Arena Stage Production Books.

76. Doug Wager, "Reinventing Arena," 1996, p. 4, box 3, fol. 19, Arena Stage Miscellaneous.

77. David Savran, *The Playwright's Voice: American Dramatists on Memory Writing, and the Politics of Culture* (New York: Theatre Communications Group, 1999).

78. Robert Brustein, "Akalaitis Axed," in *Dumbocracy in America: Studies in the Theatre of Guilt, 1987–1994* (Chicago: Ivan R. Dee, 1994), 173.

79. Guy Bergquist, in discussion with the author, January 2015.

80. Doug Wager, in discussion with the author, October 2014.

81. Zelda Fichandler, in discussion with the author, December 2012.

82. Gamarekian, "The Arena Theater in Washington Gets Ready for a Change of Cast."

83. "Meeting of the Arena Stage Communications Committee," April 27, 1993, box 122, fol. 16, Arena Stage Production Books.

84. Minutes of the Arena Stage Communications Committee Meeting, March 17, 1994, box 123, fol. 6, Arena Stage Production Books.

85. Shugoll Research, "Assessing the Image of Arena Stage," 1995, p. 4, box 123, fol. 7, Arena Stage Production Books.

86. Ibid.

87. Lloyd Rose, "Arena Stage Director Resigns," *Washington Post*, November 5, 1996, clipping from box 3, fol. 12, Arena Stage Miscellaneous.

88. Qtd. in David Richards, "Arena's Next Stage," *Washington Post*, March 31, 1996, https://www.washingtonpost.com/archive/lifestyle/style/1996/03/31/arenas-next-stage/7258ffb4-fda1-41f9-aeoc-2f4a573feebe/?utm_term=.7ff479d0a7b7.

89. Zelda Fichandler, in discussion with the author, December 2012.

90. Sumru Erkut and Ineke Ceder, "Women's Leadership in Resident Theaters," Wellesley Centers for Women (Wellesley, MA: Wellesley College, 2016), 2.

91. Molly Smith, in discussion with the author, December 2012. Amended by Smith via email, January 2018.

92. Minutes of Senior Staff Meeting, April 7, 1998, box 3, fol. 6, Arena Stage Newsletters, GMUL.

93. Alison Irvin, in discussion with the author, January 2015.

94. Minutes of Senior Staff Meeting, April 7, 1998.

95. Laura Connors Hull, "Arena Stage Identity Redesign Creative Brief," c. 1998, box 3, fol. 6, Arena Stage Newsletters.

96. Cathy Madison, "Q&A with Director, Molly Smith," *Cat on a Hot Tin Roof* playbill, 1998, p. 10–15, box 22, fol. 1, Arena Stage Printed Materials.

97. "Arena Stage Kicks Off Lillian Hellman Festival with *The Little Foxes*," Arena Stage, September 22, 2016, https://www.arenastage.org/about/press-room/press-releases/releases/16-17/Hellman%20Festival%20Release%20web.pdf.

98. Jacqueline Trescott, "Arena Gets $1.2 Million for Diversity," *Washington*

Post, October 6, 2000, https://www.washingtonpost.com/archive/lifestyle
/2000/10/06/arena-gets-12-million-for-diversity/07026ed7-2f97-432a-a01d
-33aa123052d4/?utm_term=.812ffae871ec.

99. Isaac Butler, "A Clearer Picture 2," *Parabasis* (blog), January 13, 2010, http://
parabasis.typepad.com/blog/2010/01/a-clearer-picture-2.html.

100. Harry J. Elam Jr., *The Past as Present in the Drama of August Wilson* (Ann
Arbor: University of Michigan Press, 2006), 25.

101. Harry J. Elam Jr., "Towards a New Territory in 'Multicultural' Theater," in
Uno and Burns, *The Color of Theater*, 93.

102. Dana A. Williams, "Introduction," in *August Wilson and Black Aesthetics*, ed.
Sandra G. Shannon and Dana A. Williams (New York: Palgrave Macmillan,
2004), 1–2.

103. Yvonne Shafer, "Breaking Barriers: August Wilson," in *Staging Difference:
Cultural Pluralism in American Theatre and Drama*, ed. Marc Maufort (New
York: Peter Lang, 1995), 283.

104. Jackie M. Roberts, "Healing Myths from the Ethnic Community, or Why I
Don't Teach August Wilson," *Theatre Topics* 20, no. 2 (September 2010): 147.

105. Manny Strauss, "Arena Stage's Molly Smith to Receive Helen's Star," *theatre-
Washington*, October 24, 2012, http://theatrewashington.org/content/arena
-stages-molly-smith-receive-helens-star.

106. In 1976, the Guthrie staged Lonne Elder III's *Ceremonies in Dark Old Men*.

107. For more on the history of this company, see Macelle Mahala, *Penumbra:
The Premier Stage for African American Drama* (Minneapolis: University of
Minnesota Press, 2013).

108. "Arena Seasonal Stats 98–14," Khady Kamara, email to author, July 15, 2014.

109. Anthony Byrnes and Christina Ramos, "5 Graphs That Show the Ethnic,
Racial and Gender Makeup of Playwrights at the Mark Taper Forum,"
KCRW, April 6, 2017, https://curious.kcrw.com/2017/04/graphing-the-ethnic
-racial-and-gender-makeup-of-playwrights-in-the-50-year-history-of-the
-mark-taper-forum; and "Visualizing the (Lacking) Diversity of Directors
at the Mark Taper Forum," KCRW, April 20, 2017, https://curious.kcrw.com
/2017/04/director-diversity-mark-taper-forum.

110. Diane Ragsdale, *In the Intersection: Partnerships in the New Play Sector*
(Washington, DC: Center for the Theater Commons/HowlRound.com,
2012), loc. 2455 of 3710.

111. For more on the uplift power of respectable black representations in early
musical theatre, see Paula Marie Seniors, *Beyond "Lift Every Voice and Sing":
The Culture of Uplift, Identity, and Politics in Black Musical Theater* (Columbus: Ohio State University Press, 2009).

112. Qtd. in Diane Grams, "Achieving Success," in *Entering Cultural Communi-*

Notes to Pages 179–181

ties: Diversity and Change in the Nonprofit Arts, ed. Diane Grams and Betty Farrell (New Brunswick, NJ: Rutgers University Press, 2008), 236.

113. Ibid., 237.

114. Ibid., 232.

115. Perkins and Richards, "Black Women Playwrights in American Theatre," 543.

116. Staged in 2018, *Hold These Truths* by Jeanne Sakata was the second Asian American play to receive a full production at Arena.

117. For a discussion of Anna Deavere Smith and Culture Clash, see Kondo, "(Re)Visions of Race."

118. James M. Harding, *The Ghosts of the Avant-Garde(s): Exorcising Experimental Theater and Performance* (Ann Arbor: University of Michigan Press, 2013), 186.

119. Stephen Richard, email to author, January 18, 2015.

120. Laura Penn, in discussion with the author, August 2017.

121. Cathy Madison, in discussion with the author, December 2014.

122. Anita Maynard-Losh, in discussion with the author, January 2015.

123. Stacey Stewart, in discussion with the author, January 2015. Amended by Stewart via email, January 2018.

124. This anti–affirmative action logic has gained ground especially since the election of Barack Obama, and the Donald Trump administration has officially opposed affirmative action, though applicants of color, not whites, continue to face systemic racial discrimination on the job market.

125. David Dower, in discussion with the author, August 2014. Amended by Dower via email, January 2018.

126. Ibid.

127. Molly Smith, in discussion with the author, December 2012. Amended by Smith via email, January 2018.

128. David Dower, in discussion with the author, August 2014. Amended by Dower via email, January 2018.

129. Guy Bergquist, in discussion with the author, January 2015.

130. "Arena Stage at the Mead Center for American Theater," http://www.arena stage.org/plan-your-visit/the-mead-center/ (accessed February 15, 2018).

131. Brandi Wilkins Catanese, "Taking the Long View," *Theatre Journal* 62, no. 4 (December 2010): 548–50.

CHAPTER SIX

1. Angela Pao, *No Safe Spaces: Re-casting Race, Ethnicity, and Nationality in American Theater* (Ann Arbor: University of Michigan Press, 2010).

2. Jill Dolan, *Utopia in Performance: Finding Hope at the Theater* (Ann Arbor: University of Michigan Press, 2005), 13.

3. Richard Rodgers and Oscar Hammerstein II, *Oklahoma!* (New York: Applause, 2010), 103–4.

4. Zelda Fichandler, "Thoughts on Non-Traditional Casting," November 1987, box 5, fol. 3, Arena Stage Printed Materials.

5. For a critique of meritocracy in casting, see Brian Herrera, "The Best Actor for the Role, or the Mythos of Casting in American Popular Performance," *Journal of American Drama and Theatre* 27, no. 2 (Spring 2015): http://jadt journal.org/2015/04/24/the-best-actor-for-the-role-or-the-mythos-of -casting-in-american-popular-performance/.

6. Zelda Fichandler, "Casting for a Different Truth," *American Theatre* 5, no. 2 (May 1988): 18–23.

7. Annette K. Miller, "History Corner," *Arena Arrow* 1, no. 1 (November/December 1989): 2–5; Dan Baum, "To Color American Drama," *Arena Arrow* 1, no. 2 (Spring 1990): 6, in box 8, fol. 2, Arena Stage Printed Materials.

8. For more on the controversy over *Our Town*, see Pao, *No Safe Spaces*, 169–74.

9. Jonathan Yardley, "At Arena Stage, a Casting Miscue," *Washington Post*, December 3, 1990, clipping from box 90, fol. 11, Zelda Fichandler Papers, GMUL.

10. Letter from Doug Wager to the *Washington Post*, December 3, 1990, p. 2, clipping from box 90, fol. 11, Zelda Fichandler Papers.

11. Doug Wager, in discussion with the author, October 2014.

12. Raymond Knapp, *The American Musical and the Performance of National Identity* (Princeton, NJ: Princeton University Press, 2005), 3–12.

13. Molly Smith, in discussion with the author, December 2012.

14. For an astute review of the potentials and limits of racial critique in Molly Smith's production of *South Pacific*, see Yuko Kurahashi, "*South Pacific* (Review)," *Theatre Journal* 55, no. 3 (October 2003): 536–38.

15. Molly Smith, in discussion with the author, December 2012. Amended by Smith via email, January 2018.

16. "Molly Smith Discusses *Oklahoma!*, the 10–11 season opener," YouTube video, 2:44, posted by "arenastage1," August 17, 2010, http://www.youtube .com/watch?v=Cmd5OpFd47c&feature.

17. Arena Stage, "Great American Musical," 2010–11 Inaugural Season brochure. Author's collection. "Book" or "integrated" musical means that the artistic elements from the score to the sets seem of a piece in telling a serious, realistic story as opposed to earlier musical comedies, such as Cole Porter's *Anything Goes* (1934), with loosely strung together numbers and plotlines typically about show business. However, scholars such as Tim Carter have traced the construction of this suspect evolutionary narrative, in which Hammerstein himself played a major part, and pointed to the existence of book musicals prior to 1943 such as Kurt Weill, Ira Gershwin, and Moss Hart's *Lady in*

the Dark (1941), about a fashion editor undergoing a psychological break-down. See Tim Carter, *Oklahoma! The Making of an American Musical* (New Haven, CT: Yale University Press, 2007).

18. Gerald Mast, *Can't Help Singin': The American Musical on Stage and Screen* (Woodstock, NY: Overlook Press, 1987), 214.

19. See Bruce Kirle, "Reconciliation, Resolution, and the Political Role of *Oklahoma!* in American Consciousness," *Theatre Journal* 55, no. 2 (May 2003): 251–74; and Paul Filmer, Val Rimmer, and Dave Walsh, "*Oklahoma!*: Ideology and Politics in the Vernacular Tradition of the American Musical," *Popular Music* 18, no. 3 (October 1999): 381–95.

20. "Molly Smith Discusses *Oklahoma!*, the 10–11 Season Opener," YouTube video, 2:43, posted by "arenastage1," August 17, 2010, https://www.youtube.com/watch?v=Cmd5OpFd47c.

21. See for example Peter Marks, "A Grand New State: You Just Cain't Say No to Arena Stage's 'Oklahoma!,'" *Washington Post*, November 6, 2010, http://www.washingtonpost.com/wp-dyn/content/article/2010/11/05/AR2010110507023.html.

22. Pao observes that other companies have employed this strategy of citing historical populations because contemporary U.S. audiences demand realism. Pao, *No Safe Spaces*, 136.

23. Molly Smith, "Director's Note," *Oklahoma!* playbill, published October 22, 2010, 8. Author's collection.

24. Rodgers and Hammerstein, *Oklahoma!*, 118.

25. Jill Dolan, "Diversity Drama in the 2012–2013 Season," *Feminist Spectator* (blog), May 22, 2012, http://feministspectator.princeton.edu/2012/05/22/diversity-drama-in-the-2012-2013-season/.

26. Bruce Kirle, *Unfinished Show Business: Broadway Musicals as Works-in-Process* (Carbondale: Southern Illinois University Press, 2005).

27. Michael Omi and Howard Winant, *Racial Formation in the United States from the 1960s to the 1990s*, 2nd ed. (New York: Routledge, 1994).

28. Consider for example Richard Schechner's suggestion that any person should be permitted to play any role and his observation that "slowly, race-blindness is over-taking race-consciousness. But even here, progress is slow. "Open Casting," *Critical Stages*, November 10, 2010, http://www.criticalstages.org/criticalstages3/entry/Open-Casting-1?category=2. A version of this essay was originally published as "Race Free, Gender Free, Body-Type Free, Age Free Casting," *TDR* 33, no. 1 (1988): 4–12. Critic Richard Hornby similarly argues that race should move "into the background," and he chastised reviewers of James Earl Jones: "If they were honest with themselves, they would have had to admit that they soon forgot about Jones's race in *Ghosts*, because his performance was so strong," thereby implying that virtuosic per-

formance triumphs over blackness. Richard Hornby, "Interracial Casting at the Public and Other Theatres," *Hudson Review* 42, no. 3 (Autumn 1989): 460.

29. Brandi Wilkins Catanese, *The Problem of the Color[blind]: Racial Transgression and the Politics of Black Performance* (Ann Arbor: University of Michigan Press, 2011), 66.

30. Clinton Turner Davis and Harry Newman, eds., *Beyond Tradition: Transcripts of the First Symposium on Non-traditional Casting* (New York: Nontraditional Casting Project, 1988).

31. Daniel Banks, "*The Welcoming Table*: Casting for an Integrated Society," *Theatre Topics* 23, no. 1 (March 2013): 1–18; Dominique Morisseau, "Colorblind Casting or Color-Consciousness?," *Public Theater* (blog), October 20, 2011, http://publictheaterny.blogspot.com/2011/10/colorblind-casting-or-color .html.

32. Pao, *No Safe Spaces*, 28.

33. Marvin McAllister, *Whiting Up: Whiteface Minstrels and Stage Europeans in African American Performance* (Chapel Hill: University of North Carolina Press, 2011), 50.

34. Stephanie Li, *Signifying without Specifying: Racial Discourse in the Age of Obama* (New Brunswick, NJ: Rutgers University Press, 2012), 23.

35. Lynn Riggs, *Green Grow the Lilacs* (New York: Samuel French, 1931), 161. Emphasis in the original.

36. Eduardo Bonilla-Silva, *Racism without Racists: Color-Blind Racism and the Persistence of Racial Inequality in America*, 3rd ed. (Plymouth, UK: Rowman & Littlefield, 2010).

37. For example, a study found that the same resumes with white-sounding names instead of black-sounding names received 50 percent more interview callbacks: Marianne Bertrand and Sendhil Mullainathan, "Are Emily and Greg More Employable Than Lakisha and Jamal? A Field Experiment on Labor Market Discrimination," *American Economic Review* 94 (2004): 991–1013. For a recent study on how the majority of white Americans do not believe that black people are treated worse than white people, see Pew Research Center, "On Views of Race and Inequality, Blacks and Whites Are Worlds Apart," June 27, 2016, http://www.pewsocialtrends.org/2016/06/27 /on-views-of-race-and-inequality-blacks-and-whites-are-worlds-apart/.

38. Jodi Melamed, *Represent and Destroy: Rationalizing Violence in the New Racial Capitalism* (Minneapolis: University of Minnesota Press, 2011).

39. Amrita Ramanan, in discussion with the author, December 2012.

40. "A Glance behind the Scenes at Arena Stage's 2010–11 Season Opener 'Oklahoma!,'" YouTube video, 2:58, posted by "arenastage1," October 20, 2010, http://www.youtube.com/watch?v=hKVrzCO1BUg.

41. Dan Pruksarnukul, email to author, July 10, 2012.

42. Asian American Performers Action Coalition, "Ethnic Representation on New York City Stages 2006/07-2010-11 Seasons," February 2012, http://www .aapacnyc.org/uploads/1/1/9/4/11949532/ethnic_representation_nyc.pdf.

43. Ibid.

44. "Washington (city), District of Columbia," U.S. Census Bureau, http://quick facts.census.gov/qfd/states/11/1150000.html.

45. Arena Stage, "Great American Musical," 2010-11 Inaugural Season brochure. Author's collection.

46. Dan Pruksarnukul, in discussion with the author, January 2013.

47. Harvey Young, "3 Things Actors Should Know about Race on Stage," *Backstage*, June 14, 2013, http://www.backstage.com/advice-for-actors/backstage -experts/3-things-actors-should-know-about-race-stage/.

48. August Wilson, "The Ground on Which I Stand," *Callaloo* 20, no. 3 (1997): 493–503.

49. Marvin Carlson, *The Haunted Stage* (Ann Arbor: University of Michigan Press, 2001).

50. For an example of the frequency of such productions, consider when the characters in Young Jean Lee's *Straight White Men* (2014) recall protesting an all-white high school production and parodying *Oklahoma!* by singing "O-K-K-K!"

51. Andrea Smith, "Heteropatriarchy and the Three Pillars of White Supremacy: Rethinking Women of Color Organizing," in *The Color of Violence: The Incite! Anthology*, ed. INCITE! (Cambridge, MA: South End Press, 2006), 66–73.

52. Knapp, *The American Musical and the Performance of National Identity*, 124-26. A further discussion of racial dynamics in the text proper of *Oklahoma!* is beyond the scope of this chapter. For more on how the positioning of Native Americans in this musical fortifies whiteness, see Warren Hoffman, *The Great White Way: Race and the Broadway Musical* (New Brunswick, NJ: Rutgers University Press, 2014), 56-66. For a reconsideration of casting racially specifically in order to share more Native American plays with audiences, see Courtney Elkin Mohler, "The Native Plays of Lynn Riggs (Cherokee) and the Question of 'Race'-Specific Casting," *Theatre Topics* 26, no. 1 (March 2016): 63-75. For a longer history of white male appropriation and performance of indigenous peoples to construct American identity, see Philip Deloria, *Playing Indian* (New Haven, CT: Yale University Press, 1998).

53. McAllister, *Whiting Up*, 260.

54. See Donatella Galella, "Being in 'The Room Where It Happens': *Hamilton*, Obama, and Nationalist Neoliberal Multicultural Inclusion," *Theatre Survey* 59, no. 3 (September 2018): 363-85.

55. Pao, *No Safe Spaces*, 136.

56. Josephine Lee, "Racial Actors, Liberal Myths," *XCP: Cross Cultural Poetics* 13 (2003): 95.

57. For more on how Latinx actors traverse multiple racial categories on stage and screen, see Brian Herrera, *Latin Numbers: Playing Latino in Twentieth-Century U.S. Popular Performance* (Ann Arbor: University of Michigan Press, 2015), 54–95.

58. Wayman Wong, "Nicholas Rodriguez Talks Life, Love and 'Oklahoma!,'" *After Elton*, November 30, 2010, http://www.afterelton.com/people/2010/11 /interview-with-nicholas-rodriguez.

59. Rodgers and Hammerstein, *Oklahoma!*, 13.

60. Molly Smith, in discussion with the author, December 2012.

61. Pao, *No Safe Spaces*, 38–40.

62. Amrita Ramanan, in discussion with the author, December 2012.

63. Ibid.

64. Andrea Most, *Making Americans: Jews and the Broadway Musical* (Cambridge, MA: Harvard University Press, 2004), 117.

65. Rodgers and Hammerstein, *Oklahoma!*, 63.

66. Kirle, *Unfinished Show Business*, 135; Knapp, *The American Musical and the Performance of National Identity*, 134; Derek Miller, "'Underneath the Ground': Jud and the Community in *Oklahoma!*," *Studies in Musical Theatre* 2, no. 2 (2008): 163–74.

67. See for example Misha Berson, "Provocative 'Oklahoma!' Hits 5th Avenue Stage," *Seattle Times*, February 10, 2012, http://seattletimes.com/html/thearts /2017478542_throklahoma11.html.

68. For yet another interesting case study, consider the production of *Oklahoma!* set in an all–African American town staged by Portland Center Stage in 2011. *Oklahoma!*, Portland Center Stage, http://www.pcs.org/ok/.

69. Most, *Making Americans*, 101–18.

70. According to Carter, Rodgers and Hammerstein at one point intended for the character to sing a coon song and couple with an "exotic" Latina, further suggesting his racialization. Carter, *Oklahoma!*, 90, 92–94.

71. Rodgers and Hammerstein, *Oklahoma!*, 85.

72. Ibid., 119.

73. Dolan, *Utopia in Performance*, 7.

74. Bonilla-Silva, *Racism without Racists*, 179.

75. Samuel Sommers and Michael Norton, "White People Think Racism Is Getting Worse. Against White People," *Washington Post*, July 21, 2016, https://www .washingtonpost.com/posteverything/wp/2016/07/21/white-people-think -racism-is-getting-worse-against-white-people/?utm_term=.8a30ca5d362c.

76. See for instance Bob Mondello, "*Oklahoma!*," *Washington City Paper*, No-

vember 12, 2010, http://www.washingtoncitypaper.com/articles/40015/okla
homa-at-arena-stage-reviewed/.

77. See Charles Shubow, "*Oklahoma* Is Simply Superb at Arena," *Broadway World*,
November 29, 2010, http://dc.broadwayworld.com/article/BWW_Reviews
_OKLAHOMA_is_Simply_Superb_at_Arena_20101129_page2#ixzz1tfPowdSO;
Hilton Als, "America, America: Two Plays about the Country's Complexities,"
New Yorker, December 13, 2010, http://archives.newyorker.com/?i=2010-12
-13#folio=102; and Susan Berlin, "*Oklahoma!*," *Talkin' Broadway*, n.d., http://
www.talkinbroadway.com/regional/dc/dc502.html.

78. Terry Teachout, "An OK 'Oklahoma!,'" *Wall Street Journal*, November 26,
2010, http://online.wsj.com/article/SB100014240527487042439045756305518
33719776.html.

79. Leslie Milk, "Review: Oklahoma!," *Washingtonian*, November 9, 2010, http://
www.washingtonian.com/blogs/afterhours/theater-review/review-okla
homa.php.

80. Marks, "A Grand New State."

81. Ibid.

82. For another critique of Peter Marks's flippancy, see Jessica Brater et al., "'Let
Our Freak Flags Fly': *Shrek the Musical* and the Branding of Diversity," *Theatre Journal* 62, no. 2 (May 2010): 164.

83. Marks, "A Grand New State."

84. Ibid.

85. Rebecca Ritzel, "Props for a No-Props 'Carousel' at Arena Stage," *American Theatre Magazine*, June 2, 2017, http://www.americantheatre.org/2017
/06/02/props-for-a-no-props-carousel-at-arena-stage/.

86. "Get to Know the OK! Cast: Cara and Shane," YouTube video, 2:45, posted by
"arenastage1," August 2, 2011, http://www.youtube.com/watch?v=go77iuEZ2
Zk&list=PL2465CD8DC44EB849&index=2&feature=plpp_video.

EPILOGUE

1. Zelda Fichandler, "Address to the Stage Directors and Choreographers Society in Celebration of the Third Annual Zelda Fichandler Award," Howl-
Round, November 13, 2011, http://howlround.com/address-to-the-stage
-directors-and-choreographers-society-in-celebration-of-the-third-annual
-zelda.

2. "Washington's Booming Theater Scene Is Second Only to New York,"
Diamondback, November 20, 2013, http://www.dbknews.com/archives
/article_3b8ec4ee-5246-11e3-ab79-001a4bcf6878.html.

3. David Dower, in discussion with the author, August 2014.

4. Jamie Gahlon, in discussion with the author, August 2014.

5. David Dower, in discussion with the author, August 2014.

6. Nelson Pressley, "Where Are the Kogod Cradle's New Plays?," *Washington Post*, October 12, 2012, http://www.washingtonpost.com/entertainment/theater_dance/where-are-the-kogod-cradles-new-plays/2012/10/11/1e2f9df4-0cb7-11e2-97a7-45c05ef136b2_story.html.

7. Rohan Preston, "Guthrie Theater Furloughs Most of Its Full-Time Employees for a Week," *Minneapolis Star Tribune*, January 14, 2014, http://www.startribune.com/entertainment/stageandarts/240178521.html.

8. Scott McCaffrey, "Updated: Arlington Taxpayers to Bail Out Signature Theatre a Second Time," *InsideNoVa*, December 18, 2014, http://www.insidenova.com/news/arlington/updated-arlington-taxpayers-to-bail-out-signature-theatre-a-second/article_c4cf3dd6-81fe-11e4-99cc-abaoc9ba73ce.html.

9. Crystal City Business Improvement District, "The Economic Impact of Theaters in Arlington County, Virginia," March 2009, p. 2, www.arlingtonarts.org/libraries/grants_documents/theaterstudy_final_p1.sflb.ashx.

10. See Paul Bonin-Rodriguez, *Performing Policy: How Contemporary Politics and Cultural Programs Redefined U.S. Artists for the Twenty-First Century* (New York: Palgrave Macmillan, 2015).

11. Alan Brown and Rebecca Ratzin, *Counting New Beans: Intrinsic Impact and the Value of Art* (San Francisco: Theatre Bay Area, 2012).

12. See Diane Ragsdale, *In the Intersection: Partnerships in the New Play Sector* (Washington, DC: Center for the Theater Commons/HowlRound.com, 2012).

13. Zelda Fichandler, "Remarks for the Stage Directors and Choreographers Gala," November 8, 2009, reproduced in "Remembering Zelda: The Words of a Visionary," p. 5, http://arenastage.net/zelda/images/All%20Speeches.pdf?ignoremobile=y.

14. Dean Adams, "Puttin' the Profit in Nonprofit Broadway Theatre Companies," *Theatre Symposium* 22 (2014): 60.

15. Peter Marks, "Star Broadway Team to Bring a Kinder, Gentler President to Arena Stage," *Washington Post*, January 25, 2018, https://www.washingtonpost.com/entertainment/theater_dance/star-broadway-team-to-bring-a-kinder-gentler-president-to-arena-stage/2018/01/25/0aa9341c-01d9-11e8-93f5-53a3a47824e8_story.html?utm_term=.d840edcf6de9.

16. *The Velocity of Autumn* playbill, April 2014. Author's collection.

17. Arena Stage, "The Mead Center History," https://www.arenastage.org/about-us/the-mead-center/ (accessed August 9, 2018).

18. In 2012, Center Stage, the leading professional theatre of Baltimore, celebrated its fiftieth anniversary by asking fifty prominent U.S. playwrights, "What is my America?" To see some of their responses, visit https://www.centerstage.org/plays-and-events/digital-initiatives.

19. Kelly Renee Armstrong, in discussion with the author, March 2015.

20. Arena Stage, "Audience Demographics," c. 2010, http://www.arenastage.org/about/contact/images/media%20kit%20sheet%2010-11.pdf and Amanda Noss, "Household Income for States: 2010 and 2011," U.S. Census Bureau, September 2012, https://www.census.gov/prod/2012pubs/acsbr11-02.pdf.

21. Edgar Dobie, in discussion with the author, January 2015. Amended by Dobie via email, January 2017.

22. Andrew Gans, "Arena Stage Is Developing 25 New Political Plays and Musicals," *Playbill.com*, November 30, 2016, http://www.playbill.com/article/arena-stage-is-developing-25-new-plays-and-musicals.

23. Angela Pao, *No Safe Spaces: Re-casting Race, Ethnicity, and Nationality in American Theater* (Ann Arbor: University of Michigan Press, 2010), 3.

BIBLIOGRAPHY

ARCHIVES AND SPECIAL COLLECTIONS

Arena Stage Records, 1950–2007, Special Collections Research Center, George Mason University

Donald McKayle Papers, Special Collections, University of California, Irvine

J. Burke Knapp Papers, 1960s, Special Collections Research Center, George Mason University

Lorraine Hansberry Papers, Schomburg Center for Research in Black Culture, New York Public Library

Theatre on Film and Tape Archive, Performing Arts Library, New York Public Library

Thomas C. Fichandler Papers, 1950–1997, Special Collections Research Center, George Mason University

Washingtoniana Division, Martin Luther King Jr. Memorial Library, District of Columbia Public Library

Zelda Fichandler Papers, 1950–2000, Special Collections Research Center, George Mason University

ADDITIONAL SOURCES

Abdur-Rahman, Aliyyah. *Against the Closet: Identity, Political Longing, and Black Figuration.* Durham, NC: Duke University Press, 2012.

Ackermann, Robert John. *Heterogeneities: Race, Gender, Class, Nation, and State.* Amherst: University of Massachusetts Press, 1996.

Adams, Dean. "Puttin' the Profit in Nonprofit Broadway Theatre Companies." *Theatre Symposium* 22 (2014): 48–61.

Adler, Steven. *On Broadway: Art and Commerce on the Great White Way.* Carbondale: Southern Illinois University Press, 2004.

Ahmed, Sara. *The Cultural Politics of Emotions.* New York: Routledge, 2004.

———. *On Being Included: Racism and Diversity in Institutional Life.* Durham, NC: Duke University Press, 2012.

Ahn, Christine E. "Democratizing American Philanthropy." In *The Revolution Will Not Be Funded: Beyond the Non-Profit Industrial Complex*, edited by INCITE!, 63–76.

Alexander, Bryant Keith. "'Boojie!' A Question of Authenticity." In *From Bourgeois to Boojie: Black Middle-Class Performance*, edited by Vershawn Ashanti Young with Bridget Harris Tsemo, 309–30.

Als, Hilton. "America, America: Two Plays about the Country's Complexities."

New Yorker, December 13, 2010, http://archives.newyorker.com/?i=2010-12
-13#folio=102.

Anderson, Benedict. *Imagined Communities: Reflections on the Origin and
Spread of Nationalism*. London: Verso, 1983.

Anderson, Sheila McNerney. "The Founding of Theater Arts Philanthropy in
America: W. McNeil Lowry and the Ford Foundation, 1957–65." In *Angels
in the American Theater: Patrons, Patronage, and Philanthropy*, edited by
Robert A. Shanke, 173–89.

Aono, Tomoko. "The Foundations of American Regional Theatre." PhD diss.,
CUNY Graduate Center, 2010.

Arden, John. *Serjeant Musgrave's Dance*. London: Methuen, 1972.

Arena Stage. "About Arena Stage." http://www.arenastage.org/about/ (accessed
May 7, 2012).

———. "Arena Stage at the Mead Center for American Theater." http://www
.arenastage.org/plan-your-visit/the-mead-center/ (accessed February 15,
2018).

———. "Arena Stage Kicks Off Lillian Hellman Festival with *The Little Foxes*."
September 22, 2016, https://www.arenastage.org/about/press-room/press
-releases/releases/16-17/Hellman%20Festival%20Release%20web.pdf.

———. "Audience Demographics." c. 2010, http://www.arenastage.org/about
/contact/images/media%20kit%20sheet%2010-11.pdf.

———. "The Mead Center History." https://www.arenastage.org/about-us/the
-mead-center/ (accessed August 9, 2018).

———. "Mission, Vision and Values." https://www.arenastage.org/about-us
/mission-vision-and-values/ (accessed July 31, 2018).

———. " 'The Originalist' extends its hand across the aisle and finds the
humanity in our civil discourse." http://ow.ly/1Rob3oclobf, June 5, 2017,
3:00 p.m., https://twitter.com/arenastage/status/871849184638488576.

———. "Our History." http://www.arenastage.org/about/history/ (accessed
February 25, 2015).

Arkatov, Janice. "Ron Milner's 'Checkmates' at Inner City Center." *LA Times*,
May 31, 1987, http://articles.latimes.com/1987-05-31/entertainment/ca-9156
_1_ron-milner.

Asch, Chris Myers, and George Derek Musgrove. *Chocolate City: A History of
Race and Democracy in the Nation's Capital*. Chapel Hill: University of North
Carolina Press, 2017.

Asian American Performers Action Coalition. "Ethnic Representation on New
York City Stages 2006/07-2010-11 Seasons." February 2012, http://www
.aapacnyc.org/uploads/1/1/9/4/11949532/ethnic_representation_nyc.pdf.

"ASTR/ATHE Adjunct Survey Data." *News and Press: ATHE News*, August 25, 2016,
http://www.athe.org/news/305136/ASTRATHE-Adjunct-Survey-Data.htm.

Balibar, Étienne, and Immanuel Wallerstein. *Race, Nation, Class: Ambiguous Identities.* 2nd ed. London: Verso, 2011.

Balme, Christopher B. *The Theatrical Public Sphere.* Cambridge: Cambridge University Press, 2014.

Bambara, Toni Cade. *The Black Woman: An Anthology.* New York: Washington Square Press, 1970.

Banks, Daniel. "*The Welcoming Table*: Casting for an Integrated Society." *Theatre Topics* 23, no. 1 (March 2013): 1–18.

Barnard, Rita. *Apartheid and Beyond: South African Writers and the Politics of Place.* New York: Oxford University Press, 2007.

Barnes, Clive. "Theater: Howard Sackler's 'Great White Hope.'" *New York Times,* October 4, 1968, 40.

Batiste, Stephanie. *Darkening Mirrors: Imperial Representation in Depression-Era African American Performance.* Durham, NC: Duke University Press, 2012.

Baumol, William J., and William G. Bowen. *Performing Arts: The Economic Dilemma.* Cambridge, MA: MIT Press, 1966.

Bennett, Susan. *Theatre Audiences: A Theory of Production and Reception.* London: Routledge, 1990.

Berkowitz, Gerald M. *New Broadways.* 2nd ed. New York: Applause, 1997.

Berlin, Susan. "*Oklahoma!*" *Talkin' Broadway,* n.d., http://www.talkinbroadway.com/regional/dc/dc502.html.

Bernardi, Daniel. *Star Trek and History: Race-ing toward a White Future.* New Brunswick, NJ: Rutgers University Press, 1998.

Bernstein, Robin. "Inventing a Fish Bowl: White Supremacy and the Critical Reception of Lorraine Hansberry's *A Raisin in the Sun.*" *Modern Drama* 42, no. 1 (Spring 1999): 16–27.

Berson, Misha. "Provocative 'Oklahoma!' Hits 5th Avenue Stage." *Seattle Times,* February 10, 2012, http://seattletimes.com/html/thearts/2017478542_throklahoma11.html.

Bertrand, Marianne, and Sendhil Mullainathan. "Are Emily and Greg More Employable Than Lakisha and Jamal? A Field Experiment on Labor Market Discrimination." *American Economic Review* 94 (2004): 991–1013.

Bhabha, Homi K. *The Location of Culture.* New York: Routledge, 1994.

Bianchini, Natka. *Samuel Beckett's Theatre in America: The Legacy of Alan Schneider as Beckett's American Director.* New York: Palgrave Macmillan, 2015.

Binkiewicz, Donna M. *Federalizing the Muse: United States Arts Policy and the National Endowment for the Arts, 1965–1980.* Chapel Hill: University of North Carolina Press, 2004.

Black, Cheryl, and Jonathan Shandell, eds. *Experiments in Democracy:*

Interracial and Cross-Cultural Exchange in American Theatre, 1912–1945. Carbondale: Southern Illinois University Press, 2016.

Bonilla-Silva, Eduardo. *Racism without Racists: Color-Blind Racism and the Persistence of Racial Inequality in America*. 3rd ed. Lanham, MD: Rowman & Littlefield, 2010.

———. *Racism without Racists: Color-Blind Racism and the Persistence of Racial Inequality in America*. 4th ed. Lanham, MD: Rowman & Littlefield, 2014.

———. *White Supremacy and Racism in the Post–Civil Rights Era*. Boulder: Lynne Rienner, 2001.

Bonin-Rodriguez, Paul. *Performing Policy: How Contemporary Politics and Cultural Programs Redefined U.S. Artists for the Twenty-First Century*. New York: Palgrave Macmillan, 2015.

Booth, John E. *The Critic, Power, and the Performing Arts*. New York: Columbia University Press, 1991.

Bordelon, Pamela. "New Tracks on *Dust Tracks*: Toward a Reassessment of the Life of Zora Neale Hurston." *African American Review* 31, no. 1 (1997): 5–21.

Bottoms, Stephen J. *Playing Underground: A Critical History of the 1960s Off-Off-Broadway Movement*. Ann Arbor: University of Michigan Press, 2006.

Bourdieu, Pierre. *The Field of Cultural Production*. New York: Columbia University Press, 1993.

———. "Sport and Social Class." *Social Science Information* 17 (1978): 819–40.

Braconi, Adrienne Macki. *Harlem's Theaters: A Staging Ground for Community, Class, and Contradiction, 1923–1939*. Evanston, IL: Northwestern University Press, 2015.

Brater, Jessica, et al. "'Let Our Freak Flags Fly': *Shrek the Musical* and the Branding of Diversity." *Theatre Journal* 62, no. 2 (May 2010): 151–72.

Brecht, Bertolt, and Eric Bentley. *The Caucasian Chalk Circle*. New York: Grove, 1966.

Brody, Jennifer DeVere. "Hyphen-Nations." In *Cruising the Performative: Interventions into Representation of Ethnicity, Nationality, and Sexuality*, edited by Sue Ellen Case, Philip Brett, and Susan Leigh Foster, 149–62.

Brooks, Daphne. *Bodies in Dissent: Spectacular Performances of Race and Freedom, 1850–1910*. Durham, NC: Duke University Press, 2006.

Brown, Alan, and Rebecca Ratzin. *Counting New Beans: Intrinsic Impact and the Value of Art*. San Francisco: Theatre Bay Area, 2012.

Brown, Carlyle. *The African Company Presents Richard III*. Black Drama Database. Alexandria: Alexander Street Press, 2014.

Brown, Jayna. *Babylon Girls: Black Women Performers and the Shaping of the Modern*. Durham, NC: Duke University Press, 2009.

Broyles-Gonzalez, Yolanda. *El Teatro Campesino: Theater in the Chicano Movement*. Austin: University of Texas Press, 1994.

Brustein, Robert. *Dumbocracy in America: Studies in the Theatre of Guilt, 1987–1994*. Chicago: Ivan R. Dee, 1994.

Burns, James, and Abel Bartley. *"The Great White Hope*: A Forgotten Biopic?" *a/b: AutoBiography Studies* 26, no. 1 (Summer 2011): 53–67.

Burns, Ken, dir. *Unforgivable Blackness: The Rise and Fall of Jack Johnson*. DVD, 240 min. PBS, 2004.

Burrell, Julie M. "To Be a Man: A Re-assessment of Black Masculinity in Lorraine Hansberry's *A Raisin in the Sun* and *Les Blancs*." *Continuum* 1, no. 1 (June 2014), http://continuumjournal.org/index.php/incession-content/26 -volumes/issues/vol-1-no-1-inception/vol-1-no-1-content/articles/58-to-be -a-man-a-re-assessment-of-black-masculinity-in-lorraine-hansberry-s-a -raisin-in-the-sun-and-les-blancs2.

Butler, Isaac. "A Clearer Picture 2." *Parabasis* (blog), January 13, 2010, http:// parabasis.typepad.com/blog/2010/01/a-clearer-picture-2.html.

Butler, Judith, and Gayatri Chakravorty Spivak. *Who Sings the Nation-State? Language, Politics, Belonging*. London: Seagull Books, 2007.

BWW News Desk. "Arena Stage Celebrates 25 Years of Allen Lee Hughes Fellowship Program." *BroadwayWorld*, March 4, 2016, https://www.broad wayworld.com/washington-dc/article/Arena-Stage-Celebrates-25-Years-of -Allen-Lee-Hughes-Fellowship-Program-20160304.

Byrnes, Anthony, and Christina Ramos. "5 Graphs That Show the Ethnic, Racial and Gender Makeup of Playwrights at the Mark Taper Forum." KCRW (blog), April 6, 2017, https://curious.kcrw.com/2017/04/graphing-the-ethnic-racial -and-gender-makeup-of-playwrights-in-the-50-year-history-of-the-mark -taper-forum.

———. "Visualizing the (Lacking) Diversity of Directors at the Mark Taper Forum." KCRW (blog), April 20, 2017, https://curious.kcrw.com/2017/04 /director-diversity-mark-taper-forum.

Canning, Charlotte. *The Most American Thing in America: Circuit Chautauqua as Performance*. Iowa City: University of Iowa Press, 2005.

———. *On the Performance Front: US Theatre and Internationalism*. Houndmills, UK: Palgrave Macmillan, 2015.

Carby, Hazel. *Cultures in Babylon*. London: Verso, 1999.

Carlson, Marvin. *The Haunted Stage*. Ann Arbor: University of Michigan Press, 2001.

———. "National Theatres: Then and Now." In *National Theatres in a Changing Europe*, edited by S. E. Wilmer. Houndmills, UK: Palgrave Macmillan, 2008.

———. *Places of Performance: The Semiotics of Theatre Architecture*. Ithaca, NY: Cornell University Press, 1993.

Carpenter, Faedra Chatard. "Activating the Asterisk: The Dramaturgy of

Intentionality." *Journal of Dramatic Theory and Criticism* 32, no. 2 (Spring 2018): 129–40.

———. *Coloring Whiteness: Acts of Critique in Black Performance*. Ann Arbor: University of Michigan Press, 2014.

Carter, Steve. *Nevis Mountain Dew*. Black Drama Database. Alexandria: Alexander Street Press, 2014.

Carter, Steven R. *Hansberry's Drama: Commitment and Complexity*. Urbana: University of Illinois Press, 1991.

Carter, Tim. *Oklahoma! The Making of an American Musical*. New Haven, CT: Yale University Press, 2007.

Cary, Francine Curro, ed. *Urban Odyssey: A Multicultural History of Washington, D.C.* Washington: Smithsonian Institution Press, 1996.

Case, Sue Ellen, Philip Brett, and Susan Leigh Foster, eds. *Cruising the Performative: Interventions into Representation of Ethnicity, Nationality, and Sexuality*. Bloomington: Indiana University Press, 1995.

Catanese, Brandi Wilkins. *The Problem of the Color[blind]: Racial Transgression and the Politics of Black Performance*. Ann Arbor: University of Michigan Press, 2011.

———. "Taking the Long View." *Theatre Journal* 62, no. 4 (December 2010): 547–51.

Chansky, Dorothy. "Alphabet Soup: The Acronymization of the American Theater." In *The Sixties, Center Stage: Mainstream and Popular Performances in a Turbulent Decade*, edited by James M. Harding and Cindy Rosenthal, 231–50.

———. *Composing Ourselves: The Little Theatre Movement and the American Audience*. Carbondale: Southern Illinois University Press, 2004.

Chinoy, Helen Krich, and Linda Walsh Jenkins, eds. *Women in American Theatre*. 3rd ed. New York: Theatre Communications Group, 2006.

Chong-Stannard, Joy, dir. *Donald McKayle: Heartbeats of a Dancemaker*. DVD, 57 min. Hightstown, NJ: Dance Pioneers and PBS Hawaii, Dance Horizons Video, 2002.

Christiansen, Richard. *Theater of Our Own: A History and a Memoir of 1,001 Nights in Chicago*. Evanston, IL: Northwestern University Press, 2004.

Chuh, Kandice. *Imagine Otherwise: On Asian Americanist Critique*. Durham, NC: Duke University Press, 2003.

Cima, Gibson. "Resurrecting *Sizwe Banzi Is Dead* (1972–2008): John Kani, Winston Ntshona, Athol Fugard, and Postapartheid South Africa." *Theatre Survey* 50, no. 1 (May 2009): 91–118.

Cleage, Pearl. *Blues for an Alabama Sky*. Black Drama Database. Alexandria: Alexander Street Press, 2014.

Coe, Richard L. "Arena Creates a New Stage." *Washington Post*, June 4, 1966,

http://search.proquest.com.ezproxy.cul.columbia.edu/docview/142695501
?accountid=10226.

———. "Arena Puts New Note into Pirandello." *Washington Post*, November 29,
1968, http://search.proquest.com.ezproxy.cul.columbia.edu/docview/143243
006?accountid=10226.

———. "Impulses." *Washington Post*, January 23, 1969, http://search.proquest
.com.ezproxy.cul.columbia.edu/docview/147723744?accountid=10226.

———. "London Acclaim for 'Texas Trilogy.'" *Washington Post*, February 24,
1977, https://www.washingtonpost.com/archive/lifestyle/1977/02/24/london
-acclaim-for-texas-trilogy/ac8f2e03-2221-4b63-b256-11170cc32bae/?utm
_term=.b74a1e4dd5ba.

———. "'Threepenny Opera' Opens Arena Stage." *Washington Post*, November
28, 1968, http://search.proquest.com.ezproxy.cul.columbia.edu/docview
/143394613?accountid=10226.

Cohen, Cathy J. "Punks, Bulldaggers, and Welfare Queens: The Radical
Potential of Queer Politics?" *GLQ: A Journal of Lesbian and Gay Studies*
3 (1997): 437–65.

Colbert, Soyica Diggs. *The African American Theatrical Body: Reception,
Performance, and the Stage.* Cambridge: Cambridge University Press, 2011.

———. *Black Movements: Performance and Cultural Politics.* New Brunswick,
NJ: Rutgers University Press, 2017.

———. "Drama in the Harlem Renaissance." In *The Cambridge Companion to
African American Theatre*, edited by Harvey Young, 85–102.

Cole, Catherine M. "When Is African Theater 'Black'?" In *Black Cultural Traffic:
Crossroads in Global Performance and Popular Culture*, edited by Harry J.
Elam Jr. and Kennell Jackson, 43–58.

Colleran, Jeanne. "Athol Fugard and the Problematics of the Liberal Critique."
Modern Drama 38, no. 3 (Fall 1995): 389–407.

Coyne, Bernard. "A History of Arena Stage, Washington, D.C." PhD diss., Tulane
University, 1964.

Cremieux, Anne, Xavier Lemoine, and Jean-Paul Rocchi, eds. *Understanding
Blackness through Performance: Contemporary Arts and the Representation
of Identity.* New York: Palgrave Macmillan, 2013.

Crenshaw, Kimberlé. "Mapping the Margins: Intersectionality, Identity Politics,
and Violence against Women of Color." *Stanford Law Review* 43, no. 6 (July
1991): 1241–99.

Crew, Spencer R. "Melding the Old and the New: The Modern African American
Community, 1930–1960." In *Urban Odyssey: A Multicultural History of
Washington, D.C.*, edited by Francine Curro Cary, 208–27.

Crow, Brian, with Chris Banfield. *An Introduction to Post-Colonial Theatre.*
Cambridge: Cambridge University Press, 1996.

Crystal City Business Improvement District. "The Economic Impact of Theaters in Arlington County, Virginia." March 2009, www.arlingtonarts.org/libraries /grants_documents/theaterstudy_final_p1.sflb.ashx.

Daileader, Celia R. *Racism, Misogyny, and the Othello Myth: Inter-racial Couples from Shakespeare to Spike Lee*. Cambridge: Cambridge University Press, 2005.

Davis, Andrew. *America's Longest Run: A History of the Walnut Street Theatre*. University Park: Penn State University Press, 2010.

Davis, Carol Bunch. "'Ghost[s] in the House!'": Black Subjectivity and Cultural Memory in Howard Sackler's *The Great White Hope*." *MELUS: Multi-Ethnic Literature of the U.S.* 37, no. 3 (Fall 2012): 71–95.

———. *Prefiguring Postblackness: Cultural Memory, Drama, and the African American Freedom Struggle of the 1960s*. Jackson: University of Mississippi Press, 2016.

Davis, Clinton Turner, and Harry Newman, eds. *Beyond Tradition: Transcripts of the First Symposium on Non-traditional Casting*. New York: Non-traditional Casting Project, 1988.

DeFerrari, John. "Lost Washington: The Gayety Theater." *Greater Greater Washington* (blog), January 26, 2011, https://ggwash.org/view/8040/lost -washington-the-gayety-theater.

Deloria, Philip. *Playing Indian*. New Haven, CT: Yale University Press, 1998.

Dever, Marissa. "Thawing the Cold War with Theatre." *Boundary Stones*, WETA's Local History Blog, February 2, 2017, http://blogs.weta.org/boundarystones /2017/02/02/thawing-cold-war-theatre.

DiMaggio, Paul. "Cultural Boundaries and Structural Change: The Extension of the High Culture Model to Theater, Opera, and the Dance, 1900–1940." In *Cultivating Differences: Symbolic Boundaries and the Making of Inequality*, edited by Michele Lamont and Marcel Fournier, 21–57.

Dolan, Jill. "Diversity Drama in the 2012–2013 Season." *Feminist Spectator* (blog), May 22, 2012, http://feministspectator.princeton.edu/2012/05/22 /diversity-drama-in-the-2012-2013-season/.

———. *Utopia in Performance: Finding Hope at the Theater*. Ann Arbor: University of Michigan Press, 2005.

Dudziak, Mary L. *Cold War Civil Rights: Race and the Image of American Democracy*. 2nd ed. Princeton, NJ: Princeton University Press, 2011.

Dukore, Bernard F. "John MacDonald and the Washington Stage Guild." *SHAW: The Annual of Bernard Shaw Studies* 29 (2009): 225–30.

Edney, Kathryn. "Tapping the Ivories: Jazz and Tap Dance in *Jelly's Last Jam* (1992)." In *Gestures of Music Theater: The Performativity of Song and Dance*, edited by Dominic Symonds and Millie Taylor, 113–27.

Edwards, Brent Hayes. *The Practice of Diaspora: Literature, Translation, and the Rise of Black Internationalism*. Cambridge, MA: Harvard University Press, 2003.

Edwards, Erica. *Charisma and the Fictions of Black Leadership*. Minneapolis: University of Minnesota Press, 2012.

Elam, Harry J., Jr. "Black Theatre in the Age of Obama." In *The Cambridge Companion to African American Theatre*, edited by Harvey Young, 255–78.

———. *The Past as Present in the Drama of August Wilson*. Ann Arbor: University of Michigan Press, 2006.

———. "Towards a New Territory in 'Multicultural' Theater." In *The Color of Theater: Race, Culture, and Contemporary Performance*, edited by Roberta Uno with Lucy Mae San Pablo Burns, 91–114.

Elam, Harry J., Jr., and Kennell Jackson, eds. *Black Cultural Traffic: Crossroads in Global Performance and Popular Culture*. Ann Arbor: University of Michigan Press, 2005.

Elam, Harry J., Jr., and Douglas A. Jones Jr., eds. *The Methuen Drama Book of Post-Black Plays*. London: Methuen Drama, 2012.

Elfe, James Wolfgang, James Harding, and Gunther Holst, eds. *The Fortunes of German Writers in America: Studies in Literary Reception*. Columbia: University of South Carolina Press, 1992.

Engle, Ron, and Tice L. Miller, eds. *The American Stage: Social and Economic Issues from the Colonial Period to the Present*. Cambridge: Cambridge University Press, 1993.

Engstrom, Susannah. "Twin Cities Theater in the 1960s: Negotiating the Commercial/Experimental Divide." In *The Sixties, Center Stage: Mainstream and Popular Performances in a Turbulent Decade*, edited by James M. Harding and Cindy Rosenthal, 251–72.

Erkut, Sumru, and Ineke Ceder. "Women's Leadership in Resident Theaters." Wellesley Centers for Women. Wellesley, MA: Wellesley College, 2016.

Esslin, Martin. "Brecht at Seventy." *TDR* 12, no. 1 (1967–68): 36–43.

Farrar, Margaret E. *Building the Body Politic: Power and Urban Space in Washington, D.C.* Urbana: University of Illinois Press, 2008.

Ferguson, Karen. *Top Down: The Ford Foundation, Black Power, and the Reinvention of Racial Liberalism*. Philadelphia: University of Pennsylvania Press, 2013.

Ferguson, Roderick A. *Aberrations in Black: Toward a Queer of Color Critique*. Minneapolis: University of Minnesota Press, 2003.

Ferreira da Silva, Denise. *Toward a Global Idea of Race*. Minneapolis: University of Minnesota, 2007.

Fichandler, Zelda. "Address to the Stage Directors and Choreographers Society in Celebration of the Third Annual Zelda Fichandler Award." *HowlRound*, November 13, 2011, http://howlround.com/address-to-the-stage-directors-and-choreographers-society-in-celebration-of-the-third-annual-zelda.

———. "Arena to Create a New Inter-Racial Stage Force." *Washington Star*, June 30, 1968, D-1.

———. "Casting for a Different Truth." *American Theatre* 5, no. 2 (May 1988): 18–23.

———. "Introductory Remarks at a Panel on The Open Stage," given at the International Theatre Institute Conference in New York City, June 1967, reproduced in "Remembering Zelda: The Words of a Visionary," http://arenastage.net/zelda/images/All%20Speeches.pdf?ignoremobile=y.

———. "Remarks for the Stage Directors and Choreographers Gala." November 8, 2009, reproduced in "Remembering Zelda: The Words of a Visionary," http://arenastage.net/zelda/images/All%20Speeches.pdf?ignoremobile=y.

———. "Theatres or Institutions?" *Theatre* 3 (September 1970): 105–16.

———. "Whither (or Wither) Art?" *American Theatre* (May/June 2003): 28–31, 68–73.

Fichandler, Zelda, and Edwin Wilson. "Interview with Zelda Fichandler." *CUNY Spotlight*. VHS, 1991.

Filmer, Paul, Val Rimmer, and Dave Walsh, "*Oklahoma!*: Ideology and Politics in the Vernacular Tradition of the American Musical." *Popular Music* 18, no. 3 (October 1999): 381–95.

Frazier, E. Franklin. *Black Bourgeoisie: The Rise of a New Middle Class in the United States*. New York: Free Press, 1957.

Fugard, Athol. *The Blood Knot*. Cape Town: Oxford University Press, 1992.

———. *A Lesson from Aloes*. New York: Theatre Communications Group, 1993.

———. *My Children! My Africa!* New York: Theatre Communications Group, 1990.

———. *Townships Plays*. New York: Oxford University Press, 2000.

Funke, Lewis. *Playwrights Talk about Writing: 12 Interviews with Lewis Funke*. Chicago: Dramatic Pub. Co., 1975.

Galella, Donatella. "Being in 'The Room Where It Happens': *Hamilton*, Obama, and Nationalist Neoliberal Multicultural Inclusion." *Theatre Survey* 59, no. 3 (September 2018): 363–85.

———. "Diversity in Theatre and Higher Education." In "Archiving ATHE's Thirtieth Anniversary Conference Plenaries," edited by Kelly Howe, *Theatre Topics* 27, no. 1 (2017): 5–6.

———. "*Playing in the Dark* / Musicalizing *A Raisin in the Sun*." *Continuum: The Journal of African Diaspora Drama, Theatre, and Performance* 1, no. 2 (2015): http://continuumjournal.org/index.php/component/content/article

Bibliography

/33-volumes/issues/vol-1-no-2-amiri-baraka-revaluation-and-appreciation
/vol-1-no-2-content/ysc-1-2/95-playing-in-the-dark-musicalizing-a-raisin
-in-the-sun.

Gamarekian, Barbara. "The Arena Theater in Washington Gets Ready for a
Change of Cast." *New York Times*, September 2, 1990, http://www.nytimes
.com/1990/09/02/theater/the-arena-theater-in-washington-gets-ready-for
-a-change-of-cast.html?pagewanted=all.

Gans, Andrew. "Arena Stage Is Developing 25 New Political Plays and Musicals."
Playbill.com, November 30, 2016, http://www.playbill.com/article/arena
-stage-is-developing-25-new-plays-and-musicals.

Gates, Henry Louis, Jr. "The Chitlin Circuit." In *African American Performance
and Theater*, edited by Harry J. Elam Jr. and David Krasner, 132–48.

———. *The Signifying Monkey: A Theory of African-American Literary Criticism.*
New York: Oxford University Press, 1988.

"Get to Know the OK! Cast: Cara and Shane." YouTube video, 2:45, posted by
"arenastage1," August 2, 2011, http://www.youtube.com/watch?v=go77iu
EZ2Zk&list=PL2465CD8DC44EB849&index=2&feature=plpp_video.

Giannetti, Charlene. "Arena Stage's Molly Smith—Showcasing American
Musicals and Plays." *Woman around Town*, May 9, 2012, http://www
.womanaroundtown.com/sections/woman-around-town/woman-around
-town-arena-stage%E2%80%99s-molly-smith-showcasing-american
-musicals-and-plays.

Gillette, Howard, Jr. *Between Justice and Beauty: Race, Planning, and the Failure
of Urban Policy in Washington, D.C.* Philadelphia: University of Pennsylvania
Press, 2006.

Gilmore, Matthew B. "District of Columbia Population History." *Washington DC
History Resources* (blog), 2014, https://matthewbgilmore.wordpress.com
/district-of-columbia-population-history/.

Gilmore, Ruth Ann. *Golden Gulag: Prisons, Surplus, Crisis, and Opposition in
Globalizing California.* Berkeley: University of California Press, 2007.

———. "In the Shadow of the Shadow State." In *The Revolution Will Not Be
Funded: Beyond the Non-profit Industrial Complex*, edited by INCITE!, 41–52.

Gilroy, Paul. *The Black Atlantic: Modernity and Double-Consciousness.*
Cambridge, MA: Harvard University Press, 1993.

Glover, Eric M. "By and About: An Antiracist History of the Musicals and the
Antimusicals of Langston Hughes and Zora Neale Hurston." PhD diss.,
Princeton University, 2017.

———. "What Is This 'Black' in Black [Musical Theater]?" Paper delivered at
the Association for Theatre in Higher Education, Chicago, IL, August 12,
2016.

Golden, Thelma. *Freestyle.* New York: Studio Museum in Harlem, 2001.

Gordon, Avery F., and Christopher Newfield, eds. *Mapping Multiculturalism*. Minneapolis: University of Minnesota Press, 1996.

Gordon-Reed, Annette, ed. *Race on Trial: Law and Justice in American History*. New York: Oxford University Press, 2002.

Gordone, Charles. *No Place to Be Somebody*. Black Drama Database. Alexandria: Alexander Street Press, 2014.

Gottfried, Martin. *A Theater Divided: The Postwar American Stage*. Boston: Little, Brown, 1967.

———. "What Shall It Profit a Theatre If . . . ?" *New York Times*, August 23, 1970, http://search.proquest.com.ezproxy.gc.cuny.edu/docview/117965802 ?accountid=7287.

Grams, Diane. "Achieving Success." In *Entering Cultural Communities: Diversity and Change in the Nonprofit Arts*, edited by Diane Grams and Betty Farrell, 221–47.

Grams, Diane, and Betty Farrell, eds. *Entering Cultural Communities: Diversity and Change in the Nonprofit Arts*. New Brunswick, NJ: Rutgers University Press, 2008.

Greene, Alexis, ed. *Women Writing Plays: Three Decades of the Susan Smith Blackburn Prize*. Austin: University of Texas Press, 2006.

Gussow, Mel. "Profiles: Witness." *New Yorker*, December 20, 1982, 47–49.

Guterman, Gad. "Field Tripping: The Power of *Inherit the Wind*." *Theatre Journal* 60, no. 4 (December 2008): 563–83.

Gutmann, Amy, ed. *Multiculturalism: Examining the Politics of Recognition*. Princeton, NJ: Princeton University Press, 1994.

Haedicke, Susan C. "Theater for the New Generation: The Living Stage Theatre Company's Program for Teen Mothers." In *Performing Democracy: International Perspectives on Urban Community-Based Performance*, edited by Susan C. Haedicke and Tobin Nellhaus, 269–80.

Haedicke, Susan C., and Tobin Nellhaus, eds. *Performing Democracy: International Perspectives on Urban Community-Based Performance*. Ann Arbor: University of Michigan Press, 2001.

Hall, Stuart. "Notes on Deconstructing 'the Popular.'" In *People's History and Socialist Theory*, edited by Raphael Samuel, 227–40.

———. "Whose Heritage? Un-settling 'the Heritage,' Reimagining the Post-nation." In *The Politics of Heritage: The Legacies of "Race,"* edited by Jo Littler and Roshi Naidoo, 23–35.

Hansberry, Lorraine. *Les Blancs*. New York: Vintage, 1972.

———. *A Raisin in the Sun*. New York: Random House, 2002.

———. *The Sign in Sidney Brustein's Window*. New York: Samuel French, 1986.

Harding, James M. *The Ghosts of the Avant-Garde(s): Exorcising Experimental Theater and Performance*. Ann Arbor: University of Michigan Press, 2013.

Harding, James M., and Cindy Rosenthal, eds. *Restaging the Sixties: Radical Theaters and Their Legacies*. Ann Arbor: University of Michigan Press, 2006.

———, eds. *The Sixties, Center Stage: Mainstream and Popular Performances in a Turbulent Decade*. Ann Arbor: University of Michigan Press, 2017.

Hartman, Saidiya V. *Scenes of Subjection: Terror, Slavery, and Self-Making in Nineteenth-Century America*. New York: Oxford University Press, 1997.

Harvey, David. *A Brief History of Neoliberalism*. New York: Oxford University Press, 2007.

Hemenway, Robert E. *Zora Neale Hurston: A Literary Biography*. Urbana: University of Illinois Press, 1980.

Herrera, Brian. "The Best Actor for the Role, or the Mythos of Casting in American Popular Performance." *Journal of American Drama and Theatre* 27, no. 2 (Spring 2015): http://jadtjournal.org/2015/04/24/the-best-actor-for-the-role-or-the-mythos-of-casting-in-american-popular-performance/.

———. *Latin Numbers: Playing Latino in Twentieth-Century U.S. Popular Performance*. Ann Arbor: University of Michigan Press, 2015.

Hill, Lynda Marion. *Social Rituals and the Verbal Art of Zora Neale Hurston*. Washington: Howard University Press, 1996.

Hobsbawm, Eric. *Nations and Nationalism since 1780: Programme, Myth, Reality*. 2nd ed. New York: Cambridge University Press, 1992.

Hoffman, Warren. *The Great White Way: Race and the Broadway Musical*. New Brunswick, NJ: Rutgers University Press, 2014.

Holloway, Joseph E., ed. *Africanisms in American Culture*. Bloomington: Indiana University Press, 1990.

hooks, bell. *Ain't I a Woman: Black Women and Feminism*. Cambridge, MA: South End Press, 2007.

———. *Black Looks: Race and Representation*. Cambridge, MA: South End Press, 1992.

———. *Killing Rage: Ending Racism*. New York: Henry Holt, 1996.

Hopkinson, Natalie. *Go-Go Live: The Musical Life and Death of a Chocolate City*. Durham, NC: Duke University Press, 2012.

Hornby, Richard. "Interracial Casting at the Public and Other Theatres." *Hudson Review* 42, no. 3 (Autumn 1989): 459–66.

Huneycutt, Keith L. "'The Profound Silence of the Initiated': Zora Neale Hurston's *Polk County*, Dorothy Waring, and Stage Voodoo." In *Florida Studies: Proceedings of the 2009 Annual Meeting of the Florida College English Association*, edited by Claudia Slate and Carole Policy, 39–49.

Hurston, Zora Neale, with Dorothy Waring. *Polk County*. Black Drama Database. Alexandria: Alexander Street Press, 2014.

INCITE!, ed. *The Color of Violence: The Incite! Anthology*. Cambridge, MA: South End Press, 2006.

————. *The Revolution Will Not Be Funded: Beyond the Non-profit Industrial Complex*. Durham, NC: Duke University Press, 2017.

Irwin, Cathy, and Sean Metzger. "Keeping Up Appearances: Ethnic Alien-Nation in Female Solo Performance." In *Mixing It Up: Multiracial Subjects*, edited by SanSan Kwan and Kenneth Speirs, 163–80.

Iton, Richard. *In Search of the Black Fantastic: Politics and Popular Culture in the Post–Civil Rights Era*. New York: Oxford University Press, 2008.

Jackson, Lawrence P. *The Indignant Generation: A Narrative History of African American Writers and Critics, 1934–1960*. Princeton, NJ: Princeton University Press, 2010.

Jackson, Walter A. *Gunnar Myrdal and America's Conscience: Social Engineering and Racial Liberalism, 1938–1987*. Chapel Hill: University of North Carolina Press, 1990.

Jaffe, Harry S., and Tom Sherwood. *Dream City: Race, Power, and the Decline of Washington, D.C.* New York: Simon & Schuster, 1994.

Johnson, E. Patrick. *Appropriating Blackness: Performance and the Politics of Authenticity*. Durham, NC: Duke University Press, 2003.

Jones, Corey H. "Why Regional Theater Companies Are Forsaking Their Once-Mighty Resident Acting Ensembles." *Colorado Public Radio*, June 6, 2014, http://www.cpr.org/news/story/why-regional-theater-companies-are -forsaking-their-once-mighty-resident-acting-ensembles.

Jones, John Bush. *Our Musicals, Ourselves: A Social History of the American Musical Theatre*. Hanover, NH: University Press of New England, 2003.

Jones, Margo. *Theatre-in-the-Round*. New York: Rinehart & Company, 1951.

Jones, Syl. *Black No More*. New York: William Morris Agency, 1995.

"Joyce Brown." Internet Broadway Database, http://ibdb.com/person.php?id =79156.

Kammen, Michael. *American Culture, American Tastes*. New York: Alfred A. Knopf, 1999.

Kelley, Robin D. G. *Race Rebels: Culture, Politics, and the Black Working Class*. New York: Free Press, 1994.

Kelsey, Matthew. "How Helen Hayes Helped Desegregate the National Theatre." *Boundary Stones*, WETA's Local History Blog, June 22, 2016, http://blogs .weta.org/boundarystones/2016/06/22/how-helen-hayes-helped -desegregate-national-theatre.

Kim, Jodi. *Ends of Empire: Asian American Critique and the Cold War*. Minneapolis: University of Minnesota Press, 2008.

King, Bruce. *Derek Walcott and West Indian Drama: "Not Only a Playwright but a Company," The Trinidad Theatre Workshop 1959–1993*. Oxford: Clarendon Press, 1995.

King, Woodie, Jr. *The Impact of Race*. New York: Applause Theatre & Cinema Books, 2003.

Kirle, Bruce. "Reconciliation, Resolution, and the Political Role of *Oklahoma!* in American Consciousness." *Theatre Journal* 55, no. 2 (May 2003): 251–74.

———. *Unfinished Show Business: Broadway Musicals as Works-in-Process*. Carbondale: Southern Illinois University Press, 2005.

Knapp, Margaret M. "Narrative Strategies in Selected Studies of American Theatre Economics." In *The American Stage: Social and Economic Issues from the Colonial Period to the Present*, edited by Ron Engle and Tice L. Miller, 267–77.

Knapp, Raymond. *The American Musical and the Performance of National Identity*. Princeton, NJ: Princeton University Press, 2005.

Knapp, Raymond, Mitchell Morris, and Stacy Wolf, eds. *The Oxford Handbook of the American Musical*. New York: Oxford University Press, 2011.

Kolin, Philip C., ed. *Contemporary African American Women Playwrights: A Casebook*. London: Routledge, 2007.

Kondo, Dorinne K. "(Re)Visions of Race: Contemporary Race Theory and the Cultural Politics of Racial Crossover in Documentary Theatre." *Theatre Journal* 52, no. 1 (March 2000): 81–107.

Krasner, David. *A Beautiful Pageant: African American Theatre, Drama, and Performance in the Harlem Renaissance, 1910–1927*. New York: Palgrave Macmillan, 2002.

Kraut, Anthea. *Choreographing the Folk: The Dance Stagings of Zora Neale Hurston*. Minneapolis: University of Minnesota Press, 2008.

Kruger, Loren. *The National Stage: Theatre and Cultural Legitimation in England, France, and America*. Chicago: University of Chicago Press, 1992.

Kuftinec, Sonja. *Staging America: Cornerstone and Community Based Theater*. Chicago: Southern Illinois University Press, 2005.

Kurahashi, Yuko. *Asian American Culture on Stage: The History of the East West Players*. London: Routledge, 1999.

———. "*South Pacific* (review)." *Theatre Journal* 55, no. 3 (October 2003): 536–38.

Kwan, SanSan, and Kenneth Speirs, eds. *Mixing It Up: Multiracial Subjects*. Austin: University of Texas Press, 2004.

Lacy, Karyn R. *Blue-Chip Black: Race, Class, and Status in the Black Middle Class*. Berkeley: University of California Press, 2007.

Lahoud, John. "Theatre Reawakening: A Report on Ford Foundation Assistance to American Drama." New York: Ford Foundation, 1977.

Lamb, Yvonne Shinhoster. "Arts Administrator, Playwright Vantile Whitfield Dies." *Washington Post*, January 23, 2005, http://www.washingtonpost.com /wp-dyn/articles/A29685-2005Jan22.html.

Lamont, Michele, and Marcel Fournier, eds. *Cultivating Differences: Symbolic Boundaries and the Making of Inequality.* Chicago: University of Chicago Press, 1992.

Landro, Vincent. "The Mythologizing of American Regional Theatre." *Journal of American Drama and Theatre* 10 (Winter 1998): 76–101.

Landry, Bart. *The New Black Middle Class.* Berkeley: University of California Press, 1987.

Larson, Gary O. *The Reluctant Patron: The United States Government and the Arts, 1943–1965.* Philadelphia: University of Pennsylvania Press, 1983.

Lee, Esther Kim. *A History of Asian American Theatre.* Cambridge: Cambridge University Press, 2006.

Lee, Josephine. *The Japan of Pure Invention: Gilbert and Sullivan's "The Mikado."* Minneapolis: University of Minnesota Press, 2010.

———. "Racial Actors, Liberal Myths." *XCP: Cross Cultural Poetics* 13 (2003): 88–110.

Lemoine, Xavier. "Embodying Hybridity: Anna Deavere Smith's Identity Cross-Overs." In *Understanding Blackness through Performance: Contemporary Arts and the Representation of Identity,* edited by Anne Cremieux, Xavier Lemoine, and Jean-Paul Rocchi, 237–61.

Levine, Lawrence. *Highbrow/Lowbrow: The Emergence of Cultural Hierarchy in America.* Cambridge, MA: Harvard University Press, 1988.

Li, Stephanie. *Signifying without Specifying: Racial Discourse in the Age of Obama.* New Brunswick, NJ: Rutgers University Press, 2012.

Lipsitz, George. *How Racism Takes Place.* Philadelphia: Temple University Press, 2012.

———. *The Possessive Investment in Whiteness: How White People Profit from Identity Politics.* Philadelphia: Temple University Press, 2006.

Littler, Jo, and Roshi Naidoo, eds. *The Politics of Heritage: The Legacies of "Race."* London: Routledge, 2005.

Lo, Jacqueline, and Helen Gilbert. "Topography of Cross-Cultural Theatre Praxis." *TDR* 46, no. 3 (Autumn 2002): 31–53.

London, Todd. *The Artistic Home: Discussions with Artistic Directors of America's Institutional Theatres.* New York: Theatre Communications Group, 1988.

London, Todd, Ben Pesner, and Zannie Giraud Voss. *Outrageous Fortune: The Life and Times of the New American Play.* New York: Theatre Development Fund, 2009.

Lowe, John. "Hurston, Toomer, and the Dream of a Negro Theatre." In *"The Inside Light": New Critical Essays on Zora Neale Hurston,* edited by Deborah G. Plant, 79–92.

Lowe, Lisa. *The Intimacies of Four Continents.* Durham, NC: Duke University Press, 2015.

MacDonald, Laura, and William Everett, eds. *The Palgrave Handbook of Musical Theatre Producers*. New York: Palgrave Macmillan, 2017.

Macgowan, Kenneth. *Footlights across America: Towards a National Theater*. New York: Harcourt, Brace, and Company, 1929.

Madison, Cathy. "West Probes Traumas—with No Flinching." *American Theatre* (March 1999): 46–47.

Magat, Richard. *The Ford Foundation at Work: Philanthropic Choices, Methods, and Styles*. New York: Plenum Press, 1979.

Magnus, Dorothy B. "Matriarchs of the Regional Theatre." In *Women in American Theatre*, 3rd ed., edited by Helen Krich Chinoy and Linda Walsh Jenkins, 203–9.

Mahala, Macelle. *Penumbra: The Premier Stage for African American Drama*. Minneapolis: University of Minnesota Press, 2013.

Marks, Peter. "A Grand New State: You Just Cain't Say No to Arena Stage's 'Oklahoma!'" *Washington Post*, November 6, 2010, http://www.washington post.com/wp-dyn/content/article/2010/11/05/AR2010110507023.html.

———. "Star Broadway Team to Bring a Kinder, Gentler President to Arena Stage." *Washington Post*, January 25, 2018, https://www.washingtonpost .com/entertainment/theater_dance/star-broadway-team-to-bring-a-kinder -gentler-president-to-arena-stage/2018/01/25/0aa9341c-01d9-11e8-93f5 -53a3a47824e8_story.html?utm_term=.d840edcf6de9.

———. "The State of D.C. Theatre." *Washington Post*, January 6, 2012, http:// www.washingtonpost.com/entertainment/theater-dance/the-state-of-dc -theater/2012/01/03/gIQADvwIfP_story.html.

Maslon, Laurence. *The Arena Adventure: The First 40 Years*. Washington: Arena Stage, 1990.

Mason, Jeffrey D., and J. Ellen Gainor, eds. *Performing America: Cultural Nationalism in American Theater*. Ann Arbor: University of Michigan Press, 1999.

Mast, Gerald. *Can't Help Singin': The American Musical on Stage and Screen*. Woodstock, NY: Overlook Press, 1987.

Matura, Mustapha. *The Playboy of the West Indies*. London: Oberon, 2010.

———. *A Small World*. Black Drama Database. Alexandria: Alexander Street Press, 2014.

———. *Trinidad Sisters*. Black Drama Database. Alexandria: Alexander Street Press, 2014.

Maufort, Marc, ed. *Staging Difference: Cultural Pluralism in American Theatre and Drama*. New York: Peter Lang, 1995.

Maultsby, Portia K. "Africanisms in African-American Music." In *Africanisms in American Culture*, edited by Joseph E. Holloway, 185–210.

Mayer, John. *Steppenwolf Theatre Company of Chicago: In Their Own Words*. London: Bloomsbury, 2016.

McAllister, Marvin. *Whiting Up: Whiteface Minstrels and Stage Europeans in African American Performance*. Chapel Hill, University of North Carolina Press, 2011.

McCaffrey, Scott. "Updated: Arlington Taxpayers to Bail Out Signature Theatre a Second Time." *InsideNoVa*, December 18, 2014, http://www.insidenova .com/news/arlington/updated-arlington-taxpayers-to-bail-out-signature -theatre-a-second/article_c4cf3dd6-81fe-11e4-99cc-abaoc9ba73ce.html.

McConachie, Bruce. *American Theater in the Culture of the Cold War: Producing and Contesting Containment, 1947–1962*. Iowa City: University of Iowa Press, 2003.

McGinley, Paige A. "Reconsidering 'the American Style': Black Performers and Black Music in *Streetcar* and *Cat*." *Theatre Journal* 68, no. 1 (March 2016): 1–16.

McKayle, Donald. *Transcending Boundaries: My Dancing Life*. London: Routledge, 2002.

McNally, Megan. "Washington: Number One in College Degrees." Brookings Greater Washington Research Program. Washington: Brookings Institute, 2003, https://www.brookings.edu/wp-content/uploads/2016/06/education .pdf.

Melamed, Jodi. *Represent and Destroy: Rationalizing Violence in the New Racial Capitalism*. Minneapolis: University of Minnesota Press, 2011.

———. "The Spirit of Neoliberalism: From Racial Liberalism to Neoliberal Multiculturalism." *Social Text* 24, no. 4 (Winter 2006): 1–24.

Metzger, Sean. "Charles Parsloe's Chinese Fetish: An Example of Yellowface Performance in Nineteenth-Century American Melodrama." *Theatre Journal* 56, no. 4 (2004): 627–51.

Mews, Siegfried. "'Brecht, Motherhood, and Justice': The Reception of *The Caucasian Chalk Circle* in the United States." In *The Fortunes of German Writers in America: Studies in Literary Reception*, edited by James Wolfgang Elfe, James Harding, and Gunther Holst, 231–48.

Milk, Leslie. "Review: *Oklahoma!*" *Washingtonian*, November 9, 2010, http:// www.washingtonian.com/blogs/afterhours/theater-review/review -oklahoma.php.

Miller, Derek. "'Underneath the Ground': Jud and the Community in *Oklahoma!*" *Studies in Musical Theatre* 2, no. 2 (2008): 163–74.

Miller, Henry D. *Theorizing Black Theatre: Art Versus Protest in Critical Writings, 1898–1965*. Jefferson, NC: McFarland, 2010.

Miller, Hillary. *Drop Dead: Performance in Crisis, 1970s New York*. Evanston, IL: Northwestern University Press, 2016.

Mills, Charles W. *Black Rights / White Wrongs: The Critique of Racial Liberalism.*
New York: Oxford University Press, 2017.

Mitchell, Koritha. *Living with Lynching: African American Lynching Plays,
Performance, and Citizenship, 1890–1930.* Urbana: University of Illinois Press,
2011.

Modan, Gabriella Gahlia. *Turf Wars: Discourse, Diversity, and the Politics of
Place.* Hoboken: Wiley-Blackwell, 2007.

Mohler, Courtney Elkin. "The Native Plays of Lynn Riggs (Cherokee) and the
Question of 'Race'-Specific Casting." *Theatre Topics* 26, no. 1 (March 2016):
63–75.

"Molly Smith Discusses *Oklahoma!*, the 10–11 Season Opener." YouTube video,
2:44, posted by "arenastage1," August 17, 2010, http://www.youtube.com
/watch?v=Cmd5OpFd47c&feature.

Mondello, Bob. "*Oklahoma!*" *Washington City Paper*, November 12, 2010, http://
www.washingtoncitypaper.com/articles/40015/oklahoma-at-arena-stage
-reviewed/.

———. "Remembering Zelda Fichandler, Matriarch of American Regional
Theater." *NPR*, August 4, 2016, http://www.npr.org/2016/08/04/488710159
/remembering-zelda-fichandler-matriarch-of-american-regional-theater.

Montoya, Richard, Ric Salinas, and Herbert Sigüenza. *Culture Clash in America:
Four Plays.* New York: Theatre Communications Group, 2003.

Moon, Krystyn R. *Yellowface: Creating the Chinese in American Popular Music
and Performance, 1850s–1920s.* New Brunswick, NJ: Rutgers University Press,
2004.

Moore, Thomas Gale. *The Economics of the American Theater.* Durham, NC:
Duke University Press, 1968.

Morgan, Edmund S. *American Slavery, American Freedom.* New York: W. W.
Norton & Company, 1975.

Morisseau, Dominique. "Colorblind Casting or Color-Consciousness?" *Public
Theater* (blog), October 20, 2011, http://publictheaterny.blogspot.com/2011
/10/colorblind-casting-or-color.html.

Morrison, Toni. *Playing in the Dark: Whiteness and the Literary Imagination.*
New York: Vintage Books, 1992.

Most, Andrea. *Making Americans: Jews and the Broadway Musical.* Cambridge,
MA: Harvard University Press, 2004.

———. *Theatrical Liberalism: Jews and Popular Entertainment in America.*
New York: NYU Press, 2013.

Mtwa, Percy, Mbongeni Ngema, and Barney Simon. *Woza Albert!* London:
Methuen, 1983.

Muñoz, José Esteban. *Disidentifications: Queers of Color and the Performance
of Politics.* Minneapolis: University of Minnesota Press, 1999.

Neal, Mark Anthony. *What the Music Said: Black Popular Music and Black Public Culture*. New York: Routledge, 1998.

Nemiroff, Robert, Charlotte Zaltzberg, and Robert Brittan. *Raisin*. New York: Samuel French, 1978.

Netzer, Dick. *The Subsidized Muse: Public Support for the Arts in the United States*. Cambridge: Cambridge University Press, 1978.

Newman, Danny. *Subscribe Now! Building Art Audiences through Dynamic Subscription Promotion*. New York: Theatre Communications Group, 1977.

Noss, Amanda. "Household Income for States: 2010 and 2011." U.S. Census Bureau, September 2012, https://www.census.gov/prod/2012pubs/acsbr11 -02.pdf.

Novick, Julius. *Beyond Broadway: The Quest for Permanent Theatres*. New York: Hill and Wang, 1968.

O'Connell, Sam. "Fragmented Musicals and 1970s Soul Aesthetic." In *The Cambridge Companion to African American Theatre*, edited by Harvey Young, 155–73.

———. "*The Wiz* and the African Diaspora Musical: Rethinking the Research Questions in Black Musical Historiography." Paper delivered at the Association for Theatre in Higher Education conference, Montreal, Canada, August 2, 2015.

Ohlandt, D. "Engaging the Audience: Cultivating Partners, Collaborators, and Stakeholders." *Theatre Topics* 25, no. 2 (June 2015): 139–48.

Oliver, Robert. "National Theater or Public Theater: The Transformation of the Theatrical Geography of Washington, D.C., circa 1970–1990." PhD diss., University of Maryland, College Park, 2005.

Omi, Michael, and Howard Winant. *Racial Formation in the United States from the 1960s to the 1990s*. 2nd ed. New York: Routledge, 1994.

Orenstein, Claudia. *Festive Revolutions: The Politics of Popular Theater and the San Francisco Mime Troupe*. Jackson: University Press of Mississippi, 1998.

Osborne, Elizabeth A. *Staging the People: Community and Identity in the Federal Theatre Project*. New York: Palgrave Macmillan, 2011.

OyamO. *I Am a Man*. Black Drama Database. Alexandria: Alexander Street Press, 2014.

Palumbo-Liu, David, ed. *The Ethnic Canon: Histories Institutions and Interventions*. Minneapolis: University of Minnesota Press, 1995.

Pao, Angela. *No Safe Spaces: Re-casting Race, Ethnicity, and Nationality in American Theater*. Ann Arbor: University of Michigan Press, 2010.

Parks, Suzan-Lori. "New Black Math." *Theatre Journal*, 57, no. 4 (December 2005): 576–83.

Paulin, Diana Rebekkah. *Imperfect Unions: Staging Miscegenation in U.S. Drama and Fiction*. Minneapolis: University of Minnesota Press, 2012.

Perkins, Kathy A. Interview. In *Black Theater Is Black Life: An Oral History of Chicago Theater and Dance, 1970–2010*, edited by Harvey Young and Queen Meccasia Zabriskie. Evanston, IL: Northwestern University Press, 2014, 123–38.

Perkins, Kathy A., and Sandra L. Richards. "Black Women Playwrights in American Theatre." *Theatre Journal* 62, no. 4 (December 2010): 541–45.

Pew Research Center. "On Views of Race and Inequality, Blacks and Whites Are Worlds Apart." *Pew*, June 27, 2016, http://www.pewsocialtrends.org/2016 /06/27/on-views-of-race-and-inequality-blacks-and-whites-are-worlds -apart/.

Plant, Deborah G., ed. *"The Inside Light": New Critical Essays on Zora Neale Hurston*. Santa Barbara: Praeger, 2010,

Poggi, Jack. *Theater in America: The Impact of Economic Forces 1870–1967.* Ithaca, NY: Cornell University Press, 1968.

Preserving the Legacy: Voices of the American Theatre, vol. 1. DVD. Theatre Communications Group, 2003.

Pressley, Nelson. *American Playwriting and the Anti-theatrical Prejudice: Twentieth- and Twenty-First Century Perspectives.* New York: Palgrave Macmillan, 2014.

———. "The Good Fight." *American Theatre* (October 2000): 28–32, 135–36.

———. "Where Are the Kogod Cradle's New Plays?" *Washington Post*, October 12, 2012, http://www.washingtonpost.com/entertainment/theater_dance /where-are-the-kogod-cradles-new-plays/2012/10/11/1e2f9df4-0cb7-11e2 -97a7-45c05ef136b2_story.html.

Preston, Rohan. "Guthrie Theater Furloughs Most of Its Full-Time Employees for a Week." *Minneapolis Star Tribune*, January 14, 2014, http://www.star tribune.com/entertainment/stageandarts/240178521.html.

"Race/Ethnicity of College Faculty." National Center for Education Statistics, n.d., https://nces.ed.gov/fastfacts/display.asp?id=61.

Ragsdale, Diane. *In the Intersection: Partnerships in the New Play Sector*. Boston: Center for the Theater Commons / HowlRound.com, 2012.

Ray, Glenn A. *A Basic Guide to Audience Diversity*. Richmond: Virginia Commission for the Arts, 1988.

Reddy, Chandan. *Freedom with Violence: Race, Sexuality, and the US State.* Durham, NC: Duke University Press, 2011.

Richards, David. "Arena's Next Stage." *Washington Post*, March 31, 1996, https:// www.washingtonpost.com/archive/lifestyle/style/1996/03/31/arenas-next -stage/7258ffb4-fda1-41f9-aeoc-2f4a573feebe/?utm_term=.7ff479d0a7b7.

Richards, Sandra. "African Diaspora Drama." In *The Cambridge Companion to African American Theatre*, edited by Harvey Young, 230–54.

Riggs, Lynn. *Green Grow the Lilacs*. New York: Samuel French, 1931.

Ritzel, Rebecca. "Props for a No-Props 'Carousel' at Arena Stage." *American Theatre Magazine*, June 2, 2017, http://www.americantheatre.org/2017/06/02/props-for-a-no-props-carousel-at-arena-stage/.

Rizzo, Frank. "Yale Rep Celebrates Its 50th Amid Nostalgia (and a Few Worries)." *New York Times*, October 10, 2016, http://www.nytimes.com/2016/10/11/theater/*yale*-rep-celebrates-its-50th-amid-nostalgia-and-a-few-worries.html?_r=0.

Roach, Joseph. *Cities of the Dead: Circum-Atlantic Performance*. New York: Columbia University Press, 1996.

Roberts, Jackie M. "Healing Myths from the Ethnic Community, or Why I Don't Teach August Wilson." *Theatre Topics* 20, no. 2 (September 2010): 147–56.

Robinson, Cedric J. *Black Marxism: The Making of the Black Radical Tradition*. 2nd ed. Chapel Hill: University of North Carolina Press, 2000.

———. *Forgeries of Memory and Meaning: Blacks and the Regimes of Race in American Theater and Film before World War II*. Chapel Hill: University of North Carolina, 2007.

Rockefeller Panel Report. *The Performing Arts: Problems and Prospects*. New York: McGraw-Hill, 1965.

Rodgers, Richard, and Oscar Hammerstein II. *Oklahoma!* New York: Applause, 2010.

Rodríguez, Dylan. "The Political Logic of the Non-profit Industrial Complex." In *The Revolution Will Not Be Funded*, edited by INCITE!, 21–40.

Roediger, David R. *The Wages of Whiteness: Race and the Making of the American Working Class*. Brooklyn, Verso: 2007.

Román, David. *Performance in America: Contemporary U.S. Culture and the Performing Arts*. Durham, NC: Duke University Press, 2005.

Rose, Tricia. "Hansberry's *A Raisin in the Sun* and the 'Illegible' Politics of (Inter)personal Justice." *Kalfou* 1, no. 1 (Spring 2014): 27–60.

Rosenberg, Bernard, and Ernest Harburg. *The Broadway Musical: Collaboration in Commerce and Art*. New York: New York University Press, 1993.

Runstedtler, Theresa. *Jack Johnson, Rebel Sojourner: Boxing in the Shadow of the Global Color Line*. Berkeley: University of California Press, 2012.

Sackler, Howard. *The Great White Hope*. New York: Samuel French, 2010.

Salamon, Lester M., ed. *The State of Nonprofit America*. Washington: Brookings Institution Press, 2002.

Samuel, Raphael, ed. *People's History and Socialist Theory*. London: Routledge, 1981.

Saudler, Joan, ed. *Black Theater: A Resource Directory*. New York: Black Theatre Alliance, 1973.

Savran, David. *Highbrow/Lowdown: Theater, Jazz, and the Making of the New Middle Class*. Ann Arbor: University of Michigan Press, 2009.

————. *The Playwright's Voice: American Dramatists on Memory Writing, and the Politics of Culture.* New York: Theatre Communications Group, 1999.

————. *A Queer Sort of Materialism: Recontextualizing American Theater.* Ann Arbor: University of Michigan Press, 2003.

Schechner, Richard. "Blau and Irving at Lincoln Center." *Tulane Drama Review* 9, no. 4 (Summer 1965): 15–18.

————. "Open Casting." *Critical Stages*, November 10, 2010, http://www .criticalstages.org/criticalstages3/entry/Open-Casting-1?category=2.

Selassie, Bereket H. "Washington's New African Immigrants." In *Urban Odyssey: A Multicultural History of Washington, D.C.*, edited by Francine Curro Cary, 264–75.

Sell, Mike. *Avant-Garde Performance and the Limits of Criticism: Approaching the Living Theatre, Happening/Fluxus, and the Black Arts Movement.* Ann Arbor: University of Michigan Press, 2005.

Seniors, Paula Marie. *Beyond "Lift Every Voice and Sing": The Culture of Uplift, Identity, and Politics in Black Musical Theater.* Columbus: Ohio State University Press, 2009.

Shafer, Yvonne. "Breaking Barriers: August Wilson." In *Staging Difference: Cultural Pluralism in American Theatre and Drama*, edited by Marc Maufort, 267–85.

Shanke, Robert A., ed. *Angels in the American Theater: Patrons, Patronage, and Philanthropy.* Carbondale: Southern Illinois University Press, 2007.

Shannon, Sandra G., and Dana A. Williams, eds. *August Wilson and Black Aesthetics.* New York: Palgrave Macmillan, 2004.

Shaw, Rashida Z. Interview. In *Black Theater Is Black Life: An Oral History of Chicago Theater and Dance, 1970–2010*, edited by Harvey Young and Queen Meccasia Zabriskie, 152–62.

Sheehy, Helen. *Margo: The Life and Theatre of Margo Jones.* Dallas: Southern Methodist University Press, 1989.

Shimakawa, Karen. *National Abjection: The Asian American Body on Stage.* Durham, NC: Duke University Press, 2002.

Shimizu, Celine. *The Hypersexuality of Race: Performing Asian/American Women on Screen and Scene.* Durham, NC: Duke University Press, 2007.

Shubow, Charles. "*Oklahoma* Is Simply Superb at Arena." *Broadway World*, November 29, 2010, http://dc.broadwayworld.com/article/BWW_Reviews _OKLAHOMA_is_Simply_Superb_at_Arena_20101129_page2#ixzz1tfPowdSO.

Singh, Nikhil Pal. *Black Is a Country: Race and the Unfinished Struggle for Democracy.* Cambridge, MA: Harvard University Press, 2004.

Slate, Claudia, and Carole Policy, eds. *Florida Studies: Proceedings of the 2009 Annual Meeting of the Florida College English Association.* Newcastle upon Tyne, UK: Cambridge Scholars, 2010.

Smith, Andrea. "Heteropatriarchy and the Three Pillars of White Supremacy: Rethinking Women of Color Organizing." In *The Color of Violence: The Incite! Anthology*, edited by INCITE!, 66–73.

Smith, Anna Deavere. *House Arrest*. New York: Anchor Books, 2004.

———. *Talk to Me: Listening between the Lines*. New York: Random House, 2000.

Smith, Cecil. "Stage: 'Great White Hope' a New Champion on Broadway." *Los Angeles Times*, November 17, 1968, D30.

Smith, Cecil, and Glenn Litton. *Musical Comedy in America: From "The Black Crook" to "South Pacific," from "The King and I" to "Sweeney Todd."* New York: Routledge, 1981.

Smith, Cherise. *Enacting Others: Politics of Identity in Eleanor Antin, Nikki S. Lee, Adrian Piper, and Anna Deavere Smith*. Durham, NC: Duke University Press, 2011.

Smith, Michael. "What Future for Lincoln Center Repertory?" *New York Times*, December 10, 1967, http://search.proquest.com/docview/118133144?account id=7287.

Sommers, Samuel, and Michael Norton. "White People Think Racism Is Getting Worse. Against White People." *Washington Post*, July 21, 2016, https://www .washingtonpost.com/posteverything/wp/2016/07/21/white-people-think -racism-is-getting-worse-against-white-people/?utm_term=.8a30ca5d362c.

Stecopoulos, Harilaos. "Melodrama of the Movement: Lorraine Hansberry's *A Raisin in the Sun*." In *From Bourgeois to Boojie: Black Middle-Class Performance*, edited by Vershawn Ashanti Young with Bridget Harris Tsemo, 209–31.

Stephens, Jeffrey. "Negotiations and Exchanges: Alan Schneider, *Our Town*, and Theatrical Détente." *Journal of American Drama and Theatre* 23, no. 1 (Winter 2011): 43–65.

Stern, Mark Joseph. "Scalia Fan Fiction." *Slate*, March 27, 2015, http://www.slate .com/articles/news_and_politics/jurisprudence/2015/03/the_originalist _the_new_play_about_antonin_scalia_and_his_lesbian_law_clerk.html.

Strauss, Manny. "Arena Stage's Molly Smith to Receive Helen's Star." *theatreWashington*, October 24, 2012, http://theatrewashington.org/content /arena-stages-molly-smith-receive-helens-star.

Sullivan, Dan. "'White Hope' Drama of a Fallen Champ: 'Great White Hope' at the Ahmanson." *Los Angeles Times*, December 4, 1969, C1.

Symonds, Dominic, and Millie Taylor, eds. *Gestures of Music Theater: The Performativity of Song and Dance*. New York: Oxford University Press, 2014.

Taubman, Howard. "In Culture, Is Washington a Hick Town?" *Washington Post*, December 27, 1959, http://ezproxy.gc.cuny.edu/login?url=http://search .proquest.com.ezproxy.gc.cuny.edu/docview/114634140?accountid=7287.

Bibliography

Tavernise, Sabrina. "A Population Changes, Uneasily." *New York Times*, July 17, 2011, http://www.nytimes.com/2011/07/18/us/18dc.html.

Taylor, Regina, and Michael Cunningham. *Crowns*. New York: Dramatists Play Service, 2005.

Teachout, Terry. "An OK 'Oklahoma!'" *Wall Street Journal*, November 26, 2010, http://online.wsj.com/article/SB10001424052748704243904575630551833719 776.html.

Terkel, Studs. *The Studs Terkel Interviews: Film and Theater*. New York: New Press, 1999.

Theatre Workshop. *Oh! What a Lovely War*. London: Methuen, 1988.

Thomas, Aaron C. "Watching *A Raisin in the Sun* and Seeing Red." *Modern Drama* 58, no. 4 (Winter 2015): 461–81.

Trescott, Jacqueline. "Arena Gets $1.2 Million for Diversity." *Washington Post*, October 6, 2000, https://www.washingtonpost.com/archive/lifestyle/2000 /10/06/arena-gets-12-million-for-diversity/07026ed7-2f97-432a-a01d-33aa 123052d4/?utm_term=.812ffae871ec.

"The 23rd Annual Tony Awards." DVD, New York, 1969, Theatre on Film and Tape Archive, Performing Arts Library, New York, NY.

"The 28th Annual Tony Awards." DVD, New York, 1974, Theatre on Film and Tape Archive, Performing Arts Library, New York, NY.

Ullom, Jeffrey. *America's First Regional Theatre: The Cleveland Play House and Its Search for a Home*. New York: Palgrave Macmillan, 2014.

———. *The Humana Festival: The History of New Plays at the Actors Theatre of Louisville*. Carbondale: Southern Illinois University Press, 2008.

Uno, Roberta, with Lucy Mae San Pablo Burns, eds. *The Color of Theater: Race, Culture, and Contemporary Performance*. London: Continuum, 2002.

U.S. Census Bureau. "District of Columbia—Race and Hispanic Origin: 1800 to 1990." U.S. Census Bureau, September 13, 2002, https://web.archive.org/web /20080726045433/http://www.census.gov/population/www/documentation /twps0056/tab23.pdf.

U.S. Department of Commerce. "1950 Census of Population." October 15, 1950, https://www2.census.gov/library/publications/decennial/1950/pc-02/pc -2-49.pdf.

Vandenbroucke, Russell. *Truths the Hand Can Touch: The Theatre of Athol Fugard*. New York: Theatre Communications Group, 1985.

Vogel, Shane. *The Scene of Harlem Cabaret: Race, Sexuality, Performance*. Chicago: University of Chicago Press, 2009.

Von Eschen, Penny. *Satchmo Blows Up the World: Jazz Ambassadors Play the Cold War*. Cambridge, MA: Harvard University Press, 2004.

Walcott, Derek. *The Odyssey*. Black Drama Database. Alexandria: Alexander Street Press, 2014.

————. *"Remembrance" and "Pantomime": Two Plays*. New York: Farrar, Straus and Giroux, 1980.

Wallenstein, Peter. "Interracial Marriage on Trial: *Loving v. Virginia*." In *Race on Trial: Law and Justice in American History*, edited by Annette Gordon-Reed, 177–96.

Walter, Mildred Pitts. "Black Woman Examines Two Plays by White Men." *Los Angeles Times*, February 15, 1970, Q12.

Warner, Keith Q. "From 'Down the Way Where Nights Are Gay': Caribbean Immigration and the Bridging of Cultures." In *Urban Odyssey: A Multicultural History of Washington, D.C.*, edited by Francine Curro Cary, 250–63.

"Washington (City), District of Columbia." U.S. Census Bureau, http://quick facts.census.gov/qfd/states/11/1150000.html.

"Washington's Booming Theater Scene Is Second Only to New York." *Diamondback*, November 20, 2013, http://www.dbknews.com/archives /article_3b8ec4ee-5246-11e3-ab79-001a4bcf6878.html.

Weber, Bruce. "Critic's Notebook: Power, Pitfalls and 'The Great White Hope'; A Washington Company Revisits a Shining Moment from a Decidedly Different Era." *New York Times*, September 14, 2000, E1.

Wertheim, Albert. *The Dramatic Art of Athol Fugard*. Bloomington: Indiana University Press, 2000.

West, Cheryl. *Before It Hits Home*. New York: Dramatists Play Service, 1993.

————. *Holiday Heart*. Black Drama Database. Alexandria: Alexander Street Press, 2014.

————. *Jar the Floor*. New York: Dramatists Play Service, 2002.

Wiener, Gary, ed. *Gender in Lorraine Hansberry's "A Raisin in the Sun."* Detroit: Greenhaven Press, 2011.

Williams, Dana A. "Introduction." In *August Wilson and Black Aesthetics*, edited by Sandra G. Shannon and Dana A. Williams, 1–8.

Wilmer, S. E., ed. *National Theatres in a Changing Europe*. Houndmills, UK: Palgrave Macmillan, 2008.

————. *Theatre, Society, and the Nation: Staging American Identities*. Cambridge: Cambridge University Press, 2002.

Wilson, August. "The Ground on Which I Stand." *Callaloo* 20, no. 3 (1997): 493–503.

Wolff, Geoffrey A. "Stark and Brutal Theme Is Found in 'Sergeant Musgrave's Dance.'" *Washington Post*, March 19, 1966.

Woll, Allen L. *Black Musical Theatre: From "Coontown" to "Dreamgirls."* Cambridge, MA: Da Capo Press, 1991.

Wollman, Elizabeth. *The Theatre Will Rock: A History of the Rock Musical from "Hair" to "Hedwig."* Ann Arbor: University of Michigan Press, 2006.

Wollman, Elizabeth, and Jessica Sternfeld. "After the 'Golden Age.'" In *The Oxford Handbook of the American Musical*, edited by Raymond Knapp, Mitchell Morris, and Stacy Wolf, 111–26.

Wong, Wayman. "Nicholas Rodriguez Talks Life, Love and 'Oklahoma!'" *After Elton*, November 30, 2010, http://www.afterelton.com/people/2010/11 /interview-with-nicholas-rodriguez.

Wyszomirski, Margaret J. "Arts and Culture." In *The State of Nonprofit America*, edited by Lester M. Salamon, 187–218.

Young, Harvey. "3 Things Actors Should Know about Race on Stage." *Backstage*, June 14, 2013, http://www.backstage.com/advice-for-actors/backstage -experts/3-things-actors-should-know-about-race-stage/.

———, ed. *The Cambridge Companion to African American Theatre*. Cambridge: Cambridge University Press, 2012.

———. *Embodying Black Experience: Stillness, Critical Memory, and the Black Body*. Ann Arbor: University of Michigan Press, 2010.

———. "The Long Shadow of *A Raisin in the Sun*." In *The Sixties, Center Stage: Mainstream and Popular Performances in a Turbulent Decade*, edited by James M. Harding and Cindy Rosenthal, 52–70.

———. *Theatre and Race*. New York: Palgrave Macmillan, 2013.

Young, Harvey, and Queen Meccasia Zabriskie. *Black Theater Is Black Life: An Oral History of Chicago Theater and Dance, 1970–2010*. Evanston, IL: Northwestern University Press, 2013.

Young, Vershawn Ashanti, with Bridget Harris Tsemo, eds. *From Bourgeois to Boojie: Black Middle-Class Performance*. Detroit: Wayne State University Press, 2011.

Zarhy-Levo, Yael. *The Making of Theatrical Reputations: Studies from the Modern London Theatre*. Iowa City: University of Iowa Press, 2008.

Zeigler, Joseph Wesley. *Arts in Crisis: The National Endowment for the Arts versus America*. Chicago: A Cappella Books, 1994.

———. *Regional Theatre: The Revolutionary Stage*. Minneapolis: University of Minnesota Press, 1973.

"Zelda Fichandler Public Memorial Service at Arena Stage, Washington DC— HowlRound TV." YouTube video, 2:11:00, posted by HowlRound, October 25, 2016.

INDEX

Page numbers in italics refer to images

139; and blackness, 1, 125, 128, 136;
and boojie performativity, 113; and
essentialism, 138; and *Oba Koso*,
100; and *Playboy of the West Indies*,
115; and *Polk County*, 2, 3; and
Raisin, 125, 128, 129, 137–40, 146,
147, 150
avant-garde theatre, 21, 40–42, 55; bias
toward, 5, 6; and Black Arts Movement, 128; v. regional theatre, 5–6

Bambara, Toni Cade, 82–83
Baraka, Amiri (Leroi Jones), 11, 136;
as foil for Fugard, 105; as foil for
Sackler, 105; on *A Raisin in the Sun*,
130; *Slave Ship*, 11
Barnes, Clive: on *Great White Hope*,
81, 83
Barter Theatre, 92
Bauer, Richard, 38, 162
Baumol, William, 44, 52
Behan, Brendan, 40
Bergquist, Guy, 173, 183, 188
Black Arts Movement, 50, 51, 136;
Arena Stage eschewing of, 104;
avant-garde aesthetics of, 128; and
complicity of white audience, 144;
and *Great White Hope*, 61; and
Raisin, 144
black bodies: and black theatre, 126–
27; and blackness, 59; and Jack
Johnson, 66; racialization of, 126;
violence to, 68
black habitus, 58, 59; and critical
memory, 60
black middle class, 13; and Arena
Stage audiences, 49, 91, 111, 113, 118;
and Great Migration, 111; strategic
assimilation of, 112–13
black musicals, 17–18, 99, 124, 130–31;
Arena Stage programming of, 118,

124, 150–51; and authenticity, 126,
128–29, 139; and minstrelsy, 125;
and racial uplift, 17, 144–45, 181–
82, 224; and soul music, 126. See
also *Crowns* (Taylor); *Polk County*
(Hurston); *Raisin* (musical)
black nationalism, 136–37
black plays: Arena Stage programming of, 97–99, 108, 110–12, 114–15,
117–18, 156, 172, 224; marketing of,
151, 165. *See also* black musicals
Black Power, 128, 131, 145; and *Great
White Hope*, 80
black theatre: Arena Stage engagement with, 90, 98, 102, 108, 128, 150,
174, 180; and the black body, 126–
27; definitions of, 126
blackface: in *Great White Hope*, 60,
68; and multiracial casting, 166–67;
and *Oklahoma!*, 203; in *Raisin*, 144
blackness: and Arena Stage, 12–13, 18,
42, 46, 61, 92, 107, 128–29, 191, 219,
225; and Arena Stage subscribers,
166; and authenticity, 1, 125, 128,
136; and black bodies, 59; and
black habitus, 60; and capitalism,
126; and essentialism, 126–27; and
Great White Hope, 93; and heteronormativity, 136; inclusion of, 3;
and James Earl Jones, 77; and masculinity, 136; performance of, 135,
143, 146, 147; and *Raisin*, 125, 135,
140, 143, 146, 147; and realism, 129;
as relational, 127–28; and social
struggle, 128; and soul music, 126;
in theatre, 11, 126
Blacks, The (Genet), 115, 144
Blood Knot, The (Fugard), 97–98
Bonilla-Silva, Eduardo, 10–11, 202, 213
Boston Toy Theatre, 25
Bougere, Teagle F., 117

sions of, 38; on *Raisin*, 132–33; and Russia, 28, 93; on theatre in the round, 15

5th Avenue Theatre: production of *Oklahoma!*, 210–11

Ford Foundation, 120; support for Arena Stage, 38, 49, 51–52; support for black musicals, 131; support for regional theatres, 36, 49–50

Ford's Theatre, 33, 51; and black musicals, 150

for-profit theatre, 23, 26–27, 78, 221; and fiscal responsibility, 53; as right, 21

Frohnmayer, John, 160

Fugard, Athol, 89, 97, 101–5; *The Blood Knot*, 97–98; *A Lesson from Aloes*, 104–5; *My Children! My Africa!*, 104–5; as racially liberal, 103–5; *Sizwe Banzi Is Dead*, 101–4, 107; as universal, 104; white identity of, 103

Gahlon, Jamie, 220

Gamble, Eleasha, 203, 204, 208, 209

Gardley, Marcus, 190

Gayety Theater, 27

Gilmore, Ruth Wilson: on foundations, 37; on racism and premature death, 10

Ginsburg, Ruth Bader, 13, 223

Glass Menagerie, The (Williams), 117, 194–95

globalization: and nationalism, 156–57

Goodman Theatre, 6; audience diversity at, 122

Gordone, Charles, 48, 79, 98, 164

Gospel at Colonus (Breuer), 99, 106, 151, 192

gospel plays, 137

Gottfried, Martin: on *Great White Hope*, 77, 78–79, 81–82; on left and right theatre camps, 21; regional theatres, critique of, 47

grant foundations, 36; and U.S. tax policy, 37, 52. *See also* Ford Foundation

grants: and politics, 41; and symbolic capital, 27

Great Migration: and black bourgeoisie, 111; and Washington, DC, 34, 111

Great White Hope, The (Sackler), 46–47, 55, 66, 70, 158–59, 222; ambivalence in, 58, 68, 72; antiracism of, 17, 61–62, 82–83, 86; awards for, 56–57, 61, 83–85; black feminist critiques of, 59, 77, 82–83; blackface in, 60, 68; and blackness, 93; as colorblind, 59, 73, 77; critical reception of, 77–83; earnings for, 57, 62–63; economic and symbolic capital of, 56, 103; funding for, 62, 78–79; as individualist, 68, 82; interracial relationship in, 47, 56–57, 64–65, 69–73, 75; marketing of, 73, 75; as middlebrow text, 60–61, 83; minstrelsy in, 68–69; playbill of, 74, 75; and race, disavowal of, 58, 73, 75–76, 82, 86; race erasure of, 75; and racial liberation, 59, 64–65; as racially liberal, 62, 73, 75–76, 79–80, 83, 103; realism of, 61, 69; and respectability politics, 67; segregation in, 65; spectatorship, 65; staging of, 59, 65–66; stereotyping in, 70, 80, 83; structural racism in, 67; systemic racism, disavowal of, 64–66; transfer to Broadway, 8, 16, 47, 56, 62, 125; 2000 revival of, 69; as universal, 75–76, 77, 81–82; white gaze

Mills, Charles W., 8–9

minstrelsy: and black musicals, 125; and casting, 166–67; in *Great White Hope*, 68; and Jack Johnson, 69; and multiracial casting, 203; in *Raisin*, 142, 144

miscegenation, 69–70; in musicals, 61. *See also* interracial relationships

Mitchell, Koritha, 126

Mokae, Zakes, 104

Mondello, Bob, 116

Morton, Joe, *138*, 140, 141

Most, Andrea, 210

Mount Vernon Players, 27

Moynihan Report, 137

Mrozek, Sławomir, 89

Mtwa, Percy, 103

multiculturalism: and Arena Stage, 13, 161–63, 166–72, 174, 188; and arts funding, 160; and the canon, 160; and erasure of race, 215; and financing, 161; and government theatre support, 155; and identity, 170; neoliberal, 202; and theatre patronage, 162

multiracial casting: at Arena Stage, 166–67, 192, 194–204, 214–17, 223–24; v. "colorblind" casting, 199–200; and colorblindness, 199–200; and difference, 9; and minstrelsy, 203; and national identity, 206–7; and realism, 195–96, 201; as social justice project, 200; and stereotyping, 203; and whiteness, 206

musical theatre: and whiteness, 139

musicals: as American, 195; Arena Stage programming of, 195–96, 216–17; interracial relationships in, 61; as open texts, 198. *See also* black musicals; *Oklahoma!* (Rodgers and Hammerstein); *Raisin* (musical)

My Children! My Africa! (Fugard), 104–5

My Fair Lady: Arena productions of, 216–17

nation: and Arena Stage, 15, 18; in *Oklahoma!*, 213–14; and race, 157; and theatre, 157

National Endowment for the Arts (NEA): Arena Stage, funding for, 46, 52, 62, 78–79, 96, 120–22, 161, 189; cuts to, 118; NEA Four, 122, 160; and theatre budgets, 160, 172

National Theatre, The, 33, 51

nationalism: and Arena Stage, 14; black nationalism, 136–37; and globalization, 156–57; and racial difference, 198; U.S., 5, 193

NEA Four, 122, 160. *See also* National Endowment for the Arts (NEA)

Negro Ensemble Company, 50, 85, 99, 110, 131; Arena Stage, presentations at, 99, 108

Nemiroff, Robert, 16, 98, 128, 130; on *Raisin* production, 132–33, 141, 145–46, 149

Nevis Mountain Dew (Carter), 99, 110

New Black Aesthetic, 127

New Lafayette Theatre, 50

New Voices for a New America, 167, 173–74; PlayQuest, 168

Newman, Danny, 110

Ngema, Mbongeni, 103

No Place to Be Somebody (Gordone), 48, 79

nonprofit industrial complex (NPIC), 49–50

nonprofit theatre: as left, 21; little theatres, 25, 27. *See also* Arena Stage; regional theatre

Nottage, Lynn, 182, 190, 222

white privilege, 11; and Arena Stage, 12; disavowal of, 202; and white supremacy, 157–58

white supremacy, 10–11; and color-blindness, 200; denial of, 202, 206; and *Great White Hope*, 58, 59, 64; and postrace racial project, 206; and *Raisin*, 141; social construction of, 58; and white privilege, 157–58

whiteness: and Arena Stage, 6, 49, 108–9, 167, 178; centering of, 5; and *Great White Hope*, 17, 58, 75; and multiracial casting, 206; and musical theatre, 139; as normative, 214; and *Oklahoma!*, 205, 207–8, 211; presumed, 214; and race, 157; and racial liberalism, 8; and theatre programming, 179; as unmarked, 200, 203

Wiest, Dianne, 93

Williams, Tennessee, 26, 158, 177

Wilson, August, 12, 114–15, 118, 205, 224; Arena Stage productions of, 179

Winant, Howard, 10, 127, 198

Wines, Halo, 162

Wiz, The, 131; as pseudo-lack musical, 126

Woldin, Judd, 16, 128, 131–32, 146

Woll, Allen, 126; on black musicals, 130

Wollman, Elizabeth, 131; on *Raisin*, 142–43

Woolly Mammoth Theatre Company, 118, 173, 176, 180

Woza Albert! (Mtwa, Ngema, and Simon), 103

Yale Repertory Theatre, 7–8; Fugard at, 102–3

Yardley, Jonathan, 195

yellowface, 48

Yerma (García Lorca), 163, 164, 165

Young, Harvey, 10; on black habitus, 58, 59; on multiracial productions, 204–5, 214

Zacarías, Karen, 182, 189

Zaltzberg, Charlotte, 16, 128, 130

Zeigler, Joseph, 6, 43, 45; on *Great White Hope*, 58

Zeisler, Peter, 44

STUDIES IN THEATRE HISTORY AND CULTURE